CW00517747

Gillian Perrin

PAST SOUNDS

An Introduction to the Sonata Idea in the Piano Trio

"Unlike the architect, who has to mould the coarse and unwieldy rock, the composer reckons with the ulterior effect of past sounds."

Eduard Hanslick, *The Beautiful in Music*, 1854

AUSTIN MACAULEY PUBLISHERS™
LONDON • CAMBRIDGE • NEW YORK • SHARJAH

Copyright © Gillian Perrin 2022

The right of Gillian Perrin to be identified as author of this work has been asserted in accordance with sections 77 and 78 of the Copyright, Designs and Patents Act 1988.

All rights reserved. No part of this publication may be reproduced, stored in a retrieval system, or transmitted in any form or by any means, electronic, mechanical, photocopying, recording, or otherwise, without the prior permission of the publishers.

Any person who commits any unauthorised act in relation to this publication may be liable to criminal prosecution and civil claims for damages.

A CIP catalogue record for this title is available from the British Library.

The cover image is used with permission © 2022 The Granger Collection LTD d/b/a GRANGER – Historical Picture Archive.

ISBN 9781528991599 (Paperback)
ISBN 9781528991605 (Hardback)
ISBN 9781528991612 (ePub e-book)

www.austinmacauley.com

First Published 2022
Austin Macauley Publishers Ltd®
1 Canada Square
Canary Wharf
London
E14 5AA

For Charles

On Instrumental Music

"In the contemplation of that immense variety of agreeable and melodious sounds, arranged and digested, both in their coincidence and in their succession, into so complete and regular a system, the mind in reality enjoys not only a very great sensual, but a very high intellectual, pleasure, not unlike that which it derives from the contemplation of a great system in any other science."

Adam Smith, *Essays on Philosophical Subjects*,
London and Edinburgh, 1795.

ACKNOWLEDGEMENTS

This book has been long in the making. I take full responsibility for its shortcomings, but such merits as it may have I owe to others. Firstly to the encouragement of early mentors: my inspirational teacher Anne Foster, herself a former pupil of the renowned music analyst Donald Francis Tovey; and my Oxford tutor Elizabeth Mackenzie, who placed me under the singular supervision of Egon Wellesz.

I am very grateful to David Matthews for reading the MS and for his comments, as well as for his ready willingness on several occasions to spare time for discussion.

My warm thanks for helpful comments are due to Clare Dawson, former Director of Music at The London Oratory School, and Jane Faulkner, professional violinist and Chair of the Piano Trio Society; also to David Terry for all his help notating the music examples, to Paul Robinson for so kindly recording the vocal audio clips, and to Walter Stephenson of Austin Macauley for his painstaking and sympathetic editorial work.

I am grateful to countless friends (strangers too!) pinned by courtesy to their chairs while they politely heard me out, then encouraged my ideas for this book; also to my family, who have been patient target practice for many years; most of all I thank my exceptional and long-suffering husband Charles for his incalculable support.

AUDIO CLIPS

To enable readers of the digital versions of this book to hear the sound of the notated Music Examples distributed throughout the text, Audio Clips may be accessed from a companion website by clicking adjacent icons marked 🔊.

The address of the companion website is:

https://gillianmargaretperrin.ampbk.com/

Readers of the printed book who wish to hear the Audio Clips on the companion website are encouraged to keep the site open while reading. The Audio Clips have the same numbering as in the book and can be accessed at:

https://gillianmargaretperrin.ampbk.com/musical-examples

A full list of the Audio Clips/Music Examples and the works from which they are taken may be found on pp.370-376.

Recordings of all the Piano Trios discussed are widely available.

CONTENTS

Part III
THE 20TH CENTURY

INTRODUCTION

A SENSE OF structure is an essential ingredient of understanding in most subjects. This is clearly so in the sciences, where a structure can be key to intelligibility – such as Linnaeus' classification of plant and animal species, or the periodic table of chemical elements, or the double helix of DNA. However, a sense of structure is also an important element in the appreciation of arts subjects. Students of English literature learn that the sonnet is a poem of fourteen lines, and that an infinite variety can spring from the arrangement of these fourteen lines in the different schemes and rhymes of the Petrarchan or Elizabethan types. Other students find consistent structures in the orders of classical architecture or the cruciform footprint of Christian buildings; others again study the geometrical techniques of perspective in painting or the conventions of western portraiture. As in the sciences, initiation into such topics may include a fair degree of detailed analysis.

We put ourselves through all this for good reason. Not to be burdened with dry academic facts, but to be equipped with a sense of the structure of things, a structure of expectation for future fulfilment – above all, a basis for future enjoyment. To have an insight into the "working" of literature and the fine arts raises our perception and appreciation of artistic craftsmanship. We study the sonnet, the classical column and the cruciform building because these are just a few of the great archetypes of western culture – archetypes which enrich our lives and connect us with the shared humanity and skills of our past.

The art of music has its archetypal structures too, but the formal structures which underpin music seem rarely to be studied as a general subject, being more often reserved for specialist pupils with previous experience of music and its notation, which may be thought necessary to musical understanding. Yet that great music educator Percy Buck[1]* once wrote "the bedrock condition underlying an understanding and appreciation of music is the *grasp of its structure*".

---

* Numbered endnotes can be found at the end of each chapter.

Music is tremendously widely enjoyed, but through lack of specific instruction the musical structures of the western classical tradition remain an unopened book to many people.

This is particularly so in music for instruments without voices. Listening to music involving singers and words is less difficult, since here the music is carried by the forward impetus of language and narrative. But there are no such props in music for instruments alone, and although listeners may sense that this too has a forward narrative, they feel unable to understand it without some training. They feel distanced from it by "not understanding how it works". They are frustrated because they know that music can move them deeply, and they would like to know why and how this can be so. They may also feel that they are missing out on enjoying music at a more intellectual level; they may feel perplexed by Adam Smith's comment on instrumental music in his *Essays on Philosophical Subjects*:

> "In the contemplation of that immense variety of agreeable and melodious sounds, arranged ... into so complete and regular a system, the mind ... enjoys not only a very great sensual, but a very high intellectual, pleasure, not unlike that which it derives from the contemplation of a great system in any other science."[2]

Smith's essay was published in 1795, some fifty years after instrumental music had begun to challenge the dominant position until then enjoyed by vocal music. Of course, music for instruments had existed before, but performers had a subservient role, merely introducing or accompanying the "serious" music of opera or sacred music, or falling back on arrangements of vocal originals. Music to accompany dancing or social events hardly ranked as "serious", and the best a skilled performer might do was perform variations on a well-known song or dance-tune – which was popular because the word-associated melody was easily recognised. Virtuosity tended to be admired for its own sake in the concerto rather than for the musical content of the work.

By the time of Smith's essay in 1795, all this was in the past. A new style of musical composition had come into being, focusing on a new, purely instrumental type: the sonata. From the middle of the eighteenth century the sonata idea spread rapidly across Europe. A "sonata", pure and simple, was a composition for a solo instrument. But a work for string quartet or wind quintet was also a "sonata" – for a chamber group. A symphony was a "sonata" for orchestra – and so on. Symphonies and string quartets led the way in public concerts, and in the course of time these sonatas came to consist of three or four separate movements clustered together. Habit crystallised into certain characteristics for each movement: a fast and lively movement to begin, followed by one which was slow and expressive, then an old-fashioned dance (the minuet), and probably a fast movement to close. But the first movement was widely regarded as the most important: it was sometimes called the "Long Movement". It was also the most "serious" movement and the most likely to follow a consistent formal framework, which over time became known as "First Movement or Sonata Form".

This is a title which has met with much opprobrium from scholars in recent times (of which more in the following paragraphs). But the general reader may not realise what a seminal and dominant influence this great formal structure, sonata form, has been in the history of western music in the last 250 years. The old *Harvard Dictionary of Music* (1951) actually reckoned that "80% of all the movements found in sonatas, symphonies ... and so on, from 1780 to the present day, are written in sonata form, strictly or freely applied." Excluding opera and all other vocal and choral music, this means that sonata form dominated some 80% of the concert/recital repertoire. This is why it is so unfortunate that people who do not read music nor play instruments have little formal training to help them recognise its structure – not as a dry exercise in analysis, but because it can greatly enhance their understanding and enjoyment of sonata music. And in view of the widespread practice reflected in the *Harvard Dictionary*'s statistics, it is disappointing that it is not more widely known and understood. There may be two reasons for this.

Firstly, although sonatas were written from the middle of the eighteenth century, no composer or theorist of that century ever referred to such a thing as "sonata form". The textbook title was first used by a German theorist, A B Marx, in 1824. His description was based on the contemporary nineteenth-century, post-Beethoven sonata, and written as a model for teaching pupils *how to write* sonata movements. It was not, and was never intended to be, a description of sonata practice in the eighteenth century. Because of this, many modern scholars prefer not to use the term "sonata form" for earlier works. Nevertheless, it is widely acknowledged that Haydn and Mozart represent the height of Classical sonata composition, and since salient characteristics of the subsequent sonata blueprint are evident in the sonatas of both Haydn and Mozart, it seems perverse to throw out this title merely because it was coined so much later and may not be a perfect fit with every work.

The evidence of innumerable sonata first movements from the 1760s onwards clearly points towards a widespread use of consistent characteristics of the later "sonata form". As Mark Evan Bonds points out, "... form is the manner in which a work's content is made intelligible to its audience" and "... it would be ludicrous to argue that sonata form was not at least in part an *a priori* schema

available to the composer"[3]. The differing scholarly approaches to
the subject, from the broadly musicological to the music-theoretical,
are well summarised by James Hepokoski and Warren Darcy at the
beginning of their book *Elements of Sonata Theory*.[4] Charles Rosen,
in the first chapter of his book on *Sonata Forms*, comes down on the
side of cautious use of the bad old textbook description of "sonata
form" for eighteenth-century works: "... we still need the term for
an understanding of that period as well as for those which came
after."[5] So long as we do not attempt to fit early sonatas into the
later mould, but see them as they are and against the background
of their own time, using the later description can only help to give
a more complete overview of the development of the sonata idea.
After all, when going bird-watching one needs to know what feather
markings one is looking for. But the fact that the title "sonata form"
has become a hot potato in scholarly circles may have something to
do with its omission as a topic from a general curriculum.

The second reason for omission may be the general perception
that it is notoriously difficult to describe such an intangible subject
as music to the untrained listener. Yet explaining tonality – the
relationship of musical sounds to each other – may be more of a
perceived than an actual difficulty. Another widely-respected musicologist, Donald Francis Tovey,[6] thought that he needed

> "... to convince the most general reader that, ever since he became
> fond of music at all, he has enjoyed tonality whether he knew it or
> not, just as Molière's *Bourgeois Gentilhomme*, Monsieur Jourdain,
> found that he had been talking prose all his life without knowing it."[7]

Similarly, we shall find that our own familiarity with the music of
the western tonal system, the tonality which we encounter daily in
popular music as well as in the so-called "classical" repertoire, needs
only a little guidance to turn instinctive understanding into more
sophisticated appreciation. A systematic explanation of the dynamic
relationship between the eight notes of the western scale will enhance
the listener's enjoyment of melody and assist the recognition of
recurring tunes or "themes", as well as identifying the subtlety of
tonal departure and return which lies at the heart of sonata form.

Understanding tonality will be a crucial factor in understanding
the sonata idea, for the story of the sonata is also an important part
of the story of western tonality.* But we should not be too daunted
by the prospect. We should be aware that mid-eighteenth-century

---

* Unless defined otherwise by context, references to "western tonality" throughout this book refer to the tonality of European art music from c.1650–c.1900,
known as the "Common Practice Period"; this music is characterised by its use of
the major and minor keys, its supporting harmony and metrical regularity.

audiences were not all musically sophisticated; if we can get into the minds of those listeners, we may be able to understand how they heard the new sonatas and therefore understand musical tonality as they did.

As the eighteenth century progressed, the cultured aristocratic patrons of the previous Baroque era, with their refined cultural tastes, were making way for less well-educated audiences. A wealthy new urban class was buying its way into social respectability by cultivating a taste for music and patronising public concerts. In these concerts, the complex forms and traditions of Baroque music were challenged by new programmes of songs and instrumental pieces, responding to a demand for music in a light and simple style, designed for entertainment rather than edification. Vocal music was no problem for composers, but the new instrumental music presented a challenge: the structural framework of words and stanzas had to be replaced by a new, purely musical narrative – capable of standing entirely on its own, but nevertheless comprehensible to the new audiences.

The sonata idea was conceived as a response to this challenge. We shall try to get into the minds of these audiences to understand how they heard this music – for despite the appeal of its simple surface melodies, it actually owed its intelligibility to much older, long-familiar musical traditions. Accordingly, Chapter 1 sets the scene for the arrival of early sonata music in London in the middle of the eighteenth century, but Chapters 2 and 3 then step aside for two substantial diversions describing the process by which European singers and dancers had established the deep-rooted foundations of western music. Chapter 4 returns to follow the chronological development of the sonata idea. In these early chapters it will become clear why the title *Past Sounds* has been chosen for this book; it is taken from a quotation by the nineteenth-century Austrian music critic Eduard Hanslick in *The Beautiful in Music* (1854):

"Unlike the architect, who has to mould the coarse and unwieldy rock, the composer reckons with the ulterior effect of *past sounds*."[8] [My italics.]

As well as enjoying public concerts, where symphonies and string quartets could be heard performed by professional musicians, eighteenth-century audiences also developed a considerable appetite for music for their own domestic use. Composers responded with smaller-scale "sonatas" written for solo harpsichord, or better still, for harpsichord with accompanying parts for one or more other instruments – a violin, or violoncello – so that families and friends could play music together.

These simple chamber works, written for amateurs, provide an ideal way to study sonata form. They are a practical choice for less experienced listeners because their three instruments have well-contrasted and easily-identifiable registers and tone colours, making it easier to pick out each "voice" from the texture than it would be from the monochrome of a keyboard or from ensembles consisting only of string instruments. In due course the accompanied keyboard sonata became a new chamber music *genre* in its own right – the piano trio. Its development followed a broadly similar pattern to other "sonatas" for chamber music groups and the "sonata" for orchestra: the same musical principles applied in each case, the differences being only of size and sophistication.

A further admirable reason for choosing to follow the development of the sonata idea in music for the piano trio is that there is a comparatively little-known repertoire of beautiful works written for this chamber group. Part I describes examples of sonata form in the piano trio, from the earliest ventures in the 1760s to the refined peak of the Classical period with Haydn, Mozart and Beethoven later in the century. Then as the trio leaves the private salon and takes to the concert platform in the nineteenth century, in Part II splendid examples follow in works by the great Romantic composers: Schubert, Mendelssohn, Schumann and Brahms; and in trios also by nationalist composers such as Dvořák and Tchaikovsky. Finally, in Part III and the twentieth century, against a background of profound changes in musical style there are more fine trios by Fauré, Ravel and Shostakovich, as well as several other composers.

This book may be read in the first instance as a background introduction to the development of the sonata idea in the piano trio (without pursuing the detailed analysis of each selected work described in a boxed text), but then later used as a reference guide for detailed listening against this contextual background. Audio clips of the music discussed can be heard by following links in the text to a companion website, marked 🔊:* because of these, a basic knowledge of musical notation is useful but not essential, and the boxed text includes only simple music examples. All necessary technical terms will be explained as they arise, or can be found in a Glossary at Appendix B.

To place composers and works in the context of their times, brief biographical details about each musician are included in the main text, and in both Parts I and II a chapter is dedicated to contemporary theoretical writing about the sonata idea; in Part III a section describing the introduction of serialism and atonality will provide background to piano trios continuing to follow the tonal sonata idea in the modern era. The narrative also presents the music against its

---

* See p.6 and pp.370-376 for more information.

cultural background throughout, and here again diversions discuss contemporary arts, painting, literature and philosophy as they illuminate the culture of an era and are reflected in its music.

Just as the study of great literary or architectural archetypes can lead to a rewarding appreciation of the masterworks of our cultural past, so can a deeper understanding of the formal organisation of musical sounds lead to a more rewarding appreciation of the sonata tradition. Sonata form is arguably the greatest structural archetype of the western instrumental repertoire: it need not be a closed book to all but the musically-trained. Hopefully this book may help music students, performers and general readers of all ages to a better understanding and enjoyment of the sonata's sophisticated synthesis of emotional and intellectual appeal – and to a better appreciation of the significant position it occupies in the western musical canon.

CHAPTER ENDNOTES

1   Sir Percy Buck (1871-1947), King Edward Professor of Music at the University of London, Music Adviser to the London County Council and teacher at the Royal College of Music (where he founded the RCM Junior Department).

2   Smith, Adam. *Essays on Philosophical Subjects*. London and Edinburgh: Cadell & Davies, 1795, p.172.

3   Bonds, Mark Evan. *Wordless Rhetoric*. Cambridge, MA: Harvard University Press, 1991, p.5, p.29.

4   Hepokoski, James and Darcy, Warren. *Elements of Sonata Theory*. Oxford: Oxford University Press, 2006; paperback ed. 2011, pp.3ff.

5   Rosen, Charles. *Sonata Forms* (Revised Edition). New York: W W Norton & Co, 1988, pp.2ff.

6   Sir Donald Francis Tovey (1875-1940), British musicologist and music analyst, Reid Professor of Music at the University of Edinburgh.

7   Tovey, Donald Francis. *Beethoven*. Oxford: Oxford University Press, 1944, p.4.

8   Hanslick, Eduard. [*Vom Musikalisch-Schönen* (1854)] *The Beautiful in Music* (1854). 7th edition, transl. Gustav Cohen. New York: Liberal Arts Press, 1957, p.52.

Part I

THE 18TH CENTURY

CHAPTER 1

A FASHIONABLE COMMODITY

"LIFE IS CHANGE," said the Greek philosopher Heraclitus (c.544-483BCE). And so must Louis XIV's contemporaries across Europe have felt when the Sun King died soon after the beginning of the eighteenth century. It was the end of an era. The demise of this most autocratic of rulers marked the end of absolutist patronage and ushered in far-reaching changes. The new century would be driven by the enquiring minds of the Enlightenment – a century of philosophy and revolution, of advances in science and the beginnings of industrialisation. Colonisation and economic expansion further contributed significant changes across Europe, as a new mercantile and urban class joined the old princelings and aristocratic élites as patrons of society.

These patrons displayed their conspicuous wealth with an unprecedented rise in consumer spending. A prosperous market for luxury goods sprang up as old and new purchasers sought fashionable clothes, exotic foodstuffs and expensive entertainment. The arts thrived in this climate, and none more so than music. All over Europe, music was at the heart of the consumer boom. There had been a long tradition of musical performance enjoyed by cultured people with discerning tastes – opera, church music, incidental music for social occasions – but now music blossomed anew in the great cities of Europe, in Vienna, Paris and London, as well as in Venice, Naples, Milan, Hamburg, Berlin and Madrid.

At that time London was one of the largest cities in the world, and according to the historian Roy Porter it was "a bottomless pit of consumption".[1] London, too, had an insatiable appetite for music, and the city's prosperity and enthusiasm attracted musicians from all over Europe. It was also ahead of other continental cities with an established public concert life. Although England produced few native composers who achieved recognition abroad, with its flourishing concerts it could draw on the finest musicians of the times. Of all those in the capital in the second half of the eighteenth century,

London was especially fortunate to attract J C Bach, among the most gifted of early Classical composers.

Johann Christian Bach (1735-1782) was one of the younger sons of Johann Sebastian Bach, born in Leipzig and only 15 years old when his father died in 1750. He was initially taught and cared for by his elder brother Carl Philip Emanuel, but at the age of 21 he decided to leave behind the stern Lutheran traditions of his famous family, and travelled to Italy to study under the renowned teacher and composer Padre Martini. For eight years he lived in Milan, where he converted to Catholicism, encountered the bold new symphonic style of Giovanni Battista Sammartini, and fell under the spell of Italian opera. He wrote three operas for Italian opera houses which were so successful that they attracted the attention of English opera impresarios. He was commissioned to write two more for the King's Theatre in the Haymarket, and came to London in 1762 intending to stay for a year to execute the commission.

John Bach (as he was called in London) must have arrived with high hopes that the success which he had enjoyed amongst the operatic *cognoscenti* in Naples would be repeated with the aristocratic audiences who patronised the King's Theatre. But here he was disappointed. Opera in London was a cut-throat commercial enterprise, and competition was fearsome. Furthermore, he soon learnt that the lighter style of Italian comic opera and the simpler, homegrown English ballad operas heard at the theatres in Covent Garden and Drury Lane were more popular with a large section of the public. Although Bach did eventually write five operas for the Haymarket (and achieved some success with them), he must initially have doubted he could establish a long-term career for himself in the English capital.

Then came an offer of a quite different nature. He was invited to become Music Master to George III's wife, Queen Charlotte. It was a natural fit for both sides – he was a skilled keyboard player and his fluent German was undoubtedly appreciated. Moreover, the appointment ensured his acceptance in the best social circles: a royal appointment naturally engaged a supply of distinguished patrons and pupils, and his biographer C S Terry records that he became "one of the most popular and fashionable teachers in the metropolis".[2]

This was a significant step towards earning a living in London's competitive musical environment. But Bach had also to think of other sources of income if he was to survive. Perhaps he thought of the success of one of the operas he had written for Naples before his arrival: *Catone in Utica* had been particularly commended for the expressive quality of its orchestral accompaniment.[3] Maybe he should think in terms of instrumental music for London? So this

gifted and resourceful musician teamed up with a childhood friend
from Leipzig days, Carl Friedrich Abel, who was already working in
London, to launch a concert series in which for the first time instrumental music would take precedence over music for the voice.

Bach and Abel were fortunate to procure a foothold in the social
diary of the London Season. This was the most fashionable period of
the year, when the Quality and the stylish *ton* were in town looking
for entertainment on most nights of the week: it began with the
Queen's official birthday on 18th January, and continued until the
King's birthday on 4th June. Bach and Abel secured the Wednesday
evening slot throughout the Season for their Subscription Concerts.
It was the first regular concert series in London, later much admired
by the contemporary music historian Dr Charles Burney:

> "... as their own compositions were new and excellent, and the best
> performers of all kinds which our capital could supply, enlisted
> under their banners, this [weekly] concert was better patronised
> and longer supported than perhaps any one had ever been in this
> country; having continued for full twenty years with uninterrupted
> prosperity."[4]

The Subscription Concerts became an ideal showcase for Bach and
Abel's own compositions: every week the two composers presented
the London public with symphonies, concertos, chamber and
keyboard works. Bach's first-hand experience of the light Italian
comic opera style – derived from the fast-moving pace and the
humour of its caricatured protagonists – proved invaluable. Fresh
from the theatre, the style of the *sinfonia avanti l'opera* was translated
into his new symphonies, which became immensely popular and
established these independent pieces for orchestra on the London
concert scene.

At the same time, John Bach's appointment to the royal household
opened up unforeseen opportunities. His duties included teaching
harpsichord to the royal children as well as to the Queen. He was also
charged with organising chamber concerts for the Royal Family. The
repertoire of keyboard music for amateurs at that time was limited,
and he saw an opportunity to write new works for the Family to play
– both solo harpsichord compositions as well as pieces in which a
violinist and a 'cellist could play together. (The fact that these could
be printed, with impressive dedications to members of the Royal
Family – positively ensuring good sales – was a further attraction
not lost on this enterprising musician.) Bach's post with the Royal
Family gave him a reason for writing good but simple music for
amateurs – of especial interest to us because it marks the beginning

in England of a new *genre* of chamber music, which in the course of time became the piano trio.

It soon became clear that there was a considerable market for such music for domestic use. When the Season was over and the Quality retired to their country estates for much of the rest of the year, they were delighted to add chamber music to the songs which until now had been their staple fare for domestic entertainment. Charles Avison recognised this in the introduction to his harpsichord pieces accompanied by two violins and 'cello:

> "This kind of music is not, indeed, calculated so much for public entertainment, as for private Amusement. It is rather like a conversation among Friends, where Few are of one Mind, and propose their mutual Sentiments, only to give Variety, and enliven their select Company."

At the time of John Bach's arrival in London in 1762, however, his new instrumental works were still a few years ahead. His immediate concern must have been the disparate tastes of the audience whose favour he had to secure if he was to achieve any success here with his music. Tastes ranged from the aristocrats who still admired the long, elaborate Da Capo arias of *opera seria* to those who preferred the quicksilver wit of *opera buffa*; from those who preferred oratorios and sacred music to those who relished English ballad operas; those who enjoyed the music to be heard at the Pleasure Gardens at Ranelagh, Vauxhall and Marylebone, or the catches of the gentlemen's Glee Club in the City. Apart from the conservative intellectuals, they seemed united in one thing: they had tired of the long-winded style and artifice of the Baroque era, and were now looking to music for lighter entertainment. They were looking for a change of musical style.

Who were this audience John Bach had to please? Who might come to the Subscription Concerts or buy his new music to play and enjoy in their own homes? The musicologist Simon McVeigh describes contemporary audiences as

> "... the upper reaches of polite society, a broad élite consisting of a number of strands. Of course it included the landed gentry and nobility ('the quality'), but it also incorporated a range of professionals, clergy and men of letters; indeed anyone who could pass himself off as a well-educated gentleman of good bearing. In addition, money opened doors without too many questions, and increasingly London's wealthy urban bourgeois joined this heterogeneous élite."[5]

This description gives us an idea of the wide range of tastes which Bach had to please. It also hints at powerful undercurrents. The Subscription Concerts would not be open to all London's population. Old money was still dedicated to preserving the exclusivity of social entertainment such as music: subscription lists of those deemed socially acceptable were rigorously supervised by a small coterie of society dowagers controlling access to the concerts. But new money was equally keen to gain entrance, for "Betterment" was a significant factor for the new bourgeois; and as McVeigh points out, "music ... had the advantage of involving both conspicuous spending and pretension to good taste."[6] Bach could at least be sure that a new audience would apply itself diligently to learning to appreciate good music.

For all that the old Quality and the new urban class now dressed in the same finery and sipped the same wines, their musical experiences must have been very different, and seemingly irreconcilable. How could these disparate folk settle side by side on Mrs Cornelys's* sofas with mutual understanding of brand new music? Did they share familiarities, commonplaces of musical experience, with which we do not immediately identify – what the musicologist Hugo Riemann once referred to as "lost matters of course" – which now escape us?

The idea of something missing in our own comprehension of a past time also runs through a passage by the legal historian S F C Milsom. Writing about his effort to understand the long-lost everyday assumptions of people in the Middle Ages, he wrote:

"... there is never occasion to write down what everybody knows. And when everybody has forgotten what everybody once knew, when the assumptions are beyond recall, there is nothing to put the historian on his guard. Not knowing (or even missing) the assumptions of the time, he will read the materials in the light of his own assumptions ..."[7]

Have we forgotten some eighteenth-century musical commonplace which everybody at those Subscription Concerts took for granted?

The significant element in their common experience is *dance music*,** and perhaps we do not immediately see it because – as Milsom points out – we are thinking of dance music in terms of our own experience. Social dancing to modern readers essentially means

---

* Teresa Cornelys was a flamboyant society hostess and ex-opera singer in whose Soho Square rooms the earliest of Bach and Abel's concerts were held.

** Throughout the following chapters dance music should be understood as communal social dancing, not the solo display dancing of ballet, and not Morris dancing or Highland sword dances.

couple-dancing, from the waltz of the nineteenth-century ballroom to the anything-goes of modern nightclub dances. But social dancing in the eighteenth century was very different. Dancing had been at the heart of social life for centuries: it was a communal activity, involving all those on the dance floor and requiring a long familiarity with innumerable sequences of step-patterns and movements to be fully enjoyed.* At a time when people had to make so much of their own entertainment it was a natural and easy pastime enjoyed at all levels of society, from the highest to the lowest.

As eighteenth-century dancers took to the dance floor and joined hands to commence the dance, however, it is unlikely that they were aware of the long centuries of dance tradition which had moulded the music for dance. Nor, indeed, would they have been aware of the embedded expectations dance music had given them for music in general.

To understand their reception of John Bach's music, we should step aside in the next two chapters and fill in some background understanding of his audience's experience of music which he could take for granted. Firstly, we shall see how the patterns of dance had imposed pattern and expectation on music; and secondly, recognise how their enjoyment of "a good tune" was connected to similar cultural expectations.

---

* A similar experience can still be had in the 21st century by those – across Europe and in the USA – who take part in folk dancing (whether in a live tradition or in revivalist societies), and also, nearer home, in traditional Scottish reels.

CHAPTER ENDNOTES

1   Porter, Roy. *English Society in the 18th Century.* London: Allen Lane, 1982; revised ed, Penguin Books, 1991, p.39.

2   Terry, Charles Sanford. *John Christian Bach.* London: Oxford University Press, 1929; 2nd ed, 1967, p.155.

3   Terry, *ibid*, p.53.

4   Burney, Charles. *A General History of Music*, vol.II, 1789. Modern ed. New York: Dover, 1957, p.1017.

5   McVeigh, Simon. *Concert Life in London from Mozart to Haydn.* Cambridge: Cambridge University Press, 1993, p.11.

6   McVeigh, *ibid*, p.11

7   Milsom, S F C. *A Natural History of the Common Law.* New York: Columbia University Press, 2003.

CHAPTER 2

BACKGROUND 1:
MUSIC FOR THE DANCE

PEOPLE HAVE DANCED since the dawn of human history. Moreover, many of the dances which have carried the most significant human meaning have been ring dances. These began as a simple ritual circling round a sacred object, but over the millennia, gradually added layers of increasingly complicated movement before arriving at the patterned sophistication of eighteenth-century dances. Music was an important component of ring-dancing's development, driving movement with pulse and punctuating pattern with variation of pitch.

We shall find it illuminating to look at a selection of objects and contemporary documents to illustrate how music's pulse and pitch followed the outline of this development. We begin with primitive village farming communities. Evidence of ring-dancing has been found in sites over a wide area of the ancient Near East and Southern Europe, in painted human figures circling round the rims of Neolithic pottery bowls.[1]

The archaeologist Yosef Garfinkel believes the figures in these illustrations are dancers: firstly, they hold hands and appear in dancing positions; secondly, each dancer maintains an identical stance, suggesting a common co-ordinated movement; and thirdly, each figure is an approximately equal distance from the next, suggesting the regulation of a common beat. (See over.)

Individuals in village farming communities in the sixth and fifth millennia BCE would have gathered round a significant object – perhaps a sacred fire, or a holy tree – and delineated a sacred space around it with their own bodies by joining hands. The circular shape of the dance is physically as well as symbolically reproduced on the rim of the bowl.

Painted Pottery from Iran, from the 6th or 5th millennia BCE.
Adapted from an illustration in Garfinkel, 2003

The relentless pulse and beat of the dance impelled the individual to join the rituals. Scientists do not even now know precisely how this part of the human neural system works, but it is widely acknowledged that there is an auditory-motor pathway which triggers a compulsive physical reaction in humans when they hear the insistence of a regular beat. *Homo sapiens* is a natural timekeeper, living as he does with the regular rhythm of his own beating heart, as well as locomotion on two feet (efficient bipedalism depends on a *regular* walking rhythm). Neolithic individuals were drawn into the dance by the irresistible invitation of the drumming beat.

Circle-dancing associated with religious ritual persisted down the centuries:

> "Like the Mycenaeans, the Minoans, and the Egyptians before them, the Greeks danced at religious ceremonies; they danced to ensure fertile fields and fertile women; they danced to prepare for war and to celebrate victories; they danced at weddings and funerals; they danced to overcome depression and to cure physical illness."[2]

We find evidence from the ancient Greek world between the sixth and fifth centuries BCE in a terracotta fragment depicting a group of figures. This is a votive object relating to the rites of Hera, the Greek goddess of fertility and creativity, from the former Greek colony of Poseidonia in Italy (now known by its Roman name of Paestum). It depicts two figures on a circular base; there is a part of a third figure, suggesting there may originally have been more dancers in this ring (they are probably priestesses of the goddess, since they wear her high round head-dress, the *polos*).

By the time we arrive in Athens in the fifth century BCE, words can be added to our vision of the dance. It was still a ring-dance, circling around the central focus of an altar to a god, but now performed to a poem known as the *dithyramb* in honour of Dionysus. The poem, the singing of it, the dancing to it – all are part of an indissoluble whole, embraced by the Greek word *mousike*. We do not have the evidence of actual music, but we know that, because the poetry and music were so inextricably related, the dance itself also mirrored the pattern of the words. The dancing changed direction with the stanzas, turning to the left for the *strophe*, and back to the right for the balancing *antistrophe*. The Greek word *strophe* actually means a "turning". So here is a circle dance which turns first one way and then the other, varying the pattern of movement, and in which poetry and music have become united in the delineation of the dance.

There is evidence to suggest that ring-dancing may also have been a part of early Christian worship. A Christian text, written c.180CE,

Fragment of a votive group of terracotta figures from the Sanctuary of Hera at Paestum, c.5th century BCE, Museo Archeologico Nazionale, Paestum. Photograph by author.

the Apocryphal *Acts of St John*, describes Christ himself standing in the centre of a ring dance:

> "He bade us therefore make as it were a ring, holding one another's hands, and himself standing in the midst he said: Answer Amen unto me. He began, then, to sing a hymn and to say: Glory be to thee, Father. And we, going about in a ring, answered him: Amen ... Thus, having danced with us the Lord went forth."[3]

This interesting passage clearly refers not only to Christian ring-dancing, but also to the ancient practice of "call and response" – establishing the principle of a repeating refrain – which centuries later became such a feature of poetry and music for the dance. In the early days of Christianity, however, the observances of many contemporary Greek religious cults had degenerated into frenzied, orgiastic dance. It is unlikely that Christian dance was ever orgiastic, for the early Christians were rooted in Hebrew attitudes. But the Roman authorities might not have recognised fine distinctions between types of dance: they suspected Christianity was just another of those troublesome eastern religions and tried to suppress it. Within the Christian Church itself, the joyousness of early Christian dance fell victim to the reputation of such cults, and in the fourth century the Christian Council of Laodicea took fright and dance was officially forbidden to all Christians in the west.

As a result of this formidable ban, records of dancing in Western Europe disappeared for several centuries. But people do not always do as they are told. We know that they must have continued to dance, because down the centuries we can hear the stern voice of Christian authority telling them *not* to do so. It was a long time before churchmen relented. When the concession finally came it was in the splendidly mediaeval form of an allegory: a ring-dance might achieve respectability as *a symbol for celestial motion*. Thus the theologian Honorius of Autun:

> "By the circling of the dance ... they wished the revolution of the heavens to be understood; by the joining of hands the linking of elements; by the sound of singers the harmony of the resounding planets; by bodily gestures, the movements of the constellations; by hand-clapping or the stamping of feet, the crashing of thunder ..." [4]

Here lies buried a very useful description of a contemporary twelfth-century dance: a number of dancers join hands and move round in a circle, singing, clapping their hands and stamping their feet.

The impetus for secular, social dance finally arrived with the development of modern vernacular languages in Europe in the High Middle Ages: metrical poetry and "tail" rhymes were natural bedfellows for music. Metrical verse became a powerful communication tool at a time when few people could read or write: it was an oral memory bank for shared histories as well as entertainment to fill those long and dark winter nights in northern Europe. Work by the neurologists T Turner and E Poppel has shown that metrical verse is easily assimilated by an audience:

> "The fundamental unit of metred poetry, the line, nearly always takes from two to four seconds to recite (peak distribution 2.5 to 3.5 seconds). The three-second poetic line is the salient feature of metred poetry. Its prevalence in human poetry appears to be universal ... Like the poetic line, the parcel of experience is about three seconds – the length of the human "specious present" or present moment. ... Thus it is that a speaker will pause every three seconds or so to organise the next three seconds' worth of syntax; a listener will absorb about three seconds' worth of heard speech and then pause briefly to integrate what he has heard. This three second period to bundle information together to be sent on for processing to higher cortical centres constitutes a sort of pulse ... The apparent identity between the three-second pulse of metred verse and that of the brain's fundamental auditory processing system may account for the easy memorability of metred verse..."[5]

This potent mix of words and music in new vernacular languages became established in the south of France at the dawn of the twelfth century, with Guillaume IX, Duke of Aquitaine. He was amongst the first of the *troubadours*, aristocratic poet-musicians who sang of courtly love in poetry and music. But scholars are divided as to the musical source of inspiration for these songs which occupy such a pivotal position in European literary history.

Some believe that they may be derived from the Islamic culture which flourished in the south of Spain after the Arab conquest in 711 CE.[6] There is a colourful legend which has it that when the Spanish city of Barbastro was re-taken for the Christians by Guillaume de Montreuil in 1064, he took a thousand Arab slave-girls as booty back to his master in Provence. Even allowing for indignant exaggeration of the numbers in an Arab account, this is an intriguing story: the slave girls and their repertoire of Arabic sung poetry were taken to the court of Guillaume VI of Poitiers, who was father of none other than – the *troubadour* Guillaume IX of Aquitaine.

A second strand of scholarship however points to another metrical poetic tradition nurtured within the church itself: the Christian hymn. Hymns were strikingly different from the rest of the liturgy. They were short and made up of regular, four-line verses. Furthermore, each of those lines had an equal number of syllables, falling in eight even beats (the Latin hymns of the sixth-century poet Venantius Fortunatus were said to have been influenced by the rhythm of Roman marching songs). Hymns were sung to plainsong hymn chants: the first two lines arrived at a half-close, then the second two replied with a conclusive ending. They had a purposeful shape, a sense of goal-orientated melody.

Once Western poet-musicians discovered regular metre and rhyme, they could draw on this satisfying tonal model of the hymn. Just how much European poetry and song later owed to cross-fertilisation with the user-friendly hymns of the Christian church can be heard by following a conversion of the free-flowing plainsong of the old Advent hymn *Conditor alme siderum*. Here is the original seventh-century version:

Ex. 1.1

and here it is in sixteenth-century France, transformed into a bouncing three-beats-in-a-bar *Noel* entitled *Conditor fut le non-pareil*.

Ex. 1.2

The text is now macaronic, mixing the original Latin hymn with new French words, but the pitch of every plainsong note is identical and the integrity of the modal melody remains intact. Moreover, we can hear how the symmetry of the music must have matched the symmetry of the pattern of a dance: eight steps to the left – eight steps to the right – and so on.

Finally released from the disapproval of the Church, social dance emerged as an immensely popular activity between the twelfth and the fourteenth centuries, enjoyed by boisterous peasants as well as their more refined superiors at court and in manor houses. We now find a clear description of a round dance, the *carole,* in the *Roman de la Rose* (c.1230) by Guillaume de Lorris, suggesting that this dance has acquired sophisticated turns and pattern:

> "Now see the carol go! Each man and maid
> Most daintily steps out with many a turn
> And arabesque upon the tender grass."[7]

La Danse de Carole from *Œuvres poétiques de Guillaume de Machaut,* 1350-55,
Le Remède de Fortune: Scène de danse, folio 51.
Paris, Bibliothèque Nationale.

Fewer than fifty pieces of dance music survive from before 1400, none helpfully titled *"carole"*. However, a manuscript collection of songs by the French poet-composer Guillaume de Machaut contains a fine illustration entitled *La Danse de Carole* which we can add to de Lorris's description.

The picture features five debonair courtiers in long hose, holding hands with five refined ladies with carefully coiffured curls. There is a palpable sense of movement in each bent knee, as the dancers circle round under the clipped trees with dignified gliding steps – not for these graceful creatures the hop-skip-and-jump of contemporary roistering peasants.

At the same time as these fastidious courtiers were pacing gracefully through the *carole*, country village folk were also enjoying ring-
dances. The tradition of dancing round a maypole – a late example
of dancing round a central object, which may have had a Germanic
pagan origin – became established in Britain from the fourteenth
century. A painting from the studio of the English artist Francis
Hayman in c. 1741/2 illustrates a lively maypole dance taken from
a sequence of paintings illustrating contemporary country pastimes,
which hung in the Supper Boxes of the Pleasure Gardens at Vauxhall. The dancing scene is set on a village green: the Maypole rises
in the centre and the swaying bodies of the girls indicate that the
dance is circling round it to the left. (The dancers are not perfectly
synchronised – perhaps the painter is poking fun at rustic incompe-
tence.)

Francis Hayman and studio, *Country Dances Round a Maypole*, 1741/2.
London, Victoria and Albert Museum.

★ ★ ★ ★ ★

This painting of maypole dancers summarises the long evolution of
dancing in a ring which fed into eighteenth-century dance traditions.
For in this century, country dancing, with all its ancient histories,
was flourishing in England as never before. The folksong historian
Cecil Sharp described how

"... the Country Dance of the village green, the farmhouse, and
the dancing booths of the annual fairs, was slowly invading the

parlours and drawing-rooms of the wealthy, competing in attractiveness with the Minuets, Courantes, Gavottes, and rapidly gaining favour with the upper classes."[8]

Strange as it may seem with the background of social snobbery described in Chapter 1, these dances with all their circling and turning, and their accumulation of traditional step-patterns, had become adopted by the gentry – so that the social dancing of polite society in England was now *based on old country dances*. We may have known that dancing was very popular in the eighteenth century, but perhaps we had not realised precisely what that dancing might have been like.

Let us go back to the first principles of the dance in all those centuries of dancing *round* an object. If you had an immoveable object in the middle of your circle – such as an altar, or a maypole – you could not move across the circle, you could only go *round* the object, or close *up to it*, and then *back again*. Thus dancing became a perpetual pattern of circling and returning, going to the centre and back again. And when you no longer had to worry about the existence of a central object, you continued with the idea of circling and returning, going forward and coming back, *because that was what dancing now meant to you.*

These are the movements described in an immensely popular dance manual published by the enterprising English publisher John Playford between 1651 and 1728. His *English Dancing Master, or Plaine and easie Rules for the Dancing of Country Dances, with the Tune to each Dance* was an immediate hit. (It remained so popular that it went into eighteen editions and eventually included about nine hundred tunes.) Playford's dances are sequences of "figures" – circles, swinging, turns, weaving, "gips", "heys" and so on, and he provides not only the tunes but an accompanying description of each dance. Most importantly, *each sequence takes eight steps* to execute, and then a *further eight as the figure reverses* and the dancer returns. (In practice, musicians accompanying the dances simply repeated the short tunes over and over again – as many times as was necessary for the dancer to complete all the figures of the dance.)

As published by Playford, none of the tunes have words, and many bear curious titles (for instance "*Jenny Pluck Pears*" and "*Jockey was a dowdy lad*") which suggest that they were originally dance *songs*. However, a few texts do survive elsewhere, and here is one of them – "*If all the world were paper*": *

---

* These are the traditional words and music, neither to be confused with Shirley Temple's 1938 version!

If all the world were paper,
And all the sea were ink,
If all the trees were bread and cheese –
What would we have to drink?

The musical pulse of this short quatrain accompanies the dance like this:

If àll the wòrld were pàpèr and àll the sèa were ìnk,
[steps] 1   2   3 4   5   6   7   8 [turn]

If àll the trèes were brèad and chèese – what wòuld we hàve to drìnk?
        1   2   3   4   5   6   7   8
                                                                                                                      [home]

(4)

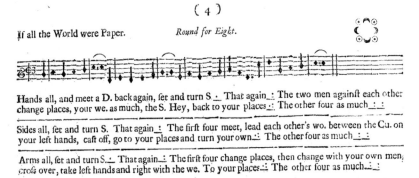

If all the World were Paper.   *Round for Eight.*

Hands all, and meet a D. back again, fet and turn S .·. That again.·: The two men againft each other
change places, your we. as much, the S. Hey, back to your places .·: The other four as much .:.:

Sides all, fet and turn S. That again.·: The firft four meet, lead each other's wo. between the Cu. on
your left hands, caft off, go to your places and turn your own.·: The other four as much .:.:

Arms all, fet and turn S.·. That again.·: The firft four change places, then change with your own men,
crofs over, take left hands and right with the we. To your places.·: The other four as much.:.:

Facsimile of Dance, From Playford's *English Dancing Master: If all the world
were paper:* Round for eight showing diagram of 8 dancers in a circle and
    instructions for several step sequences. From the 10th edition (1698).

Ex. 2

Every dance is built up from selected figures, each consisting of
8 + 8 steps. It will immediately be obvious that the pattern of the
dance, which is the pattern of figures executed by steps, coincides
precisely with the pulse and tonality of poetry and music as we heard
poetry and music coinciding in *Conditor fut le non-pareil.* With Playford's precise instructions now before us, we see how dance, poetry

and music must have been working together like this for a very long time.

(And we can also understand how the human brain's auditory processing system (see p.29) had been a factor in the long development of music for the dance – going back through Christian hymns and Roman marching songs, perhaps even to the beginnings of western civilisation in the villages of the ancient Near East.)

Music's own powerful contribution to song and dance in the west – just as potent as pulse and rhythm – was its tunefulness: the rise and fall of melodic lines helped to endorse the ends of poetic lines, especially those with "tail" rhymes, which so define the dance songs. (This contribution had come through the goal-oriented melody learnt from Gregorian hymn chants.)

Now listen again to Playford's tune *"If all the world were paper"*. At the end of the second line there is a pause on the word "ink" which produces a brief sense of *hiatus*. Imagine you have just danced the first 8 steps of a figure: you will sense the music *here telling you* that the figure is not yet completed – that *there is more to come*. Then listen through to the fourth line, where the tune ends with a sense of arrival and fulfilment (endorsed in the song by the expected rhyme of "drink" with "ink"). In music these line-endings are called "cadences". It is music's tunefulness which enables the listener to hear whether the end of the metric line is a hiatus or a full stop – a weak, "imperfect" cadence, a half-close (signifying a temporary stop), or a strong, "perfect" one, a full-close (signifying a distinct close).

By Playford's time the words had dropped out of use, but the metrical lines stayed on in dance tunes. If the tunes were taken away from the dance and used independently of either words or dance, the framework of cadences remained perfectly intelligible to audiences because the tonal idea of half-closes and full-closes was so familiar to them. So when John Bach came to write tunes to please his London audiences, he followed the same simple tonal template. Here is a little tune with a half-way pause and final close which he wrote not long after arriving in London:

Ex. 3.1

Ex.3 J C Bach: *Allegro*

It has the same simple pattern of expectation and fulfilment as Play-ford's dance tune. If you count each accented note as you hear it, you will sense the hiatus in the 8th bar, before Bach goes on to complete the little tune on the 16th accent.

This is the true significance of all that social dancing down the centuries: it hard-wired the simple tonal structure of the dance-song into the musical subconsciousness of people at every social level, all over Europe. It was the embedded expectation in dance music – an unfinished pause halfway, followed by a final close – which audiences now brought to their reception of John Bach's new music for instruments.

CHAPTER ENDNOTES

1   Garfinkel, Yosef. *Dancing at the Dawn of Agriculture*. Austin: University of Texas Press, 2003, p.19, pp.79ff, p.182.

2   Jonas, Gerald. *Dancing – the Power of Dance Around the World*. London: BBC Books, 1992, p.40.

3   From *The Apocryphal New Testament*, transl. M R James. Oxford: Clarendon Press, 1924, vv.94,97.

4   From Honorius of Autun, *Gemma Animae*, lib.I, cap.139 (*PL* 172.587). Quoted by Stevens, John, in *Words and Music in the Middle Ages: Song, Narrative, Dance and Drama, 1050-1350*. Cambridge, University Press, 1986, p.160; in turn citing from Gougaud, L, 'La Danse dans les Eglises', *Revue Historique Ecclésiastique* 15 (1914), pp.16-17.

5   Quoted by Rose, Gilbert J. *Between Couch and Piano – Psychoanalysis, music, art and neuroscience*. Hove and New York: Brunner-Routledge, 2004, pp.11-12.

6   Menocal, M R. *The Arabic Role in Medieval Literary History*. Philadelphia, University of Pennsylvania Press, 1987, p.28.

7   Quoted in Weiss, Piero and Taruskin, Richard, ed. *Music in the Western World: A History in Documents*. New York, Schirmer, 1984, pp.58-9.

8   Sharp, Cecil J. *The Country Dance Book* Part II. London: Novello and Co Ltd, 3rd edition, 1927, p.9.

CHAPTER 3

BACKGROUND 2: A GOOD TUNE

IN ADDITION TO the familiarity with dance music we have taken as a matter of course for eighteenth-century audiences, there is another important assumption we can make about their musical experience: they would have been familiar with what might broadly be described as the "tunefulness" of music. We might probably go further and assume that contemporary listeners realised that "tunes" were built from the eight notes of a musical scale, rising from a low note to a higher one in a consistent pattern of intervals. (The name "scale" incorporates the concept of "rising": it derives from the Latin *scala*, meaning "ladder".)

What eighteenth-century audiences might not have realised was that the tunes and the scale from which they were derived were part of a musical system which had arisen uniquely in western culture; nor that, like all systems, it was subject to regulation, in this case the natural laws of the properties of sound. On account of these laws, the notes of the western scale enjoyed complex relationships with each other which were well understood by composers: it was their skill in arranging the notes and manipulating the relationships which could make music so effective. So to understand how composers like John Bach made sure his music would appeal to audiences, we should begin with his raw material – *sound*.

Each individual sound or musical note contains – in addition to the fundamental note heard most strongly by the human ear – a rainbow-like spectrum of higher, ever-rising, ever-softer sounds, called *harmonics*. Only the first few of these are audible to humans, who however find them consonant with the sound of the fundamental, and therefore pleasing.

The 1st (the fundamental sound) and the 2nd harmonic, being the loudest, have the most powerful relationship (the 2nd is exactly double the frequency of the fundamental and is clearly audible to humans). These two harmonics sound an *octave* apart. The name *octave*, from the Greek *okto* (eight), records the distance of eight notes from top to bottom of the western scale. As an example, it is the interval – i.e. the difference in pitch – between the first two notes of the well-known song from the 1939 film *The Wizard of Oz* – "Somewhere over the rainbow".

Because of the special quality of this octave interval, almost all world music systems are structured around it – the science journalist Philip Ball calls it "grounded in the neurology of audition".[1] Each culture has evolved its own style of filling in the aural space between these anchor-points, choosing larger or smaller intervals to suit its own preference. Oriental music systems, for instance, favour many small intervals, while others cling to a larger one (a fourth) with only a few infilling notes (and this is the basis of the *pentatonic* scale, found in Scotland and Ireland and over a wide geographic area extending eastwards to Indonesia and westwards to North America). In ancient Greece the space was filled with combinations of two intervals – one small, one slightly larger; we recognise these today as the intervals in our own western scale.

The next harmonic, the 3rd, sounds at the interval of a *fifth* above the 2nd harmonic, and can also be heard by the human ear. The name *fifth* describes the distance between itself and the bottom note of the scale. This is the interval between the first two bars of the nursery-rhyme "*Twinkle, twinkle little star*".

In fact intriguing evidence has been unearthed by the French acoustic archaeologist Iégor Reznikoff which suggests that the audibility of these harmonics to humans may have been exploited in Palaeolithic times. Aware that caves have powerful natural resonance, Reznikoff went to the French Pyrenees to conduct some acoustic experiments.[2] He travelled methodically through the famous painted cave systems at Niaux and Le Portel, using his own voice at different pitches to pick up the natural vibrating frequency of each open space. He frequently picked up both 2nd and 3rd harmonics, sometimes simultaneously, so that powerfully reverberant musical sounds of fifths (and octaves) welled up from the darkness as he combed the galleries.

EXPERIMENT

A simple experiment on a traditional piano with strings will also reveal these harmonics: silently depress the note of middle C to lift the damper off the strings; then, keeping this key down, strike C an octave below middle C; release the low C and you will hear the pitch of middle C sounding as its strings vibrate in sympathy. This can be repeated with the higher notes G and C also sounding in sympathy with the low C.

Reznikoff made two significant findings: firstly, that there was a remarkably high correlation between the location of wall-paintings and key resonance points (90% in Niaux and 80% in Le Portel); and secondly, that in the Jammes Gallery at Le Portel, black and red wall markings seemed to direct him precisely to the resonance points of the 2nd and 3rd harmonics, suggesting that the positions of the markings were purposefully calibrated for resonance. He became convinced that in many instances the locations for paintings had been tested and chosen for their sound value.

All the pitches which he found were low, suggestive of a man's voice. In Palaeolithic times religious rituals were controlled by a shaman, who acted as sorcerer, diviner, healer and fount of all knowledge to his people; the shaman went into trance to connect with the superior world of supernatural powers, and to provide a link between humans and the spirit-realms. Reznikoff found that by pitching his voice at exactly the right frequency the shaman could have set the caves alive with resonating sound. It is easy to imagine what an extraordinarily powerful effect this would have had on ignorant, primitive peoples: they would readily have believed that the very spirits of the cave were responding to the shaman's call. We might imagine such people stumbling out into the daylight after one of these mesmerising experiences, with *the sound of the natural harmonics* ringing in their heads – for hours, perhaps days, on end.

Primitive peoples have an acute sense of hearing, but of course we can never know whether this was how the intervals of octave and fifth were first acknowledged in the west. The fifth is however known to be an important interval in many musical traditions all over the world, as far apart and diverse as the musics of China and India and that of small tribes in the islands of Oceania. Aniruddh Patel has proposed that its widespread incidence suggests there is "something about the human auditory system [which] biases people toward choosing this interval in building pitch relations in their musical sound systems".[3]

As it happens, the human voice itself sits comfortably within the pitch range of an octave – not only in song, but also in speech. Julian Jaynes writes that "In ordinary speech, we are constantly changing pitch, even in the pronunciation of a single syllable ... Speech reels around all over a certain portion of an octave (in relaxed speech about a fifth)."[4] It is possible that the harmonics' interval of the fifth has also affected the pitch range of spoken language. Whatever the original source, it is clear that at some far distant point in time, our human ancestors heard this beautifully consonant interval and it became hard-wired into their auditory consciousness.

The most important thing to realise about the 3rd harmonic, however, is that in the context of the fundamental, its frequency is *heavily out-numbered* (not least because the next one, the 4th harmonic, is exactly another octave above the 2nd – i.e. it is another "fundamental" sound, two octaves higher). Because of this, although the fifth blends well in the context of the fundamental and its upper harmonics, it must cede to the superior volume of fundamental sound. This is at the heart of understanding the special relationship between the fifth and the two octave sounds above the fundamental: *it is naturally pulled to return to one or other of them*, either down a 5th or up a 4th. Thus it was that when early societies based their music systems on the physical properties of sound, they (consciously or not) used the melodic intervals of octave, 5th and/or 4th to act as tonal anchors.

There is evidence of this relationship being effectively exploited in the music of the early Christian church, in the chanting of Psalms. Here everything flowed from the requirement that the sacred words should be heard and understood. If the priest was to be heard, he had to raise his voice – better still, to sing, since by singing he ensured the sound would carry well. So he began on a low note, then raised his voice to intone the first half of the verse at a higher pitch, usually a fifth above (known in the chant as the *tenor*), with a pause at the end of it; then he held the listener's attention at this higher pitch for the second half, until the final fall and close sealed the conclusion of the verse. This characteristic melodic shape is described by Willi Apel:

"The basic design of a Gregorian melody is that of an arch ... The most elementary embodiment of this design exists in the psalmodic recitative with its upward-leading intonation, its tenor recitation, and its downward-leading termination. It represents the prototype of the Gregorian phrase ..."[5]

There are a number of details to note here:

First is the sense of expectation set up by the two parts of the verse; the listener hears the "half-finished" pause halfway, before the more complete close on the final cadence at the end of the verse. *Second*, this pause is endorsed by the nature of the tonal relationship between the *tenor* and lower pitch of the mode – that strong "pull" of the fifth back down to the starting-point. *Third*, the chant trained listeners to follow the unfolding melodic line, so that as it became longer and more florid, the underlying stability of the two tonal anchor-points released all intervening notes to perform a purely decorative function.

This is a melodic line *with goal-orientated purpose*, which we have already encountered in the Christian hymn, but now we are better informed to understand the binding relationship between the *tenor* and the low *finalis* note. The sense of a falling close was so marked and so consistent that it was reflected in the descriptive name given to the final notes: the origin of the name "*cadence*" (see p.35) came from the Latin *cadere*, to fall. We shall find the principle of *cadences acting as musical punctuation* immensely important.

As we saw in the previous chapter, hymns were in the tradition of metrical verse, with their short four-line structure, and syllables to every one of the eight notes of each line. They were well suited for adaptation to this tonal model. The first two lines would arrive at a half-close, perhaps on the *fifth*; the second two would reply with a conclusive cadence, increasingly often ending on the *finalis* note of the mode itself. They had the purposeful shape, as in the Psalm tone, of melody governed by the dynamic of the relationship derived from the harmonics. Hymns were *tuneful*.

So now with this additional information we are in a better position to understand the success of the cross-fertilisation between sacred hymns and secular verse, such as we saw in the sixteenth century macaronic *Noel* in the previous chapter (p.30). Metrical verse brought regular pulse and rhyme schemes to dance-songs, but, crucially, music also endorsed the rhymes with rising and falling cadences – with its *tunefulness*. Only a century later Playford was publishing the first of the dances in his *English Dancing Master*.

★ ★ ★ ★ ★

There is, however, more to western tunefulness than two or three notes. In the middle of the eighteenth century, composers had five other notes in a scale at their disposal, making up the total of eight notes to an octave. The chart below names the eight notes in three different ways *(to accommodate what may be readers' own different experiences)*:

- the first line gives the degrees of the scale numbered by their position in it;

- the second the 'proper' name for each degree of the scale;

- the third gives the solmisation names for the notes (which are included here because, thanks to Julie Andrews in Rodgers and Hammerstein's *The Sound of Music,* they are widely known).

- the last line describes the intervals between each note.

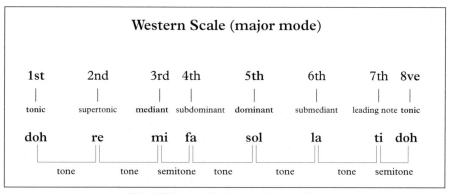

Fig. 1 Western Scale (major mode)

Ex. 6   Major Scale

(The solmisation names were not actually an idea dreamed up by Rodgers and Hammerstein: they were in fact coined by a most inventive late tenth-century monk, Guido d'Arezzo. He noticed (or perhaps he made up) a hymn tune, in which each line begins with a note of a rising scale, and then he used it as musical *mnemonic:*

"**Ut** queant laxis / **Re**sonare fibris / **Mi**ra gestorum/ **Fa**muli tuorum / **Sol**ve polluti / **La**bii reatum/ Sancte Johannes."

Ut was changed to *doh* and *ti* added in the nineteenth century.)

It is important to realise that for John Bach *these inherited eight notes have distinctive inter-relationships* which impact powerfully on western notions of tunefulness.

Once the home starting note has been sounded, all other notes are governed by the over-riding strength of the relationship between its own 1st, 2nd and 4th harmonics. These double octaves of fundamental sound set the home pitch of any tune using this scale, so this is generally known as the *tonic* (from the Greek word *tonos,* meaning "a thing stretched", i.e. the string of a musical instrument), its "note" or the "pitch" at which it sounds. The next in this hierarchy is the fifth: it is not for nothing that the fifth is known as the *dominant* (it can pull back to the tonic more conclusively than any other note in the scale). But there is another strong note in the major scale too: the third, or *mediant*. It is strong because it is the next harmonic, the 5th one (sounding at the interval of a third above the 4th harmonic) and therefore it is beautifully consonant with the tonic and dominant; in the west we regard this note in the major scale as having a cheerful, positive ring to it.

What of the remaining notes? We can see (*Fig. 1*) most are a **tone** apart, such as *doh* to *re, re* to *mi*, and so on. The tone is a relaxed interval, happy to act as a foil to stronger notes and simply pass between them. The **semitones**, as the name implies, are smaller intervals, but they are also much more sensitive. Because *doh* and *mi* are strong notes, the adjacent semitones *ti* and *fa* are unstable – *ti* and *fa* long to move to their strong neighbours, *doh* and *mi* respectively, and there is a reassuring sense of relief when they do so. Exploiting the dynamics of the inter-relationships of these eight notes – what Aniruddh Patel neatly describes as their "hierarchy of stability"[6] – is the way in which a composer makes music interesting and expressive, as well as stable and satisfying. In considering musical examples, we shall constantly be aware of these dynamics.

The western system has another scale too – the minor scale. This is set in the same overall framework as the major one, so that it is governed by strong tonic and dominant notes, but here the semitones are differently placed. Its most critical difference is the minor third, which is a semitone lower than the major third. This note comes from one of the higher harmonics in the harmonic series, and is not so closely related to the tonic and the dominant; although it associates satisfactorily with them, it does not – again by common western consent – produce the "cheerful, positive" sound of the major third, but a "plaintive, insecure" one. Its remote position in the series is basis enough for its fragility; but the continuing perception of the minor third as "sad" dates back as far as the Renaissance, and "... any cultural tradition that has persisted for so long takes on a certain importance even if it is based on nothing more than custom"[7]. The other semitones in the minor scale can be variable: as in the major scale, the sharpened 7th, or *leading note*, longs to move up the semitone home to the tonic; but the 6th note, or *submediant*, can be dropped by a semitone ("flattened") so that it produces a yearning, unstable semitone above the dominant, longing to fall down onto it and help it lead home to the tonic. These are the notes of the "harmonic" minor scale.

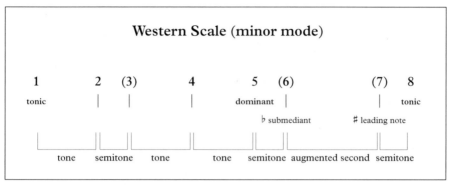

Fig. 2 Western Scale (minor mode)

Ex. 7.1 Minor Scale (harmonic)

In practice, the angular, awkward sound of the augmented second interval between ♭6th and ♯7th is often mitigated by 6th and 7th moving together. They can be raised as they progress upwards, and lowered coming downwards. This produces the more ingratiating "melodic" minor scale.

Ex. 7.2 Minor Scale (melodic)

(To hear the difference in sound quality between the major and minor modes, listen to some well-known pieces in the major mode, such as Handel's *Hallelujah* chorus, Beethoven's *Ode to Joy* from the 9th Symphony, or Chopin's *Minute* waltz. Then compare them with pieces in the minor mode such as Purcell's *Dido's Lament*, Mozart's 40th Symphony in g minor, or Rachmaninov's 2nd piano concerto in c minor.)

Most of the new instrumental music in the eighteenth century was written primarily in the major mode, because people wanted to be *cheerfully* entertained. However, composers often dropped into the minor mode of the home tonic to create a *serious* contrast. But this entailed changing several of the notes of the major scale. They could cast a temporary shadow over a sunny piece of music more easily by letting it slip into the minor mode of a nearby neighbour: this entailed altering only a single note (raising the 5th by a semitone). This neighbour stands in the relationship of 6th, or submediant, to the tonic and shares many of the same notes. Because of its close relationship, this minor scale is known as the "*relative minor*" of the major scale. This is a relationship we shall hear frequently in the music of the eighteenth and nineteenth centuries – but it is best understood as a melodic one, as just explained. The following chart demonstrates the closeness of the relationship:

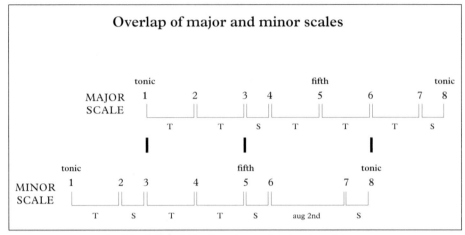

Fig.3 Overlap of major and minor scales

★   ★   ★   ★   ★

Up to this point most references have been of necessity to the melodic lines, or "tunes" of vocal music, because western music was primarily vocal in origin. Melody is the horizontal aspect of music: the notes of a tune are understood by being heard consecutively, not simultaneously. But there is also a vertical aspect to music, when other voices accompany the tune with different notes which we do hear simultaneously. This vertical aspect is called "harmony" and it is a feature of the western music system which sets it apart from all other music systems – the ethnomusicologist Bruno Nettl called it "the hallmark of Western music".[8] Scales are the notes which define either the *major* or the *minor* mode, but harmony comprises the groups of notes (or "chords") which support those notes, especially in the cadences which define the "home tonic" sound. It is a crucial element in establishing the tonality of a piece. To understand the basic essentials of harmony in the eighteenth century, we must turn again to the physics of sound.

The human ear finds consonant sounds attractive, therefore composers found that the most pleasing sounds to accompany a note were – naturally – those nearest to it in the harmonic series. Beginning on the 1st note, or tonic, they added the consonant 3rd and 5th above it, three notes which, sounded together, became known as the "tonic triad". This home tonic sound is the centre of gravity in a piece of western music, the tonal core always pulling towards return.

We have already understood why the 5th (the dominant) note in the scale relates so closely to the tonic. The triad built up on the dominant (the 5th, 7th and 2nd notes of the home scale) pulls strongly towards the tonic – not only because its root is the closely-related home 5th, but also because its third note is the 7th (the home leading-note) which longs to move up the semitone home to the tonic.

All the notes of the tonic and dominant triads can be found in the home tonic scale. There is one more triad which can also be derived from the scale: starting on the 4th note, the subdominant triad consists of the home 4th, 6th and tonic octave notes. The harmonics of the 4th and 6th notes are far from the home tonic base, and therefore this triad does not sound as strong as the tonic or dominant. The subdominant triad therefore sets up an element of relative uncertainty, best smoothed away by movement from it to the dominant triad leading back to the tonic.

The three triads thus provide the *functional harmony* which supports the sense of home tonality – known as "*key*" – in a piece of music. Underpinning a melodic line with these strong chords helps to establish and sustain the home key, particularly at cadence points. Here is a chart of the *primary triads* showing how they can accompany any note of the home scale which may be used in a tune:

Notes of scale	tonic	2nd	3rd	4th	5th	6th	7th	tonic	
	doh	re	mi	fa	sol	la	ti	doh	
tonic triad (I)	1	-	3	-	5	-	-	8	
fifth triad (V)	-	(2)	-	-	5	-	7	-	2
fourth triad (IV)				4	-	6	-	8	

Fig. 4 Primary Triads

Accompanying a tune was more important than it may sound. As musical style became simpler during the course of the eighteenth century, the listener's attention focused more on the melodious line of the treble instrument. Underlying parts became less interesting, but they were supplying harmony-as-accompaniment and this was functionally rather important. Composers used the harmony of the

primary triads to endorse the direction of the treble tune, punctuating it and reinforcing the cadences which made the new instrumental music intelligible. This will become clear as we listen to the music
itself.

Ex. 8 Major Scale harmonised by primary triads

I   V   IV   I   IV   I   V   I

Ex.8 Major scale harmonised by primary triads

We should also note two important changes taking place in the
practice of western music in the first half of the eighteenth century.
Until the middle of the previous century, song and dance tunes had
been derived from the interval patterns of the old mediaeval modes.
But gradually, between c.1650 and c.1700, the two scales we have
just considered (which had been Church modes XI and IX) became
by far the most popular, and all the rest fell into disuse.

While in most respects this was a welcome simplification, it was
not without problems. If instruments were to play together, they
had to be tuned to the same scales, but at the turn of the century
many were not compatible. So the second important change was the
introduction of a new system of tuning which could be applied to all
instruments, including keyboard and fretted ones.

The system, known as *equal temperament*,[9] divided the octave into
twelve equal semitones; and although it produced fifth and third
intervals which were acoustically impure, as William Thomson has
observed, "the human perceptual agency is liberally forgiving",[10] and
it became an acceptable compromise to most ears: J S Bach wrote
the forty-eight preludes and fugues of *Das Wohltemperirte Clavier*
(1722) in celebration of it. It had a further great advantage: it gave
composers a previously impossible degree of freedom to move not
only between the two scales, but also between many more different
keys. The transition to the new tuning was gradual, but by the middle
of the eighteenth century it had become an accepted norm (for most
musicians other than some recalcitrant French and English organ-
ists, who took another century or so to come round to it).

The freedom to move between keys opened up previously
undreamt-of vistas of tonal exploration for the composer. A scale
could be set up on any of the twelve notes as a starting-point – one
only had to observe the scale sequence of *tone-tone-semitone-tone-*
tone-tone-semitone and a sense of key could be established at any

pitch. It would then be possible, temporarily and for local colour and variation, by altering only a few notes to slip into a neighbouring key such as the dominant, the subdominant or the relative minor (and in the course of time – as we shall see – much further away than that).

(For purposes of quick reference, the customary musicians' shorthand for chords built on the notes of the scale will be used throughout this book. Each note is numbered as in the chart in Fig. 1, p. 43, and the chords follow the same numbering with capital Roman numerals for major triads (e.g. tonic major = I, dominant = V), and lower case for minor triads (i.e. tonic minor = i).)

A diagram of a piano keyboard follows so that the reader with little or no experience of musical notation can have a point of reference (should s/he so wish) for the twelve names and notes of the western system. From the middle of the eighteenth century a composition was known by its generic title (such as symphony or sonata) but also, taking its tonic as starting point, by its key (such as "Sonata in B♭ major"). Readers not familiar with notation or a keyboard may find it helpful to see how scales are built up, and especially where the semitones are situated: the distance between each note, black or white, is a semitone; 2 semitones = a tone. (For reference purposes, this diagram is also reproduced at Appendix A, together with the key signatures of major keys and their relative minor keys). This diagram may also be helpful to an understanding of how composers became more adventurous about moving between different keys as the sonata idea developed.

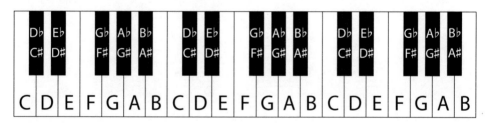

♯ sharp = semitone *above* a named note;
♭ flat = semitone *below* a named note.

Fig. 5 Diagram of note names

* * * * *

The system of equal temperament tuning became accepted over a long period of time. Beginning in 1651, the dances in Playford's *English Dancing Master* began as an assortment of modal tunes, but by the time of its final edition in 1728 they had all been trimmed into either the major or the minor mode. By then the dropping of little-used modes in favour of these two was widespread, and Bach and Abel's eighteenth-century London audiences would have been entirely comfortable with the tuning in contemporary performances. The ancient tonality handed down in the dance encompassed that of the major and minor modes from which tunes were now built.

The history of social dancing has demonstrated that centuries of moulding to the dance experience had made dance music quintessentially fit for purpose. Its embedded expectations had given everyone a simple but profound sense of *tonality* – a simple acceptance of *tonic as home*, and at a deeper level a sense of the *dominant as a temporary hiatus* always requiring the resolution of *return to the home tonic*. The fact that the gentrification of country traditions led to fewer dances which were "Rounds" and more "Longs-for-as-many-as-will" (to suit the shape of Assembly Halls and Long Rooms in gentry houses) did not matter: by now the dancers had inherited this sense of tonality which would be the essential background to the sonata idea.

CHAPTER ENDNOTES

1   Ball, Philip. *The Music Instinct*. London: Bodley Head, 2010.

2   As recounted by Devereux, Paul. *Stone Age Soundtracks: The Acoustic Archaeology of Ancient Sites*. London: Vega, 2001, pp.107-113.

3   Patel, Aniruddh D. *Music, Language and the Brain*. Oxford: Oxford University Press, 2008, p.93.

4   Jaynes, Julian. *The Origin of Consciousness in the Breakdown of the Bicameral Mind*. Boston: Houghton Mifflin, 1976; reprinted London: Allen Lane, 1979, p.264.

5   Apel, Willi. *Gregorian Chant*. Bloomington & Indianapolis: Indiana University Press, 1958; First Midland Book edition, 1990, p.249.

6   Patel, *ibid*, p.201.

7   Aldwell, Edward and Schachter, Carl. *Harmony and Voice Leading*. San Diego & New York: Harcourt Brace Jovanovich, 1989, pp.19-20; as quoted in Hepokoski, J and Darcy, W, *op.cit*, p.307.

8   Nettl, Bruno. *The Study of Ethnomusicology*. Urbana and Chicago: University of Illinois Press, 1983; new ed. 2005.

9   For a full account, see Isacoff, Stuart. *Temperament*. London: Faber and Faber, 2002.

10 Thomson, William. *Schoenberg's Error*. Philadelphia: University of Philadelphia Press, 1991, p.67.

CHAPTER 4

THE *GALANT* ACCOMPANIED HARPSICHORD SONATA: J C BACH, SCHOBERT, HAYDN

AN EASY UNDERSTANDING of tonic and dominant tonality, a penchant for a nice well-rounded tune – London audiences in the 1760s were ready to hear what John Bach had to offer them.

Within a year of his arrival Bach was exploring the idea of writing symphonies for the forthcoming Subscription Concerts, and also some little pieces in the same popular Italian style for his pupils. He called these pieces "sonatas".

The title *sonata* was not new: towards the middle of the eighteenth century it had already been in use for some two hundred years. It was originally derived from the Italian word *suonare* – a *sonata* being a "sounding" piece of music for instruments, as opposed to a *cantata,* a "singing" piece for voices. It is important to realise that the title had been applied to a number of earlier musical types which have little to do with the later sonata. The Baroque trio sonata, for instance, the most popular chamber music work of its era, which might be thought from its title to be the direct forerunner of the piano trio, is nothing of the sort: it actually required four, not three performers – two melody instruments (usually violins) and a 'cello with the harpsichord. The harpsichord player in these works was merely the accompanist for the rest, with no independent written part, forced only to follow the bass line and to improvise a suitable part from figured notes indicated by the composer. Harpsichordists were highly skilled, but not regarded as solo instrumentalists in these trio sonatas. "Keyboard accompaniments in chamber music did not evolve from continuo improvisations to obbligato parts," writes David Fuller, "they disappeared ... along with the continuo itself".[1]

From the beginning of the eighteenth century the role of the keyboard player in chamber music underwent a profound change on account of the growing realisation of the unexplored solo potential of contemporary keyboard instruments. Early harpsichord and organ concertos, as well as the brilliant style of new works such as J S Bach's keyboard suites (written c.1715 in Weimar) and Handel's eight "Great" Harpsichord suites (published in London in 1720) established the harpsichord as a solo instrument, and created a small but distinguished repertoire of works for performance by skilled players. In Paris the music of the *clavecinistes* was popular in the salons, especially the miniaturist *genre* pieces of François Couperin, and it was here that the focus on the harpsichord as a solo instrument reached a notable point with the publication in 1734 of the French composer Mondonville's *Pièces de clavecin en sonates avec accompagnement de violin*, op 3. In spite of their equivocal title, these *pièces* gave equal weight to violin and harpsichord, and signalled the beginning of the solo violin and piano sonata (and hence of the great tradition of solo instrumental sonatas with piano).

It was only a matter of time before further chamber music *genres* involving a keyboard instrument would appear. The string quartet had already taken off in the wake of the early symphony, but it had two advantages: firstly, that the string instruments were well balanced with each other in tone, and secondly, that it could be performed in public by professional players. The first sonatas for a harpsichord accompanied by both a violin and a 'cello appeared in the early 1750s in Mannheim, and, given the new emphasis on the harpsichord, they became known as "accompanied sonatas" for harpsichord (in fact, the string parts were often optional). At around the same time Leopold Mozart produced a similar set in Salzburg, while Felice Giardini brought the Neopolitan style to London with his *Six Sonatas with obbligato keyboard.*

John Bach arrived in London just as demand for accompanied sonatas was gaining momentum. He was himself a skilled harpsichord player, and as well as having already written and performed several concertos, he had also composed some accompanied sonatas in Milan. He was therefore well placed to contribute new works to this fledgling sonata *genre*. He was also shrewd, and could see ways of addressing two difficulties which had already arisen with the accompanied sonata.

Firstly, there were problems of balance between strings and harpsichord. Although the upper register of the keyboard was clear and bright, in the middle and lower registers it tended to be drowned out by the stronger tone of a string instrument. Adding a low part for a 'cello to double the left hand of the harpsichord had proved to be an effective solution, so Bach decided to write his new sonatas for a harpsichord with a 'cello as well as a violin (or flute).

Bach's second problem was that there was likely to be inconsistency between the skills of the performers for whom these new pieces were intended. As we have seen, the new accompanied sonatas were not for public performance, but for private domestic enjoyment. The harpsichord players were chiefly the ladies of the house, who enjoyed music and were often quite talented; moreover, they dedicated much of their ample leisure time to diligent practice, so they were also skilled performers. The ladies of that time, however, were not permitted to play any of the other common chamber music instruments: not the violin, certainly not the 'cello, nor any of the woodwind instruments – because performance on these instruments was deemed unacceptably unladylike. So the accompanying instrumental parts had to be taken by the gentlemen, family members or friends of the household. They might enjoy music, but they had a somewhat cavalier attitude towards practice, primarily because they thought that musical performance was not really the province of English gentlemen, but rather of foreign professionals (who at that time ranked more or less as household servants). Advice to young men had often been distinctly hostile to the study of music. James Puckle, writing in 1713, advised his son that

> "Musick takes up much time to acquire to any considerable perfection … It's used chiefly to please others, who may receive the same gust from a mercenary; consequently, it is scarce worth a gentleman's time, which might be much better employ'd in the Mathematicks, or what else would qualify him for the service of his country."[2]

The quality of the gentlemen's performance, in short, was unpredictable: the accompanying instrumental parts had to be simple.

Let us try to get inside John Bach's head as he writes these pieces for his pupils. He must ensure that they are not too long, not too difficult, yet at the same time must have a flavour of the idiom which would prove so popular at the Concerts: they must be *galant* pieces in miniature.

He begins with his own starting-point – his lessons from Johann Sebastian. His father's teaching methods were recorded by another pupil, Gerber, who said that the great master began lessons with the keyboard music of his own (so-called) French and English suites. The suite was a collection of movements based on the rhythm of stylised French court dances, such as the *menuet* from Versailles, the *allemande,* the *gavotte* and the *gigue*. The *gigue* was known for its jaunty triplet rhythm; it was in fact derived from the sixteenth-century English "jig", a rustic dance which had travelled to France and achieved gentrification at court – composers traditionally rounded off suites with a *gigue* as a rousing finale. Here is a description of one with which John Bach would have been familiar:

J S Bach: *Gigue* from Suite no 4 of Six "English" Suites BWV 809

It is soon clear that this music will have none of the continual pausing on half-closes and cadences associated with dancing – these are stylisations of the dance. It is as though on the very first note the composer puts his foot on the treadle of a spinning wheel, setting in motion a flow of notes which scarcely pause from the beginning to the end of each piece. Taking the familiar rhythms of the dance as a starting-point, Bach creates a duet between the performer's right and left hands. We hear the opening motif at different pitches, until there is a temporary halt in the key of the fifth, the dominant, at the end of the first part; the first part is repeated. The second part then takes off from where the first left off – in the dominant key – and works its way back to the opening tonic key.

Note the device of *sequence*: a "sequence" is a type of repetition. It is a hallmark of Baroque style. A musical phrase is stated (it can be short or equally quite long) and then repeated at a different pitch (usually a tone above or below). The ear immediately picks up the repetition and there is a sense of pleasurable anticipation in the expectation of another hearing. It is "a harmonic movement with the propulsive force of rhythmic repetition" (Rosen) and because of its effectiveness as a compositional tool we shall encounter this device in continual use through the Classical period and beyond.

Johann Sebastian's suite movements are superb: subtle, intricate and highly intellectual, constantly slipping from one key to another in search of change and tonal contrast. But they also have an old and familiar groundplan. If we compare this *gigue* with *If all the world were paper*, we can see that (shorn of its length and complexity) it is actually an extended version of the dance:

If all the world were paper

(16 beats: 8 + 8)

tune   〰〰〰 ' 〰〰〰

note   1   5   5   1

J S Bach: *gigue*

(52 bars: 24 + 28)

music   〰〰〰〰〰〰〰〰〰 ' 〰〰〰〰〰〰〰〰〰〰

key   I   V   V   I

Fig. 6 Tonal groundplan: dance song and *suite* movement

The dance pauses on the fifth *note* of the scale, then returns to close in the tonic; the *suite* movement pauses halfway in the *key* of the fifth, and also returns to close in the tonic. This is the parallel between the tonal structure of dance and *suite* movements, and, importantly, how the sense of beginning and ending in a "home" key is fundamental to both.

John Bach has undoubtedly known and loved this music all his life. It was by studying the craft of composition in the contrapuntal texture of such works that he himself began to learn the techniques of composition. He also recognises the tried and tested tonal framework, with its secure division into two parts, the repeats of those parts, and the satisfaction of the final return to the home key. But he knows too that his audience has tired of both the repetitiveness and also the complexity of the Baroque style. He thinks of the neat brevity, the simple tunefulness and the changes of mood and texture he has heard in Italy. So he takes the little tune he has invented (see p.35) and he builds around it a movement which will have the secure ground plan of Johann Sebastian's suite movements, but the light touch of an Italianate tune.

J C Bach: 2nd movement *Allegro* from Sonata in G major op 2 no 2 W B44

The movement begins with the little tune with its halfway pause and repeat.

Ex. 3.2

Having established his home key (G major), Bach now moves swiftly away. We hear the bass line falling to settle on another note: it is proposing another dominant, which takes us to a firm close in the *home dominant key* of D major. This ends the first part, which is then repeated.

The second part opens with the beginning of the little tune (still in D major), but then the harpsichord drifts away into a couple of sequences. We hear the bass halt, and then remain on the same note for 6 bars, creating a feeling of *anticipation* (we sense this is the *home* dominant note, wanting to return …). The anticipation is happily resolved by the reappearance of the opening tune, now safely back in the home tonic key. Bach then repeats almost all of the first part, in the home key to the end. The second part is also repeated.

Let us first look at the little tune itself. It is just the sort of tune Bach's audience will appreciate – a dance pattern of 8 bars + 8 bars, making 16 bars in all. He has built it up from several small repeating motifs:

motif + *repeated* + *another motif* + *repeated* + *rounding off on V*
2 bars + 2 bars + 1 bar   + 1 bar   + 2 bars   = 8 bars
the whole repeated, but turned at end to cadence not on V, but on I
2 bars + 2 bars + 1 bar   + 1 bar   + 2 bars   = 8 bars

Note how the temporary dissatisfaction of the weak cadence in the middle is entirely resolved by the strong closing cadence on the tonic. This is not a rambling succession of notes, but a carefully-constructed sequence of separate motifs, made cohesive by the use of repeats (at both the same and at different pitches) and also by the balance of its two halves. This is a perfect example of a Classical tune, an archetypical 16-bar period structure.[3] Its two balanced 8-bar phrases add up to the neatest little design in time.

We shall find that it is a typical example of the procedure which Classical composers adopt to build up the tunes or "themes" of their sonata movements. Balancing motifs and phrases not only meets the audience's predilection for symmetry and intelligibility, but we will see that it also gives composers a considerable degree of flexibility. (This theme, for instance, might have cadenced after the first half back in I, leaving the second half to cadence on V and continue moving on immediately.) The tune is typically *galant* in style: it is prettily melodious, it has breathless pauses between phrases and is decorated with tiny trills.

The *galant* in music is often regarded as the equivalent of the *rococo* in the fine arts, characterised by lightness and elegant decoration. Essentially it marked a pronounced change of tone after the Baroque. By the middle of the century the daily experience of music had moved from church and opera house into the *salon*, grandeur had been replaced by conversational pleasantry and wit. Musically it was characterised by tunefulness, short phrases, little dotted rhythms and *appoggiaturas*, emphasis on tunes in the upper voices of violin or the treble register of a keyboard with simple functional accompaniments below. *Galant* was perhaps best defined by Voltaire, who said that "being *galant*, in general, means *seeking to please*."

Typical of the symmetry of a classical musical structure, quite different from the rambling continuity of the Baroque suite, this tune also parallels the symmetry of contemporary decorative design. If we look at Thomas Chippendale's designs for the splat (the decorative back panel) of three chairs dating from c.1754, we can see that on either side of each central vertical line the carved patterning is duplicated. No wonder the *galant* style was popular: both tune and chair satisfy the contemporary desire for mirror-image symmetry.

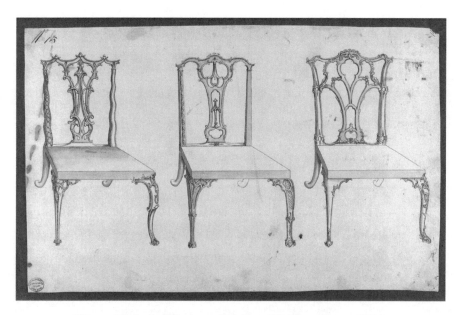

Three Chairs by Thomas Chippendale, London, c.1754.
New York, Metropolitan Museum of Art.

The second point to note in Bach's *Allegro* is the family likeness with the binary suite movements. Listeners were used to hearing these dance movements in which the second part was a little longer than the first – extended by extra material between the double bar and then a return to the opening idea. The Classical period adopted the same footprint, and this *Allegro* is essentially the same. The difference is that, with less rapidly-changing harmony, John Bach's move to the dominant in the first half is made earlier, and the tonic returns correspondingly earlier in the second half. But he fills in the space between the double bar and the return with sequences, just like Johann Sebastian – and we should note this expansion in the middle of a binary movement, already here in place long before this space, became the focus for development in sonata movements.

This short piece is the second movement of the set of six sonatas published as Bach's op 2 in 1763. They were dedicated to Princess Augusta, the King's sister, and described on the title page as *Six Sonatas for the harpsichord accompanied by a Violin or Flute and a Violoncello*. Because of its position at the end of the work, it was intended to be a light-hearted finale, and therefore shorter, less serious and more condensed than the first movement. It affords an ideal opportunity to see the bare bones of early classical structure. While it is unusual to begin by listening to the last movement of a work, our excuse is that this little movement has given us such a clear insight into the working of early sonata practice. The theorist

Johann Mattheson actually advised his students in 1737 to begin their studies with

> "a little minuet, so that everyone may see what the structure of such a little thing consists of, when it is not a monstrosity, and so one might learn to make a sound judgment by moving from the trifling to the more important"[4]

Here is a description now of the opening movement of this sonata:

J C Bach: 1st movement *Allegretto* from Sonata in G major op 2 no 2 W B44

The harpsichord takes the lead and presents a pleasant 4-bar tune (**1**), characterised by a smooth semiquaver turn (**a**), and a crisp dotted rhythm (**b**) – this expands to fill the first eight bars.

Ex. 9.1

With the tonic established, the violin takes over (a), and then heads away into a transitional passage of sequences high in its register. This ends in three bars of emphatic cadencing on the chord of A (V of home V, D major). A new tune (2) follows in the dominant key (D), incorporating a *galant* figure of staccato semiquavers shared between the harpsichord and violin.

Ex. 9.2

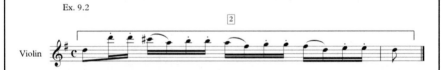

Six further bars cadence firmly in the dominant. Repeat.

The second part begins with the opening 8 bars in the dominant, but then the semiquaver motif (a) takes us into e minor (the relative minor key of the home tonic). The minor mode persists for 14 bars, until 3 bars of home V re-instate the tonic tonality, and the violin picks up (a), safely returned to the home key. The rest of the material from the first part then follows in the home tonic. Repeat.

John Bach's natural flair for pleasing melody and the attractive flow of 8-bar "tunes" may initially mask the close links this movement still has with the suite. Again it is set out in two parts, both of which are marked to repeat; and again the tonal footprint – travelling to the dominant at the double bar, and home again at the end – remains the same.

However, there is a significant new feature. Once the opening tune has run its course and Bach has gone on to establish the dominant key with that emphatic cadencing on the V of V chord, he introduces a second, *new and different*, tune in the dominant key. This signally announces his arrival in the dominant, making a much more distinctive feature of the new key than in the old *suite* movement. He also introduces further new (though not so distinctive) material in the last 3 bars of the first part, firmly rounding off the section in the dominant key.

Leaving the home tonality so emphatically like this *sets up a sense of unrest at a deep level of the listener's perception*. It is in fact a longer, deeper version of the hiatus after the 8 steps of the dance, or half-way through John Bach's little tune in the *Allegro* movement. The second tune has *drawn attention to the difference between the tonic and dominant keys*. Charles Rosen calls the new key "essentially a dissonance raised to a higher plane", since "a passage in a tonal work that is outside the tonic is dissonant in relation to the whole piece".[5]

Because this unrest goes so deep, it follows that when the home tonic key does finally return in the second part (as listeners expect), the material which was originally heard in the dominant key must now be heard in the tonic to achieve a resolution of the unrest. We noted the moment when John Bach returned to home tonality: from that transitional moment onwards, all the material which was heard in the dominant in the first part – transition, second tune, closing 3 bars of cadences – is now scrupulously repeated in the home tonic.

Rosen comments:

"Material presented outside the tonic must have created, in the eighteenth century, a feeling of instability which demanded to be resolved ... Today, our harmonic sensibilities have become coarsened by the tonal instability of music after the death of Beethoven, and the strength of this feeling is perhaps difficult to recapture."[6]

You may not think you have heard the instability at this moment, but you assuredly will do so at the end of the first part. Listen with eighteenth-century ears for *the return to the tonic* on the repeat of the first part, and *the return to the dominant* after the repeat of the second: these are the moments to hear the difference between tonic and dominant keys and to experience eighteenth-century tonality as contemporaries did. The repeats of each part (observed in contemporary performance) are important: not only to familiarise the listener with the contents of the first part, but to hear the tonal contrast and the satisfaction of final resolution in the second part.

As in the *Allegro* second movement, John Bach organises his material very differently from J S Bach. His two "tunes" are neatly packaged into 8-bar tonal boxes. These boxes are moments of tonal stasis, enclosed in firm cadences (either tonic or dominant). The intervening passages – more loosely defined, often consisting of scales and arpeggio figures in sequence – move on again, carrying the listener to the next box and the next stage in the unfolding tonal story. Listen to the bass line in the harpsichord and 'cello to sense the harmonies moving, and expect insistent preparation on a new dominant as they create tonal stability for the next "tune".

The simplicity of this movement by John Bach enables us to hear very clearly how composers exploited the distinctive difference in the relationship of tonic and dominant, and thus to understand the concept of "dissonance" introduced by the dominant, and the crucial importance of eventual "resolution" in the return of the tonic. This tonal concept would be the mainspring of the sonata idea.

★   ★   ★   ★   ★

The year after John Bach's accompanied sonatas were published, Leopold Mozart arrived in London with his two prodigiously gifted children. With his royal connections and native German tongue, John Bach naturally made the arrangements for them to be presented at court. Wolfgang was eight years old and John Bach was still only twenty-nine. There are charming anecdotal descriptions of the child sitting between the young man's knees as they improvised together for Queen Charlotte.

But what is especially interesting is a letter which Leopold, back in their lodgings, wrote shortly afterwards to his wife, describing Wolfgang "seated at the harpsichord *preparing to play one of Bach's Trios*". These were the sonatas of op 2 (and it is noteworthy that Leopold actually refers to them as "trios" and not "accompanied sonatas"). They were among a number of works by Bach which Mozart encountered at this time, all of which made a deep impression on the child. There are only a few recorded instances of the two musicians meeting, but every time Mozart mentions Bach it is with warmth and appreciation. Fourteen years later he writes to Leopold from Paris that "I love him (as you know) and respect him with my whole heart". The charm of Bach's *galant* style and the Italianate flair in his elegant writing had a lasting influence on Mozart – there are certain turns of phrase which we may think of as characteristically

Mozartian but which were in all probability absorbed from Bach. (And it was one of Bach's arias, *Non so d'onde* (from his opera *Alessandro nell'Indie)* which Mozart once called *"meine favorit Sache"* – "my favourite piece".)

It is fascinating to think of the child Mozart seating himself on the harpsichord stool to play this music at sight, recognising the new idiom and drawing it into his musical consciousness. Many years later, he wrote to his father that he could "accept and imitate pretty well any type and style of composition". Here is early evidence of that ability: he was so excited by Bach's sonatas that he immediately dashed off six accompanied sonatas of his own in imitation of Bach, K.10–K.15, which were engraved in London during their stay. But these are immature works, now rarely performed, and Mozart felt the influence of the older composer at a deeper level later in his life.

On their way to London, the Mozart family had spent five months in Paris. Thanks to the mediation of a fellow countryman, Baron Grimm, they had secured invitations to perform at several aristocratic houses, including that of the Prince Conti. One of the city's most successful young musicians, Johann Schobert (c.1735-1767), was employed by the Prince, and he also had made an immediate and considerable impression on Wolfgang.

Very little is known about Schobert's life. He was probably born in Silesia, but settled in Paris in c.1760. The French capital was habitually dominated by opera, but in the middle of the eighteenth century a number of German musicians arrived, notably from Mannheim. Schobert was one of these, and he made his name as a harpsichordist and composer of sonatas, concertos and symphonies – later in his career Mozart adapted a movement from these sonatas in one of his own piano concertos, and used others for teaching. The final known fact of Schobert's short life is that he – together with his wife, a child, a servant and four guests – met a most unfortunate and gruesome death by eating poisonous toadstools, refusing to believe they were not mushrooms.

Grimm's funeral eulogy sang Schobert's praises as a harpsichordist: "he had a great talent, a brilliant and bewitching technique" he said. Burney wrote that Schobert's "pieces for the harpsichord [had] been for many years the delight of all those who could play or hear them"[7]. This is one of a set of *Trois Sonates pour le Clavecin avec accompaniment de Violin et Basse ad Libitum* published in Paris as his op 6 in 1765:

J Schobert: 1st movement *Allegro* from Sonata in B♭ Major op 6 no 3

The lively opening bars (1) attract attention like an operatic overture, moving down a sequence of falling 3rds and fully establishing
the home tonality.

The violin rises above the harpsichord to be heard, further endorsing the tonic key in sustained high notes. Four bars later the bass
line is heard rising firmly up a semitone (always a significant
interval) to endorse arrival on a new dominant – C major (the V
of home V, F major). Shortly afterwards a second tune (2) (with
an offbeat rhythmic figure) in the dominant is heard alternating
between the harpsichord and the violin.

This is followed by 12 bars re-affirming this key (prominently heard
in the bass line when a harmless note D (the home 6th) suddenly
adds piquancy by falling down a semitone through D♭ to arrive on
C and re-emphasise the dominant key). Repeat.

The second part opens with the lively 6-bar "overture" tune in the
dominant. The next chord comes as a surprise: Schobert plunges
from F major to D major – which involves the note F (the home
dominant) rising a semitone to F sharp. But this turns out not such
a surprising chord after all, since it is none other than the dominant
of the relative minor of the home tonic (i.e. V of vi, g minor – but
this was an unusual way of getting to it). The harmonies then drift
in a sequence which lands conventionally on the home dominant.
But now a strong sense of anticipation builds up in the next five
bars, enhanced by the composer's instruction to the performers
to play *pianissimo* – and then he actually writes a pause sign ...
The suspense is broken by the jovial return of the 6-bar opening

> "overture" tune, safely back in the home key. Thereafter almost all the material of the first part is repeated, all in the home tonic. Repeat.

There are both similarities and differences between this movement and John Bach's. The tonal framework is similar to Bach's: it is in two parts, both repeated; it moves to the dominant by the double bar, and returns to the tonic in the second part; the early modulation to the dominant is endorsed by the introduction of a second tune; the section immediately after the double bar (apart from its harmonic surprises) drifts into sequences in the relative minor key. The difference is obviously the dramatic way in which Schobert engineers his return to the tonic in the second part, and the fact that he then repeats all the material of the first part, including the opening "overture" tune. Both the drama and the comprehensive return of material are unusual in the 1760s.

Two further movements follow: an *Andante* and a Minuetto and Trio. The *Andante* has the binary structure of the suite; it is written in two repeating parts with the usual modulation to the dominant half-way through, a repeat of the opening material (in the violin) after the double bar and the return of both tonic key and much of the thematic material in the second part. The serene opening theme, immediately sonorously repeated by the violin in its lowest register, is especially expressive: the mood and style of this movement may reflect the "poetic stance" which Mozart's biographer Dyneley Hussey thought Mozart had derived from Schobert. The Minuetto and Trio hold no surprises for any of the instrumental parts and are the most conventional of the three movements.

It is not difficult to see why Mozart was impressed by Schobert's compositions. In addition to the innovative detail described above, the first movement has a purposeful sense of direction behind its vivacity and bustle, and bears out Burney's comment in his *General History* that

> "The novelty and merit of Schobert's compositions seem to consist in the introduction of the symphonic, or modern overture style, upon the harpsichord, and by light and shade, alternate agitation and tranquillity, imitating the effects of an orchestra."[8]

Other contemporary comments on his music could be more disparaging: Grimm said Schobert "wrote with great ease" and implied that he indulged in empty passagework and a good deal of repetition. However, Grimm also said that he "knew perfectly the effects and magic of harmony"[9] and the surprising modulation in the second half of the *Allegro* endorses that comment. The serenity of the *Andante*, its use of the warm tone of the violin in its lowest register, and its frequent dynamic markings are all unusual at this time; also the fact that this movement is not in the usual tonic key, but in the key of E flat, the fourth of the home key. Schobert was only about thirty years old at the time these sonatas were published: they show exceptional imagination, great vivacity and a very pleasing warmth of expression, and it is tempting to wonder how his style would have developed had his life not been so abruptly cut short only two years later.

Leopold Mozart was of course astute in his choice of the cities which he visited with his children. As we have seen, London and Paris in the middle of the eighteenth century were both well placed to attract musicians and composers from all over Europe. At the centre of the Austro-Hungarian empire, Vienna was also a magnet to musicians. The court itself had a long tradition of music patronage, the Austrian nobility was very numerous and many had their own musical establishments; but performances were also enjoyed by the lesser nobility and some of the new merchant élites. Copies must have circulated in manuscript, however, as there does not appear to have been much printed music available before 1760; nor does there seem to have been much demand for the accompanied sonata before that time. The most notable composer of the pre-Classical period, Christoph Wagenseil (1715-1777), began writing solo keyboard *divertimenti* from 1753, but these short works were only gradually becoming emancipated from the suite and did not contribute to the development of the trio idea.

The most productive composer of accompanied keyboard sonatas in Vienna up to 1760 was the young (Franz) Joseph Haydn (1732-1809). He had lived in the Imperial City since becoming a chorister at St Stephen's Cathedral at the age of eight; he sang in the Cathedral Choir and also sometimes at court. Legend has it that his well-documented sense of humour was the cause of his dismissal ten years later: he was accused of testing the effectiveness of a new pair of scissors by cutting off the pigtail of a fellow chorister.[10] After this he had to set about earning his living as a keyboard player and violinist, and so he became an independent teacher, performer and composer. Fortuitously, he was engaged to give lessons to the daughter of a family in the diplomatic service who occupied part of the vast Michaelerhaus on the Kohlmarkt: they gave him free board in one of the attics of the house in return for three years of tuition. As it happened, the first floor of this great building was occupied by the Dowager Princess Esterházy, and the third floor by the court poet Metastasio. The introductions which these well-connected neighbours effected for Haydn set him up for the rest of his working life. He met all Vienna's great musicians, including Gluck and Wagenseil, and some of his earliest compositions were sonatas and trios for aristocratic pupils.

In c.1758 he became Musikdirektor to Count Morzin, and although this involved spending the summer months on the Count's Bohemian estate, he still spent the winter in Vienna. Haydn probably wrote about thirteen accompanied works for harpsichord, violin and 'cello in the decade between 1750 and 1760, all except two of which have survived.[11] Dating and confirming authenticity of these early works have been problematic for scholars for many years, however, and they are rarely performed, not least because later in his life Haydn went on to write no fewer than twenty-nine more piano trios whose mature style makes them of greater interest. All the later works were separated from this first group by the long years of Haydn's employment with the Esterházy family, when he wrote very little chamber music with keyboard.

One of Haydn's earliest accompanied sonatas is a work originally entitled *Divertimento*, which for some time was thought to have been written by Wagenseil but is now identified as Haydn's Hob.XV:C1 (listed as Trio no.2 in Georg Feder's revised numbering). The ascription to the older composer may have been based on the title (which betrays the lingering relationship with the old suite), or the fact that the sonata includes a minuet complete with trio, or that it ends with a set of variations (which Wagenseil often wrote).

F J Haydn: 1st Movement *Allegro moderato* from Divertimento in C major Hob XV:C1

The movement begins with an assertive tonic tune (1) in a neat 4-bar tonal box – 2 bars for solo harpsichord with an immediate response from the violin – cadencing firmly in the home key.

Ex. 11.1

Shortly afterwards both instruments make off in an exchange of motifs, until halting on an emphatic cadence which romps up and down the dominant chord of the home V key (D major leading to G major). With the new key thus established, the violin introduces a second, gentler tune in the dominant (2), a new falling phrase in slow sustained notes,

Ex. 11.2

Violin

p

followed by 4 bars of firm cadencing at the double bar. Repeat.

The second part returns to the opening, now in the dominant, which is then followed by a change of mood – an extended section of sequential repetition which leads to the sombre key of the relative minor (vi). In due course Haydn heads back towards the home key, but just as we begin to hear tonic tonality he suddenly seems loathe to leave the minor mode, and inserts a *minor* third (E♭) into a scale run. But this turns out to be a mischievous joke: in the very next bar the opening theme returns sunnily, back in the major mode, and the repeat of the entire first part, all in the tonic key, follows without further incident. Repeat.

Haydn's economy of expression in this movement is particularly noticeable. The first part is a mere 20 bars long, and both parts together total only 54 bars. Compared with John Bach's sonata (*Allegretto*: 1st part – 33 bars, total – 80 bars) and Schobert's (*Allegro moderato*: 1st part – 45 bars, total 106 bars) this is appreciably shorter than both. Yet within these self-imposed limits Haydn has included two contrasting ideas and attractive intervening passage-work. Much of the added length of the second half can be attributed to the 18 bars of sequential repetition in the excursion into minor modes – none of which seem to be related to any of the material in the first part. Like Schobert, Haydn returns to repeat all the material of the first part in the return to the home tonic in the second part – the opening tonic theme as well the dominant's second tune.

A striking feature of this movement is the active and interesting part assigned to the violin. Not only is there a good deal of independent interplay between its part and that of the harpsichord, but the sustained second idea only appears in the violin (it would be unsuited in fact to the short duration of harpsichord tone). A possible explanation for all this might be that it was a piece written for the Countess Wilhelmina Morzin. She was his pupil between c.1758 and 1760 and it has been suggested that while she played the harpsichord part, Haydn himself may have played the violin – and therefore wrote a more interesting "accompaniment" for himself.

There are two further movements: a Menuet and Trio, and an *Adagio* theme with six variations. Both are in the home tonic key (except for the Trio, which is traditionally in the minor mode), suggesting a persisting link with the Viennese suite, and both tend to look backwards in style to the Baroque. The variations are also old-fashioned in that it is the bass harmonies of the theme which are embellished rather than the theme itself: they follow traditional Baroque practice, gradually building up the velocity of varied figuration in the upper instruments, especially in the harpsichord part. By the final variation there is no trace of the original theme.

A. Peter Brown[12] describes Haydn's early style in works such as this as "in the mainstream of the Viennese tradition". Brown continues by adding:

"... But the examination of Haydn's use of many of the same movement types, figurations, and other rhythmic and melodic materials commonly used by his predecessors and contemporaries only heightens our appreciation of his accomplishments before his first mature works, from the mid-1760s."

* * * * *

Before moving on to the next decade in the story of the keyboard trio, it may be useful to summarise the evidence of these early accompanied sonatas. Haydn, John Bach and Schobert represent three strands of typical *galant* activity: they were all German or Austro-German in origin, all influenced by the ubiquitous Italian style, and all working in thriving musical cities. As it happens, they were also born within a few years of each other – Haydn in 1732, John Bach in 1735 and Schobert probably also c.1735.

As we have seen, what audiences were demanding in the middle of the century was essentially a change of style: they now wanted to be entertained rather than edified. Composers thus had a dilemma: they needed to respond to demands, but they had to do so in a way that audiences would find musically comprehensible.

The solution was simple. To make the new sonata movement easily grasped, composers retained the familiar tonal footprint of the suite movement, a long-standing binary structure with proven effectiveness. But to respond to the audience's changing tastes, the internal style and content of the movements within the satisfying tonal framework was now very different from Baroque style and content. The *galant* style was concise, elegant and pleasing. The three composers wrote simple treble tunes which they underpinned with stereotyped accompaniments in the harpsichord part; pretty little 2- and 4-bar phrases were packaged into 8-bar tonal boxes, decorated with characteristic dotted and "Scotch" snap rhythms, little interpolated runs of triplets, a generous sprinkling of *appoggiaturas*; the boxes were separated by stylised figuration designed to draw the listener on to

the next tonal halting-place, where arrival was advertised by conspicuous dominant chord preparation.

Thus at the beginning the new sonata movement was essentially
a two-part tonal, harmonic concept. The early distinction between
tonic and dominant keys drove the need to characterise the keys with
two separate "tunes"or musical ideas; the same distinction emphatically drove the consequent need to restore tonic tonality by repeating
the tunes in the home key in the second part. All the accompanied
sonatas we have heard fulfil these requirements. The difference was
that John Bach returned only the dominant's "tune" and material to
the tonic at the end, whereas Schobert and Haydn repeated virtually
all the original thematic material.

It is important to note that both solutions to the necessary tonal
resolution are equally satisfactory. Conditioned by our previous
knowledge of later sonata works, which follow Schobert and Haydn
with full repeats, we may tend to think that Bach's sonata is only an
immature staging-post on the way to the fully-developed form. But
Hepokoski and Darcy regard this sonata-type (which they identify as
a "Type 2" sonata – see p.92) as valid in its own right:

> "... the Type 2 alternative coexisted as a viable option ... even
> though it was one less often adopted ... Deciding which option to
> select seems to have been a matter of preference and compositional
> convention. ... The Type 2 sonata is by no means a "not-fully-
> worked-out" structure as opposed to a satisfactorily complete one.
> Assessed by its own standards, the Type 2 sonata lacks nothing."[13]

For Haydn and Schobert, the actual moment of return to the tonic
had become highly sensitive: as we saw, Schobert milked it for all the
suspense he could; Haydn, being Haydn, delayed it with a joke.

The passage between the double bar and the return to the tonic
seems the least satisfactory section of these sonatas. Written in a
less concentrated style than the first part, it often employs the old
Baroque device of sequence, and roams through more rapid key
changes before lingering in the gloomy regions of the minor mode.
It is linked neither thematically nor tonally with the rest of the movement, and at this early stage in the development of the sonata idea, it
has yet to find itself a satisfying role.

In all three of the sonatas we have heard so far, the need to write
for amateur performers has a significant effect on the instrumentation. They are not yet true chamber works, with equal parts for each
instrument. The harpsichord takes the lead in each case, introducing
almost all the "tunes" and carrying the burden of the most intricate
accompanying figuration. The violin parts are variable: John Bach's
are the simplest (perhaps his English gentlemen presented him with

the greatest problem); Haydn's are the most difficult (perhaps he would play them himself). But the violin is given a reasonable share of interesting lines, frequent opportunities for interacting with the harpsichord in the exchange of sequences, and many stretches of passagework doubling the keyboard in thirds or sixths below.

It is the 'cello which always has the most tedious part, merely plodding along with the outline of the harpsichord's left-hand part. We should realise, however, that it was not at this time regarded as a solo instrument: that would not follow until the nineteenth century (together with the role of the heroic tenor singer in opera). But neither should we overlook the importance of its two functions here. Firstly, it is essential to the balance of the ensemble that the 'cello reinforces the bass line, since the shallow tone of the harpsichord would not sound strongly enough without its help; secondly, it is crucial to the new sonata style that the listener can hear clearly all the signposting of harmonic changes which the 'cello signals. It is not for nothing that Caplin heads his book on *Classical Form* with a quotation from Schoenberg's *Fundamentals of Musical Composition:* "Watch the harmony; watch the root progressions; watch the bass line."[14]

CHAPTER ENDNOTES

1   Fuller, David. 'Accompanied Keyboard Music' in *Music Quarterly*, vol lx, no 2 (April 1974), p.226.

2   Quoted in Leppert, Richard. *Music and Image*. Cambridge: Cambridge University Press, 1988, p.21.

3   As described by Caplin, William in *Classical Form*. New York: Oxford University Press, 1998; paperback ed, 2001, pp.49,65

4   Mattheson, Johann. *Kern Melodischer Wissenschaft* 1737, p.109. Quoted by Mark Evan Bonds in *Wordless Rhetoric*. Cambridge, MA: Harvard University Press, 1991, p.84.

5   Rosen, Charles. *The Classical Style*, 1971. Revised ed. London: Faber and Faber, 1997, p.26.

6   Rosen, *ibid*, p.73

7   Burney, *op.cit*, p.956.

8   Burney, *op cit*, p.957

9   Turrentine, Herbert C. 'Schobert, Johann' in *Grove Music Online*, 2001.

10 Geiringer, Karl. *Haydn: A Creative Life in Music*. Sydney: George, Allen & Unwin, 3rd ed, rev, enlarged, 1982, p.24.

11 Published in *Joseph Haydn Werke*, revised Georg Feder, Reihe XVII, Bd 1. Munich: G Henle Verlag, 1970.

12 Brown, A Peter. *Joseph Haydn's Keyboard Music*. Bloomington: Indiana University Press,1986, p.289.

13 Hepokoski and Darcy, *op.cit*, p.366.

14 Caplin, *op cit*, p.2

CHAPTER 5

ENTER THE FORTEPIANO

IN THE SIXTEEN years which intervened before John Bach published his last two accompanied sonatas, he continued to work in one of the most competitive businesses of the era. To be success-ful as a musician and composer in London in the 1770's meant being sensitive to the ever-changing tastes and fickle whims of an unpredictable audience. Mrs Gertrude Harris, mother of the first Earl of Malmesbury, had a less than charitable expectation of some members of her sex: "...fine ladies are so capricious," she said, "'tis hard to say what they would have."[1] Bach's often-quoted remark that his brother Carl Philip Emanuel Bach "lives to compose, whereas I compose to live" was not just a wry witticism – it was all too true. During this time he wrote five operas, contributed arias to *pastiches*, and wrote popular strophic songs for outdoor performance at the Pleasure Gardens; he composed and conducted endlessly for the Subscription Concerts, and invested in a lavish new concert room in Hanover Square in an effort to outdo other concert venues; he even travelled down to Dorset in the summer months (in spite of having been robbed by a highwayman on an earlier country journey with his friend the painter Gainsborough), to put on concerts for the Quality during the annual Race Week in Blandford Forum (maybe he also went to the races – Leopold Mozart did so, taking Wolfgang and Nannerl racing on their way to Dover at the end of their London visit); and of course his Royal Patrons constantly required attend-ance as well as compositions, and his aristocratic pupils also needed lessons and further attention. In all these ventures, to please his audiences – whether at Concerts, in the Pleasure Gardens, in palaces or in private drawing rooms – was Bach's absolute priority.

For some time, although there was a steady market for music for amateurs, the unequal balance between the harpsichord and strings discouraged composers from taking the keyboard trio seriously. But then came a catalyst for real change – the commercial introduction of the *fortepiano*. Up to this time, the two main domestic keyboard instruments had been the clavichord (especially in Germany) and the harpsichord. The clavichord was a quiet, intimate instrument, its sound produced by metal tangents striking the strings; the harpsichord had a bigger tone, its strings plucked by quills. The new fortepiano was different; its strings were struck by hammers but its tone was stronger and brighter than the clavichord, and it had the potential for more variety and sustaining power than the harpsichord. As its name, *forte* and *piano*, implies, it produced a range of dynamics from loud to soft, depending on how hard the keys were struck. Thus it could not only produce graduated *crescendos* and *diminuendos*, but also allow the performer to shape the dynamics of a musical phrase. This sensitivity to touch revolutionised not only keyboard playing itself but also the music written for the new fortepiano.

(Note – The title of the new instrument appears to have been interchangeable from the outset – contemporary title pages refer to both fortepianos and pianofortes. In modern practice, however, many performers tend to refer to earlier instruments as *fortepianos*. I have opted to follow this, using *fortepiano* for instruments up to c.1800, and *pianoforte* thereafter. This is merely to suggest the contrast in tone colour between the two, and it should be realised that it is a distinction without a difference, and does not necessarily follow eighteenth-century practice.)

Fortepianos were first made in Italy in the early years of the eighteenth century by an ingenious instrument-maker called Bartolomeo Cristofori. But it was another half century before the potential of the instrument was fully realised and the difficulties in replicating its complicated mechanism were overcome, enabling fortepianos to be made on a commercial scale. The earliest manufacturer in England was the immigrant Johannes Zumpe, who arrived from Saxony and began production of the new keyboard instruments by the mid 1760's. One of his square fortepianos was first heard in public accompanying a singer in 1767, but it was John Bach – well-placed as ever – who gave one of the earliest public solo performances in an Assembly Room on 2 June 1768, playing one of his own solo sonatas.

Bach's connection with the Royal Family ensured the instrument's immediate respectability and success. (The price was a further attraction: it cost roughly half the amount of a single-manual harpsichord, and much less than one of the early grand pianos.) Square fortepianos were attractively housed in a rectangular mahogany case, not unduly large, and could easily be accommodated in even the most modest of drawing-rooms. The tone was not loud enough for concert performance, but for domestic music-making it was ideal, and a better balance than the harpsichord for chamber music with strings. From now onwards there was a lasting demand for music for fortepiano which amateurs could play at home.

John Bach's last two accompanied sonatas were written with the new fortepiano and not the harpsichord in mind – although the continuing option of playing the keyboard part on the harpsichord was naturally advertised on the title page (it would have been foolish to exclude a substantial raft of potential purchasers). Ten years or so after his historic first performance, the new instrument makes a significant contribution to the style and development of the sonata idea in the trio *genre*.

Bach's collection of *Four Sonatas* ★ *and two Duetts for the Piano Forte or Harpsichord with accompaniments* were published as his op 15 in 1779. This is the first movement of the first Sonata:

J C Bach: *Allegro* from Sonata for fortepiano with accompaniments in C major op 15 no 1 W B49

Bach begins with an engaging 8-bar melodic idea first heard in the fortepiano alone (1), promptly repeated by the violin.

Ex. 12.1

Tonic tonality thus established, two bars of scale passages lead to a tuneful transitional passage, mainly involving the fortepiano, in which we hear the home tonic note C gradually metamorphosing into new V tonality. (Listen for the Mozartian moment in the forte-piano when the note D (V of home V) slips down through C♯ to C – and we hear it not as the home tonic any longer, but now the seventh above the new V of V, a dominant seventh, waiting to fall another semitone onto the new 3rd). To emphasise arrival in the dominant key, 6 bars of cascading arpeggio cadences follow. The

★ Only the first two sonatas of the set are trios, the second two do not have 'cello parts and therefore are more properly violin sonatas; the Duetts are for two performers on one keyboard instrument.

violin then begins a second tune, high in its register (2a), slowly rising up the chord of G over the next 4 bars.

As this closes it is heard again two octaves lower (wonder of wonders) in the 'cello. The fortepiano and violin respond with another new idea (2b), rising up together a third apart, then repeat it.

A cheerful cadence figure follows and then the section closes emphatically in the dominant key. Repeat.

The second part begins with the opening idea heard now in the dominant, but it soon drifts into a soulful sequence falling step-by-step in the violin; this works its way down to cadence on a chord of E major (the V of a minor, the home tonic's relative minor) where the violin and the 'cello (again) echo each other over the next four bars; they close firmly, still on E. The fortepiano responds unexpectedly with something like (although not quite the same as) the first idea in the relative minor key – but by the 3rd bar has lost its nerve, and slips down into home V tonality; the violin tries to respond with its own version of the first idea, but is also forced to modify it to accord with the home dominant harmonies now being hammered out by the fortepiano and 'cello. With the home tonality now very close Bach returns triumphantly to the cascading transitional arpeggios of the first part, leading securely into the second tune in the violin and 'cello, safely back in the home tonic key of C. A full repeat of the rest of the material follows (all in the home key). Repeat.

This delightful work shows how some ten years of living with a fortepiano, playing and composing for it, have transformed John Bach's keyboard writing. Whereas in his op 2 sonatas we heard a good deal of diligent writing and figuration for harpsichord, now there is an expressive and idiomatic part for the fortepiano. The melodic invention of the ideas positively invites sensitive phrasing from the performer, and in between the different ideas the passage-work is lively and clear. Here we can see too how Bach has drawn on all his London experiences: in those songs written for the opera and for Vauxhall he has found his own distinctive melodic voice. This is the composer who Mozart admired so much, whose style Leopold Mozart called "natural, easy and flowing", and who Burney described as "this excellent master", who brought about "a total revolution in our musical taste".

We find evidence also for Burney's important comment that

> "Bach seems to have been the first composer who observed the law of *contrast*, as a *principle*. Before his time, contrast there frequently was, in the works of others; but it seems to have been accidental. Bach in his symphonies and other instrumental pieces, as well as his songs, seldom failed, after a rapid and noisy passage to introduce one that was slow and soothing."[2]

The piano was well suited to make such contrasts effective, and this is another indication how far Bach has travelled from the mono-chrome dynamics of the suite movement and his own earlier sonatas.

We can hear too how Bach's wide experience of orchestral colour has influenced the way he now writes for the group of three instruments. The expressiveness of the fortepiano enables the violin to play a more equal part against it, and even the 'cello is given several opportunities to participate in its own right. This is not yet the sophisticated interplay of the three instruments which we shall hear in Mozart's trios, but it is a positive step in the direction of real piano trio music. It is written for competent amateur pupils, simple without being condescending. The second movement – a *Tempo di Minuetto* in C major and contrasting trio in a minor – is even more simple, and well within their capabilities.

At this point we should stand back for a moment and see how this movement meets contemporary expectations of the accompanied sonata. Regardless of the attractiveness of Bach's tunes, it is the harmonic framework which is paramount, and this sonata movement is still dominated by the two-part harmonic structure which underpins it.

John Bach's task is thus to invent attractive ideas, and incorporate them into the recognised framework. "Constructing a sonata-form movement was a task of *modular assembly*: the forging of a succession of short, section-specific musical units (spaces of action) linked together into an ongoing linear chain" say Hepokoski and Darcy.[3]

The musical ideas are arranged in order of significance: first the opening idea, then the second idea in the dominant, then cadential figuration to close the first part; these ideas then reappear in the second part with orientation back to the tonic for tonal resolution. John Bach has no difficulty inventing attractive material which he then defines within the harmonic framework by appropriate *cadences*.

The importance of cadences to the intelligibility of the sonata movement was all-important. We have already noted Charles Rosen saying "The cadence is the basis of all musical form". Contemporary theorists knew it, too, and in summarising their writing Mark Evan Bonds writes

> " All authors stress that a hierarchy of cadences articulates various degrees of rest within a [movement]: authentic cadences are generally reserved for the conclusion of a major section or an entire movement, while half, deceptive, and inconclusive cadences articulate closures of ever-decreasing strength and importance ... There is ... a consistent emphasis on the underlying need for ... points of articulation. Without them, individual phrases would be indistinguishable from one another; a movement consisting of unintelligible phrases would be unintelligible as a whole. And the ease with which a work's ideas can be comprehended by the listener is one of the most important qualities in any rhetorical art."[4]

In one respect John Bach's sonatas still lack an important feature of the mature sonata idea: the section after the double bar is nebulous, not playing a significant part in the movement. Bach tends to fill the space with sequences designed to carry him elegantly from the dominant to the relative minor, and he uses passage work to do so, rather than bringing in any of the material heard in the first section. "All in all," says Newman,

> "... Christian's "developments" create no more tension than would be expected in forms that are characterised not by drama and passion but by lyricism, charm, fluency, and a certain discursiveness."[5]

Moreover Bach continues to follow the expanded binary sonata model for his return to the tonic. His audience will have followed him to that emphatic pause on the dominant chord E major; from there he could easily have slipped home and the fortepiano could shortly have struck up with the opening melodic idea in the tonic key. Bach now gives us a different but perfectly good solution – he hints (perhaps mischievously) at the opening material his audience half-expects, but temporarily foils expectations by *putting it in the minor mode*. Hepokoski and Darcy describe a similar passage in a quartet by Haydn, where the return of the principal idea is "bludgeoned onto an ominous, minor-mode vi [the relative minor], somewhat dizzily seeking its way back home".[6] This is a happy description and perfectly fits this moment in Bach's sonata. Immediately afterwards the expectations of home tonic tonality are amply satisfied by the cascading arpeggios and Bach arrives safely back in the tonic. He gets home, and all the former dominant tonality is turned to tonic. And in the sonata, that is what matters.

With hindsight, we know that this movement is not yet a fully-developed chamber work for the three independent instruments of the piano trio in the mature Classical style. But this is a winning example of a *galant* sonata, and lays the framework on which the High Classical sonata would build: a secure tonal structure, tuneful ideas as thematic content, definition of those ideas by functional harmony emphasising cadences, and a satisfying resolution of all tonal tensions by the end of the second part.

Can we form a view as to how Bach's London audience might have received this sonata, and judge how they would have heard and enjoyed it?

Inevitably, we have no record of a performance of this actual work, but we can come quite close to its atmosphere of domestic music-making in a near-contemporary painting of an English family – who, as it happens, had a London house near Bach's new Hanover Square concert room (it is tempting to wonder whether they joined the neighbours' chorus of protests when the project was announced and noisy building work began ...).

This painting by Johan Zoffany* of *Lord Cowper and the Gore family,* was commissioned and executed in 1775. Clearly this is not a London house, but probably the *Villa Palmieri* in Fiesole: its owner, George Nassau Clavering-Cowper, 3rd Earl Cowper, stands in the centre, carefully poised in the conventional cross-legged portrait pose of the true gentleman. He is surrounded by the family of Charles Gore, to whose youngest daughter (standing behind the square fortepiano on the left) he is engaged to be married. Miss Hannah Anne Gore has secured a pompous, somewhat portly, but very patrician catch. Lord Cowper is only 36 at the time of this painting (he perhaps looks older) but has already been in Florence for some 15 years. He had originally arrived on his Grand Tour, but remained to pursue a number of inconclusive dalliances, beginning with an

---

* Zoffany was one of Bach's circle of artists and musicians and also a close friend – his wife was a witness to Bach's Will and the painter himself was one of only four people to attend Bach's funeral in 1782.

Italian *marchesa* and ending with a Florentine lady (shortly before the arrival of the Gores). He is a keen music-lover, hosting musical entertainments at his Villa and becoming (in due course) the principal adviser in musical matters to the Grand Duke Pietro Leopoldo.

If this is Cowper's villa it is very unlikely that the painting on the wall behind Hannah Anne could really have hung there: this is probably an instance of Zoffany's notorious sense of humour. It depicts (appropriately) a classical allegory in the form of a wedding ceremony in the Temple of Hymen, Greek goddess of matrimony, and (rather less appropriately) an impersonation of Calumny (being forcibly repelled, which appears to refer to Cowper's *affaires*)[7]. Perhaps Cowper's classical reading was rusty, or he was broad-minded enough to enjoy the joke; there appear to be no records of any of the sitters objecting to it, and the painting remained in the family by descent until 1977. What we should read into the picture (Zoffany's wicked humour apart) is a general appreciation: this background of a Baroque allegorical painting endorses the sitters' impeccable cultural credentials. The sense of theatricality which is conveyed by the drapery of its dark green curtain (conventionally added by artists to suggest "performance") is echoed by the drapery of the red curtain slung artfully over a convenient vine: this is a performance too, by the Gores for their future son-in-law.

The Gores were a very wealthy family: they had a country estate in Lincolnshire as well as the house in Hanover Square, and Charles had married Mary Cockerill, heiress to a shipbuilding fortune, (presumably) Cockerills of Scarborough. (This had been a feature of Cowper's interest in Anne: each daughter would have "fifty thousand pounds apiece, which would be very well," he wrote to a cousin*). This is a useful reminder that although the artist Rowlandson might lampoon new money in unkind sketches of farmers' wives affecting gentility, new money could also give new life to the purchasing power of old families and their wellbred tastes.

Everything about this family is elegant and sophisticated: the ladies wear silk dresses lavishly trimmed with lace and frills, the gentlemen are also dressed in fancy silk waistcoats and neckties. The picture is carefully littered with evidence of their cultivated interests and occupations. The presence of a square fortepiano, played by one of Anne's sisters, is of course especially interesting for us: this picture announces the fashionable musical credentials of the Gore family. But there is also something very natural about the way Charles Gore leans forward to read the bass line over his daughter's shoulder. Mr Gore was an amateur artist, and we can see his marine drawings on

---

* The value of this sum in today's money would be over £3m – "very well", indeed!

the chair behind the fortepiano (perhaps too this is an indirect reference to the shipbuilding business). We also notice that Mrs Gore is reading. The book in her hand may have been a guidebook, but it was equally likely to have been a novel – she continues to mark her place in its open pages, despite the distraction of being painted.

The fact that Mary Gore has chosen to be painted with book in hand is not without significance. We should remember that only about fifty years earlier, reading for pleasure had been comparatively rare, even amongst educated people – they would read the Bible and Shakespeare, and semi-devotional books like *Pilgrim's Progress*. But then came the novel and with it a revolution in reading habits; by the second half of the century a huge number of people were reading new fiction.[8]

Johan Zoffany, *Lord Cowper and the Gore Family*, 1775.
Yale Center for British Art, Paul Mellon Collection.

One of the most significant books of the eighteenth century was Samuel Richardson's *Pamela, or Virtue Rewarded* which was published in London in 1740. The story concerns a simple lady's maid who contrives to defend her virtue from the would-be seduction of her aristocratic employer. The revolutionary aspect of this novel is that it is the serving-maid's voice and viewpoint which is heard throughout: she is the heroine of this cliff-hanging love-story, and it is the aristocrat who eventually capitulates by actually *marrying* her – an unheard-of solution. Obviously it had instant appeal for the new readership in the socially-climbing ranks of the *bourgeoisie*, but for the well-bred also its sexual *frissons* were a riveting departure from writers like Bunyan. It rapidly went through numerous editions and revisions, even the addition of a two-volume sequel. By the time the artist Joseph Highmore dashed off a series of twelve scenes from the novel in 1744 the bandwagon was well on its way.

What helped to keep it rolling was what today would be "the film of the book" – in eighteenth-century terms, stage entertainments. *Pamela* sped off to Europe, where both Voltaire and Goldoni put her on the stage with the neatest of final twists: in the closing moments it was revealed that after all, this poor maiden in distress was not really a servant at all, but – *brava!* – an aristocrat fallen on hard times! That made the idea far more palatable, and although the novel remained controversial the continental stage versions seem to have been widely acceptable.

Goldoni then realised that his play had an ideal plot for a comic opera. He turned it into a libretto with another twist: Pamela became a gardener's girl. Several composers set his *La buona Figliuola*. John Bach himself contributed a couple of songs to an English version, *The Maid of the Mill*, and even Mozart set a *Pamela* opera – the aristocratic garden girl turns up again in another Italian opera libretto, *La Finta Giardiniera* in 1775. There must have been at least fifty plays and operas drawing on Richardson's original novel by the end of the century.*

The importance of *Pamela* however is the *cult of sensibility* which it triggered. Undoubtedly with bourgeois roots, it became a European as well as an English sensation, and its influence shows how the moral stance and purchasing power of the Middling Sorts began to make their mark on classical culture – through women's reading in the first instance, but gradually infiltrating both middle and upper levels of society, male and female. We hear such a lot about *sensibility* after this. Hume (in a beautiful simile based on sympathetic harmonic vibrations) wrote

"As in strings equally wound up, the motion of one communicates itself to the rest; so all the affections readily pass from one person to another; and beget correspondent movements in every human creature."[9]

---

* As an example of how far *La buona Figliuola* travelled, perhaps the most exotic recorded performance was given, some time before 1778, by Italian Jesuits at the Chinese Court in Peking.

And in 1775 (the year of Zoffany's painting), "sensibility" was described in a newspaper as "a lively and delicate feeling, a quick sense of the right and wrong, in all human actions, and other objects considered in every view of morality and taste".

The addictive sensibility of novels is strikingly illustrated in contemporary paintings of eighteenth-century readers. In c.1746 Jean-Siméon Chardin painted an interesting portrait of his wife, which he called "Domestic Pleasures". She is comfortably settled in a large chair, reading; her fingers mark the place in a book on her lap, but she has looked up from it and is now utterly lost in a daydream. A contemporary observer writing in 1748 confirms this – he says "... To judge by the sort of languor that pervades her ... we guess she was reading a novel and that the pictures it has conjured up made her daydream ...."*

Women readers of these times are often, like Mary Gore and Chardin's wife, depicted with fingers in books, carefully marking the place they have reached in the narrative, as though to say that they will not be kept away for long. Here are two more examples:

Joseph-Siffred Duplessis, *Madame Lenoir*. 1764. Paris, Musée de Louvre

Jean-Étienne Liotard, *Madame d'Epinay*. 1759. Geneva, Musée d'Art et d'Histoire de Geneve

---

* Chardin's painting, in the Nationalmuseum in Stockholm, can be seen at: https://commons.wikimedia.org/wiki/File:Domestic_Pleasures_(Jean_Sim%C3%A9on_Chardin)_-_Nationalmuseum_-_17789.tif.

These pictures tell their own story of how avidly women at this time entered into the world of their reading.

What, however, of the tastes of contemporary gentlemen? Returning to Zoffany's painting, we are clearly meant to infer that both Lord Cowper and Charles Gore were men of educated taste, and that they particularly enjoyed music.

As good sons of the Enlightenment, young English gentlemen were put to study a broadly-based curriculum. They were educated to be rational, analytical, with a rigorous and no-nonsense attitude to life. They were taught languages, arithmetic, geometry, algebra and geography; also history, theology and some natural philosophy (the contemporary term for science); and naturally Latin and Greek, together with law, logic, ethics and rhetoric. They also enjoyed a range of physical exercise. But drawing, dancing and music in general came low on their list of accomplishments, added as final refinements. They might enjoy music and the arts as indications of their good breeding and cultivated tastes, but no more than that. Advice to young men continued to be hostile to the study as well as to the practice of music: the notoriously crusty Lord Chesterfield had this admonition for his son in 1749:

> "If you love music, hear it; go to operas, concerts, and pay fiddlers to play for you; but I insist upon your neither piping nor fiddling yourself. It puts a gentleman in a very frivilous *[sic]*, contemptible light; brings him into a great deal of bad company; and takes up a great deal of time, which might be much better employed."[10]

However, as already noted, this did not preclude a competent gentleman (as we imagine Charles Gore probably was) playing chamber music with his family or intimate friends. Secondly, dislike of performance certainly did not imply a dislike of music itself. These men were intelligent, well-read and intellectually curious, and the breadth of their education enabled them to appreciate a wide variety of matters. Studies in maths, geometry and logic, for instance, helped them to appreciate the pleasing equilibrium and proportions of architecture. Many Englishmen (like Lord Cowper) on their Grand Tour fell in love with the beauty of classical buildings, and came home to refine and define the English countryside with houses in the Palladian style. Men who could appreciate the symmetry which flowed from central pediment through supporting columns and flanking wings would intuitively have found a parallel in the equilibrium of the sonata's two matching parts and the logic of its tonal footprint; they might also match the rhythm of decorative detail with the recurrence of themes, testimony to the pleasure to be derived from pattern and uniformity.

But it is clear that contemporary gentlemen at this time had some difficulty in applying their enquiring minds to the problem of *instrumental music as art*. Their classical education had taught them that the purpose of art was to prompt an emotional response from the beholder. When music was associated with words in opera or song, it had proved very capable of emulating rage, sympathy, love, hatred, or whatever emotion was demanded by the dictates of plot and text. But music for instruments alone did not have such clear emotional pointers: it required a new and different approach. As a way of directing listeners *how to listen to instrumental music*, contemporary writers and theorists frequently therefore resorted to discussing instrumental music by analogy with rhetoric. Gentlemen familiar with the art of rhetoric (as they all were) could hear music as "an oration in sound" (Mattheson, 1739), an ordered succession of musical thoughts which would be arranged within conventional patterns. Thus gentlemen could now apply themselves diligently to *listening* to the new sonata idea.

A crucial feature of the sonata idea in all its forms was that it *demanded to be listened to*, not merely heard in the background (we should realise that audiences at that time did not expect to listen to music either quietly or attentively, and there is reason to believe that London audiences were especially talkative and noisy – as late as 1799 the Duchess of Brunswick was said to have insisted that in her presence the orchestra *"must play softly so as not to disturb her card-playing"*). Sonatas were different. If a listener did not follow the musical ideas, and sense the underlying tonal narrative, the whole purpose of the piece could be lost.

It was the superior education of gentlemen which prompted them in the second half of the eighteenth century to engage with music in this different way from their wives and daughters. Thus for well-educated gentlemen taught the classical art of oratory – *the persuasive presentation of argument* – the music of John Bach's sonatas might indeed now be understood as a sophisticated tonal metaphor for rhetoric. The following analogy between rhetoric and the music of the sonata idea shows how the technical skill of the composer – assembling the harmonic framework, inventing the musical ideas, defining the whole with careful cadences – might enable an educated listener to follow the thrust of the musical argument without too much difficulty:

"An orator would behave unnaturally and contrary to the goal of edifying, persuading, and moving [his audience] if he were to give a speech without first determining what is to be his main idea, his secondary ideas ... As musical works of any substantial length are nothing other than speeches for the sentiments by which one seeks to move the listener to a certain empathy and to certain emotions, the rules for the ordering and arrangement of ideas are the same as in an actual oration. And so one has, in both, a main idea, supporting secondary ideas ... A musical work in which ... ordering is so arranged that all thoughts mutually support and reinforce one another in the most advantageous way possible, is well ordered."[11]

For women the appreciation of music was rather different. We may guess that the experience of music went deeper for women than it did for men. Eighteenth-century ladies, whether aristocratic, Quality or Middling Sorts, might hear the sonata as an emotional as well as a musical narrative, often made all the more real by their own participation and performance. As listeners or performers, music gave them the opportunity to enter the emotional world of the novel and engage with contemporary sensibility – we have seen from the French paintings how readily they would immerse themselves in a world of fantasy. An imaginative lady might sense a sunny introduction to a set of characters, a distant threat of impending disaster in the minor mode of the middle section, but eventually a happy resolution. Her more imaginative approach was captured by the classicist Thomas Twining, writing in 1789, when he said:

" ... in the best instrumental music, expressively performed, the very indecision itself of the expression, leaving the hearer to the free operation of his emotion upon his fancy, and, as it were, to the free choice of such ideas as are, to him, most adapted to react upon and heighten the emotion which occasioned them, produces a pleasure, which nobody, I believe, who is able to feel it, will deny to be one of the most delicious that music is capable of affording."[12]

For such ladies, carefree melody and return to tonal security might be a metaphor for "happy ending". Which was indeed exactly what the sonata aimed for – the resolution of tensions in a happy tonal outcome.

We know that John Bach's symphonies and concertos were popular with English audiences, and there is no reason to suppose that the accompanied sonata which we heard at the beginning of this chapter was not equally popular amongst the amateur performers for whom it was written. John Bach's music drew on a broad range of contemporary trends, but his gift for lyrical melody – part Italian, part English ballad and folk song, but chiefly his own genius for writing good tunes (we should not forget he was a son of Johann Sebastian) – was developed in response to his London audience.

By the time of his last accompanied sonatas their taste for conventional song and dance structures had matured. The introduction of the fortepiano enabled amateur performers to shape his pretty tunes with true sensibility; the thematic tonality of his sonata first movements encouraged structured listening on rhetorical lines. Together John Bach and his London audiences shaped his distinctive contribution to the accompanied sonata idea.

CHAPTER ENDNOTES

1   Harris, Mrs Gertrude. *A series of letters of the first Earl of Malmesbury, his family and friends, from 1745 to 1820*. London, 1870. 2 vols: i: p.287. Quoted in Terry, C S, *op.cit*, p.143.

2   Burney, *op.cit*, vol.ii, p.866.

3   Hepokoski and Darcy, *op.cit*, pp.15-16.

4   Bonds, *Wordless Rhetoric*, p.72.

5   Newman, William S. *The Sonata in the Classic Era*. Chapel Hill: University of North Carolina Press, 1963, p.714.

6   Hepokoski and Darcy, *op.cit*, p.271.

7   See *Exhibition Catalogues:* i) Mary Webster (1976) for National Portrait Gallery, 1977: *Johan Zoffany* 1733-1810, pp.60 – 63. ii) Kate Retford (2011) for Yale Center for British Art and Royal Academy of Arts, London, 2011-12: *Johan Zoffany RA: Society Observed*, pp.233-235.

8   Outram, Dorinda. *The Enlightenment*. Cambridge: Cambridge University Press, 1995, pp.19-20.

9   Hume, David. *A Treatise of Human Nature, 1739-40*. Modern ed. London: Penguin Books, 1985, p.626.

10   Quoted in Leppert, *op.cit.*, p.22.

11   Forkel, J N. *Allgemeine Geschichte der Musik*, I, 1788, p.50; quoted in Bonds, *Wordless Rhetoric*, p.123.

12   Twining, Thomas. *Aristotle's Treatise on Poetry*, 1789. 2nd ed (London 1812), pp.73-75.

CHAPTER 6

A PLAN OF MODULATION

ELSEWHERE IN EUROPE, different circumstances prevailed. In some places public concerts were less well established, in other places music was still mainly written for private performance in aristocratic palaces, and in Italy opera continued to dominate. But there were common traits too: cultured tastes were universal and publishers were producing ever more music. A "Catalogue of Vocal and Instrumental Music" on the back page of one of the English publisher John Bland's publications nonchalantly describes the contents as "Printed & Sold by J. Bland ...and may be had in most parts of Europe". Music in the same style was popular everywhere and musicians travelled widely in spite of the multiple dangers and discomforts involved.

With such universality of style it is hardly surprising to find a universal use of the same formal structures, since familiarity was an important part of audience comprehension and enjoyment. The two-part tonal model for the first movement, which we heard and considered in the preceding chapters and which Mozart had heard in his travels across Europe, now became widely adopted. It was never prescriptively defined as *Sonata Form*, to be rigorously followed, but it was nevertheless a well-recognised structural *process* which was frequently described by contemporary theorists.

The first movement of a sonata work was often known as the "long movement", and the process of composing it is described by the German musician A F C Kollmann (born in the same year as Mozart) in his *Essay on Practical Musical Composition*, published in London in 1790, as follows:

"In its *outlines*, a long movement is generally divided into *two sections*. The first, when the piece is in major, ends in the fifth of the scale [the dominant], and the second in the key [i.e. the key of the work] ...These two sections are either separated by a double bar or repeat ... But though pieces are not calculated for a repetition, the above distinction of two sections is required in them, if they shall create an expectation at the beginning, and give a satisfaction at the end; without which they cannot be truly entertaining."

Kollmann gives the alternative keys which would be used for movements in a minor mode, and descriptions for further subdivisions of the two sections by key, before concluding:

"The above is the plan of modulation, which will be found attended to in most sonatas, symphonies, and concertos ... of all great Composers, because it is the most reasonable one, and the most adapted to the nature of our attention, and our feeling, hitherto known."[1]

It is clear from this description that Kollmann sees the process in terms of keys – he specifically says that this is "the plan of modulation". He does not specifically refer to keys being differentiated by distinctive themes, although he allows for "a sort of elaboration" within the subsections. Nevertheless, his outline plan for the long movement is essentially the same as "Sonata Form" as we shall find it labelled and precisely described by theorists in the early decades of the nineteenth century.

This is the groundplan for the High Classical works of Mozart and Haydn, and at this stage in the development of the sonata idea, it was widely understood and adopted. We saw in Chapter 4 that many features of the later sonata form were in fact evident in the 1760s. In order to establish a terminology which will not only be appropriate now but also carry through to later stages, we may construct a chart giving the basic outline of this eighteenth-century sonata plan as it was understood and employed by Classical composers:

18th CENTURY SONATA FORM
(for works in the major mode)

SECTION I: tonal progression from Key I to Key V

SECTION II: tonal progression from Key V to Key I

SECTION I: tonal progression from Key I to Key V

EXPOSITION:
- introducing the thematic material of the movement:

1st Subject*, or group of subjects in the home tonic key
Transitional passage, ending in cadence on V of V
2nd Subject, or group of subjects in home dominant key
Cadence group (reinforcing home dominant key)

SECTION II: tonal progression from Key V to Key I

DEVELOPMENT:
- a free section, beginning in the home dominant key (or near-related key such as relative minor) and then travelling freely into other keys, generally using thematic material (either whole themes, or motifs derived from themes) from the Exposition
- the final focus of this section is the anticipation of the return of the home key and the 1st subject: for this reason it must progress to a passage of home V chord preparation which leads into the

RECAPITULATION:
- returning to the thematic material of the Exposition, all in the home key. Typically this will have a "Double Return" – i.e. simultaneous return of 1st subject and home key, but sometimes composers omit the return of the 1st subject and begin the Recapitulation by returning to the home key with the 2nd subject

1st Subject group in the home tonic key
Transitional passage, ending in home V cadence
2nd Subject group in the home tonic key
Cadence group (reinforcing home key)

Fig. 7 18th century Sonata Form

---

* "Subject" is another word for a musical idea, tune or theme.

The eighteenth-century Exposition retained its relationship with the suite and was played through twice; after 1780, the repeat of the second section was less often observed.

In works in the minor mode the two-section structure is the same, the only significant difference being that the 2nd subject group is generally in the **relative major** key; in the Recapitulation the composer has the option of returning either to **tonic major or minor** throughout.

All of this is already familiar to us. To follow the earlier diagram (at Fig.6, p.56), see Fig.8 on the next page, showing the tonal ground-plan with the sonata added for comparison.

This is the formal process most commonly used by composers for the first – the longest and therefore the most serious – movement of sonata works in the final quarter of the eighteenth century, in solo sonatas, chamber music and orchestral symphonies. We should note at this point that, not surprisingly given its logical evolution from the ubiquitous two-part suite movement of the preceding Baroque era, as outlined in Chapter 4, sonata form had a number of close relatives. None of these challenged the supremacy of the form for the first movement as outlined above, but as these variants were often employed in other movements of sonata works, this is a good moment to introduce them.

Hepokoski and Darcy define five co-existing sonata form types:[2]

Type 1 Sonata Form: the simplest type, comprising Exposition and Recapitulation only, with no central Development section

Type 2 Sonata Form: in which the Recapitulation does not begin with the Double Return, but with the 2nd Subject (or preceding transitional material) in the tonic key, i.e. only the material previously heard in the dominant (see John Bach, Sonata op 15 no 1, pp.75-76ff).

Type 3 Sonata Form: 1st Movement or Sonata Form proper, as outlined in the chart above

Type 4 Sonata Form: the principle of Sonata Form combined with the idea of a recurrent rondo (*see below*) theme, often used in the last movement of a sonata

Type 5 Sonata Form: Sonata Form adapted for concertos (not relevant to the piano trio)

If all the world were paper

(16 beats: 8 + 8)

tune 〰〰 ' 〰〰
note   1   5   5   1

J S Bach: *gigue*

(52 bars: 24 + 28)

music   〰〰〰〰〰〰 ' 〰〰〰〰〰〰
key   I   V   V   I

J C Bach Sonata op 2 no 2 (1st movement)
(80 bars: 33 + 47)

music   〰〰〰〰〰〰
key   I   V
music   '〰〰〰〰〰〰〰〰〰
key   V   I

18th century Sonata Form

theme 1   2 group   CG
music 〰〰〰〰〰〰〰〰
key   I   V   V
         EXPOSITION

theme   1   2 group   CG
music '〰〰〰〰〰〰〰〰〰〰〰〰
key   V I   I   I
         DEVELOPMENT   RECAPITULATION

(Themes have been added to the Sonata Form diagram; the dotted line in the key segment of the Development indicates freedom to travel into other keys)

Fig. 8 Tonal groundplan: dance song, *suite* movement, 18th-century Sonatas

★ ★ ★ ★ ★

Of these five sonata variants, Type 1 needs no further comment; Type 2 has been discussed with John Bach (who happens to be one of its champions); Type 3 is the focus of this book; Type 5 is not relevant to the piano trio and therefore need not concern us here. Type 4 will often be encountered in the last movement of trios: the following therefore serves as an introduction to its close relationship with Type 3 sonata form.

The rondo began with the idea of a recurring refrain or chorus (from the French *rond*, a "ring", and hence a poem with repeating lines which "come round again"). It is probably an idea of considerable antiquity, since an unadorned refrain could be memorised by people who could not read and this would have enabled them to take a simple part in musical performances. On the evidence of pieces such as the macaronic French *Noel, Conditor fut le nonpareil*, which we encountered in Chapter 2, refrains with energetic rhythms had become an established part of merry-making by the sixteenth century. "Italian *rondos*" with recurrent refrains were a feature of early opera around 1600, and the popularity here too of triple-metre rhythms is reflected in the fact that dances in triple metre frequently concluded these early operas with a "happy" dance. The eighteenth-century dance *suites* also traditionally ended merrily with a triple-metre dance – the *gigue* – but rondo finales probably came into the sonata from *opera buffa*.

Both these strands – the idea of a recurrent, easily-recognised tune, and the traditional "cheerfulness" of tunes with triplet rhythms – came together to establish a common habit of including a rondo as the final movement of a sonata. (When we come to Haydn's trios shortly, we shall find a well-known example in his *Rondo all' Ongarese*.) Hepokoski and Darcy describe the rondo as

"… a structure built primarily by the juxtaposition of discrete sections, each of which is normally marked by memorably tuneful ideas. Its defining feature is the recurrence of a tonic-key refrain (or "rondo theme") separating the appearance of differing or contrasting episodes (or "couplets"), which are often, though by no means always, in nontonic keys."[3]

The most basic type of instrumental rondo may be summarised as follows (A representing the rondo theme, other letters contrasting episodes):

$$A - B - A - C - A$$

Longer, more extended rondos have the pattern:

$$A - B - A - C - A - D - A$$

It is only a short distance from the latter, longer rondo to incorporation into the framework of sonata form; with only a little tonal modification, the 1st subject became a (frequently-reappearing) rondo theme, and thus, as defined by Hepokoski and Darcy, a Type 4 sonata.

A	–	B	–	A	–	C	–	A	–	B	–	A
(R)	–	B	–	A(R)	–	C	–	A(R)	–	B	–	A (R)
		(2nd subj in V)								(2nd subj in I)		

Here again the rondo theme is in the home tonic key on every appearance; B as 2nd subject appears in the dominant in the Exposition, but the tonic in the Recapitulation; and C (which functions in place of the Development) can be in any key of the composer's choice.

The primary requirement of a rondo theme is that it is worthy of constant repetition. Sonata Rondos are typically found as the option for a fast finale: we shall find many exuberant rondos closing piano trio works in uplifting style.

CHAPTER ENDNOTES

1   A F C Kollmann, *An Essay on Practical Musical Composition*, London, 1790, 5-7; quoted in Weiss and Taruskin, *op.cit*, pp.317-318.

2   See Hepokoski and Darcy, *op.cit*, introductory paragraphs to Chapter 16, pp.343-5.

3   See Hepokoski and Darcy, *op.cit*, p.388.

CHAPTER 7

THE CLASSICAL FORTEPIANO
TRIO: HAYDN

WE LEFT HAYDN in Chapter 4 in 1760, shortly before he took up a post with the Esterházy family, one of the great noble landowners of Hungary. Although employment with such a family offered musicians welcome security in the eighteenth century, there was no escaping the unpalatable fact that they were treated as common household servants. Haydn's contract stipulated that he "be considered and treated as a house officer", and that performing before company, he and all his musicians "shall appear in uniform ... in white stockings, white linen, powdered, and either with a pigtail or hairbag...".[1]

Less than eleven months after he had appointed Haydn as his ViceKapellmeister, Prince Paul Anton Esterházy died and was succeeded by his brother, Prince Nikolaus. This Prince insisted on spending much of the year on his country estate at Eszterháza, culturally isolated deep in the Hungarian countryside. Furthermore, he was not initially minded to share Haydn's compositions with a wider public, so that at first Haydn was obliged to grant the Prince exclusive rights to his work. Yet all this was mitigated not only by the person of the Prince himself – he was an ardent music lover as well as a competent performer – but also by the sumptuousness of the palace which the fabulously wealthy Nikolaus the Magnificent (as he was called) went on to build for himself at Eszterháza between 1776 and 1784. The palace contained two great halls (often used for musical performances) as well as its own chapel, a picture gallery and a library; and it boasted an opera house as well as a marionette theatre. The musical opportunities open to Haydn were endless – indeed, the post of *Kapellmeister* to the Esterházys was surely one of the key musical positions in Europe at that time.

For many years the isolation and the restrictions do not seem to have troubled Haydn unduly. He famously said to his biographer Griesinger:

> "My prince was always satisfied with my works. Not only did I have the encouragement of constant approval, but as conductor of an orchestra I could make experiments ... and be as bold as I pleased. I was cut off from the world; there was no one to confuse or torment me, and I was forced to become original."[2]

And in time his patience brought its own reward. In spite of the isolation of Eszterháza the opportunities for composing were so numerous, and he worked so industriously, that the reputation of his inventive genius spread far beyond Hungary. Recognising the reputation of his *Kapellmeister*, in 1779 Prince Nikolaus signed a new contract which not only considerably increased the annual salary, but also omitted the clause giving the Prince exclusive rights to Haydn's compositions. From this date onwards, he was free not only to write whatever he chose (subject to being able to find the time to do so around his commitment to the Prince's insatiable appetite for opera), but also to have his works published across Europe.

Haydn's employment with the Esterházys affected his composition of fortepiano trios – or rather, accompanied sonatas, as he continued to call them. For the first 16 years he had little time to write more of these, because the Prince required him to write for his own instrument, the baryton (a stringed instrument like the viol). The composition of 126 baryton string trios crowded out the possibility of chamber music with keyboard.

In the 1780s, however, set free by his new contract, Haydn made contact with both Viennese and English publishers, and as a result embarked on the composition of a new sequence of fourteen accompanied sonatas. The first six were produced between 1784 and 1785 with the harpsichord still in mind as the keyboard instrument, but as Haydn encountered more contemporary music in the few winter weeks he was able to spend in Vienna, he became more aware of the potential of the new fortepiano. This was partly because, in Vienna, it *was* still new: the first instruments were introduced in 1763 but had been slow to gain in popularity. But in the 1780s enthusiasm for the fortepiano as a domestic instrument was growing, and just as we shall find Mozart doing between 1786 and 1788 in the next chapter, Haydn now turned to writing for this lucrative amateur market.

Accordingly, Haydn wrote to the Viennese publisher Artaria in 1788 and offered to compose either three string quartets or three accompanied sonatas. The reply came back within a week: they would prefer the sonatas.[3] Haydn set to work with his customary thoroughness, and feeling that he needed to be more familiar with the fortepiano, acquired an instrument from the Viennese manufacturer Wenzel Schanz. He was impressed by its light, fast touch, and the clear, bell-like tone produced by its little leather-covered hammers. The three accompanied sonatas were duly completed and published together in 1789. We have a rare glimpse of eighteenth-century performance in a charming illustration from the title page of another collection of Haydn's trios published by Artaria. We can see three amateur players clustered together, the string players' music conveniently propped up on the lid of the small "bentside" fortepiano:

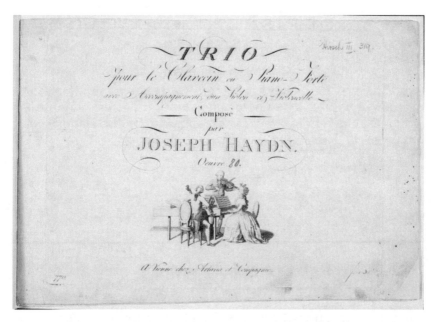

Title page of Artaria's edition of Haydn Trio XV:10, published as op.80.
London, British Library, Hirsch Collection.

We shall listen to the second of the 1789 set, the Trio in E minor, Hob.XV:12. This will be the first time that we have encountered a trio in a minor key. Of all the forty two trios written by Haydn, only eight were in minor keys; this is chronologically the third of them. Hepokoski and Darcy describe the minor mode as

"generally interpretable within the sonata tradition as a sign of a troubled condition seeking transformation (emancipation) into the parallel minor mode ... The possibility of a tonic-minor-to-tonic-major trajectory (or the represented inability to attain that transformation) is rich in metaphorical implication ... Minor-mode sonatas contend with the initial presence of the tonic minor – often a turbulent or threatening expressive field – either to overcome it or to be overcome by it."[4]

In the case of this Trio Hob.XV:12 Haydn moves to the relative major for a substantial part of the Exposition, but then opts to return to the minor key throughout the Recapitulation – achieving this by omitting the Exposition's major-key details. He redresses the balance of good cheer by using the major mode for both the following movements.

F J Haydn: 1st movement *Allegro moderato* from Accompanied Sonata in E minor Hob XV:12

1st Section:

Exposition: A loud chord in all three instruments introduces the **1st subject** with its arresting opening motif (**a**) – three notes from the tonic minor triad immediately followed by the leading note, compulsively demanding resolution on the tonic.

Ex. 13.1

Fortepiano

The next 17 bars grow organically from this opening, as it fragments into derivative motifs and dynamic contrasts. The home key is confirmed with (**a**) again at bar 18. But this time the continuation leads into a transitional passage which moves towards the V of the relative major key, and shortly afterwards we sense our arrival indeed in G major for the **2nd subject**. This begins with the same four notes of (**a**), which now sound far less painfully angular in the major mode; two more distinctive ideas follow – 2(**b**), a lively phrase with a distinctive twist in its tail as it slides playfully down three falling semitones in its second bar (**x**),

Ex. 13.2

Fortepiano

and 2(c), which introduces busy semiquavers.

Ex. 13.3

All this closes in a sequence of scales by way of a cadential send-off.

2nd Section:

A short, highly-concentrated **Development** section follows. The four-note motif (a) re-appears, accompanied at first by (x) from the 2nd subject; but then (a) dominates the texture with increasing energy, ending with a loud statement in G major which unexpectedly slips onto the home V, so that Haydn is swiftly back in the home tonic minor ready for the Recapitulation

Recapitulation: The opening statements of the 1st subject faithfully follow the Exposition, but after the 15th bar the motif (a) – having featured so strongly in the Development – now disappears from both the transition and the opening of the 2nd subject. 2(b) and (c) reappear, but now in the minor mode, not the major mode of the Exposition. The last surprise comes near the end of the movement, when the cadential scales of the Exposition are brilliantly displaced by a final emphatic reappearance of motif (a) in all three instruments in unison.

The second and third movements are in the home tonic major key. The second movement *Andante* is in a slow, gently-lilting triplet metre, its opening tune in the fortepiano accompanied by *pizzicato* chords in the strings, gently hinting at the contemporary *siciliano* dance type. There are two parts to the tune, both of which are beautifully ornamented with subtle variants. The *Presto* finale sees Haydn experimenting with the sonata rondo idea, incorporating ebullient 8-bar dance phraseology and the contrast of a minor mode section with elements of the tonal return of the sonata.

From the point of view of the development of the sonata idea, the first movement shows that Haydn is not afraid to experiment. He retains the distinct cadences demarcating the tonal areas of the 1st and 2nd subjects, but then achieves a contrast between them – not by introducing new material, but rather by re-using the same motif (**a**) *in the major mode*. As just noted, he then sidesteps the problem

of how to deal with this major mode 2nd subject in the Recapitulation simply by omitting (a) here altogether. The later sections of
the 2nd subject, with their playful semitone decorations, lend themselves naturally to transference into the minor mode, after which (a)
is repositioned near the end to ensure a final thematic balance.

The use Haydn makes of his material is especially interesting,
notably the organic growth of the 1st subject in the Exposition, and
the concise development with its focus on (a) and – unexpectedly –
the development of the potential of that playful motif (x) from the
2nd subject. Although this is not an extensive movement, it is packed
full of original details and the attention to thematic development is a
significant pointer to future directions.

We should not be surprised to find, for all the new awareness of
the fortepiano, that this is a polished work. Haydn was fifty-six in
1788, and already widely experienced, with his reputation based
on the composition of some ninety-two symphonies and over forty
string quartets. We can sense the background of his orchestral and
chamber music in the craftsmanship of the interplay between fortepiano and violin; and if the 'cello continues for the most part to
double the left hand of the keyboard, this is because the fortepiano's
shallow tone still needs support.

Perhaps the most striking feature of this accompanied sonata,
however, is the new richness of its musical vocabulary. If we think
back to our identification of the simple major scale on pp.47-48,
and the three primary triads – the functional harmony of I, V and
IV – which could be drawn from its basic eight notes, we sense that
Haydn now goes much further than John Bach in introducing extra-
neous notes. These are the "foreign" semitones which lie between
the original eight notes.

Such foreign notes are more properly described as "chromatic" to
the home key (literally, "coloured"), and there is no better description of the effect of a "chromatic" note than Percy Buck's, who
called it "a sudden touch of colour to monochrome – *like a poppy in
a cornfield*". This is because a chromatic note sets up a *dissonance* in
the setting of the familiar scale. In a tonal context, a dissonance is a
problem which demands *resolution*.

Tunes in minor keys are especially prone to chromatic decoration, since by their nature they abound in semitones. Haydn does
not limit chromaticism to his melodic line, however, but extends it
also to the accompanying harmony. By introducing dissonant chromatic notes into *chords*, he creates a fleeting hiatus which makes the
immediately-following *resolution* more satisfying. Using chromatic
notes in this way was not new: chromaticism had been used for
effect since the early history of opera, and an immensely rich vocabulary of chromatic harmony had been developed by composers of

the Baroque period, notably J S Bach. But Haydn and his Classical contemporaries now use chromatic harmony in a very specific way in the sonata – to reinforce the harmonic progressions at significant cadences. These punctuation points, underlining arrival in a new key or return home to the tonic, or heralding the presentation of an important new theme, all these are an important part of the way in which the composer unfolds the narrative of each sonata story. Chromatically-enhanced harmony now *sign-posts the narrative*.

The Classical composer had a kitbag of chromatic chords which he could use for this purpose. These ranged from the so-called Neapolitan sixth* to three other chords which contained augmented sixth intervals** (rather abstrusely known as Italian, French and German sixths); these were used immediately before the V chord to enhance the sense of strong arrival on V before resolution on I. In addition there was the ubiquitous dominant seventh chord,*** created by stacking another minor third interval on top of the V triad; this was not actually a chromatic chord, but it was striking because of the discordant 7th note the additional third produced. There was also the arresting chord of the diminished seventh,**** an immensely needy chord which could be resolved in a number of different and satisfying ways.

For general purposes, it is enough simply to hear these chromatic chords and recognise them as momentary decoration: the human ear tends to prefer consonant intervals and welcomes swift resolution, so chromatic chords were effectively used to endorse functional harmony. These rogue interruptions enhanced the impact of arriving back in a familiar, anticipated place, so that paradoxically their function was actually to stabilise the tonal context, not destabilise it. Haydn's use of such devices has become masterly.

★ ★ ★ ★ ★

There was a further pause of five years in Haydn's composition of fortepiano trios after 1790, when his life changed course following the death of Prince Nikolaus Esterházy. The Prince's son was not

---

* Essentially a version of the triad on the 2nd note of the scale, but *flattened* (♭II) and therefore heard exotically as a mere semitone above the tonic.

** The augmented sixth interval is typically created between two chromatic notes (the minor ♭6th note and a sharpened 4th), both longing to resolve onto the dominant (♭6th falls down a semitone, ♯4th rises up).

*** This 4-note chord contains the leading note longing to rise a semitone to the tonic, as well as its discordant 7th (the home 4th) longing to fall a semitone to the 3rd.

**** Another 4-note chord, a stack of minor third intervals, occurring naturally in the minor scale with its ♭6th, but widely used with chromatic alterations.

interested in music, and disbanded the Eszterháza musical establishment, so that Haydn found himself suddenly free to go and do whatever he wished. The impresario Salomon promptly persuaded him to
accompany him to London, so that two visits and the composition
of twelve new symphonies occupied much of Haydn's time for the
next five years. Contact with the English capital's flourishing musical
life, the rich variety of both public and private concerts and working
with its large and proficient orchestras greatly extended his musical
experience. The city also provided the stimulus for fifteen further
fortepiano trios which Haydn wrote during or after his second visit
in 1794/5.

That stimulus came first and foremost from the fortepiano instruments which Haydn encountered in London. By this time there was
a flourishing market for making and selling keyboard instruments,
and all over Europe manufacturers were vying with each other to
improve the quality of the fortepiano. In London John Broadwood
had taken out a patent for a new action in the 1780s; housed in a
case with a curving bentside like a small grand piano, Broadwood's
fortepiano had additional notes at each end of the range, and three
strings to each note. By the time that Haydn met them, Broadwood's
instruments had a fuller, rounder tone than the Viennese fortepianos, and they could produce a good *cantabile* (literally, "singing")
tone. Moreover, London's well-established enthusiasm for the piano
had attracted many more foreign *virtuoso* keyboard performers to its
musical scene than there were in Vienna – such as Clementi, Dussek
and Cramer.

The second stimulus for Haydn's late fortepiano trios came from
the performing standards set by two notable women pianists –
Rebecca Schroeter and Therese Jansen. It is interesting that here we
still encounter women as significant performers on the instrument:
neither of them could be professional but both were highly competent amateurs. Haydn dedicated a set of three trios to each of them.

Although Therese Jansen was undoubtedly the more brilliant
performer, Rebecca Schroeter had other musical attributes which
intrigued Haydn. She was the widow of Johann Samuel Schroeter,
a musician from Leipzig who had settled in London and who on
John Bach's death in 1782 succeeded him as music master to Queen
Charlotte. Burney said that Schroeter was "the first who brought
into England the true art of treating [the piano]" (*Rees's Cyclopae-
dia*), and the lengthy Obituary published in the *European Magazine*
after his death stated that

> "the grand Piano Forte was Schroeter's favourite instrument. His
> stile of playing was distinguished by that peculiar elegance and
> delicacy, which a chaste and correct taste improved by science,

alone can acquire ... he possessed the most complete domination of his instrument... His manner of playing an Adagio was unrivalled ..."[5]

Schroeter's performing style must have been a formative influence on his talented pupil Rebecca Scott, whom he had married in 1775. When Haydn arrived in London she had been widowed for three years. As she was already such a competent player it was not surprising that she applied to him for further fortepiano lessons, and as the dedication of the trios shows, she became one of Haydn's most favoured pupils.[6] The fortepiano lessons were conducted in Rebecca's own house and on her late husband's Broadwood grand fortepiano – and in these lessons we have this happy vignette of Haydn introduced to the double stimulus of a truly pianistic performance style as well as the characteristic tone and technical advances of her London instrument.

There is another strand in the story of Rebecca Schroeter which is interesting for us because it illustrates the continuing ambivalence in the English attitude at this time towards musicians. Rebecca Scott's family permitted her to take music lessons from Schroeter because they believed that playing the fortepiano well could improve her chances of making an advantageous marriage: the Scotts' considerable wealth had come from merchant trading and they were avidly concerned to preserve the gentry lifestyle and reputation which it had bought for them. They were incensed when Rebecca – being very musical – was so inspired by her music master that she actually wanted to marry him. They saw Schroeter only as a person of low birth committed to a servile profession; worse still, he was a foreigner – and Catholic to boot. In order to retain Rebecca's dowry of £15,000 (in today's money around £1m) and to dissociate themselves from the match – it is not clear which of the two weighed more heavily with them – when Rebecca insisted on going through with the marriage, the family took her through the Court of Chancery. Schroeter's obituary suggests that there was a settlement – of sorts: the Scotts bought him off with an annuity of £500 on condition "that he was to relinquish his profession so far as never to perform at any public concert". Fortunately for Schroeter, the prohibition was overtaken by events:

"The Prince of Wales heard him play at a private concert, and expressed the highest admiration of his performance. His Royal Highness's household was then about be established, and without any solicitation Schroeter was appointed one of his band of music, with a liberal salary." [7]

We must now return to the set of fortepiano trios which Haydn dedicated to Rebecca Schroeter in 1795.

F J Haydn: 1st movement *Allegro* from Piano Trio in D major Hob.XV:24.

1st Section: **Exposition:** First a firm chord in the home tonic, and then the **1st subject**, six bars in all the instruments which play beautifully to the *cantabile* strength of the English piano.

Ex. 14.1

Haydn cadences on the dominant and we expect an answering phrase to return to the home key. But then, he suddenly gives us the same rhythm and (roughly) the same contours, beginning on an entirely unexpected note (on the supertonic, the key of e minor). After this escapade he has some work to do to re-establish the home key, but he soon turns deftly back into the home tonic, and follows with an 8-bar passage full of rising scales and neat little cadences, and then repeats it on the violin, just to make sure. But Haydn is not yet done with surprises: the first six notes of the 1st subject (**x**) appear in another foreign key, which soon explains itself as a chromatic decoration of the V of the home V key, in anticipation of the **2nd subject**. When that duly follows – it turns out to be none other than the opening notes (**x**), now peaceably settled into a more conventional theme and firmly tied down in the dominant:

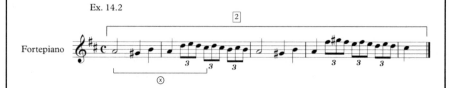

Ex. 14.2

It is followed by 6 bars of leaping octaves. A bright sequence of *staccato* quaver figures as cadential material bring the Exposition to a close.

2nd Section: The **Development** immediately plunges into distant keys, but all is made comprehensible because there is scarcely a single bar in which we cannot hear the six-note *motif* (**x**) in one or other of the instruments. We follow Haydn's train of thought until we hear the staccato quavers of the cadential material and the leaping octaves from the 2nd subject, and then hear the piano and the 'cello settling on the home dominant. Our expectations are raised – and happily satisfied when –

the **Recapitulation** begins, quietly, with the return of the 1st subject in the tonic. Apart from the immediate jump onto the key of the supertonic, there are no more surprises and the whole section progresses peacefully, omitting the wayward excursions of the Exposition, but retaining (x) as the 2nd subject as before; in the final stages the *staccato* figures bring the movement to an energetic close.

The *Andante* second movement gravitates into the minor mode. It is short, featuring a dignified theme with a dotted *motif* which dominates the whole much as the 6-note *motif* dominated the first movement. Again, there is a perfect balance between the 8-beat phrase and the 8-beat reply which constitute the tune. After the brief central section based on the dotted *motif*, listen to the return of the opening theme, where the 'cello doubles the tune in the pianist's left hand and gives it weight which it would not have without this support. It leads without a break into the last movement.

The final *Allegro ma dolce* might have been a *Minuetto*: it has the graceful flow of Haydn's symphonic minuets, with a central section like a trio. Hear how Haydn's opening 8-bar section grows organically from the first note to the last and has no need of a strict rhythmic definition to explain its structure. It is a measure of the extent to which the old dance has a new life of its own as an independent instrumental piece.

We cannot leave Haydn's accompanied sonatas for Rebecca Schroeter without hearing one of the best-known movements of the entire piano trio literature: the *Rondo all'Ongarese* from the trio in G major Hob XV:25. In this *Presto* finale Haydn combines the contemporary taste for "exotic" music with the popularity of the rondo formula. The exotic element is the so-called "Hungarian" (*all'Ongarese*) style. Haydn was better qualified than most eighteenth-century composers to produce Hungarian music: he had been born in eastern Austria, near the Hungarian border, and as we have seen, spent much of his working life at Eszterháza. In both he would have come into contact with folk traditions as well as gypsy musicians. So in between the three statements of the rondo theme he gives us two extensive episodes of vibrant "Hungarian" dance music. In characteristic units of four bars of duple rhythm, and simple but strong tonic and dominant harmony, these robust interludes give us an apotheosis of dancing energy. (Notably both rondo and episodes are all *in the same key*, giving the movement a distinct sense of rustic music-making in action.) The whirling rondo theme, packaged as always into neat 8 + 8 bar tonal boxes, undoubtedly suited the admirable technique which Rebecca Schroeter had learnt from her gifted husband, whose fingering was said to be "so peculiarly easy and elegant".

Ex.15 F J Haydn: *Presto all'Ongarese* from Piano Trio in G major Hob XV:25

Given what is known of her relationship with Haydn, the three trios dedicated to Rebecca Schroeter have a particularly personal flavour. This applies also to the subsequent set of three Trios, Hob. XV:27-29, dedicated to Therese Jansen. She was known to be one of the best of the famous pianist Clementi's pupils, and she too became a personal friend of Haydn's during his London visits – he acted as a witness at her marriage in 1795 to the son of the famous engraver Bartolozzi.

We should not forget that by virtue of their sex, because it was considered socially unacceptable for ladies to do so, neither Rebecca Schroeter nor Therese Jansen would have been permitted to play at public concerts. However both would have performed in the semi-public surroundings of a private, but probably quite large, reception room, which is suggested by Haydn's provision of "noise-killer" openings in some of these trios. Used to the hushed attentiveness of the small Eszterháza audiences, he had learnt to begin concert pieces for London with at least one loud chord to cut across the hubbub of English audiences' conversations and attract their attention.[8] Rebecca Schroeter's trio begins with a loud chord (which never reappears again); Therese Jansen's XV:27 opens with a *forte* flourish.

The first of Therese Jansen's accompanied sonatas stands out for the virtuosity of the fortepiano part; Charles Rosen says she "must have been a more than ordinary pianist"[9] and Peter Brown thinks this sonata was "certainly beyond the reach of most of the nonprofessional London pianists"[10]. The first movement abounds with technical difficulties such as third and octave runs, fast passage work, crossing of hands and constantly changing textures; it is undoubtedly the most difficult of all Haydn's trios, and in spite of Jansen's officially amateur status, it takes these late piano trios into the realm of chamber music for professional performers.

F J Haydn: 1st movement *Allegro* from Piano Trio in C major Hob XV:27

1st Section: The **Exposition** opens with the **1st subject** – four bars which alternate loud spread chords (a) with a soft reply, first on the II chord and then on I. A succession of short momentarily-suspended dissonances follow (x), which quietly resolve, repeat, then resolve again, until a firm cadence signals the end of the opening statement.

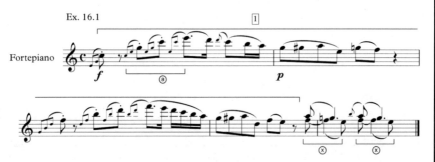

Bravura octaves in the fortepiano lead off into a short transitional passage which ends in V, G major. Here we hear another sequence of arpeggiated chords, now the first part of the **2nd subject** (a),

soon followed by a distinctive 2 (b) with little runs of triplet semi-quavers.

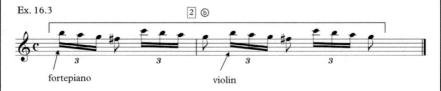

After a brief minor-mode clouding, a merry little cadential figure – heard only in the fortepiano – brings the Exposition to a close.

2nd Section: The **Development** focuses at first on (x), the innocuous tailpiece from the 1st subject. After only 8 bars the fortepiano pauses expectantly on a low note G (the home V), as though Haydn is about to return to I. But a moment later all three instruments rise up a semitone (as we have seen, always a surprising effect) and the fortepiano returns to the 1st subject's spread chords in the key of A♭ (the ♭VI of the home tonic). This gains momentum as all three instruments join in a rush of semiquavers which land eventually on E (the V of the relative minor). Are we about to go there? (It is a traditionally popular destination in Classical developments.) It seems inevitable, although none of the themes from the Exposition can be heard – but soon Haydn drifts away from this a minor key. Finally, a busy triplet semiquaver accompaniment in the pianist's left hand circles round the home V, and as the dynamic level drops to a suspenseful *pianissimo*, excitement begins to build in the strings – until finally two bars of churning harmonies lead into the **Recapitulation**. This follows the Exposition closely, although it omits the sequence of suspended dissonances (x) heard in the Development, and just before the close returns to the bravura octaves of the transitional passage and the merry cadential figure – now also splendidly delivered in octaves.

Unusually, the slow movement *Andante* is in the key of A major – presumably Haydn is thinking of it as the major mode of the relative minor key. Typically, it is in three contrasting sections: the first sets out a spacious theme comprising two distinct parts, the second introduces the contrast of the minor mode, and the third returns to reprise the opening. Although the fortepiano as usual first introduces the theme, the violin also has a full share of it, and the 'cello makes a number of strikingly independent and telling contributions to the texture which add to its beautiful richness.

Ex. 16.4

Fortepiano

Ex.16 F J Haydn: *Andante* from Piano Trio in C major Hob XV:27

The *Presto* finale finds Haydn in a particularly playful mood, inventing a nimble 8-bar opening theme which leads us to expect a rondo finale. But, as Hans Keller has pointed out, Haydn sometimes teasingly leads his listener to "expect a form, not in view of his successive structural events, but in view of the sheer character of his themes."[11] This movement turns out to be neither a rondo nor even a sonata rondo, but a regular sonata form, with a repeating Exposition and an exhilarating Coda in extra celebration of the 1st subject. With its breathless energy and the agility expected of the pianist, not to mention the powerful sonorities produced by the writing near the end, Therese Jansen's performances of this trio must have brought the house down.

Ex. 16.5

Ex.16 F J Haydn: *Presto* from Piano Trio in C major Hob XV:27

We have now seen the story of the fortepiano trio develop over four decades, and Haydn has featured at almost every stage, from the early Hob.XV:C1 in c.1760, to XV:12 in 1788/9, and finally XV:24, 25 and 27 in the mid-1790s. His view of the *genre* has remained consistent: even the last of these are still accompanied sonatas. Haydn did not write trios for three independent chamber instrumentalists; instead he came from the standpoint of contemporary keyboard instruments. He understood both harpsichord and fortepiano, and recognised that both had innate deficiencies as chamber participants, so he used the strings to make these good. Because both still had relatively quiet tone, his violin parts support melodic lines and add colour and warmth whenever required; because they had a weak bass sound, he ensured that the 'cello gave the texture strong harmonic underpinning. Haydn's trios may lack an interplay of parts, but the fortepiano leads a beautifully integrated ensemble of instruments.

Moreover Haydn's musical imagination is no less original simply because his fortepiano continues to lead the ensemble. We have seen his ideas about the sonata gradually develop from simple, suite-like beginnings to Hob.XV:12, with its carefully-planned thematic integration, neatly-demarcated layout and concise organisation. With Hob.XV:24 and 27 we sense that we are now in new territory – and recall Haydn's remark that the pattern of his career had "forced [him] to become original". So what is different, and what can we still recognise?

The starting-point is still there: the structural layout of the binary tonal template, which moves from I to V, then back from V to I, resolving dissonances. But perhaps it is not quite so easy to follow Haydn's progress through the Exposition, which is now written in a more continuous style than before: there is less differentiation between themes in tonal boxes and the character of intervening passagework, less insistent play on dominants. And Haydn also clouds matters by introducing harmonic surprises – he loves surprises – perhaps he is still at heart the prankster who cut off that pigtail – and he loves to tease his listener with musical jokes.

At first these may seem confusing, but we have to take a long view: unexpected harmonies are chromatic decorations, and as such, dissonances requiring resolution. And with Haydn resolution always follows, so that unexpected harmonic surprises – and there are many of them scattered throughout Hob.XV:24 and 27 – are really only Haydn's piquant way of emphasising home or dominant tonalities. Thus, however different the content of these late sonata movements, the framework remains that of the binary trajectory from tonic to dominant, then back to tonic.

However, the sonata idea as we now hear it in Haydn has become far more than the infilling of a tonal footprint. Contemporary theorists like Kollmann continue to give precise rules for laying out the harmonic framework, but they all agree that the process of inventing musical ideas cannot be taught, and must be down to the individual talent of the composer. The genius of Haydn and – as we shall see in the next chapter – Mozart lay in their ability to invent memorable and attractive themes, not only lyrical ideas for slow movements, or lively dance-like rondo themes for finales, but also the distinctive ideas with which they populated their first movements. Such ideas had to bear repetition and development so that they could be imaginatively used. For instance, 1st subjects might be continued into transitional passages to generate momentum, or principal themes and innocuous motifs might unexpectedly be combined together; or the same material for both first and second subjects might sometimes produce a monothematic movement, sometimes not. We know from his biographer Griesinger that

> "Haydn completed his compositions in one outpouring; for each section he set down the plan of the main voice by noting the prominent passages with a few notes and figures."

Only later did the composer "breathe spirit and life into this dry skeleton by means of the accompanying voices and through artful transitions."[12]

This again places a burden of careful listening on both performers and audience, who need to recognise recurrences of themes and motifs in order to appreciate the composer's skill and to enjoy this music. The enjoyment of the opening of XV:24, for instance, depends on recognising the 6-note theme (x) in no fewer than four keys. Haydn is able to use his material so freely because he can rely on his contemporaries' previous experience of the sonata idea. Indeed, as we have just seen, he can associate themes and motifs with daring harmonic surprises which, far from derailing tonal stability, actually contribute to enhancement of it. Such a sophisticated level of tonal and thematic recognition was now expected, as the Scots poet and philosopher James Beattie wrote in 1778:[13]

"… harmony must be studied a little in its principles by every *person* who would acquire a true relish for it … When once [a person] can attend to the progress, relations, and dependencies, of the several parts; and remember the past, and anticipate the future, at the same time he perceives the present: so as to be sensible of the skill of the composer, and dexterity of the performer; – a regular concerto, well executed, will yield him high entertainment, even though its regularity be its principal recommendation."

The importance of themes and the use now made of them by Haydn and Mozart do, however, have a significant impact on the concept of the first movement as a two-part structure. Tonally, as we have seen, it remains so, but longer development sections, taken up by extended exploration of thematic material, put such an emphasis on this section that it is perverse to continue regarding it merely as a constituent of the second half of the movement. The development has now actually found the focus and purpose which was lacking in the early sonata, but in so doing it demands to be recognised as its intellectual heart – and the sonata form bids to be experienced as a ternary, rather than a binary structure.

This is a dichotomy which has caused a great deal of trouble in scholarly circles. Is sonata form a binary or a ternary form? James Webster decisively declares in his article on Sonata Form for the *Grove Music Online* that

"The old dispute, whether sonata form is binary or ternary, is idle and superficial. Sonata form is a synthesis of binary and ternary principles: it integrates three sections into a two-part structure."[14]

I suggest that we may – serendipitously – find an interesting parallel for these simultaneously binary and ternary aspects of sonata form in the architecture of the place where Haydn spent so much of his life, Prince Nikolaus's palace at Eszterháza.

The glory of Eszterháza is the perfection of its symmetry: if we imagine a straight line drawn from the apex of the pediment in the central block in the foreground to the entrance gates at the top, we have two identical, mirror-image parts, a living incarnation of classical Palladian principles which we can appreciate at a glance. Our experience of music, however, is not as static as this experience of architecture. So to draw a closer parallel between the design of music and that of architecture, we have to inject a little movement into our engagement with the image of the palace.

Aerial photograph of Palace of Eszterháza, Fertőd, Hungary

Supposing we were to begin, not with the pediment, but with the *gates* to the palace? If we focus on the centre of the gates, then travel round and down the left-hand side until we come to the central rectangular block, we become aware of this block as a highly distinctive feature in its own right, stylistically identical but nevertheless a significant protrusion from the east-west flow of the corner wings. The eye travels over the repetition of pattern on the block's façade, recognising and savouring the crescendo of variations, before retracing the sequence of buildings up the opposite right-hand side. We might see this architectural footprint as a metaphor for the developed Classical sonata form: the mirror-imaging of flanking wings as initial Exposition and final Recapitulation, and the detail of the central block as Development – a third component which is both wholly integrated and also wholly distinct, an integral part of what is essentially a two-part design.

Haydn and Mozart were the great masters of High Classical style and form, whose works have the same symmetry and balance, repetition and variation as we recognise in the architecture of Eszterháza. The extension of the Development section does not distort the fundamentally binary tonal concept of the sonata, but by concentrating on its thematic material it enhances its rhetorical aspect, standing out as a significant third component of the musical discourse.

CHAPTER ENDNOTES

1   Geiringer, *op.cit*, pp.43-5.

2   Geiringer, *op.cit*, p.71.

3   Brown, *op cit*, p.126.

4   Hepokoski and Darcy, *op.cit*, p. 306.

5   Quoted in Hobday, Peter. *The Girl in Rose: Haydn's Last Love*. London, Weidenfeld & Nicholson, 2004, pp.109-11.

6   For further details of their relationship, see Hobday, *ibid.*

7   Obituary printed in *The European Magazine*, probably written by Charles Burney; quoted in Hobday, *ibid*, p.110.

8   See Somfai, László. 'The London Revision of Haydn's Instrumental Style', *Proceedings of the Royal Musical Association*, vol.100 (1973-74), pp.159-174.

9   Rosen, *Classical Style, op.cit*, p.358.

10   Brown, *op.cit*, p.382.

11   Keller, Hans. *The Great Haydn Quartets: Their Interpretation*. London, Dent, 1986, p.133; quoted in Hepokoski and Darcy, *op.cit*, p.399

12   Griesinger, Georg August. *Biographische Notizen über Joseph Haydn*, 1810; quoted in Bonds, *Wordless Rhetoric*, p.114 (bibl.ref. p.56).

13   Beattie, James. *An Essay on Poetry and Music as they Affect the Mind*. Edinburgh, 1778, pp.155-6; available to view online at https://archive. org/details/essaysonpoetrymu00beat/page/n5

14   Webster, James. 'Sonata Form', *Grove Music Online, 2001*. See also Hepokoski and Darcy, *op.cit*, p.366, note 24, and Caplin, *op.cit*, pp.71-72.

CHAPTER 8

THE CLASSICAL FORTEPIANO TRIO: MOZART

WE SAW IN the previous chapter how isolation at Eszterháza and Prince Nikolaus's obsession with the baryton effectively prevented Haydn from writing further fortepiano trios until late in his career. No such limitations applied to Wolfgang Amadeus Mozart (1756-1791). At the same time that Haydn (in his early thirties) was settling into employment with Prince Nikolaus, the child Mozart (then between the ages of seven and ten) was travelling with his father Leopold and sister Nannerl around the courts of northern Europe. We met them in London between 1764 and 1765, but the tour lasted another eighteen months before they finally returned to Salzburg at the end of 1766 – Wolfgang's head full of all the music they had heard on their travels.

Leopold Mozart's employment as deputy Kapellmeister to the court of the Prince-Archbishop Schrattenbach held him officially in Salzburg, but he contrived to take Wolfgang away again on three visits to Italy between 1770 and 1773. Here the teenage composer heard the stimulating Italian style at first hand, and visits to principal cities – notably Milan (where he met Sammartini and Piccinni) and Bologna (where he visited John Bach's mentor Padre Martini) – influenced the composition of his early stage works, symphonies and string quartets. Wolfgang's musical experiences were further broadened by visiting Vienna again, where he encountered more of Haydn's music, and Mannheim, where he heard performances by the famously innovative orchestral players as well as much chamber music.

At the end of 1778 Wolfgang himself was formally employed as court and cathedral organist at Salzburg. A new Prince-Archbishop, Hieronymus Colloredo, had been appointed in 1772 and permission to travel became increasingly difficult to obtain. To make matters worse, Mozart was expected – like Haydn – to submit to a life of servitude, always at the unsympathetic Colloredo's beck and call; after the adulation he had enjoyed on his travels Mozart looked on such treatment with increasing resentment. Matters came to a head in 1781, when the Archbishop and his retinue were in Vienna for the coronation of the Emperor Joseph II. Mozart was refused leave to perform for the Emperor and after a defiant exchange was literally kicked out of the Archbishop's lodgings. Thereafter he lived in the Imperial city, independent but impecunious, for the rest of his life.

After the break with Colloredo, Mozart earned an unpredictable living performing and composing for the aristocracy, in whose chambers and private theatres operas and orchestral music flourished. These private performances were a source of income which could also lead to further patronage – such as participation in the regular Sunday concerts of music by J S Bach and Handel at the diplomat Baron Gottfried van Swieten's house. Long after London, public concerts were at last becoming established in Vienna and these also provided a welcome platform for Wolfgang's symphonies, concertos and concert arias. The Viennese loved to dance, and he wrote sets of orchestral dances for balls at the Redouten rooms: according to his biographer Georg Nikolaus von Nissen, Mozart "passionately loved dancing, and missed neither the public masked balls in the theatre, nor his friends' domestic balls."[1]

In 1782 Mozart bought himself a fortepiano from Anton Walter, the acclaimed manufacturer who had set up a workshop in Vienna a couple of years earlier. He found a useful source of steady income in teaching and publishing keyboard works for the Viennese public. Sets of keyboard variations on well-known tunes were especially popular, and a set of twelve variations on a popular tune in C major, K.265, date from this time. We shall find it illuminating to step aside and consider this solo keyboard work before moving on to his piano trios, because it takes us to the heart of the decorative Italian style he had initially met in John Bach's music, but had now wholly absorbed into his own idiom. These variations will also be a useful example because the tune is as familiar to modern listeners as it was in Mozart's time, and therefore any variation of it will be recognised immediately.

The tune of the artless little air, *Ah! vous dirai-je, maman,* was probably picked up during Mozart's stay in Paris in 1778, where it was popular at the time.[2] The original text (a love poem entitled *La Confidence*★) featured a poem of the pastoral type widely enjoyed in the eighteenth century: a shepherdess confides to her mother that she has been the victim (albeit not reluctant, nor indeed unco-operative)

★ For the original French text see https://fr.wikipedia.org/wiki/Ah ! vous dirai-je, maman of seduction by one Silvandre. The poem was parodied in a version for children (essentially substituting *bons bons* for *amour*) and the simple tune became so celebrated that it travelled far beyond the borders of France. Across the Channel in 1806 it was given the words by Jane Taylor by which it is still known and loved as one of the most popular of all English nursery rhymes: *Twinkle, twinkle little star.*[3]

Our familiarity with it enables us to hear these variations unfold just as Mozart's contemporaries would have done. He begins by presenting the simple melody absolutely unadorned, save for three little twiddly trills at cadence-points. Thus the metre of the French verse dictates the outline:

A: 4 bars + 4 bars cadencing on the tonic (A repeated)

B: 4 + 4 cadencing on the dominant

C: 4 + 4 returning to the tonic (B and C together repeated)

After this the air becomes decorated by a succession of different ornaments and accompaniment figures. The well-known tune is almost always audible (unlike Haydn's old-fashioned set in his sonata Hob.XV:C1), and the final variation concludes with a flurry of rapid notes guaranteed to appeal to a Viennese audience.

However, Mozart does not only pander to popular taste for display, he also coaxes the theme into different moods. Variation no.5 adopts a jaunty character and no.8 pitches soulfully into the minor mode, while no.9 packs contrapuntal imitation into every second bar. The theme itself uses only notes in the major scale, but now and again – such as in the second part of variation no.5 – the simple contours of the tune are enlivened by "foreign" notes. Mozart loved to exploit the effect of introducing emotional chromatic semitones into his melodies. There are bright poppy colours in all these variations, often, as in no.10, introducing harmonic as well as melodic colour. But he shows his true mastery of its effect in variation no.11, where he slows the pace to *Adagio* and the little nursery rhyme is transformed into a spacious melody, sparingly but beautifully tinged with chromatic colour. These variations show Mozart in complete mastery of the technique of keyboard variation: it is not easy to be so *perfectly* simple.

The mastery had been achieved by a long process of assimilation. Wherever Mozart encountered a new musical idea on his travels, since as we have seen he could "accept and imitate pretty well any type and style" (cf. p.63), he emulated it compulsively and immediately tried it out in a composition of his own. Any worthwhile

elements of the idea then became absorbed into his own idiom. Wolfgang's own maturing as a composer in fact coincided with the transition from the *galant* to the High Classical style. The short works
of the *galant* had relied mainly on simple primary triads to propel
the musical action from one key to another. As the style matured,
the movements became longer, more expansive, more sophisticated.
Mozart held the listener's attention throughout the additional length
by a process of subtle musical variation in which chromaticism –
both melodic and harmonic – played an important part in achieving
the "heightened sense of harmonic richness and colour"[4] of the new
style.

Another feature of the *galant* which we noted in Chapter 4 was its
tendency towards different regional styles. These evaporated in the
universality of High Classicism. As we have seen, despite the considerable difficulties of long-distance travel, the best musical ideas from
all over Europe were widely known and exchanged, so that Mozart's
synthesis of style and idea were perfectly understood and enjoyed in
Vienna in the 1780s.

★   ★   ★   ★   ★

We have now arrived at the trios for fortepiano with violin and
'cello which Mozart wrote in Vienna in the space of only two years
between 1786 and 1788. His works for this combination of instruments were composed in response to the same boom in demand for
piano trios from the Viennese, both the aristocracy and the general
public, as that which stimulated Haydn in the 1780s: in the same
way that John Bach produced chamber works for English amateurs,
the Viennese were also keen to acquire new works they could play
for themselves. But Mozart would make far fewer concessions to
amateur performers than Bach had done: in performance in private
salons, he took the fortepiano part himself and expected both string
players to have the same degree of performing skills as he required of
the string players in the rest of his chamber music.

It was no accident that all his mature piano trios date from this
comparatively late stage in Mozart's career. After the six harpsichord
Sonatas with Accompaniments which he dashed off as a boy after
meeting John Bach, he had written no more chamber music with
keyboard for many years. During much of this time the fortepiano
remained a technically imperfect instrument, and his keyboard works
tended to be written without discriminating between harpsichord
or fortepiano; thus his early keyboard writing concentrated on solo
keyboard sonatas or concertos, and in chamber music he turned his
attention to the string quartet. But on his way to Mannheim in 1777,
Mozart had passed through Augsburg and visited the workshops of

the noted fortepiano manufacturer J A Stein. Construction techniques were steadily improving and Mozart was very impressed by
the even, reliable tone of Stein's instruments, which seem to have
prompted a new realisation of the expressive potential of the fortepiano and its sensitivity to touch. He began writing solo sonatas in
a new style which reflected the individuality of the instrument, and
explored the potential for a true chamber style in sonatas for violin
and fortepiano; these were no longer works for keyboard with a mere
accompaniment for a violin, but had independent parts for each
instrument. Between 1782 and 1786 Mozart also wrote no fewer
than fourteen keyboard concertos, many distinguished by innovative
interplay between the soloist and the instruments of the orchestra,
so that by the time he turned to fortepiano trios in Vienna in 1786,
he had a good deal of varied experience of writing for a keyboard in
combination with other instruments. His different attitude is at once
clear in the titles – he himself calls them "Trios".

By this time Mozart had written most of the works he was to
produce in all *genres* – operas, symphonies, concertos, string quartets and quintets, sacred music and the rest – and in the same two
years he completed *The Marriage of Figaro* and *Don Giovanni*, as well
as the three last great symphonies. In spite of his youth – he was
only 25 when dismissed by Colloredo in 1781 – Wolfgang was widely
known. *Grove Music Online* cites a *Wiener Zeitung* review of 1785
which referred to his "merited fame" and said he was "universally
valued". His fame had indeed spread far across Europe: his death a
few years later would be referred to in the diary of an English lady in
distant Middlesex as an "irreparable loss".[5]

Mozart actually wrote six fortepiano trios between the beginning
of July 1786 and the end of October 1788. Of these one is not relevant to us because it is scored for clarinet, viola and fortepiano, and
two others are slight in character and are generally assumed either
to have been substantially written at an earlier date, or intended as
sonates faciles for pupils. The three trios which Artaria published as
Mozart's op.15 in 1788 – K.502, K.542 and K.548 – are however
not only a landmark in his own works, but also in the *genre*. To see
how Mozart makes use of the accepted framework of the early sonata
form as described by Kollmann, we shall compare the first movements of all three trios, and then additionally listen to the remaining
movements of the last trio of the three, K.548.

The earliest is the fortepiano trio in B♭, K.502, written in July
1786. *(Listen intently to the opening: if you miss any element of the first
two bars it will be like missing the scenes which introduce a thriller film –
scenes which later turn out to have been the crucial motivation for the rest
of the plot.)*

W A Mozart : 1st movement *Allegro* from Piano Trio in B♭ major K.502

1st Section: The **Exposition** begins with a buoyant 2-bar phrase as **1st subject**, establishing the home tonic tonality. We should especially note the rhythm and chromatic decoration of the opening 4-note motif **(a)**; and also a jaunty comment **(b)** added by the violin.

The rhythm of this jaunty motif drives the continuation until the opening is heard again. This time it slides away into the minor mode, but shortly we sense the beginning of the transitional passage with (b) sounding in V tonality; then the 'cello (distinctly heard scored below the fortepiano) embarks on a sequence based on the rhythm of (a) which finally takes us to the anticipated V of V. 11 further bars of purposeful preparation end in a rising chromatic scale as we anticipate the arrival of a new 2nd subject.

But Mozart foils our expectations: his 2nd subject is none other than the buoyant 1st subject again, now chromatically decorating dominant tonality. But this time there is no jaunty repartee from the violin – instead the strings respond with the 1st subject themselves, accompanied by twittering trills in the fortepiano. One by one, all the instruments take up the 4-note motif (a), culminating in a long trill before cadencing in V. Now, surely, we shall hear new cadential material to close the Exposition: but no, the Cadence passages too are based on (a), and 4 bars later the Exposition closes softly in the dominant key.

2nd Section: After so much clever variation and re-use of his 1st subject material, Mozart decides to give the violin an entirely new and lyrical tune to open the **Development**; listen for the counter-statement in the fortepiano (high in its range) soulfully doubled by the 'cello (in its tenor register). Soon however the jaunty motif (b) returns as the basis of imitation between fortepiano and violin, and drifts through contrasting minor keys. This passage ends poised on the V of the relative minor (still some distance from the home V and the expected return of the 1st subject) when suddenly the fortepiano cheekily and prematurely announces the chromatic decoration (a) from the 1st subject. The strings scramble to join in but the harmony remains doggedly on D as V – until with a neat shift it lands on the home V. The 'cello hammers out the rhythm of (a) low on the dominant note itself, the violin chips in for good measure with its comment (b), and only 2 bars later order is restored and the fortepiano nonchalantly begins the **Recapitulation** with the buoyant 1st subject back in the home tonic key.

After this there is no further insubordination. Mozart re-introduces all the variants of (a) and (b) as in the Exposition, dextrously maintaining minor mode colouring as before, but turning all earlier V tonality into the home tonic key. Like the Exposition, the movement ends quizzically with a soft cadence.

This is another example of a monothematic sonata movement, which uses (basically) the same thematic material for both its main subjects. Mozart wrote fewer of these than Haydn, but seems to have written more towards the end of his career in the 1780s – perhaps under Haydn's influence. He introduces so many subtle variants and treats each appearance in such skilfully altered ways that we never feel that his motifs are overworked. The following two movements are both Rondos, but very different in character. The second is a slow movement (marked *Larghetto*) in E♭, the last movement a Rondo *Allegretto* in the home tonic.

Next we come to the piano trio in E major K.542, written in June 1788.

W A Mozart : 1st movement *Allegro* from Piano Trio in E major K.542

1st Section: The **Exposition** opens with a pianistic **1st subject** (one loud bar followed by three soft, then another loud one before three more soft), whose first half gently descends in colourful chromatic semitones; this is followed by a brief tailpiece of two fifths, falling in sequence (x).

Ex. 18.1

The strings join in to repeat all of this, extending the tailpiece by several more bars to cadence again in the home tonic key. After introducing so much chromatic decoration in this opening, Mozart adds a second part to his 1st subject – a further 8 bars of soft static phrases which gently consolidate home tonic tonality over a low tonic pedal in the 'cello. A brief transitional passage driven by rising scales in the fortepiano ends with an expectant pause on V of V.

A **2nd subject** follows, with long, expansive phrases in the violin marked *dolce* ("sweetly"), and in due course it is taken up by the fortepiano.

Ex. 18.2

The serenity of this mood is shattered by a sudden harmonic shift in the fortepiano, moving abruptly up a semitone from home V of V (F♯) to its ♭VI (G♮). The 'cello retorts loudly with the expansive phrases of the 2nd subject in less docile mood, followed two bars later by the violin in the same vein; the fortepiano enters softly, clouding the scene with minor tonality, but the 'cello saves the day by working chromatically back to the expected F♯ (so that with hindsight we hear the wayward G major harmony as a chromatic decoration of the V of V). The cadence figure which follows harks back to the chromatic fall of the 1st subject, but now at greater length and picked out in short quavers rather than smoothly-moving crotchets.

2nd Section: After the falling chromatic scale of the cadence group Mozart avoids returning to the 1st subject at the beginning of the **Development**: instead he picks up with its little tailpiece of falling fifths (x). After two bars this acquires a robust little wriggling counter-subject and all three instruments become involved in exchanging these two motifs in a passage of exquisitely-crafted counterpoint; it begins softly and passes through the home key's relative minor (c♯) before gathering momentum. The strings join forces against colourful broken chord figuration in the fortepiano in a succession of powerful falling sequences which arrive on the home V chord; after a fractional pause the 1st Subject returns to begin the **Recapitulation**. As before it is first heard in the fortepiano only, but is then repeated in the minor mode by the strings. The falling fifths tailpiece again triggers colourful sequences which however soon return to tonic tonality, followed by the peaceable second part of the 1st subject. The **2nd subject** follows regularly in home tonic tonality, with the same interruption by ♭VI harmony (C major) which is again explained as a chromatic decoration, this time of the home V (B) before the final return to the tonic for the chromatic cadence figure and an affirmatively loud close in the home key.

The E major Trio is said to have been Chopin's favourite of all Mozart's trios. Again it has two Rondos as its following movements, contrasted in mood: the second is an *Andante grazioso* in A major, and the last an *Allegro* in the home key (whose rondo theme is a perfect example of a Classical "sentence"[6] – an 8-bar theme built from two 4-bar phrases, the first consisting of a repeated 2-bar basic idea).

Finally we come to the piano trio in C major, K.548, written only a month after K.542 in July 1788.

W A Mozart: 1st movement *Allegro* from Piano Trio in C major K.548

1st Section: The **Exposition** begins with a loud fanfare (a) on all three instruments, bounding up the notes of the tonic triad in the home key. This is immediately counterbalanced by a softer, conciliatory phrase with four repeated notes (b) on the fortepiano (a characteristic Mozart counter-reply), which is then taken up by the violin. All of this comprises the first theme (**1st subject**), packed into a tidy home-key tonal box.

Ex.19.1

Next the fortepiano dives into fast-moving scales in a Transitional passage, and the harmonies slip away from the home key to arrive in the home V.

Two contrasting musical ideas comprising the **2nd subject group** follow in quick succession. They too are packed in tidy tonal boxes (all in the dominant key): first, a graceful phrase in the fortepiano, 2(a):

second, some busy semiquavers in the violin, 2(b), taken up by the fortepiano and ending with a definitive cadence in V:

But then, unexpectedly, instead of a cadence group of stereotyped figures, the opening fanfare (a) reappears *softly* (a subtle Mozartian touch) twice (all in the dominant, not the home tonic) before the section ends positively.

This Exposition is then repeated (note the effectiveness of just having re-heard that fanfare – it connects back to the beginning; listen for the clear tonal contrast between V and I when the repeat turns back to I).

2nd Section:

The beginning of the **Development** connects again with the fanfare, but now it sounds out loudly and menacingly in the dominant minor mode (v minor) as the fortepiano is answered by the strings in unison at a distance of two octaves; there is a morosely introspective reply from the piano, with drooping chromatic semitones contrasting effectively with the ebullience of the fanfare motif. The fanfare persists, but then the elements of the morose reply fracture between all three instruments and a long passage of exquisite three-part counterpoint for the three instruments follows, coming to a halt on the chord of E major (V of home relative minor). Suddenly the violin seems to have had enough of this gloominess: it tentatively introduces the four repeated notes (b) which we recognise as part of the 1st subject. The tension builds as each instrument takes this up in turn; Mozart keeps us on tenterhooks, deliberately delaying the return to the tonic … finally he settles on the home dominant, and all three instruments pause expectantly …

The **Recapitulation** finally begins:

The 1st subject fanfare (a) reappears, delighted to be back in the home key, followed by the repeated notes (b) in the fortepiano in a positive mood again. As if to punish it for its cockiness, the strings come back with (b) in the minor mode, but this cloud is soon banished by the cheery Transition. The two parts of the 2nd subject return, now packed into tidy *home-key* boxes.

We expect the fanfare – masquerading as cadence group – to follow, but instead Mozart plays another trick: he launches off into the introspective chromatically-descending motif from the Development. This cadences soberly in the home key, but is then followed by the expected quiet fanfare before the movement ends with bright figuration.

Before looking at the two following movements of this trio, we should consider the three movements we have just heard. Comparing the formal framework of all three, it is clear that little has changed since John Bach, Schobert and Haydn in Chapter 4. We recognise the fundamental outline of the two-part model, with its first section setting up the "dissonance" of 2nd subject material in the dominant key, which becomes resolved in the tonic key in the second part. Mozart also preserves the repeating symmetry between the Exposition and the Recapitulation; the following table of bar lengths shows how closely the Recapitulation mirrors the length of the Exposition:

	Exp	Dev	Recap	Total
K.502	82	35	80	197
K.542	101	34	107	242
K.548	62	40	77	179

Furthermore, the thematic material remains clearly delineated: the 1st and 2nd subjects are carefully presented in tonal boxes which are distinctly separated by the surface figuration typical of transitional and cadential passages.

For all the process itself may be little changed, however, the character of the contents is very different. The thematic material in tonal boxes is transformed by Wolfgang's incomparable gift for musical invention. His trios teem with memorable themes, with infectious momentum in the opening *Allegro*, heart-stopping expressiveness in the slow movements, and sparkling vigour in the rondo finales. Mozart is an inventive genius indeed, but he is also a superb craftsman. We sense that his thematic material has been devised with great care. It is no accident that in all three trios motifs from the 1st subject (and it is usually the 1st, not the 2nd) provide the impetus for much that follows: for instance, the initial (a) and (b) motifs in the monothematic K.502, the characteristic chromatic descent (a) and falling fifths (b) in K.542, and the fanfare motif in K.548.

With this careful crafting of useful motifs comes the implicit expectation that the audience, along with anticipating the structure of the tonal framework, would also recognise thematic material as it reappears; making this easier for the listener was the purpose of continuing to repeat the first section. This is clear from Mozart's dramatisation of the double return to home key and theme at the beginning of the Recapitulations: in both K.502 and K.548, motifs from the 1st subject taunt the listener before the tonal return is achieved – audiences needed to cotton on to these references if the drama of these moments was to be fully appreciated.

It is the Development section which is most different from the Development in the *galant* trio, and which gains most from Mozart's inventiveness. Although still much shorter than the Exposition or Recapitulation, he finds a purpose for it by making it the intellectual heart of his first movements. Not only can it counter any imbalances in the preceding Exposition (such as providing a new theme to counter the monothematicism of K.502, or new chromaticism to balance the triadic assurance in K.548), it can also take on far-reaching tonal exploration, plunging into minor keys and tonal areas which would be beyond the reach of the Exposition (as in all three trios). Perhaps most significantly, however, it provides a space for the players to come together in the musical equivalent of rhetorical debate as they take part in the "persuasive presentation of argument". The recognising listener can hear the adventures of a motif, paralleling the narrative of the novel as well as the persuasion of rhetoric, as each instrument takes motifs in turn and weaves them together in Mozart's peerless counterpoint.

Contrapuntal writing was a skill Mozart had been learning all his life – first from Leopold, then from Padre Martini in Bologna, from the venerable theorist Fux (through Haydn) and finally from J S Bach (through van Swieten). It is typical of his genius that he draws on it now to write so innovatively and beautifully for the three instruments of the piano trio. Much earlier experience is also here – Mannheim's inspiring instrumental style, Haydn's string quartets, Mozart's own violin sonatas as well as his piano concertos – all distilled in writing for the trio medium which for the first time approaches a true chamber music style. Freed from pedantically following the keyboard bass line (since the fortepiano's growing sonority was beginning to make this less necessary), the 'cello now sings in its tenor register or provides a resounding bass below the keyboard. The fortepianist is still the leading player, and the brilliance of the keyboard writing is a reflection of the piano concertos and Mozart's own performances; but the violin is an independent participant and carries a substantial share of the musical argument; the strings together make an indispensable contribution to the kaleidoscopic variety and sonority of textures throughout.

★   ★   ★   ★   ★

In the same way that all instrumental types adopted the sonata form procedure, the sequence of movements in each type also stabilised. However, where the symphony and the string quartet had settled into a pattern of four movements, as we have seen in Haydn's trios the piano trio adopted instead the concerto's formula of three: *fast – slow – fast*. So after the strenuous activity of the first movement in the Trio K.548, Mozart follows with a slow movement in more lyrical and contemplative mood. In all three trios the slow movements are set in the key of the fourth degree of the home tonic scale, the subdominant, which has a soft, gentle relationship with the home key[7] (as opposed to its brighter, sharper relationship with the dominant) – we are expected to carry the sounds of these contrasting tonal areas from movement to movement.

The second movement of Mozart's trio in C major, K.548, is also in sonata form, which is relatively uncommon in slow movements; however, it nicely illustrates for us how flexibly this tonal template can accommodate very different music.

Mozart: 2nd movement *Andante cantabile* from Piano Trio in C major K.548

The Exposition teems with gentle themes, still contained in balanced tonal boxes, but moving seamlessly from one idea to the next with none of the cadential posturing of the first movement. The Development uses two motifs, one taken from the 1st subject

and the other from the 2nd subject

unravelling them and then combining them again in a persuasive new argument. The eventual return to the Recapitulation has none of the drama of the *Allegro*: it does not play anxiously on the home dominant but instead pauses on a single note (which is *not* the home dominant), then with unruffled calm uses it as a pivot and turns it into – *the first note of the 1st subject* (i.e. it becomes the third of the home key). This is, at this date, an unusual progression, although Schubert later adopted it and used it to great effect. The Recapitulation resumes the contemplative mood of the opening, completing the symmetry of the movement with a regular return of all the music of the Exposition.

Basil Smallman describes this *Andante cantabile* as "one of the most profound of all Mozart's trio movements". Here we find the real Mozart, sensuously fingering the melodic potential of the major scale; as he lingers over the semitones a sentient phrase by an Arab musician, Simon Shaheen, springs to mind – that melody is "*a group of notes in love with each other*". This is the essence of the expressive style Wolfgang had first encountered in John Bach's music – and it is the measure of Bach's legacy to western music that he was the source of this inspiration to the genius of Mozart.

This movement is another good example of Mozart's transformation of John Bach's keyboard-dominated sonata style into an interactive ensemble of independent players: the strings are an integral part of this music. The Exposition is given a sense of spaciousness by the repetition of themes by both violin and 'cello; in the Development both strings add important commentaries to the fortepiano part, and they contribute subtlety and variety to the texture throughout.

The final Rondo *Allegro* provides an exhilarating contrast with the slow movement. Mozart's opening rondo theme is so full of apparently artless *joi de vivre* that we feel we could never have enough of it. But though it may *sound* artless, this movement is nothing of the sort. Mozart develops it as a modified Type 4 sonata rondo, with most of the thematic material – transitional passages, 2nd subject, contrasting central episode in the tonic minor mode – all so neatly derived from the bubbling rondo theme itself that we feel its presence throughout. Yet none of it, whether it is the complete theme or its many derivatives, ever fails to delight on each reappearance.

Listen carefully to the rondo theme as it is first announced by the fortepiano. You will find it is shaped like our old friend, a basic binary dance tune. It is eight bars long, and it pauses momentarily on the fifth halfway ... Mozart was well aware of the listening habits of his contemporaries, and knew they would easily assimilate and enjoy its familiar pattern. We might also recognise Mozart himself – the man who was said to have "passionately loved dancing" – in its infectious gaiety. Charles Rosen describes the Classical style as

> "… in its origins, basically a comic one … the pacing of classical rhythm is the pacing of comic opera, its phrasing is the phrasing of dance music, and its large structures are *these phrases dramatised.*"[8] [My italics.]

The description fits Mozart and this music like a glove.

Ex.19 W A Mozart: 3rd movement *Allegro* from Piano Trio in C major K.548

Looking back, we might now see John Bach's two accompanied sonatas as markers in the life of the piano trio *genre* – fledgling growth in op 2 of the 1760s, growing-up with op 15 of the late 1770s. But with Mozart's piano trios in the 1780s we have arrived at works with which, as Basil Smallman wrote, "the piano trio came finally of age as a fully-developed *genre*, significant not solely for its own time but also for its promise of later development."[9]

CHAPTER ENDNOTES

1   Quoted by Lindmayr-Brandl, Andrea in 'Dance', *The Cambridge Mozart Encyclopedia,* ed C Eisen and S P Keefe, Cambridge: University Press, 2006, p.134.

2   The tune appears to have been published for the first time as an instrumental *Divertissement Champêtre* in Paris in 1761; see http://gallica.bnf.fr/ark:/12148/btv1b90790216/f2.image

3   First published in *Rhymes for the Nursery.* London: Darton & Harvey, 1806.

4   Newman, *Sonata in the Classic Era,* p.127.

5   Quoted in Hill, Mary. *Hampstead in Light and Shade.* London: Baines and Scarsbrook, 1945, p.37.

6   As defined by Caplin, *op.cit,* pp.35ff.

7   See Chapter 3, p.47.

8   Rosen, *Classical Style,* p.96.

9   Smallman, Basil. *The Piano Trio.* Oxford: Clarendon Press, 1988, p.24.

Part II

THE 19TH CENTURY

CHAPTER 9

INTO A NEW CENTURY: HUMMEL

"IN A WEALTHY mercantile nation," observed the Anglo-Irish father and daughter Edgeworths[1] drily in 1801, "there is nothing which can be bought for money, that will long continue to be an envied distinction." Of all the envied cultural commodities now available for purchase across Europe, perhaps none continued to be more widely enjoyed than music. As a result of the shifting social pattern of musical patronage, by the closing decades of the eighteenth century music could be heard not only in princely palaces and aristocratic salons, but also in public halls and concert rooms in all major cities, at meetings of musical societies as well as in innumerable private drawing rooms.

These performances might be supported by audiences with very different experiences of music, but whether they were *Connoisseurs* or *Amateurs*, they would gather together for what was still essentially a social occasion to a background of musical accompaniment. Music was rarely heard in dutiful silence and musicians would try to claim attention with a variety show of vocal and instrumental items to please all tastes. Some indication of the enormous appetite for music as a form of entertainment can be glimpsed in performance records of no fewer than 16,558 symphonies in Europe and the New World before 1800.[2]

To hear a symphony of course required a live performance in a venue large enough to accommodate both an audience and a number of players. For the great majority this could hardly have been a daily experience, and for much of their personal enjoyment of music most people were thrown back on their own resources. Friedrich Blume describes the effects of domestic music-making in Germany and Austria:

"The most vigorous and the most valuable centre for the cultivation of music ... was now the house of the middle-class citizen, where the new piano and chamber music as well as the song in all its forms found their place … Here … the true foundation was laid upon which rested the entire practice of music in the Classic-Romantic period: 'Hausmusik', music-making in the home of the amateur. Its importance for the evolving history of music cannot be over-estimated."[3]

Across Europe, much of this music played and heard continued to lie in familiar 8-beat structural frameworks. Dancing continued to be the mainstay of social entertainment. Where else but on the dance floor, engaged in dancing, would Evelina have captured the attention of the incomparable Lord Orville (Fanny Burney, *Evelina*, 1778) or Elizabeth Bennett the notice of the supercilious Mr Darcy (Jane Austen, *Pride and Prejudice*, 1813)? The four-square patterns and symmetry of dance music remained a commonplace, and a fundamental part of musical experience across Europe. But songs were the most popular form of domestic music-making, and they were frequently strophic, so that here too the old regular patterns were heard over and over again. Similarly strophic, folksongs were also widely enjoyed and a staple of after-dinner drawing-room entertainment. The enterprising publisher George Thomson of Edinburgh published several volumes of Scottish, Welsh and Irish folksongs in "classical" arrangements for voice and piano trio by "the greatest living European Composers". These volumes included nearly 400 arrangements by Haydn and nearly 170 by Beethoven. Variations on popular songs from operas or fashionable airs bridged the gap between vocal and instrumental music. Often written for piano, or for a piano trio, they were performed not only by amateurs but also by professional musicians in both private salons and public concerts.

As well as these accessible arrangements of vocal music, amateur performers continued to enjoy the considerable number of piano trios which, as we have seen, were produced for this flourishing market by enterprising publishers. Composers wrote chamber music for amateurs in the same style as their symphonies, and the piano trio was a popular *genre*. Although on a smaller scale, chamber music gave amateurs first-hand contact with the symphonic sonata idea and it laid a foundation for appreciation. In amateur performances, women continued to take the keyboard part, since stringed instruments continued to be regarded as unsuitable for women until much later in the nineteenth century.

Gradually, however, the perception of the piano trio as merely music for amateurs began to fade, and increasingly it became a more serious *genre* for performance by professional players. There were a number of reasons for this rise in the status of the piano trio. Undoubtedly the quality – as well as the increasing difficulty – of works by composers such as Mozart and Haydn showed what the trio could achieve. But the continuing advance in manufacturing techniques of all three instruments was also an important contributory factor.

In the closing decades of the eighteenth century the great French *archetier* François Tourte (1747-1835), popularly known as the "Stradivari of the Bow", significantly developed violin and 'cello bows so that they made a rounder, fuller sound. He did this by standardising the previously haphazard dimensions of bows so that they became consistently a little longer, a little heavier at each end, and uniformly made of *pernambuco* wood from Brazil. He also increased the number of horsehairs so that the bow became wider (between 150 and 200 hairs for a violin bow, and a few more for a 'cello), and added a screw so that the tension of the hairs could be adjusted. The additional length and width were especially suited to playing in the popular *cantabile* style, and the firmer tension facilitated more varied ways of using the bow (such as the sudden accent – *sforzando*). A number of structural alterations were consequently made to the violin and 'cello to accommodate the additional pressure now exerted by the Tourte bow: for instance, the height of the bridge was increased, and longer strings, wound with finest wire, were used for the lowest strings. At the same time the neck was lengthened and tilted back a little, and the fingerboard was extended, so that it was easier for the player to finger the strings with his left hand. All this combined to increase the tone and power of the string instruments, so that their sound carried better in the larger spaces of the new concert halls where professional musicians performed.

It might be thought that superior string tone might adversely affect the balance between strings and keyboard, requiring further doubling of the fortepiano/pianoforte in order that the keyboard part could be clearly heard. In fact, simultaneous developments in piano manufacturing enabled new pianofortes to match this fuller string sound, and indeed from this time the increasing strength of piano tone decidedly reversed the old *status quo*. From now onwards it became a continuing concern that piano volume and writing should not overwhelm the strings, which must always be allowed to sound through the accompanying piano texture.

The two principal centres of piano manufacture were London and Vienna, and rivalry between English and Viennese piano makers continued. In London Broadwood led the field, producing some 400 instruments every year, but around 1800 other English manufacturers were also experimenting. Iron bracing to the frame was introduced to support the increased tension of thicker, tauter strings; the hammers were made sturdier and covered with harder felt, producing a richer, stronger tone and more volume; and the compass of the instruments was extended. The Viennese manufacturers Walter,

Streicher and Graf were content to go on using their tough old inter-locking wooden frames; the hammers which struck their strings were covered in hard leather, and their pianos were always much admired for their light, clear tone and sensitivity to touch. Perhaps the most significant outcome of all the technical improvements was the increased reliability and consistency of the new pianofortes, which gave them a considerably greater appeal to professional performers.

The army of domestic pianists must have looked on with aston-ishment and envy when a generation of travelling professional *virtu-osi* now arrived on the European scene. The *virtuosi* were mainly pianists and violinists (as yet the 'cello was not regarded as a solo instrument). Brilliant performer-composers journeyed round the principal cities of Europe, giving concerts of their own compositions designed to show off their considerable technical accomplishments. Their programmes often included chamber music such as a piano trio, when they would be joined by the best local players available in the places they visited. These trio performances greatly contributed to the rise in estimation of the *genre* – even as they also marked the beginning of the end of the piano trio as a work for amateur perfor-mance.

One of the most popular *virtuoso* pianists of the day was Johann Nepomuk Hummel (1778-1837). He had been a child prodigy, able to read music at the age of four, play the violin at five and the piano at six. Two years later his family moved to Vienna and he became a pupil of Mozart – actually living in the Mozart household. He made such outstanding progress that between the ages of 10 and 14 he was taken by his father on an extended concert tour of northern Europe. Bypassing Paris on account of the French Revolution, they arrived in England in 1790, a few months ahead of Haydn on his first visit. Hummel enjoyed two successful years performing in London before returning to Vienna.

At the height of his career, Hummel was widely held to be the finest pianist of his generation. His performances were typical of the travelling *virtuosi*: his programmes would include a solo concerto, some improvisation or variations, and chamber music with piano. As a boy Hummel must have encountered the contemporary piano trio repertoire wherever he went, but especially in 1780s Vienna, where the *genre* was so popular and his two years of study coincided with Mozart's piano trio composition. Hummel's own first essay was published while he was in London in 1792, but it is an immature work, still entitled "Sonata" and now seldom performed. His next work, the Trio in E♭, although it was not issued until 1804, may have been written a few years before publication. Listening to it we feel very close to Mozart; indeed its opening theme surely bears more than a passing likeness to Mozart's clarinet quintet K.581.* We also hear the same subtle interplay between the three instruments, the same adroit counterpoint and elegant chromatic decoration. To this impeccable inheritance Hummel adds distinctive gifts of his own: a natural flair for attractive melody, and fluent writing for the piano which shows off his famous clear and rapid fingerwork (he was known to favour the Viennese piano).

J N Hummel: 1st movement *Allegro agitato* from Piano Trio in E♭ major op 12

Exposition: The piano begins with two introductory bars, as though expecting a singer about to begin – the violin duly obliges with the **1st subject**, which consists of four falling third intervals (**a**), each emotionally decorated with a rising semitone.

The spacious opening sets out the generous proportions of the movement which follows: as the 1st subject is repeated Mozart can be heard in the piano's graceful chromatic decoration of (a). All the instruments become involved in a transitional passage of fleet staccato scales and we sense the harmony shifting to land on the V of the home V. Here the opening phrase (a) reappears as the **2nd subject** in the violin, immediately answered by a chirruping falling phrase in the 'cello to differentiate it from the 1st subject. A second section features rippling triplet quavers in the piano – designed to show off Hummel's deft finger work and the clarity of the Viennese instrument. The cadential passages take up the scales of the earlier transition and end in a robust final cadence in the home V.

Development: The 'cello and violin in turn linger over the expressive semitones of (a), after a time moving into the key of c minor (relative minor of the home I). More scale passages and beautifully-executed counterpoint carry through a number of elegant sequences to arrive finally on four bars of expectant V: the violin slinks chromatically and conspiratorially up to the first note of (a) for the

---

* Compare Mozart's 2nd subject in the first movement of K.581.

> **Recapitulation:** This follows regularly. Listen for the moment when the 'cello is heard announcing the return of the 2nd subject, as noted by a contemporary reviewer "with the same effect as a beautiful tenor voice soaring out in a vocal piece", while the violin takes over the chirruping response. Hummel adds a further 20 bars at the end of the Exposition material – a Coda – which is not thematically significant, just a final virtuosic flourish of chromatic harmony, emphatic V – I chords and a cadenza-like flurry of semi-quavers in the last 2 bars.

The extra 20 bars tacked onto the end of the Recapitulation were doubtless added as an excuse for Hummel to show off his admirable technique by closing the movement with flamboyant passage-work. Such a passage was known as a Coda (from the Italian *coda*, a "tail" or "ending") and became increasingly common in sonata movements after this time.

In spite of its later date of composition, this is a work written in the vein of Mozart's trios of the 1780s, not Haydn's of the 1790s. It flows lucidly, with themes set out in the balanced 8-bar symmetry with which audiences were so familiar, and precisely-defined sections with firm cadences and neatly-turned linking passages. In the Development Hummel engages all the instruments in thematic material woven into academic counterpoint, which he writes as gracefully as Mozart.

It is not difficult to understand why Hummel had such popular appeal. But as Joel Sachs points out, his "very gift for melodic writing could be treacherous".[4] Each theme is complete in itself, and not really suited to development. By using the same theme for his 2nd subject moreover, he loses the obvious opportunity to introduce new and contrasting material. Perhaps he saw the work as a whole as having contrast enough in its reposeful *Andante* second movement and insouciant *Presto* finale. Yet here again he was conservative: his contemporary Beethoven by this time had introduced a fourth movement into the piano trio after the model of the symphony and string quartet. Hummel doggedly continued providing only three movements in his trios to the end of his life.

Hummel's early popularity as a composer did not last: though his style became ever more brilliant, it also became more repetitive and long-winded. His initial appeal had lain in the ease with which his music could be comprehended, the pretty themes fitting comfortably into his audience's expectations of four-square tunes. Audiences had also been attracted by Hummel's brilliant performances – Sachs quotes one occasion when "an audience stood on their seats to better see his double trills". But here was the beginning of a slippery slope, where music could become more a public spectacle than a musical performance. Easy melodiousness and technical fireworks might appeal to those who continued to regard music merely as entertainment, but there were growing signs that other people were beginning to look at it in a rather more intense and serious way, and that Hummel was not one of them.

We should remember that the early decades of Hummel's life were played out against a backdrop of tremendous social changes: the aftermath of the French Revolution, a growing resentment of the autocratic domination of the landowning classes, the inexorable advance of industrialisation and a dawning realisation of its human cost. We may find it illuminating to look at a couple of contemporary landscape paintings alongside this trio by Hummel.

These are two paintings by the German-born Philippe-Jacques de Loutherbourg (1740-1812). *"Coalbrookdale by Night"* (1801) depicts the flaming colours of an iron foundry lighting up a night sky in Shropshire, prompting the viewer not only to admire its extraordinary beauty but also to recognise its power, and the suggestion of ferocious heat and danger endured by workers at the foundry.

Philippe-Jacques de Loutherbourg: *Coalbrookdale by Night,* 1801.
London, Science Museum

The other painting, of *"An Avalanche in the Alps"* (1803), is not merely a stirring evocation of wild dark mountains in stark contrast with the whiteness of an advancing avalanche, but it also invites an emotional reaction from the viewer who sees the broken bridge and the desperate plight of the puny human figures in the foreground.

Philippe-Jacques de Loutherbourg: *An Avalanche in the Alps*, 1803.
London, Tate Gallery

In both paintings the artist has chosen to paint wild scenes and interpret them in ways which prompt an emotional response from the onlooker.

Comparing these paintings with the Classical poise of Hummel's trio, we can hear that his music, though roughly contemporary with de Loutherbourg's paintings, is not ruffled by any such dramatic imaginings; nor does it seem to be aware of a new movement amongst painters, poets and philosophers at the turn of the eighteenth century. We might compare Hummel's style more effectively with Zoffany's painting of Cowper and the Gores (see p.81), done some twenty-five years earlier. We admire the technical musical detail – the formal symmetry and neat counterpoint, the adornment of expressive semitones and the pianistic figuration in the right hand of the piano part, just as we are invited to admire Zoffany's artistic technique – a painterly exercise in conventional pose and classical allusion, contrasting textures of polished wood and the sheen of soft silk. Hummel is still locked in an earlier ideal: like Zoffany, he sets out to please, not to rack his listeners with de Loutherbourg's vivid imagination or violent emotion.

"Vivid imagination" and "violent emotion" – these we now clearly recognise as hallmarks of the nineteenth-century "Romantic" movement in literature and the arts. That title was actually used by contemporaries, and was derived from the word "Romance" in the sense it had been used from the beginning of the seventeenth century. This was not in its modern sense of a love-story but more specifically denoting a *fictitious* tale or poem, which had its origins in its author's imagination (such as Sir Walter Scott's verse romances and novels of archaic chivalry). At the end of the eighteenth century, such a tale was at the opposite end of the spectrum from the scientific Enquiry or the intellectual Treatise of the Enlightenment, and indeed the Romantic movement was to a great extent just this – a reaction to the dominant rationalism of the eighteenth century and a re-statement of the importance of the human capacity for fantasy and emotion. Artists were reconsidering their role, seeing that a faithful record of their time should present not only the outward appearance of people and events, but also some sense of their inner feelings.

Paradoxically, one of the most influential sources for this changing attitude had sprung right from the heart of the Enlightenment itself. In 1757, five years before John Bach arrived in London, a youthful Edmund Burke (1729-1797) had published an essay entitled *"A Philosophical Enquiry into the Origin of Our Ideas of the Sublime and Beautiful"*. It drew on a seemingly most rational text: a classical Greek treatise on Oratory – we are never far from rhetoric in the eighteenth century. This text had defined the arousal of powerful emotions as the ultimate goal of a skilful writer or orator; the listener should be led to a state of non-rational, emotional exaltation, "not merely to persuasion but to ecstasy"; in other words, to a "sublime" reaction.

Burke's essay took the same starting-point, but went on to distinguish between the sublime and the beautiful. Beauty could be recognised and appreciated in pleasing and elegant lines (the artist William Hogarth (1697-1764) had identified his "serpentine line" of Beauty only four years earlier),[5] but there were quite other prompts for "sublime" emotions. These were dangerous and destructive, notably seen in the passion of fear, and prompted by sensations of vastness, peril, magnificence or "whatever is fitted in any sort to excite the ideas of pain and danger", because such things are "productive of the strongest emotion which the mind is capable of feeling."[6]

Burke's *Philosophical Enquiry* was widely read, and its emphasis on emotion was sympathetically received. It was a short step from the sublime in rhetoric to the sublime in the natural world, and by the end of the eighteenth century a number of artists across Europe were producing paintings like de Loutherbourg's, depicting sublimity in the grandeur and violence of nature.

Translated into German in 1773, Burke's arguments also found sympathetic resonance in contemporary philosophical and aesthetic thinking. He had argued that a sense of terror could overwhelm the power of reasoning, transporting an individual into a "higher state".

This resonated with the German philosophy of Idealism (a revival of another Greek original), which posited that a higher form of reality existed in an invisible but all-powerful world of the spirit, the transcendental source of Truth, the Infinite, the Absolute. The wildness and terror of nature, the ability of the creative artist to inspire profound emotion – all these things could offer glimpses of this other world. "Within the idealist aesthetic," writes Mark Evan Bonds, "the power of any given artwork lies in its ability to reflect a higher ideal and in the beholder's ability to perceive that ideal".[7] Thus artistic appreciation was becoming a two-way process between artist and observer, reader and listener.

The dramatist and poet Schiller (whose personal philosophy was much admired by Beethoven), writing in 1795, believed that "the ability to perceive the sublime" was "one of the most glorious capacities of the human spirit". Three years later, in his *Lines written a Few Miles above Tintern Abbey*, the English poet William Wordsworth (1770-1850) described the visual beauty of the scenery on the banks of the River Wye and then in glowing language drew "sublime" inspiration from it:

> "… And I have felt
> A presence that disturbs me with the joy
> Of elevated thoughts; a sense sublime
> Of something far more deeply interfused,
> Whose dwelling is the light of setting suns,
> And the round ocean, and the living air,
> And the blue sky, and in the mind of man,
> A motion and a spirit, that impels
> All thinking things, all objects of all thought,
> And rolls through all things."

Painting and poetry had centre-stage roles in this new aesthetic. For them it presented no difficulty, since art and literature had for centuries been concerned with *mimesis*, the representation of the physical world of people, places and objects. We might think that music, with its operatic tradition of depicting conquering heroes and traumatised heroines, would become a natural bedfellow in such an aesthetic, and that music might therefore instantly play a vigorous part in all this. In due course, as we all know, music did indeed play a leading role in the Romantic movement. But not yet.

For all the widespread enthusiasm for music, in the closing years of the eighteenth century there was still a problem with the perception of it as *an expressive art*. It was a historical problem. For centuries music had been largely functional: it had provided rhythm (for working songs, marches, or social dances) or mood-setting

accompaniment (solemn for church services, pleasing for social
occasions). Music had only been required to be *expressive* when
associated with words. Then, with the meaning provided by a text or
libretto, it had taken its place alongside the other arts and set itself,
like them, to *mimesis*, the imitation of the physical world. Thus whenever the libretto referred to upward or downward movement, the
accompanying music would obligingly rise or fall in pitch; similarly
rapid notes would accompany indications of speed; a seamless flow
of even notes a murmuring stream or twittering trills the sounds of
birdsong.

The problem was that many eighteenth-century commentators
could not see that music without the rationale of words could ever
be *serious*: "concertos, symphonies, sonatas and solos" made "a not
disagreeable sound, even a pleasant and entertaining chatter," wrote
the encyclopaedist J G Sulzer in the 1770's, "but nothing that would
engage the heart."[8]

Rousseau had gone even further in his definition of *Sonata* in his
Dictionnaire de Musique:

"Nowadays ... *sonatas* are extremely fashionable, along with
Symphonie [by which he means instrumental compositions
in general] of all kinds ... Purely harmonic music [i.e. without
a text] is short on substance ... the word is the means through
which music most frequently determines the object whose image
it offers, and it is by means of sounds in conjunction with the
human voice that this image awakens at the bottom of our hearts
the sentiment it is its purpose to produce. Who does not sense how
far pure *Symphonie*, in which nothing is sought but instrumental
brilliance, is from such an effect? Can all the violinistic fireworks
of M. Mondonville evoke in me the tenderness the voice of a great
singer produces in two notes? *Symphonie* can enliven song and add
to its expressiveness, but it cannot supplant it ... I dare predict
that so unnatural a taste will not last."[9]

So it is in the context of such still widely-held views that Kant
could write in 1790 that instrumental music was "*mehr Genuß als
Kultur*" ("more pleasure than culture"), and was, like wallpaper,
"... an abstract art that gave pleasure through its form but lacked
content and was therefore inferior to vocal music."[10]

The High Classic style was deep in Hummel's bones and he would
remain throughout his life committed to the sonata idea as a vehicle
for Classical symmetry, elegant melody and the display of "learned"
counterpoint. This was indeed not *mimesis*, but neither did it display
sublime emotion; the depth of Hummel's emotion can be measured
in his use of chromatic semitones, and these – whether melodically

lingering, or harmonically fleeting – amounted to little more than
an infinite number of prettily-delayed, decorative resolutions. It was,
as Kant said, primarily "an abstract art that gave pleasure through
its form". (Given what we have seen of the music of Mozart and
Haydn, we would take issue with the rest of Kant's statement about
instrumental music lacking content.)

As we shall see, there would shortly be a profound change in
such attitudes to instrumental music, allowing musicians to play a
full part in the Romantic movement. So it was not surprising that
Hummel's popularity gradually declined, as his contemporary and
rival Beethoven took up the challenge posed by nineteenth-century
writers and artists and injected a powerful emotional content into
his instrumental music. But although the High Classical style had
run its course, in time we shall see that Hummel's lingering Classicism was to be an important link between Mozart and later nineteenth-century composers.

CHAPTER ENDNOTES

1   Richard Lovell Edgeworth (1744-1817) and his novelist daughter Maria (1768-1849) wrote together on contemporary issues ranging from economics to education.

2   LaRue, Jan. *A Catalogue of 18th Century Symphonies*, vol. 1: Thematic Identifier. Bloomington: Indiana University Press, 1988; quoted in Bonds, Mark Evan, *Music as Thought: Listening to the Symphony in the age of Beethoven*. Princeton and Oxford: Princeton University Press, 2006, fn.1, p.1.

3   Blume, Friedrich. *Classic and Romantic Music: A Comprehensive Survey*. Transl. M D Herter Norton, New York and London: W. W. Norton & Company, 1970, p.85.

4   Sachs, Joel, rev. Kroll, Mark. 'Hummel, Johann Nepomuk', *Grove Music Online*, 2013.

5   Hogarth, William. *The Analysis of Beauty*. London, 1753.

6   Burke, Edmund. *A Philosophical Enquiry into the Origin of Our Ideas of the Sublime and Beautiful*. London, 1757.

7   Bonds, *Music as Thought*, p.14.

8   Bonds, *ibid*, p.8.

9   Rousseau, Jean-Jacques. 'Sonata', *Dictionnaire de Musique*, Paris, 1768; taken from the extract in Weiss & Taruskin, *op.cit*, transl. by R Taruskin, pp.287-8.

10   Kant, Immanuel. *Kritik der Urteilskraft*, 1790; quoted by Bonds, *op.cit.*, p.7.

CHAPTER 10

BEETHOVEN AND
THE PIANO TRIO

1790, THE YEAR of Kant's dismissive comments on instrumental music, also marked the beginning of the decade in which Ludwig van Beethoven (1770-1827) was establishing his career as a musician. The son of a family of obscure musicians in the service of the Elector of Cologne in the provincial town of Bonn, he had early music lessons on the piano and violin from his father, but his considerable musical gifts were not recognised until C G Neefe was appointed to the Electoral court in 1779. Neefe gave him J S Bach's *Das Wohltemperirte Clavier* to study, and created many of the young boy's earliest musical opportunities. As a result, Ludwig acquired several admiring patrons, one of whom was Count Waldstein: this aristocrat was connected to many of the noble houses of the Austro-Hungarian empire, and he encouraged Beethoven to go to Vienna to study with Haydn.

Beethoven arrived in Vienna in 1792, shortly before his 22nd birthday. He acquired a Walter pianoforte, and thanks to his introductions from the Elector at Bonn, from Waldstein and from Haydn himself, was immediately launched as a pianist at the soirées of aristocratic families and prominent citizens. He was a brilliant performer and became an instant success. He played works by Mozart and Haydn, but also his own music – many of the early piano sonatas and variations date from this time. He also wrote chamber music for the salons, and indeed the first works which he deemed satisfactory enough to be given an opus number were a set of piano trios.

Some of the music of these trios may have been composed earlier in Bonn and revised on arrival in Vienna. This was unlikely, however, to have been under the influence of Haydn, with whom Beethoven appears to have studied counterpoint, but not free composition. The young pianist had arrived in Vienna with a *Stammbuch* in which Count Waldstein had written his conviction that Beethoven would "receive the spirit of Mozart from the hands of Haydn", and the three trios of op.1 already begin to fulfil this famously prophetic statement. Beethoven's ambitions for the *genre* are clear as he ranks his op.1 trios alongside the symphony and string quartet and writes four, not three, movements for each one. But now all have a fashionable *Scherzo* in place of the conventional minuet.★ This title translates as "joke" or "play", and Beethoven transforms the staid old dance in witty rhythms which offset the mood of other movements.

The first two trios are Classical in style, containing much of Haydn's teasing good humour as well as the graceful fluency of Mozart's writing for the three instruments, but Beethoven's distinctive musical voice can also be heard. Haydn is thought to have heard all three trios performed at a soirée given by Prince Lichnowsky (to whom they were dedicated) at the end of 1793, shortly before he left for his second London visit. Haydn was impressed, but advised Beethoven not to publish the third. Beethoven reacted angrily – it was his favourite of the three – but Haydn was well-placed to know the amateur Viennese market of that time, and may simply have feared for its reception: he sensed that this dramatic minor mode work was new and different.

The key of c minor was to inspire several of Beethoven's best-known works – such as the *Pathétique* piano sonata, the third piano concerto, the fifth symphony. This must be one of his first essays in this significant key:

L van Beethoven: 1st movement *Allegro con brio* from Piano Trio in C minor op.1 no 3

Exposition: The 1st subject has two parts: (a) a restless, searching motif, which turns out to be the introduction to (b), a tonally more secure 8-bar theme with an insistent repetitive rhythm. The whole of this opening section is marked *piano*.

★ The third movement of no 3 is still entitled *Menuetto*, but its character is more that of scherzo than minuet.

The Transition uses (a) and (b) again and lands purposefully on the V of the relative major key. Two gently lyrical 8-bar themes (in E♭ major) comprise the two parts of the **2nd subject** which follow in quick succession.

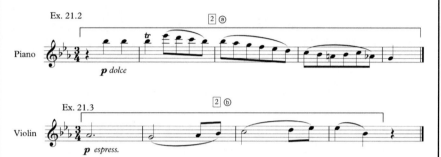

After dramatic staccato chords in all three instruments, the motif 1(a) reappears, but with a new conclusion, and is followed by 1(b) now recast as Cadential material.

Development: This section begins with 1(a) prompting a series of dramatic harmonic sequences, modulating widely and finally landing in C major (not as the home tonic major mode, but the V of home IV key, f minor). 1(b) reappears softly in the piano, until interrupted by the 'cello with the same motif, now in the key of A♭ (i.e. beautifully turning the minor third of f into a new tonic). This bold new key is shortly explained as the ♭VI of the home tonic; it duly falls down a semitone to accentuate the home V of G (this is now a familiar Classical progression), where 16 anticipatory bars usher in the

Recapitulation: The opening motif 1(a) is now heard triumphantly fortissimo (not *piano* as in the Exposition). It dominates the texture, passing through C *major* and D♭ before the Transition leads into the 2nd subject, where we hear more beautiful key shifts, before the dramatic staccato chords reinforce the home tonic minor key. At the end of the Recapitulation there is a brief pause, ushering in a

Coda: The original Cadential passage of the Exposition is expanded to 30 additional bars, drawing on earlier thematic material. Significantly these are almost entirely thematic – not simply an exhibition of technical difficulties.

The final Coda is an interesting tailpiece. It is not only quite different from Hummel's *bravura* display of pianistic fireworks, but functions as a final thematic commentary on what has gone before. Even

without it, we would have a distinct sense that the movement well fits
Hepokoski and Darcy's description of a minor mode ending "overcome" by the "turbulent or expressive field" of the minor mode (see
p.99-100). The added Coda enhances our sense that Beethoven's
trio has a dramatic, driving intensity which was missing in Haydn's
e minor Trio Hob.XV:12. This is not a criticism of Haydn, but rather
a reflection on the difference between his sardonic dramatisation of
the High Classical style, and the gritty reality inherent in Beethov-
en's music.

The "difference" of this trio was significant. Here were distant but
unmistakeable rumblings from de Loutherbourg's avalanche (see
p.141). It indicated that Beethoven was beginning to pick up on the
new movement in contemporary arts which we saw in de Loutherbourg and Wordsworth. It may also have reflected the beginnings of a
critical shift in contemporary attitudes to instrumental music. Ques-
tioning Rousseau's dismissal of the sonata idea, the composer J A P
Schulz had already suggested in the early 1770s that the symphony
was "especially suited to the expression of the grand, the solemn, and
the sublime",[1] and by the end of the century Kant's views of 1790
were being widely challenged. In 1800 the poet Herder (1744-1803)
did a complete *volte-face*: he declared that, far from being inferior,
instrumental music was actually *the highest form of all the arts* because
it provided a means of glimpsing that unknown realm, the Infinite,
or Absolute. Bonds writes:

> "The notion of the artwork – and the work of music, in particu-
> lar – as an earthly manifestation of the Absolute won widespread
> acceptance in the first decade of the nineteenth century. The
> vocabulary of idealism pervades much of the criticism written
> during this time: Music is widely described as 'supernatural',
> 'mystic', 'holy', 'divine', 'heavenly'. The mechanical associations
> with the passions were no longer the central concern they had
> been only a short time before; instead, the emphasis had shifted
> toward the premise that music is the reflection of a higher, more
> spiritual realm."[2]

With this crucial change of attitude to instrumental music, attention focused on the symphony as the most important type of instrumental music – or to be precise, on the *German* symphony, since by
the end of the eighteenth century the symphony was most extensively produced in German-speaking countries. (In fact, an anony-
mous writer in 1806 commented that "the world has the Germans to
thank, above all Haydn and Mozart," for "the grand symphony for
full orchestra" which "represents the highest and most radiant peak
of the latest instrumental music".[3])

This then was the background to Beethoven's music as the new century dawned and he entered his thirtieth year: ideally placed, one might have thought – relatively carefree, ready to respond to an eager and admiring public. But only a year later, in a letter to his friend Wegeler, Beethoven admitted to what must be the worst possible fear for a musician – that he was growing inexorably more and more deaf.

In the eight years before the composition of his next two piano trios, external events in Beethoven's life conspired to shape him both as man and musician. Not only did he have to suffer the impending catastrophe of deafness, but also bear Napoleon's invasions of Vienna, which caused him considerable physical and mental distress. He was in any case a rough square peg in the smooth round hole of the aristocratic society in which he moved – he was comparatively provincial, even boorish. Although he had a number of friends, he was not good at handling close personal relationships; he was often unwell, and with loneliness exacerbated by deafness, he became misunderstood, cantankerous, domineering – even violent. His unhappiness reached a climax in the drafting of the so-called *Heiligenstadt Testament,* a letter written to his brothers which indicated that he was contemplating suicide. This letter was drafted, but never sent, thanks to his own consciousness of his extraordinary musical gifts. For Beethoven was one of the most brilliant and original of musicians, "probably the most admired composer in the history of western music". In his own words, he came through the crisis:

"... it was only my art that held me back. Ah, it seemed to me impossible to leave the world until I had brought forth all that I felt was within me ..."[4]

The works which Beethoven wrote at this time are often referred to as dating from his "heroic" period. The real-life tragedies of deafness and what he saw to be Napoleon's betrayal of trust (in declaring himself Emperor) seemed to sharpen a consciousness of himself as a heroic individual battling against adversity. This is reflected in the intense style of many of the works of the decade from 1800, which include not only two great symphonies – the *Eroica* (1803)* and the Fifth (1807) – but also the *Razumovsky* string quartets as well as some large-scale choral and dramatic works, chamber music and piano sonatas. The easy-going entertainment of Haydn's "universal" Classical style is left behind and replaced by music which is altogether more deeply felt. The two piano trios of Beethoven's

---

* Originally entitled *"Sinfonia Buonaparte"*, but Beethoven destroyed the title page and its dedication when Napoleon was crowned Emperor in Rome in 1804.

op.70 were written during these turbulent years – so let us see how he approached the sonata form idea in the first trio (nicknamed the *"Ghost"*). We should also note that by this date Beethoven had exchanged his Walter piano for an instrument made by the French manufacturer Erard.

Beethoven: 1st movement *Allegro vivace e con brio* from Piano Trio in D major op.70 no 1, *Ghost*

Exposition: 1st Subject: The first 10 bars release three distinct musical ideas, one after the other. We must identify:
– a helter-skelter rush of rising scale-fragments (note especially the opening 4-note motif (**a**));
– after the initial rush, a pause for breath on a very unexpected note (**x**) – this is the *minor* third of the home key, so unexpected that we should note it carefully (in Patrick McCreless's admirable phrase, it should be "marked for memory"[5]). We suspect it may have a role to play later, but for now this moment swiftly passes;
– a lyrical fragment in the 'cello, marked *dolce* (comprising (**b**) and (**c**)).

Ex 22.1

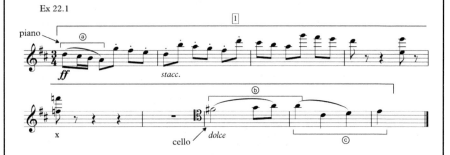

All the instruments continue singing the *dolce* phrase, developing it between themselves, until a sudden chord on its ♭VI effects a delightful key change towards the home V. The helter-skelter notes return and slide without a break into scales accompanying the **2nd subject**: all the instruments in turn punctuate the scales with its taut new rhythmic motif.

Ex. 22.2

At length, semiquavers shimmer high in the piano register, ready to cadence. Three notes (c) derived from the *dolce* phrase close on the home V chord with lovely effect: it has been approached not from its own V chord, but from IV, making a softer, gentler cadence sound.

Development: Listen for
– extracts from the helter-skelter 1(a) used (softly) in 3-part counterpoint;
– the *dolce* phrase broken down into separate motifs (dwelling especially on the second)

Beethoven works all these motifs together simultaneously in skilful counterpoint. We can hear the harmony settling on what feels like the home V, getting ready to lead back into the Recapitulation. The semiquavers of 1(a) gather momentum and finally rush back headlong into the 1st subject.

Recapitulation: We hear the 1st subject in full. It is repeated, but when the *"marked for memory"* note reappears it suddenly *itself* becomes a new V, leading into the key of B♭. After several tender appearances of the *dolce* phrase a rising bass line signals returning home tonality. But now, in another twist, the 2nd subject returns, at first in the key of G (IV), and the final cadences are approached from this "soft" tonal area.

Unusually, Beethoven specifically requires a full repeat of the second part.

Coda: A brief coda follows the repeat. Starting softly (and with 4 more bars of IV) but growing rapidly in intensity, first the piano and then the strings in unison sing out the *dolce* phrase, extending it each time to a full 8 bar length – a final lyrical apotheosis of the motif which has formed so much of the musical substance of this movement.

Beethoven presumably required the repeat of the second part so that his material could be clearly heard and understood – an indication of the co-operation now expected between composer and listener. But he no longer makes it easy for the listener to follow his formal structure by placing themes in tidy, carefully-delineated tonal boxes, with strong dominant cadences to define and close each section. Nor does he parade a classical "procession of themes" (1st subject, transition, 2nd subject group, cadence group, and so on). On first hearing, the ten bars of the 1st subject may sound lacking in immediate appeal, condensed, intense – more like Haydn, not as lyrical as Mozart. But Beethoven gradually reveals that his theme has hidden depths, and indeed a character which is not fully revealed until the very end of the movement. Its three "energy-laden"* motifs dominate the Exposition and the Development in such varied forms that the return to the Recapitulation is as eagerly awaited as ever – we look forward to hearing the full version of the theme again. But where the return to home key and principal theme was itself the high point of the Classical sonata, now there is a final Coda with more to say. In the Coda of this trio the *dolce* motif is heard in a final lyrical transformation, a sort of *apotheosis* of the thematic content of the movement.

There is a clear parallel here with classical rhetoric. Indeed, contemporaries continued to draw such parallels. In his *Musical Dictionary* of 1802, the theorist H C Koch describes the treatment of a musical *Hauptsatz* ("principal subject"):

> "Just as in a speech the principal idea, or theme, provides the essential content of the same, and must contain the material for the development of principal and subsidiary ideas, so it is in music, with respect to the modifying of an emotion that is possible through the principal subject, and just as an orator moves on from his principal subject to subsidiary subjects, antitheses, dissections etc., and employs rhetorical figures which all serve to give more strength to his principal subject, so the composer will act in the same manner in the treatment of a principal subject."[6]

But, as Dahlhaus points out, Koch first defines the word *Hauptsatz* in aesthetic terms:

> "[The] principal subject or theme is that melodic component of a piece of music which denotes the chief character thereof, or presents the emotion that is to be expressed therein in a comprehensible picture or image."

In the first movement of this trio we hear the 1st subject in the opening bars, but we come to realise that we have not fully understood its potential until the final Coda.

It is the slow movement of this trio, *Largo assai ed espressivo*, which has earned it the nickname of *"Ghost"* by which it is generally known. It is very unusually scored, with *tremolo* effects at extreme pitches on the piano, and it sounds unlike anything else Beethoven had ever written. Similar drafts were found on the same sketchbook page as preliminary jottings for an opera on Macbeth. The opera was

---

 * This splendidly descriptive phrase has been borrowed from Blume, *op.cit*, p.46.

abandoned (it would have been "too gloomy", he said) but rather than jettison every idea perhaps Beethoven used some of them for the slow movement of the trio instead. If the sense of the sublime had its origins in rhetoric, so too does the music which is heard here. It unfolds with the same relentless purpose which we sense in de Loutherbourg's painting and Wordsworth's poetry. Beethoven's interpretation of the sublime is purely musical, operating in the gradual dimension of time rather than the immediacy of a painted canvas or a written page. But it does not need extra-musical associations to be intelligible to us: its "energy-laden" units and cumulative intensity tell their own musical story.

After the concentration of this and the first movement, Beethoven decides not to include a fourth movement, and concludes the trio with a light-hearted *Presto* which doubles as both scherzo and finale.

★ ★ ★ ★ ★

Whatever Beethoven himself may have intended by the works of his "heroic" period, once he had completed his 5th Symphony he reached a landmark in the reception of his music: he was anointed as high priest of musical Romanticism by the Berlin lawyer, music critic, musician and writer E T A Hoffmann (1776-1822). Reviewing Beethoven's 5th Symphony in 1810 – which he described in full-blown Romantic language and considerable analytical detail – Hoffmann pronounced that:

> "Music is the most romantic of all arts ... Music reveals to man an unknown realm, a world quite separate from the outer sensual world surrounding him, a world in which he leaves behind all feelings circumscribed by the intellect in order to embrace the inexpressible ... Beethoven's music sets in motion the machinery of awe, of fear, of terror, of pain, and awakens that infinite yearning which is the essence of romanticism."[7]

He went on to claim that of the three great Viennese composers, Beethoven was the most original genius, the ideal Romantic artist, "the first to show us the art in its true glory".

The year after Hoffmann's review of the 5th Symphony, Beethoven began work on another piano trio. Written in the space of three weeks in March 1811, it turned out to be not only his finest work in the *genre*, but also what is generally accepted to be one of the greatest pieces of chamber music in the western repertoire. We will consider all four movements separately to see what makes this music so exceptional.

The trio in B♭ op.97 has become known as the "Archduke" trio, because it was dedicated to one of Beethoven's most loyal patrons, the Archduke Rudolph. The Archduke was also an excellent pianist, and probably enjoyed playing the piano part himself.

Beethoven: 1st movement *Allegro moderato* from Piano Trio in B♭ major op.97, *Archduke*

Exposition: The wonderfully sonorous **1st subject** in the piano which begins this work may prove to be made up of several units (and indeed as we shall see, it is); however it creates a first impression of gently-unfolding lyricism. It establishes the home key by going straight to the heart of its most sensitive intervals: the tonic note, a rise to the major 3rd, a fall to the 7th, which then nestles back up to the tonic before dropping to the 5th (the dominant) (a). This is counterbalanced by a rising scale figure (b) which pauses not on the strong sound of the dominant chord, but on the softer fourth (which we heard Beethoven use so effectively in the *Ghost* trio).

Ex. 23.1

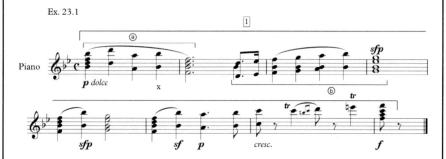

We get an immediate sense of the expansive proportions of the movement when this 1st subject is repeated in full. Motif (a) then becomes the basis of a passage in which the keys drift far away from conventional home I and V as the key of G major (VI) becomes established (with its major third (B♮) this is a long distance from home I of B♭: this is not g minor, which would have been the relative minor, and therefore unusual but not impossible in the context of B♭; nor does it bear a close relationship with the conventional V, F major). In this striking key the 2nd subject follows: it has three distinct sections (2 (a), (b), (c)) which follow rapidly one after the other, all in G major.

Ex. 23.2

At the end of the Exposition Beethoven slips easily back, and with a single bar of home dominant harmonies he is ready to return and repeat the Exposition – or move on to the Development.

The **Development** now sets about a detailed discussion of the 1st subject. We might think this would be repetitious, but Beethoven does not yet let us hear it again in its entirety. We hear only fragments: first the opening notes (a) sung lyrically, and then bandied about more strenuously between the instruments with distorted accents. The 'cello intervenes to remind us of the rising scale figure from the second half of the theme (b), picked up by the violin soaring gloriously into high registers. The 'cello responds again, this time with the scale played *pizzicato* – the notes plucked mysteriously at a low pitch. Both strings continue playing *pizzicato*, joined by short *staccato* notes in the piano, and in a masterly passage of suspense the tension builds, quietly but inexorably. A loud climax is reached. Beethoven is now poised firmly on the home dominant and we sense that the Recapitulation is very near. But still the instruments have to wait, hovering like coiled springs, until finally a long trill on the piano dissolves into the 1st subject and we are home again.

Recapitulation:

After all that suspense, the pleasure of hearing the lovely theme again is immensely rewarding – and increased by a simple but heart-stopping *appoggiatura* decoration added to the melodic line at x. The violin and 'cello sing out their approval with a couple of impromptu cadenzas, and then the 'cello returns to the original version (well, almost) and the recapitulation moves on, faithfully repeating the sectional 2nd subject, all now conventionally in the tonic key throughout.

Coda:

As the Recapitulation closes all the instruments join together in one last exhilarating statement of the 1st subject, drawing out its leaping intervals finally to swirl round the notes of the home tonic triad.

Perhaps the most striking feature of this wonderful movement is its treatment of the conventions of sonata form procedures, for in spite of Beethoven's digression into the distant key of VI instead of V in the Exposition, sonata form remains the driving force behind much of its dramatic effect. How are we to hear this VI key? Is it a dissonance, in the same way that Charles Rosen has defined the dominant as dissonant from the tonic? (See Chapter 4, p.61.) This VI key does after all *displace* the home tonic note B♭ – which has no place in G major. Susan McClary suggests that in "later Beethoven and especially Schubert, the submediant often substitutes for the too-conventional, too-rational dominant in the second key area."[8] Beethoven deals with consummate ease with a potential problem point at the double bar (the transition back to B♭ for the return to the beginning of the Exposition) and then all sense of dissonance is resolved by the Recapitulation, which is profoundly in B♭ throughout.

Thematically, we are introduced to a lyrical subject, hear it subsequently dissolve into those "energy-laden" units, and Beethoven's tantalising delaying tactics at the end of the Development only enhance the emotional reappearance of it which sonata form guarantees we may expect. And then, as in the *Ghost* trio, this musical narrative culminates in the final apotheosis of the theme in the Coda. What is perhaps most significant about the thematic content of this first movement, however, is that Beethoven here achieves a perfect synthesis between the opposing demands of romantic melody and classical rhetoric – those potentially warring elements dividing classical from romantic tastes. His principal theme is essentially lyrical, but it has been so skilfully constructed that it can be dismembered into elements suitable for musical development. Beethoven's themes are as artfully devised as any rhetorical topic by any eighteenth-century master of oratory. They can be manipulated, transformed: think only of the 2nd, 3rd and 4th notes of the 1st subject and how that nestling sequence of lyrical sounds can be made to snarl so menacingly in the Development (in much the same way, we might think, that the viewer's initial admiration of the vivid colours of de Loutherbourg's scarlet sky becomes modified by the realisation of its human cost).

After the lyricism of the first movement, Beethoven now reverses the traditional order and places his Scherzo and Trio in second place, with the slow movement to follow.

L van Beethoven: 2nd movement Scherzo *Allegro* from Piano Trio in B♭ major op.97, *Archduke*

Scherzo:

The 'cello begins with an insouciant rising scale, but we should not be deceived: it takes a highly-skilled craftsman to be wittily simple.

Ex. 23.5

An absolutely classical paragraph unfolds from this opening, reversing direction in the violin to cadence neatly on the 5th; repeating the opening in the dominant, then turning deftly back to the tonic. It is some time before the piano joins in, but when it does so more and more ideas unfold from this traditional 16-bar outline, as the movement dances through a set of delightfully simple variants.

Trio:

The contrast between the gentle humour of the Scherzo and the Trio which now follows could hardly be greater – but this is obviously Beethoven's intention. A new sort of humour emerges in the Trio: the 'cello is heard growling in low-pitched semitones, trying to rise but apparently mired down as though caught in some sort of primeval sludge. Ludicrously turning this noise into the subject of a brief fugal exposition (as only Beethoven's imaginative genius, tongue in cheek, would think to do), each instrument in turn tries to rise. Only the piano suddenly succeeds in dragging itself up and out – whereupon it breaks into a sort of antic waltz. Passages of semitone sludge and antic waltz alternate until finally the piano finds a way out and back into the sunshine of the Scherzo.

The semitones threaten to return at the close, but this time all the instruments are on the alert and scamper up the Scherzo scale before they can be bogged down again.

The luminous Air and Variations of the third movement is in the unusual and bright key of D major, the third of the home key (it is almost as though Beethoven is openly defying conventions – G major from B♭ in the first movement, and now D with its sharp third). It provides a welcome point of repose – Tovey says that variations are used at this moment "in order to express a sublime inaction".[9]

Sets of variations were immensely popular at the turn of the eighteenth century. Most composers wrote several sets, on well-known airs from operas, fashionable songs of the day, or tunes of their own devising. Like Hummel, most *virtuoso* performers used them to display their own technical accomplishments: audiences would marvel at the increasing difficulty and sheer number of notes introduced into each successive variation. Beethoven had too much integrity as a musician to stoop to the level of pyrotechnical display now prevalent amongst brilliant performers, but he had other weapons in his armoury. Improvisations – which might include variations on a theme – were a feature of his own performances, when the pianist Czerny recorded that his playing had

> "such an effect upon every hearer that frequently not an eye remained dry, while many would break into loud sobs; for there was something wonderful in his expression in addition to the beauty and originality of his ideas and his spirited style of rendering them."[10]

Even allowing for the hefty dose of contemporary sentimentality in this account, we may conclude that Beethoven's improvisations were exceptional. We can sense this in his published variations: he had already written over twenty sets before the turn of the century. They give us a fascinating glimpse into the quality and variety of his musical imagination as well as his working methods – for it is in his variations that Beethoven honed the skills which made the development sections of his symphonies and sonata works so innovative and interesting. With Beethoven a set of variations was not simply an accelerating display of technique, it became a narrative account of a musical idea – which might rely on moments of reflection as well as bombast to make its effect. Here are the variations in the third movement of the *Archduke* trio:

Beethoven: 3rd movement *Andante cantabile ma però con moto* from Piano Trio in B♭ major op.97, *Archduke*

Beethoven's theme is simple but profound (**Tema**). Bound by a repeating rhythmic sequence, it rises gradually from the third note of the scale, pauses serenely on the harmonies of II (e minor) before continuing upwards, then falls back to cadence on V; repeats all this; then rises again and finally falls back to the note on which it had begun (a classic 8-bar + 8-bar construct, with the final 4 bars repeated: second nature to his audience). But this dry description gives no sense of the melodic tension that builds up in the rising pattern of the rhythmic sequence, as the listener expects to hear ever-higher notes – the *highest* note in a phrase will always be its climax – and after this satisfaction has been achieved, the gentle falling back to the dominant; and the final descent down an octave in the last line, the instruments hugging each semitone as the melody sinks to its point of repose.

Ex. 23.6

It is unnecessary to describe each of the five variations in detail: Beethoven's music and the introduction of new and varied decorations, motifs and rhythms can speak for themselves. Notice, however, that the final variation, far from being a whirling climax, returns to the theme itself; not in the piano alone, as at the opening, but as a melody distributed between all three instruments. It is the basis for a final variation of great beauty, a "valedictory" return to the original (almost in the manner of a Recapitulation) which allows the listener to luxuriate in the beautiful theme and luscious harmonic colouring for one last time.

The ephemeral "now-you-hear-it, now-you-don't" nature of listening to variations was perfectly captured by one of Beethoven's contemporaries, C F Michaelis, writing in 1803:

"… if the basic theme, the main melody, appears clothed in a new manner, under a delicate transparent cloak, so to speak, then the soul of the listener obtains pleasure, in that it can automatically look through the veil, finding the known in the unknown, and can see it develop without effort. Variation demonstrates freedom of fantasy in treatment of the subject, excites pleasant astonishment in recognising again in new forms the beauty, charm, or sublimity already known, attractively fusing the new with the old without creating a fantastic mixture of heterogeneous figures … Variation arouses admiration insofar as everything latent in the theme is gradually made manifest, and unfolds [into] the most attractive diversity."[11]

The last chord of the Variations leads without a break into the Rondo finale (described by Tovey as "a marvellous study in bacchanalian indolence"[12]):

Beethoven: 4th movement *Allegro moderato / Presto* from Piano Trio in B♭ major op.97, *Archduke*

An effervescent Rondo theme (R) begins the *Allegro moderato* finale; it has a tailpiece at bar 20 with a rustic accent (displaced onto the second beat) which is an inseparable part of it.

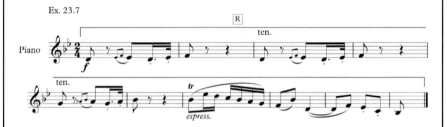

Ex. 23.7

The movement is in a fairly orthodox Sonata Rondo Form. There is a good deal of pairing of the strings against the piano, but all are now – thanks to the technical advances in the manufacture of instruments and Beethoven's skilful scoring – able to hold their own. Beethoven's sense of humour is here again too: at the end of the Development the violin is waiting to return with the Rondo theme, finally loses patience and begins – right theme, right key, right pitch – even though the piano is still a long way off. The piano has to concede and eventually swings back with tonic harmonies.

There are more harmonic twists in the long Coda with which the movement ends. The angular Rondo theme is transformed into a very fast triple-rhythm (still, however, with two beats per bar). We sense that the music is moving into distant keys, and so the Coda has to continue at some length in order to re-anchor the end of the movement in the home tonic. This final section is a particularly effective example of how Beethoven's ingenious transformation of thematic material was derived from his experience of writing variations: the effervescent Rondo theme can always be heard even through the "delicate transparent cloak" of brilliant decoration.

Beethoven's biographer Thayer recorded the first public performance of the *Archduke* Trio on 11 April 1814 in Vienna, with Beethoven at the piano. A truly pathetic account of the occasion was given by the violinist Louis Spohr, who described how

"In the *forte* passages the poor deaf man pounded on the keys until the strings jangled, and in *piano* he played so softly that whole groups of notes were omitted … I was deeply saddened at so hard a fate."[13]

After this there were no more public performances as a pianist; nor did Beethoven write any more piano concertos, nor another full-scale piano trio. For such a brilliant pianist and peerless musician the loss of hearing is unimaginable. The bleak facts speak for themselves.

★ ★ ★ ★ ★

Beethoven's legacy to posterity, however, was six outstanding piano trios. These were not only a landmark in the repertoire of the *genre*, but also in his handling of the High Classical sonata form of Mozart and Haydn. From them he inherited: an old dance-derived binary model with tonal differentiation between I and V, and three distinct divisions within the model which followed an accepted organisation of thematic material. There are two shifts of emphasis in Beethoven's treatment of the form: firstly in connection with tonality, and secondly in his development of theme.

To begin with tonality. Of course the tonality of Beethoven's sonata movements is still defined by the I – V relationship: he continues to endorse arrival in keys by emphasis on V, and observes the necessity of resolving overall dissonance by returning to I throughout the Recapitulation. Both these are especially obvious at the end of his Developments, where there is invariably a passage of significant V preparation before return to I (to ensure that the Recapitulation is soundly anchored in home tonality).

But Beethoven is also very interested in the characteristic tone colour of other areas of the home key, and he frequently enlivens the tonal framework by modulating to different keys. These modulations have to be carefully controlled to be appropriate to the moment and the purpose – he must never distort what Elaine Sisman calls his "harmonic long-range planning".[14] However, Tovey identifies four different ways in which he is able to insert new colour:

> "It is a most vital distinction in Beethoven's, as in all great music, whether the modulation asserts a key-relation directly, explains it circumstantially, digresses at large, or deliberately mystifies."[15]

We have seen all these techniques in the three trios under consideration:

1) *Asserting a key-relation directly* is the most obvious progression – the familiar endorsement of a new key by introduction of preparation with its own dominant harmonies.

2) *Explaining a key-relation circumstantially* can be illustrated by the numerous occasions when Beethoven introduces ♭VI harmony,

then follows with a semitone drop onto the home V, *explaining* its emphatic harmonic purpose. There were telling examples of this progression in the c minor trio (a single chord at the end of the Exposition, a longer passage at the end of the Development) and the *Ghost* (Transition to 2nd subject in the Exposition).

3) *Digressing at large* – the 2nd subject and Cadential groups in the Exposition of the first movement of the *Archduke* must be a *locus classicus* for this; there are also 31 bars in the key of A major in the Coda at the end of the last movement, which cause Beethoven to write a further return of the Rondo 1st subject by way of redressing the tonal balance.

4) *Deliberately mystifies* – another *locus classicus* is the unexplained F natural which appears near the beginning of the *Ghost,* but is only finally explained when, on its appearance in the Recapitulation, it turns into the V of Bb and effects a lovely key change. A few bars later, this is all explained circumstantially when Bb becomes a bVI, which colours the semitone drop to A as home V leading back to I.

Beethoven has a particular fondness also for certain chords and their associated tonal areas. He often uses IV instead of V where this is possible, for instance at the end of the Exposition in the *Ghost,* and again in the Recapitulation – in fact the *Ghost* is full of this gentle IV "plagal"* colouring. It is also a significant colour effect in the *Archduke,* where it is a feature of the 1st subject (4th and 5th bars) in the 1st movement as a lovely little resting-place. As well as IV he also enjoys using VI – as we saw in the *Archduke* – and frequently plays on both rising and falling thirds, i.e. between submediant, tonic and mediant progressions. (We have glimpsed these third progressions in John Bach and Mozart too, but it will be Schubert who finally makes them his own.) All these tonal colours are most skilfully incorporated into the sonata framework:

> "He [Beethoven] was a formidable musical architect, but typically filled out … structural mapping with imaginative and surprising expressive events, which strain the formal frameworks without quite breaking them."[16]

Beethoven's second shift of emphasis in the sonata is in his development of theme as narrative. He relies – absolutely relies – on his

---

* A "plagal" cadence features the progression IV – I (it will be familiar to Anglican churchgoers as the cadence used for "Amen" to the 1st and 2nd Collects, as opposed to the "perfect" cadence V – I used for the 3rd Collect).

audience's familiarity with the form, but he fills it with a new and dramatic intensity. The old dance-derived model becomes the basis of a musical narrative, travelling through *statement – amplification – restatement* to a climax in the final Coda. The precise classical divisions between sections become less clear, so that the whole tends to be heard as a continuous argument. Beethoven may introduce a number of contrasting musical ideas, and then have us guessing which he will proceed to exploit in the Development; he glories in thwarting and delaying the return to the Recapitulation to increase the dramatic effect of returning to his 1st subject; and, to conclude the goal-orientated trajectory of his argument, he presents the principal subject to us at the end in a final dramatic apotheosis in a Coda. (Inevitably, this will result in the formal addition of a fourth part to our definition of sonata form.)

At the same time, Beethoven was demonstrating that the intellectual rigour of classical form and the lyricism of romantic music were not necessarily incompatible. "Sonata form and style," said Tovey, "arise just at the breaking-point between lyric melody and dramatic music." The *Archduke* trio was written as Beethoven emerged from the *angst* of his first decade in the new century, for a brief period at ease with himself and the world. In a handful of other similarly serene works written at this time (such as the *Harp* string quartet, the 6th and 7th symphonies and the *Lebewohl* piano sonata),* he showed that rhetoric and melody were not necessarily fractious opposites, and that in music there might be a deeply satisfying synthesis of the sublime and the beautiful, the learned and the *galant*, seriousness and sensibility. We have already mentioned his admiration for Schiller, and perhaps he was inspired by the poet in this, for it was central to the poet's philosophy:

> "[Schiller] viewed the rational and the sensuous not as irreconcilable opposites but as complementary forces whose fusion, through the activity of aesthetic contemplation, could restore wholeness to the individual and ultimately to society in general."[17]

This demonstration came at an opportune moment. The change of attitude which now saw instrumental music as "the highest form of all the arts" and Hoffman's identification of Beethoven as the "ideal Romantic artist" focused attention on the composer and his music. Beethoven became the gold standard for "serious" musicians for the rest of the nineteenth century, against whom all others would henceforth be measured. But fully to appreciate music in the sonata tradition was an intellectual exercise requiring no small effort

---

* The *Lebewohl* sonata was also dedicated to the Archduke Rudolph.

of concentration, and inevitably a gap began to open up between "serious" and "popular" music – based on the easily-understood song-melody types which proliferated everywhere. The importance of Beethoven's music was his synthesis of old and new, of Classical form with Romantic expressiveness. Thus he crucially paved the way for Romantic composers to follow him with instrumental music which could inspire an emotional response without losing its musical integrity.

CHAPTER ENDNOTES

1   Bonds, *Music as Thought*, p.46.

2   Bonds, *ibid*, p.26.

3   Bonds, *ibid*, p.88.

4   Quoted by Stanley, Glenn. 'Beethoven at Work' in *The Cambridge Companion to Beethoven*, ed. Glenn Stanley, p.27. Cambridge: Cambridge University Press, 2000.

5   See McCreless, Patrick. 'Schenker and Chromatic Tonicization: A Reappraisal', in *Schenker Studies*, ed. Hedi Siegel. Cambridge, Cambridge University Press, 1990, p.131.

6   Koch, Heinrich Christoph. 'Hauptsatz' ("Principal Subject"), *Musikalisches Lexikon*, 1802; quoted by Carl Dahlhaus in *Ludwig van Beethoven: Approaches to his Music*; transl. M. Whittall, Oxford: Clarendon Press, 1991, p.121.

7   Taken from 'E T A Hoffman's Musical writings: Kreisleriana, The Poet and The Composer', *Music Criticism*, transl. Martyn Clarke, ed. David Charlton, Cambridge, 1989, pp.236-23; quoted by Scott Burnham in chap. 16 of *The Cambridge Companion to Beethoven*, Cambridge: University Press, 2000, p.275.

8   McClary, Susan. *Conventional Wisdom: the Content of Musical Form*. Berkeley: University of California Press, 2000, p.123.

9   Tovey, *Beethoven*, p.132.

10 Article in *London Musical Miscellany*, 1852; cited in Thayer-Forbes, p.185; and in turn by Glenn Stanley, *op.cit*, p.16.

11 Michaelis, Christian Friedrich. *Über die musikalische Wiederholung und Veränderung*, AmZ 13 (1803), cols. 197-200; quoted by Elaine Sisman, *The Cambridge Companion to Beethoven*, p.60.

12 Tovey, *op.cit*, p.102.

13 *Thayer's Life of Beethoven*, rev. and ed. Elliot Forbes, Princeton, NJ, 1964, vol.1, pp.577-8.

14   Sisman, *op.cit*, p.56.

15   Tovey, *op.cit*, p.40.

16   Kinderman, William, 'The piano music' in *The Cambridge Companion to Beethoven*. Cambridge: Cambridge University Press, 2000, p.106.

17   Bonds, *Music as Thought*, pp.73/4.

CHAPTER 11

THE AUSTRO-GERMAN MAINSTREAM 1: SCHUBERT

THE EXPECTATIONS PLACED upon Beethoven's successors were formidable. He had put the art of music in a spotlight, centre-stage of the nineteenth-century Romantic movement. Had not E T A Hoffman declared, on hearing Beethoven's 5th Symphony: "Music is the most Romantic of all arts ... the only one that is genuinely Romantic, for only the Infinite is its Subject"?

Expectations were especially high of musicians in the Austrian Empire and the German Confederation to its north: we noticed in Chapter 10 a contemporary comment of 1806, that the "highest and most radiant peak of the latest instrumental music" was in German-speaking countries. These composers thought of themselves as following in the footsteps of Haydn, Mozart and Beethoven. It will be useful to have a name for reference to this inherited tradition, and from now onwards I shall borrow a well-known phrase from a lecture by Tovey entitled "The Main Stream of Music". (Tovey's lecture actually covered the waterfront of western development from the fifteenth century to Wagner, but, as he said, "the notion of the main stream is a better metaphor for my subject than the term 'classical'." [1]) As the nineteenth century wears on, we shall need to differentiate between this "serious" Austro-German mainstream tradition and the sonata as it evolved elsewhere in Europe.

For now, for those who aspired to follow Beethoven, the sonata was no longer merely for entertainment, but for "serious" listening. Eighteenth-century composers had been craftsmen producing elegant examples of a universal type, but after Beethoven originality became prized as the hallmark of "genius", and from this point onwards new music had to be distinctive, different from anything that had gone before. With a good deal of overblown language flying around, those sedulously continuing in the Austro-German mainstream tradition had to live up to exalted expectations – while at the same time connecting with a purchasing public.

Franz Schubert (1797-1828) was nearest in age to Beethoven. He was born some twenty-seven years later in Vienna itself, but he died only a year after Beethoven at the early age of 31. He was the son of a schoolteacher and showed a precocious talent for music at an early age, becoming a choirboy at the Imperial Court Chapel in 1808. This greatly widened his musical experience: as well as choral works he came into contact with a range of orchestral and instrumental music. After his studies were over, the bespectacled youth taught at his father's school for a time, but was then persuaded by friends to drop teaching for a more congenial, albeit considerably more precarious, career in music. For the rest of his life he was short of money, but never lacking generous friends, who often provided him with lodging and invariably admired his music. Apart from his songs, relatively few of his compositions were published during his own lifetime, but a certain amount of his music was quite widely known and enjoyed in Vienna by the time he was twenty.

The compositions known in Vienna at that time, however, were not those for which Schubert is now so widely known and admired. What his contemporaries knew was mostly music for piano, especially piano duets, and also songs, part-songs and a good deal of dance music. His friends, however loyal, were not influential aristocratic patrons such as supported Beethoven; nor were they Vienna's leading musicians. Furthermore, where Mozart and Haydn came to rely on the Viennese public's appetite for purchasing new music or attending public concerts, Schubert seems "to have lived almost exclusively in relation to his friends."[2] They were drawn from the administrative and professional middle classes, or were poets, writers and artists, and they had wide cultural interests. They enjoyed nothing more than a weekly *Schubertiad* in their own houses, where their poetry could be united with Schubert's music in his songs, and they could at the same time enjoy good conversation and dancing. For many years the music by Schubert which was known in Vienna was the music he produced for this circle of friends.

During these early years, however, Schubert also wrote a great deal of other music: sonatas, string quartets, theatre and religious music, and no fewer than seven orchestral symphonies. These works were neither known nor performed because Schubert was both too shy and too modest to promulgate them himself. In 1823 he even declared that he had "nothing for full orchestra which I could send out into the world with a clear conscience": he felt himself too much overshadowed by the genius of Beethoven.

In 1822 a personal catastrophe seems finally to have prompted a mood of self-affirmation: the onset of syphilis, which he knew would inevitably shorten his life. He embarked on what John Gingerich has described as his "Beethoven Project",[3] a determination at last to try his hand at composing works in the *genres* in which Beethoven himself had been so successful. Tragically late, yet not too late, between 1824 and his death four years later Schubert produced a succession of masterpieces – the "Great" C major symphony, the final piano sonata and duets, more string quartets and the quintet in C, the Octet and more songs, including the *Winterreise* cycle. This outpouring, the intensity of which undoubtedly hastened his death, also included his two great piano trios. Apart from two isolated movements these were the only works which he wrote for the medium.

The Trio in B♭ op.99, D 898 was probably written before its companion in E♭. For all it is truly a trio in the Grand Sonata style, it had no formal public performance, being played for the first time at a *Schubertiad* in the house of one of the most loyal of all Schubert's friends, Joseph von Spaun.

F Schubert: 1st movement *Allegro moderato* from Piano Trio in B♭ major op.99, D 898

Exposition: In one of the most exhilarating openings in the piano trio repertoire, the strings together swing buoyantly up the notes of the tonic triad of B♭ (**1st subject**) to a throbbing accompaniment in the piano.

Ex. 24.1

This opening theme is expansively repeated in a distant key (as Haydn did in his trio in D, Hob.XV:24) and then followed by what seems to be a bridge passage of classical precision, ready to lead off to the 2nd subject. But Schubert has not yet finished with his theme and it is heard again, now back in the tonic and in the piano as the roles reverse. The classical cadencing returns and he has us guessing what will follow next. The answer is as surprising as it is bewitching: the 'cello picks up the last note of the cadence (which happens to be A), repeats it with high-pitched insistence, and then the piano drops down to a low note F, serenely explaining that this note is now the third of F major (after all, the conventional (V) key for a 2nd subject – albeit here so unusually approached). The 'cello continues, turning the note A into the beginning of an ardent melody (**2nd subject**) which plunges between emotive 6th and 7th intervals and exploits the sensuous semitone between B♭ and A.

Ex. 24.2

Cello

pp

Its rhythms and the semitone interval dominate extensions of this 2nd subject until the buoyant opening bars return and Schubert returns us to the beginning of the Exposition (the repeat is still marked).

Development: This is a long and eventful section. Playing together, an octave apart, the strings embark on an impassioned discussion of the 1st subject with the piano, the violin climbing high into its register while the piano plunges down equally low; the keys range in sequence with strong V chords leading each statement, until all the instruments cluster on a single note C. The tension drops as the same radiant key change as before ushers in the 2nd subject, now passing sweetly between the 'cello and the violin as it traces a trajectory of falling third modulations. Nineteenth-century ears would hear the piano landing on the home dominant note (F), where a long passage over a low pedal follows. Tension builds as the pedal is emphasised by momentary ♭VI lifts (on the chord of G♭, a semitone above V). We expect a prompt return to I and the 1st subject, but again Schubert thwarts our expectations: when the 1st theme does return, it sidles in softly and gently, not with its original exhilaration, but in this alien key of the ♭VI, G♭. After several modulating re-statements, the tonal

Recapitulation finally follows. It skips past the original opening to pick up from the third statement in the piano (as before, *piano*). After this the recapitulation is regular, the now-familiar falling third key change pivoting securely on the note D to B♭, safely back in the tonic key for the 2nd subject.

Coda:

The movement ends with a short but effective coda: this begins with an amplified statement of the opening theme, which immediately turns into another sequence at falling third intervals. But then it draws to a close, not thunderously, but dropping a few Classical curtsies before two final emphatic chords.

This is a wonderful movement, all the more remarkable for being only the second work for piano trio medium which Schubert had written. He fills the old sonata framework with vibrant thematic material – a robust 1st subject which opens the movement by ranging up the tonic triad to establish the home tonality with buoyant panache, and a melodically more static 2nd subject with a sensuous sixth interval rising to savour the expressive semitone between the 3rd and 4th.

Contemporary reviews of Schubert's music mentioned his idiosyncratic harmonies.[4] There are a number of striking moments in this movement – made possible because Schubert knew he was working against a background of established ease with the sonata conventions. When he goes off in unexpected directions, he will explain the excursion. For instance, in the striking sequences which open the Development, he gives the listener clear V – I guidelines. But he does not always use a V to approach a new key: several times in this movement he follows the falling thirds trajectory which draws the listener less overtly but equally effectively towards his tonal goal. (This was the sequence heard very simply in the opening of Schobert's sonata – here the idea now comes of age.)

Another hallmark of Schubert's modulations also involves a falling third: his magical manipulation as a single note (heard as the root of V) becomes the major 3rd of a new key. We hear it in all three appearances of the 2nd subject. Again, earlier composers have used this (see also Mozart, p.129), but it is Schubert who makes it his own: this is the same technique as the much-loved fall into the 2nd subject in the first movement of his string quintet in C major, D 956.

The most unusual moment in this movement is the return to the Recapitulation, when after a long period of obvious V preparation, the thematic return comes a full 28 bars *before* the tonal return. The thematic return opens with the 1st subject in the key of Gb, a third below the tonic and some tonal distance away from home. However, we have just heard plenty of Gb harmony decorating the home V in the preceding bars (as also at the end of the Exposition) – this is our old friend, the time-honoured chromatic, semitonal decoration of V by the bVI. So we now hear it as a tonal obfuscation, delaying the return to home I so that we will feel the resolution even more keenly when it comes 28 bars later. (Martin Chusid points out[5] that we have had a "marked for memory" note to alert us to this event, right at the beginning of the movement, when in the 9th bar the pianist decorated a low Gb with a trill before falling to F, the dominant note.)

The actual tonal return comes after no fewer than four further statements of the 1st subject, in a succession of different keys which eventually end on the home V. At last the piano returns to its script: but by now we have rejoined the Exposition halfway through its presentation of the 1st subject. The rest of the Recapitulation follows regularly. Why does Schubert do this? Perhaps simply for variety's sake, to keep us listening carefully; or perhaps because that opening buoyant energy might lose its appeal if heard too often: better to reserve it for its final *fortissimo* reappearance in the Coda.

Schubert also writes with a real understanding of the potential of each instrument to contribute to the trio ensemble. Note the intensity of expression at the beginning of the Development, when the strings, in unison but an octave apart, alternate with the piano, and explore the extremes of their pitch range. Note, too, Schubert's sympathetic use of the tone quality of the 'cello above middle C, as he explores its expressive potential – "that infinite yearning which is the essence of romanticism" (Hoffmann again; see p.155).

At the end of his life, Schubert's E♭ trio, op.100 seems to have been better known than its sister in B♭. It was performed at the only recorded public concert of his works in March 1828 and published shortly before his death. (The B♭ trio did not achieve publication until 1836.) It remained the more popular of the two for much of the nineteenth century, although in the twentieth century the B♭ seems to have overtaken it.

F Schubert: 1st movement *Allegro* from Piano Trio in E♭ major op.100, D 929

Exposition:

On first hearing the Exposition seems to present a bewildering array of different thematic material. It is arranged in three tonal plateaux:
i)   the bold unison 1st subject in the tonic key
ii) the first two sections of the 2nd subject, in unconventional "distant" keys
iii) two more sections of the 2nd subject, back in the conventional home V.

The challenge is to realise that only the opening bars of the 1st subject and the first two sections of the 2nd subject are different thematic ideas: virtually everything else is derived from a "germ" motif first heard as the continuation of the 1st subject in the 'cello.

So, from the beginning, we hear:

1st subject: a bold opening, all three instruments establishing the tonic triad in unison. It repeats, but then the 'cello innocuously introduces the all-important "germ" (x) – twice. Listen carefully to its chromatic decoration of the dominant note, and the following rise of a third.

Ex. 25.1

Immediately all the instruments pounce on the motif and use its rhythm to move on through shifting harmonies to the first two sections of the **2nd subject** : two nicely contrasted ideas featuring 4 repeating quavers 2(a),

Ex. 25.2

and gently meandering triplet quavers above the same repeating quavers 2(b);

Ex. 25.3

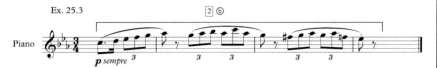

2(a) begins in ♭vi (minor mode), but the harmonies shift back and pause on a firm cadence in the expected home V. Then the "germ" motif (x) reappears as the basis of a third section of the 2nd subject (c), and again (in flowing quavers in the pianist's right hand) of a fourth section (d). *(See Ex. 25 below.)*

Finally, in an augmented form (i.e. lengthening its first four notes and adding a neat little counter-balancing phrase on the end of it), the "germ" becomes a lyrical Cadence figure with more falling third progressions. Immediately afterwards the piano and 'cello kick off a vigorous close based on the opening rhythm (listen to the harmonies as Schubert powers through distant key changes, finally dropping beautifully from a chord of A major to F (home V) – the conventional V of V – this chromatic harmonic colouring adds an exhilarating touch to the end of the Exposition).

Development:

The Development counterbalances the concentrated energy of the Exposition by devoting itself almost entirely to the motif (x) as we heard it in its lyrical incarnation as the Cadence figure (and note there is no question here of a traditional return to the opening material in V). This section is cast in three expansive paragraphs, each beginning with all three instruments singing sweetly together like a string quartet, and then the strings and the pianist's left hand pass the expanded "germ" from one to another against a translucent accompaniment in the pianist's right hand. The harmonies glide smoothly through distant keys until finally coming to rest on the home V. A sense of anticipation builds up, endorsed by the violin twice fluttering up and down the dominant triad with the rhythm of the expected 1st subject.

Recapitulation:

The 1st subject reappears triumphantly, and proceeds to repeat all the thematic material and unusual keys of the Exposition, duly transposed and skilfully turned so as to return to the home tonic.

Coda:

After the dominance of the "germ" motif throughout the Development, it is barely heard in the robust Coda. Instead, Schubert seems to redress the balance of the movement by returning briefly to the repeated quavers of 2(a), and then in the closing bars romps home via the bold opening notes from the beginning of the 1st subject.

Here we have Schubert again flouting sonata traditions, but in a different way from the B♭ trio. That now seems rather more conventional, with its two happily contrasting subjects, both equally important to the development of the sonata argument throughout. In this first movement of the E♭ trio we have no shortage of contrasting themes, but as we have just heard, most of it is derived from that opening "germ" in the 'cello. Hear how spontaneously it all seems to develop before discovering how much careful planning lies behind that spontaneity. This is true Beethovenian motivic development, ingeniously varying a motif, and then generously repeating it. It is subtly done, and so well handled that we are never tired of it.

Ex. 25

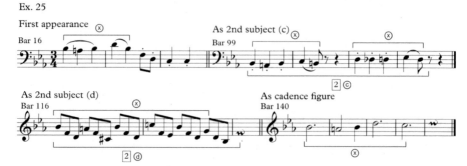

Ex.25 F Schubert: *Allegro* from Piano Trio in E♭ major op.100, D 929

Furthermore, the Development seems to reverse normal roles: the Exposition has the driving force, as the "germ" generates momentum in ever-varying ways, but then the development slows down and Schubert allows himself to explore the lovely cadence derivative in a myriad different harmonic guises. So instead of an opening Exposition followed by a driven Development, here we have a driven Exposition followed by a reflective, lyrical Development. It is also a very long one – longer than either the Exposition or the Recapitulation. But what a wonderful movement it is, alternately gathering momentum and then luxuriating in lyricism in so many original and effective ways.

Once again, this movement is full of surprising harmonies as Schubert colours each repetition and variation of his motifs with rich modulations. We have to hear the excursions as just this: harmonic *colouring*. The pattern of falling third sequences can be heard throughout, but especially in the three paragraphs of the Development.[6] If we take a long-term view of the tonal trajectory from beginning to end of the movement, we shall see that any unusual keys in which themes first appear are, long-term, simply decoration of the home V. We feel safely in the home I by the end, and in 1828 that is still what matters.

We can confidently expect a slow movement with song-like qualities from Schubert, and indeed he does not disappoint.

F Schubert: 2nd movement *Andante con moto* from Piano Trio in E♭ major op.100, D 929

The composer is caught in song-writing mode as the piano begins with two bars of what is clearly an accompaniment, and we sense a soloist waiting to begin. It is the 'cello who enters, and a haunting minor mode theme of singular beauty slowly unfolds (1).

Ex. 25.4

It passes to the piano, and finally closes in the relative major key. A lyrical second theme follows, which seems to draw its graceful falling phrases from the closing bars of the opening theme. A climax is reached, halting on an expectant home V chord, and after a brief pause the first theme returns, once more in the home tonic minor mode. (Schubert sets this movement in a modified sonata rondo format.) After a stormy episode, the second theme returns, but this time in tonic major key. Not the least effective moment in this lovely movement comes when the shadow of the minor mode falls across the score again as the opening theme returns to haunt the close with its wistful phrasing.

After this peaceful movement, we expect action again, and Schubert follows convention by continuing with a Scherzo and Trio:

F Schubert: 3rd movement Scherzo *Allegro moderato* from Piano Trio in E♭ major op.100, D 929

Here we have another seemingly carefree movement underpinned by great technical ingenuity. Beneath the insouciant running figures of the **Scherzo (S)** lies the academic rigour of a strict canon, as the strings and piano toss the lead role from one to another.

Ex. 25.5

Piano

*sempre **p***

This persists throughout most of the section, even incorporating some of Schubert's signature falling third modulations. It takes a great deal of technical skill for such academic writing to sound so natural.

The **Trio** provides an arresting contrast with the jovial tramp of a peasant dance. It is momentarily interrupted near the end by the repeated-note figure from the 2nd subject of the first movement.

As we hear the jaunty opening figure of the finale we expect it will be a typical Rondo finale: it is, however, in a sonata form of voluminous proportions, with three themes discursively developed in ample paragraphs:

F Schubert: 4th movement *Allegro moderato* from Piano Trio in E♭ major op.100, D 929

Exposition: The jaunty 1st subject features triplet quavers;

Ex. 25.6

Piano

p

the contrasting **2nd subject** drops the triplet motion for rapidly repeating notes and four beats in a bar in c minor (the relative minor key);

the **3rd subject** presents us with another triplet rhythm with added rushing semiquavers in the expected V key.

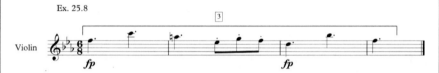

The **Development** mostly deals with the 2nd subject, and an exhilarating new idea which grows from the 1st subject's opening triplet quaver figure and falls jubilantly down two octaves. A little later, quite unexpectedly and with considerable effect, the haunting 'cello theme from the second movement is heard through falling *arpeggios* in the piano (in the ♭vi key of the home I).

The **Recapitulation** follows, reasonably regularly (although the 2nd subject is heard in an unexpected key – f minor – before returning to I for the 3rd subject).

It is succeeded in turn by a long **Coda**. The 2nd subject again leads into the jubilant new theme and we seem set for a majestic close. However, at the last minute another of those minor mode clouds drifts across the sunlight and suddenly we hear the haunting 'cello theme again, this time in the home i. We resign ourselves to a sober ending in the minor – but in the closing moments, in a master-stroke of surprise, Schubert sends the violin to join the 'cello and the minor turns to major: the cloud melts away and the movement ends in triumph.

Again, a striking feature of this movement is Schubert's writing for the trio medium. He knows where in its register the distinctive tone of each instrument will sound best, and how to combine the three in unusual and effective ways. Time and again, we note the intensity of expression which he achieves, not only when exploring the tone quality of the 'cello, but also when he scores the strings an octave apart to sing out against imaginative figuration in the piano part. We can also hear the sound of piano duets in octave-doubled melodies in the piano part. Smallman says of this finale that it contains "some of the most brilliant and exciting piano trio writing in the repertoire".[7]

But this movement has acquired a history of provoking very different listener reactions. There are those who find it too long, in spite of cuts which Schubert himself made after its first hearing. One musicologist even describes it as "little more than written-out vamping, entertainment music on a bad night."[8] There are others who would have the cuts re-instated and regard it as an exceptional, visionary movement, far ahead of its time in connecting thematic material across different movements of the work.[9] All four movements are connected by the repeating four-note motif first heard in 2(a) and (b) of the first movement: we noted its return in the Coda. This repeated note figure is transformed into the accompaniment to the melody of the *Andante*; then transformed again in both the Scherzo and fleetingly in its Trio; and finally dominates extensive tracts of the 2nd subject in the finale.

The most striking quotations, however, are two heart-stopping returns of the 'cello's haunting *Andante* theme in the finale, and especially its final return at the very end of the work, when its minor mode is radiantly transformed into the major. In addition to these obvious appearances, Janet Schmalfeldt finds a number of small detailed connections between material in the *Andante* and the finale, and also a "marked for memory" motif from within the theme buried in 2(b) of the first movement's Exposition. Schubert's purposeful inclusion of this motif has been endorsed also by Brian Newbould's discovery that it was not present in the first draft of the work: "It seems likely that Schubert added it after completing his slow movement, and perhaps the finale."[10] Smallman notes moreover that Schubert's cuts excised a third reference to the *Andante*.[11]

This scholarly detective work is very interesting, but it does not of itself explain the innovative idea of quoting from one movement in another. Why might Schubert have done this?

Schmalfeldt finds an answer in Schubert's cultural background. We have touched on contemporary notions of sensibility and the sublime in Chapter 9; we have also noted Schubert's membership of a circle of cultivated and intellectual Viennese friends. They were undoubtedly in touch with contemporary philosophical ideas about art and music, which Schmalfeldt describes as follows:

"So many of the ideas about art, and especially about music, that we have come to associate with the early nineteenth century – organicism, originality and imagination as artistic requirements, the emergence of the concept of a musical work … instrumental music's claim to autonomy, the power of Beethoven's music to transport us into the 'spirit-realm of the infinite' – such ideas gain new meaning when one considers them as inextricably linked to the moral bases of expressionist philosophy ... the cultural milieu in which all of the above-mentioned ideas mingle and flourish is one in which inwardness had become a pre-occupation."[12]

She continues by observing that "notions of inwardness in nineteenth-century music have become common-place", and continues by referring to

"... processual formal techniques that draw new kinds of attention to deeply-felt, song-inspired interior movements and secondary (as opposed to main) themes. In such pieces, the music itself would indeed seem to 'turn inward': an interior moment, or movement, becomes the focal point of the complete work – the center of gravity toward which what comes before seems to pull, and from which all that follows seems to radiate. I see processes of this kind as a key to Schubert's music in general ..." [13]

Schmalfeldt identifies the return of the haunting *Andante* theme as an "inward turning" in the finale of the E♭ trio.

The *Andante* theme is indeed singularly beautiful, but why should Schubert use this theme as an expression of "interiority"? The theme itself perhaps needs to be identified. Schubertian tradition has it that it is based on a Swedish song which he heard sung at the house of Viennese friends. The original has been traced, but as Smallman comments, "... apart from sharing the same key (C minor) and a similar marching rhythm, it bears only a very marginal resemblance to Schubert's superb theme."[14] Schmalfeldt reproduces both text and translation of the song, but apart from its melancholy subject-matter of lost hope (which may indeed be relevant), the rest does not seem particularly relevant to Schubert at this juncture.

There is a similarity between this theme and the funeral march in Beethoven's *Eroica* symphony. The contours of the opening bars, rising from the fifth below the tonic up to the minor third above, have much in common, and the grim plodding of Schubert's chordal accompaniment could hardly be more indicative of a funeral march. Beethoven had died in March 1827, and the sketches for this E♭ trio are dated only eight months later, November 1827. Intent on his Beethoven Project and with the master's death so recent, it is possible that the *Andante* is intended as an *In Memoriam* tribute to Beethoven. And if we are to look for "interior" meaning in the transfer of the theme to the finale, might it not be seen as representing not only Schubert's sense of the loss of Beethoven, but also of his own impending mortality (his health was already broken and he died only twelve months later*). Thus we would have a purely musical reference (between the *Marcia Funebre* and the *Andante*) and a purely emotional intention in Schubert's cross-referencing between his *Andante* and finale.

Since we have strayed into realms of speculation, however, there is one more hypothesis to be mentioned – which can no more resolve the problem than any other, but which merits airing because it is so intriguing. This hypothesis was included in the Schubert scholar Brian Newbould's compilation of articles about Schubert published in 1988.[15] It is a paper by a medical practitioner, Roger Neighbour, which addresses a number of problems associated with Schubert's life and personality. This medical writer was prompted by contemporary pictures of Schubert – his very short stature and certain facial characteristics – to believe that the composer was affected by IUGR (intra-uterine growth retardation); this leads Neighbour to propose that behavioural "conundrums" in Schubert's life might be clinical symptoms of the fact that he could have been the singleton survivor of a "blighted twin" pregnancy, whose pre-natal memory of an intra-uterine catastrophe had profound psychological consequences (Neighbour cites research by clinical psychologists on the phenomenon of foetal memory in support of this proposal). At the end of a carefully-reasoned paper, Neighbour suggests that Schubert may have been "a man whose creative imagination was thereby predisposed to express an abiding sense of loss and incompleteness" – the character, indeed, so bleakly portrayed in Schubert's own setting of Heine's poem *Der Doppelgänger.*

If we are looking for a meaningful source for Schmalfeldt's "inward-looking" aspect of the E♭ trio's finale, might this not have something to do with it? Given the intensity of this moment, as he writes a theme for his *Andante* worthy of Beethoven and faces his own mortality, might not the abiding sense of loss which may have overshadowed his entire life be the "interiority" which he must now express – "the center of gravity toward which what comes before seems to pull, and from which all that follows seems to radiate." The final wonder is Schubert's radiant transformation of his theme into the *major* mode – one last *redeeming* statement.

Schumann made a habit of forming shrewd opinions about the music of his fellow-musicians. His judgment of Schubert's E♭ trio was that it "had passed across the face of the musical world like some angry portent in the sky". In due course we shall find that Schubert's relaxed attitude to the rigidity of the sonata framework,

---

* It is generally assumed that the syphilis which Schubert contracted in about 1822 was the cause of his death; it was probably aggravated by the side-effects of mercury, which was at that time the standard treatment.

and the piquancy of his decorative harmony, were indeed far-sighted portents of what was to follow later in the nineteenth century. But for the moment we should also note that he was only able to experiment in these ways because he could rely on his audience's familiarity with sonata form, and because of the unconditional tonal security it offered him.

CHAPTER ENDNOTES

1   Tovey, Donald Francis. 'The Main Stream of Music, the Annual Lecture on Aspects of Art of the British Academy', read on 29 June 1938, and published as *The Main Stream of Music and other Essays*, Cleveland and New York: Meridian Books (World Publishing Co), 1959, p.340.

2   Gramit, David. 'The passion for friendship: music, cultivation and identity in Schubert's circle', in *The Cambridge Companion to Schubert*, ed Christopher H Gibbs, p.58. Cambridge: Cambridge University Press, 1997.

3   Gingerich, John M. *Schubert's Beethoven project: The Chamber Music, 1824-1828*. Ph.D.diss, Yale University, 1996.

4   Cited by Leon Botstein in 'Realism transformed' in *The Cambridge Companion to Schubert*. Cambridge: Cambridge University Press, 1997, p.33.

5   Martin Chusid in 'Schubert's Chamber Music' in *The Cambridge Companion to Schubert*. Cambridge: Cambridge University Press, 1997, pp.191-192.

6   For a detailed analysis, see Smallman, *op.cit*, p.73.

7   Smallman, *op.cit*, p.80.

8   Kramer, Lawrence. *Franz Schubert*. Cambridge: Cambridge University Press, 1998. p.158; quoted by Janet Schmalfeldt in *In the Process of Becoming: Analytic and Philosophical Perspectives on Form in Early Nineteenth-Century Music*, Oxford: Oxford University Press, 2011, p.152.

9   John Gingerich, Brian Newbould and Janet Schmalfeldt; see Janet Schmalfeldt, *op.cit*, pp.154-5.

10   Newbould, Brian. *Schubert: the Music and the Man*. Berkeley: University of California Press, 1997, p.372; quoted in Schmalfeldt, *op.cit*, p.152.

11   Smallman, *op.cit*, p.80.

12   Schmalfeldt, *op.cit*, pp.134-5.

13   Schmalfeldt, *op.cit*, p.136.

14   Smallman, *op.cit*, p.75.

15   Neighbour, Roger. 'The Doppelgänger Revealed?' in *Schubert the Progressive*, ed. B Newbould, Aldershot: Ashgate, 1988, pp.139-149.

CHAPTER 12

SONATA FORM DEFINED

WE HAVE NOW followed the development of the sonata idea in the piano trio for some 70 years. We began with the birth of the instrumental structure as described by Charles Rosen:

> "The demands of an urban class eager to appropriate high culture, coinciding with the development of an efficient tonal system containing the symmetrical range of modulation of the well-tempered scale, and a neoclassical aesthetic, which stressed simplicity and clarity of structure ... – all these contributed to the creation of the sonata forms."[1]

The simplicity of the structure was evident in Kollmann's description of his plan of modulation (see Chapter 6) and we have become familiar with the tonal symmetry which underpinned the sonata concept. We have understood how contemporaries were able to follow the harmonic progressions as well as to hear the presentation and reappearance of thematic material, mirroring their experience of the process of rhetoric. At the same time, we have seen a gradual increase in sophistication in all these things. The piano trio as a work for competent amateurs has become a Grand Sonata for performance by professional musicians in a public arena – it has caught up with the string quartet and the symphony as a "serious" musical composition. It benefits too from the newfound popularity of instrumental music, and contemporary theoretical writing about the sonata applies to the piano trio as much as any other *genre*.

There was, indeed, a good deal of writing going on. We should be aware, however, that this was directed not towards listeners by way of clarification for the better enjoyment of sonatas, but rather towards composers who had ambitions of following in Beethoven's footsteps and writing successful sonatas. It is significant that three of the most influential writers had direct contact with Beethoven: two of them produced important books in his lifetime, and the third had been a pupil and knew him well.

Although Bohemian by birth, Antoine Reicha (1770-1836) lived successively in Bonn and Vienna during two periods of his life, coinciding with Beethoven and enjoying a good friendship with him. Reicha settled in Paris in 1808, became a professor at the Conservatoire and published a number of important theoretical works. He was particularly interested in musical forms, setting out a framework for what he called a "*Grande coupe binaire*" ("Great Two-Part Form") for use in (inter alia) "instrumental music for the first movement of sonatas, duos, trios, quartets, overtures, symphonies and large concertos."[2] In his *Traité de haute composition musicale* (1824-26) he added the following diagram of it to illustrate his text:[3]

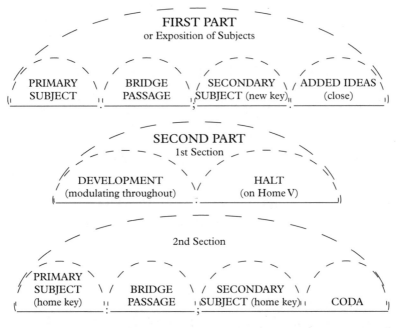

Fig. 9 Antoine Reicha: *Grande coupe binaire* [translation GP]

We recognise this as the pattern of sonata form to which we have become accustomed. John Irving draws attention to the fact that although Reicha is at pains to point out that his *Coupe* has two parts, "Première" and "Seconde Partie", his diagram is displayed on three levels, the *Développement* clearly occupying the whole of the middle level. This reflects the importance which Reicha attaches to the differentiated themes of the first level ("*première idée mère*", and "*seconde idée mère*"), so that "their subsequent development was so significant an act as to require a dedicated section in which to dissect these materials ...". Clearly, says Irving, "within Reicha's *Grande coupe binaire* there lurked a three-stage pattern of exposition, development and recapitulation, which was steadily to become the norm for nineteenth-century conceptions of sonata form."[4]

Adolf Bernard Marx (1795-1866) was a German music theorist, editor of the famous musical periodical the *Berliner Allgemeine Musikalische Zeitung* and a lifelong admirer of Beethoven, a biography of whom he published in 1859. Marx was the first writer actually to use the term *"Sonatenform"*. In 1824, discussing the historical period of Haydn and Mozart, he noted that it was characterised by

> "... more extended musical ideas and a richer sequence of melodies: the sonata- and rondo-form became prominent ... By the first term [*Sonatenform*], we mean the joining of two sections of melodies (the first in the tonic, the second in the dominant – or the first in the tonic minor, the second in the relative major), usually repeated after an interpolation [i.e. development section], with the second section transposed ... into the tonic, as in almost all movements of symphonies, quartets and sonatas."[5]

Carl Czerny (1791-1857) spent almost his entire life in Vienna. He began playing the piano at the age of three, made his concert début at the age of nine, and became a pupil of Beethoven. He built up a reputation as an outstanding teacher of the piano: his pupils included Liszt who acknowledged his indebtedness to Czerny's early discipline. His publications included several performance and composition manuals, such as the *School of Practical Composition* of c.1840, in which appeared the following description of "sonata form":

> "The first movement consists of two parts, the first of which is usually repeated.
>   This first part must comprise:
>   1. The principal subject.
>   2. Its continuation or amplification, together with a modulation into the nearest related key.
>   3. The middle subject in this new key.
>   4. A new continuation of this middle subject.
>   5. A final melody, after which the first part thus closes in the new key, in order that the repetition of the same may follow unconstrainedly.
>   The second part of the first movement commences with a development of the principal subject, or of the middle subject, or even of a new idea, passing through several keys, and returning again to the original key. Then follows the principal subject and its amplification, but usually in an abridged shape, and so modulating, that the middle subject may likewise re-appear entire, though in the

original key: after which, all that follows the middle subject in the first part, is here repeated in the original key, and thus the close is made."[6]

Note that the return to the home key in the Recapitulation remains (of course) obligatory, and that the "middle" (i.e. the 2nd) subject, must be in "the nearest related key" (i.e. the dominant, or the relative major in the case of a movement in a minor key). There is still provision for a repeat of the first Part: listeners must become thoroughly familiar with its thematic material in order fully to appreciate the treatment of it in the second Part, although there is now no expectation that the latter will also be repeated.

A growing preoccupation with thematic material is evident in all these writers. We might see this especially as a result of the demand for "originality" after Beethoven, but it also perhaps reflects the contemporary spirit of de Loutherbourg's paintings and Wordsworth's "sense sublime" (see Chapter 9) – perception and appreciation of inspirational originality is part of the new musical experience. Theorists had for some time debated "the well-known controversy as to whether harmony or melody takes precedence, whether a piece of music can be reduced ultimately to melody or harmony,"[7] but without resolving the issue had also acknowledged that whereas harmony was a subject which could be learnt by a diligent musician, the invention of truly attractive melodies could only come from a composer with real musical talent: it could not be taught. The Italian theorist Francesco Galeazzi (1758-1819) was one of the first who actually described the sonata process in terms of its distribution of themes, and he pointed out in his *Elementi teorico-pratici di Musica* of 1796 that

"We have in fact a vast quantity of authors who have written with varying degrees of success on the subject of harmony, but there is not a single one, so far as I know, who has dealt with the principal element of modern music, that is, melody ..."[8]

Note that Galeazzi has put his cards on the table: "the principal element of modern music," he says, "is melody." Theorists might not be able to teach inspiration, but they could give aspiring composers useful guidelines on a suitable style for themes.

Heinrich Christoph Koch (1749-1816), already encountered (on p.154), described the 1st subject as "a somewhat noisy/boisterous theme, expanded or bound together in several melodic parts", and the 2nd as "a cantabile theme".[9] From the examples of the trio first movements we have heard up to this point, there is nothing very new here. Burney had extolled John Bach's introduction of "contrasts" into his accompanied sonatas, and from the beginning of the sonata idea contrasting thematic material had been an important part of defining different tonal areas. If we think back to Mozart's C major Trio K.548, the tonic key is emphatically defined by the fanfare on the tonic triad which opens the first movement (what better way of establishing home tonality than using those fundamental harmonic sounds?), and then the graceful 2nd subject identifies the arrival in the dominant with a very different, chromatically-ingratiating theme.

But the theorists were now in full swing. Czerny puts forward his proposals for the contrasting 2nd subject:

"Now follows the middle subject, which must consist of a new idea. A good middle subject is much more difficult to invent, than the commencement; for *first*: it must possess a new and more beautiful and pleasing melody than all which precedes; and *secondly*, it must be very different from the foregoing, but yet, according to its character, so well suited thereto, that it may appear like the object or result of all the preceding ideas, modulations or passages ..."[10]

A point of no return was reached when Marx famously proposed that the opening *"Hauptsatz"* (principal theme) should be *"Männliche"* (masculine), in contrast with the *"Seitensatz"* (secondary theme) which should be *"Weibliche"* (feminine). This was an idea which could easily be grasped by everybody, composers and listeners alike, and it coloured not only the sonata repertoire, but listeners' perceptions and anticipation of what style of music might follow. It had unfortunate consequences in that in some quarters it trivialised the sonata repertoire as composers scrambled to invent gender-charged material to please the purchasing public. To an extent it also distorted the historical view of sonata form, as students struggle to see how Haydn's monothematic sonata movements (for instance) can fit into the mould of the supposed importance of contrasting themes.

The distortions in the historical record created by nineteenth-century theorists have largely been corrected. The Classical sonata is now seen as both a harmonic and a thematic construct, both binary and ternary in concept. "Musical form in the Classical era", says Bonds, "was conceived of thematically in both the musical and rhetorical senses of the term: the elaboration of a central idea was seen to shape the trajectory of subsequent ideas (including the recurrence of the central idea) throughout a movement."[11] So the First Part of the old binary framework remains the same, following the trajectory of I to V, but the melodic content (thematic material) which so illuminates that first part has acquired such a life of its own that – before the Second Part can return to fulfil the old intentions

– it must be allowed to run its course in a free development section, a freedom which applies to both the harmonic as well as the melodic content. Thus, as we saw in Chapter 7, the new three-part thematic concept works *with*, not *against*, the old two-part harmonic structure.

The trivialising tendency of the masculine/feminine description was less easily countered. We have seen that although the eighteenth-century composer's inherited baggage of the 8-bar dance-song gave his audience a basis for understanding classical tonality, in practice musicians had not always slavishly relied on tidy 8-bar "tunes" for thematic material. Themes were broken down into smaller components, smaller phrases and motifs used as the basis of organic growth; we have seen such motifs used as the basis of transitional material, or cadential themes; in the far-ranging sequences of development sections, or even transformation into new themes. This was an intellectual process far more difficult to achieve than merely stitching pretty tunes together. Over the first half of the nineteenth century, the metaphor of rhetoric applied to music gradually declined. This was partly due to the fact that the academic discipline of rhetoric itself fell into decline, but also because rhetoric had served its purpose for music – it had helped to encourage listening habits. Listeners could now hear and detect organic musical growth for themselves.

But if it was easier to *compose* pretty tunes than to devise the organic growth and majestic development of "marked for memory" motifs, it was also easier to *listen* to pretty tunes. And listeners often took the easier option, so that during the following years of the nineteenth century there was a great deal of sonata music for piano trio in different styles to be found across Europe. We shall follow sonata form in the "serious" Austro-German mainstream, but also seek out its development elsewhere, bearing in mind Charles Rosen's warning at the end of his great book on *Sonata Forms*:

"The prestige of [Sonata] form was a conservative force in Romantic and post-Romantic music, and it acted as a brake on the most revolutionary developments. It also, indeed, sometimes provided a well-built but artificially-designed channel for the newer modes of expression. Yet the discontinuity in the history of sonata form has an odd consequence: the most original uses of the form – those of Brahms and Bartók among others – do not take over from the work of the previous generation and build on what they have done but return to Haydn, Mozart, Beethoven and Schubert.

After Beethoven, the sonata was the vehicle of the sublime. It played the same role in music as the epic in poetry, and the large historical fresco in painting. The proof of craftsmanship was the fugue, but the proof of greatness was the sonata."[12]

CHAPTER ENDNOTES

1   Rosen, *Sonata Forms,* p.11

2   Reicha, Antoine. *Traité de mélodie,* Paris, 1814, p.48; quoted by Bonds, *Wordless Rhetoric,* p.151.

3   Reicha, Antoine. *Traité de haute composition musicale,* 2 vols, Paris: Zetter (1824-26), II, p.300; reproduced in *Music Theory in the Age of Romanticism,* ed. by Ian Bent, Cambridge: Cambridge University Press, 2008, in Peter Hoyt, 'The Concept of développement in the early nineteenth century', Part III, p.142.

4   Irving, John. *Understanding Mozart's Piano Sonatas.* Farnham: Ashgate, 2010, pp.33-34.

5   Marx, Adolf Bernard. *Berliner Allgemeine Musikalische Zeitung,* vol.I, 1824, pp.444-8; quoted in Bonds, *Wordless Rhetoric,* pp.37-8, fn.50.

6   Czerny, Carl. *School of Practical Composition,* transl. J Bishop, 3 vols, London: Robert Cocks, c.1848; quoted in Bonds, *Wordless Rhetoric,* p.32.

7   Koch, Heinrich Christoph. *Versuch einer Anleitung zur Composition.* Leipzig: A F Böhme, 1782-3, vol.II, pp.47-50; quoted in Bonds, *ibid,* p.45.

8   Galeazzi, Francesco. *Elementi teorico-pratici di Musica.* Rome, 1796, vol.II, p.xvii; quoted in Bonds, *ibid,* p.48.

9   Koch, *ibid,* 1793, vol.III; quoted in Hepokoski and Darcy, *op.cit,* p.118.

10   Czerny, *School of Practical Composition,* vol.I, p.35; quoted in Bonds, *ibid,* p.33.

11   Bonds, *ibid,* p.114.

12   Rosen, *op.cit,* p.366.

CHAPTER 13

VIRTUOSO PERFORMERS: CHOPIN, SPOHR

THE FIRST HALF of the nineteenth century was *par excellence* the era of the travelling *virtuosi*. After Hummel came the pianists Clementi, Cramer, Moscheles and Ries, and the violinists Rode, Kreutzer, Spohr, Lafour and Boucher. But even the brilliance of performers such as these was as nothing compared with the sensational technical prowess of Nicolò Paganini (1782-1840) and Franz Liszt (1811-1886). It was Paganini's prodigious mastery of his instrument – the innovatory passage-work and double-stopping – which inspired Liszt to do for the piano what Paganini had done for the violin. We will return to Liszt later, but first we should follow the consequences of the demands made by the piano *virtuosi* on the instrument itself – because they have a direct influence on the music written for the piano trio ensemble.

As performance techniques improved and expanded, performers wanted ever more from the instrument. They wanted its compass extended: where Mozart's piano had 5 octaves, and Beethoven's over 6, they now expected to be able to match the range of the orchestra with yet more treble and bass notes. They also wanted a wider dynamic range (from *fff* to *ppp*) and a more powerful sound to fill the larger performing spaces of concert halls. French workshops entered the piano manufacturing market shortly after 1800. At first they copied the action of English pianos, but soon they far outdistanced them with inventions and improvements of their own. One of the most successful of the French manufacturers was Ignace Pleyel (later joined by his son, Camille). Pleyel pianos had a light touch and a clear sound, said to have been enhanced by the soundboard of mahogany veneer which ran across pine boards beneath the strings. Another innovative French manufacturer was Sébastien Erard, who in the 1820s introduced a double escapement mechanism which

allowed for more rapid repetition of a single note than had previously been possible.

The quality of the sound of Pleyel pianos particularly appealed
to a young and unknown Polish pianist, who produced a piano trio
outside Germany in the year after Schubert's E♭ trio.

Fryderyk Chopin (1810-1849) was born near Warsaw. His exceptional musical ability was recognised early, but Warsaw was culturally isolated from the rest of Europe and although "Mr Schoppin"
performed in public for the first time at the age of eight, the fluent
and expressive piano technique he subsequently developed was
largely self-taught. It grew from an intuitive understanding of the
sound effects possible on the new nineteenth-century instrument,
coupled with a lively appreciation of the rhythmic vitality of his native
Polish folk music, which he had often enjoyed on summer holidays
in the country. Chopin heard Hummel perform in 1828, and the
following year Paganini also came to Warsaw. The young teenager
was inspired by these two brilliant executants to write his first piece
of chamber music, the piano trio in g minor. It was dedicated to
one of his aristocratic patrons, Prince Antoni Radziwill – who was an
accomplished amateur 'cellist and himself took the 'cello part. The
year following its completion Chopin left Warsaw to become the idol
of the Paris salons.

Although this is such an early work – and Chopin's only piano trio
– it is written with tremendous confidence. The piano part is fluent
and accomplished, but the strings are by no means second-class
observers, both participating freely in the presentation of thematic
material. Moreover in spite of the intricacy of the piano writing, it
never drowns the string parts.

The first movement is marked *Allegro con fuoco*:

**F Chopin: 1st movement *Allegro con fuoco* from Piano Trio
in G minor op.8**

Exposition: The movement opens resolutely with five firm chords,
1(a), followed by 8 quasi-improvisatory bars – ending enigmati-
cally on a forceful diminished 7th chord. This could lead anywhere,
but actually slips down to c minor, which colours two extended
statements of another sentence which follows, 1(b): this is a lyrical
rising phrase characterised by off-beat accents.

Ex. 26.1

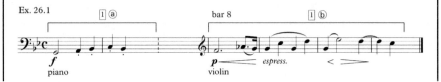

Chopin marks the closing cadence *ritardando* ("slowing down") as though emphasising the demarcation between the home tonic area of the 1st subject and the transitional passage we now expect. This duly features lively new dotted-quaver figures and leads to a firm V cadence – but it is still the home V. Nevertheless, we sense arrival at the **2nd subject** area – and now we have none other than 1(b) again, with further figurative accompaniments, all still in the home key. At bar 53 a new motif (2) makes a brief appearance,

but then 1(b) returns to feature again in the cadence figures. After a piquant interrupted cadence (taking us up a semitone to E♭ major) the Exposition closes back in the home tonic of g minor (the repeat is marked).

The **Development** veers immediately away into the minor mode of home V: 1(a) is heard loudly in the piano answered by 1(b) in the strings in octave unison. This motif dominates most of the section, either by the strings in unison or answering each other above agile decorative semiquavers in the piano. An abrupt interrupted cadence leads up the semitone from G to A♭: a series of long pedal notes racks up the tension as they rise from A♭ to the home V of D.

The **Recapitulation** returns with 1(a) and then 1(b) as previously heard in the Exposition; but after the transition the repeat becomes less faithful as a parody of (2) is heard in d minor (the minor mode of the home V). This time the interrupted cadence takes us to 1(b) in the relative major (B♭), but the minor mode returns with the home key and continues to brood over scintillating piano figuration in a **Coda** which brings the movement to a brilliant close.

Sonata Form was not a structural framework to which Chopin was often to turn. In all he wrote only five such works: three sonatas for solo piano and one for 'cello and piano, in addition to the present piano trio. Significantly perhaps, all are in minor keys; and in the later works Janet Schmalfeldt has demonstrated that although Chopin's musical language "firmly remains within the domain of the tonic-dominant axis" he became particularly fond of ascending-third harmonic progressions, i.e. I – III – V.[1] We look in vain for many of these in this early trio; however, we can hear piquant experimental harmonies and there are some instances of third progressions in this first movement. Rather curiously, Chopin retains the home tonic minor key almost throughout the Exposition; the only relief comes in the transitional passage, where he moves from g minor to B♭ major (i – III – i: a "closed, symmetric harmonic foundation"[2]). Almost perversely, in the Recapitulation he moves out of i into the dominant *minor* key for the 2nd subject, but then shifts down a third back to III (B♭ major) before ending in g minor (i.e. following a descending thirds trajectory D – B♭- G).

However, this first movement has other attractions. The piano part is beautifully written, giving us some idea of how Chopin himself might have sounded in performance, whether he is stepping in with a *bravura* punctuation or supporting the strings with an accompaniment of filigree patterning. The string parts in turn carry a good deal of thematic weight, often extracting motifs from themes and exchanging these in fine quasi-contrapuntal textures, or passionately asserting a theme doubled at the octave as in the Development. The violin part lies comparatively low in its register, which adds extra sonority to the texture, allowing the piano to glisten in the higher octaves.

The choice of the minor mode for this work is an interesting one. This is only the third trio in a minor key we have so far encountered, and like Beethoven's op.1 no 3 it fulfils Hepokoski and Darcy's description of the minor mode as "a sign of a troubled condition", here again with more involvement than the Classical detachment of Haydn's Hob XV:12. The first and last movements are in the home tonic minor, and in both it suits well: the first because it fits the mood of Romantic melancholy, and the last because it reflects the minor mode inflections of Polish national music.

The second and third movements are respectively in G major and E♭ major, thus tracing an overall progression from i – I – ♭VI – i. The order of the movements follows Beethoven's precedent, the second being a Scherzo and Trio, and the third an *Adagio sostenuto* (a beautifully lyrical movement with emotional chromatic harmony).

As we might expect of a composer who wrote so many short dances and *genre* pieces for piano – *polonaises, mazurkas, waltzes* and so on – the most innovative movement is the finale, which is enlivened by the rhythm of a traditional Polish dance. The *krakowiak* has two beats to the bar, the first beat typically having two quavers leading to an unusual accent on the second.

F Chopin: 4th movement *Allegretto* from Piano Trio in G minor op.8

This is a straightforward **Rondo** movement, in which the *krakowiak* theme serves as the rondo subject,

Ex. 26.3

Piano

sotto voce

alternating with another dance-like theme with a similar rhythm as 2nd subject. Chopin gives us a pleasing surprise later in the movement, when the rondo and the 2nd subject are heard simultaneously. Finally, the violin and then the 'cello return to the rondo theme, and the piano finishes the movement with brilliant fingerwork against the simple *krakowiak* in the violin.

R – 2nd subj – **R** – 2nd subj – **R**+2nd together – **R**

This finale is an early example of a sonata work enlivened by a national folk idiom (although we have already heard another in Haydn's trio Hob XV:25). We shall hear more of these during the second half of the nineteenth century, as music began to play a part in nationalist movements across Europe. Here we have a lively variation on classical traditions, and not surprisingly, it is well-suited for use in a Rondo finale: the compact, regular structure of the *krakowiak* fits well into the formal setting, and its constant return seems eminently appropriate – constantly return is, of course, exactly what a dance tune does … Its energising rhythm gives the movement forward impetus as well as distinctive character. It is Chopin's brilliant writing for his own instrument, however, which makes this movement exceptional. Pleyel pianos were renowned for their "bright, silvery sound", and we can hear exactly why Chopin favoured them. This would be just the clarity required for the tracery of fingerwork which he writes as accompaniment to the rhythms of the dance.

★ ★ ★ ★ ★

Public performances of chamber music seem to have been less popular elsewhere across the continent than in Germany and Austria. In Italy there was little interest in instrumental music because the people were permanently in thrall to opera. As the mantle of Rossini passed to Bellini and Donizetti, outside Italy this operatic style came to be regarded by many as increasingly shallow. (It is worth noting, however, that during the second quarter of the nineteenth century the tenor replaced Rossini's female contralto, successor to the old *castrato*, as the traditional voice for the hero: it was felt that the *timbre* of the tenor voice added more dramatic intensity to heroic roles. We shall see that it is about the same time that composers of piano trios send the 'cello soaring into its upper registers to deliver melodies with a similar emotional intensity – although it would be some time before virtuoso 'cellists emerged whose playing compared with that of violinists and pianists.)

In Paris, too, opera continued to be the most popular form of musical entertainment. But during the first half of the nineteenth century there was also a great deal of music to be heard in the salons of wealthy industrialists, bankers and the prosperous commercial classes. There was little appetite here for chamber music, however. Visiting Paris in the early decades of the century, the German musician Louis Spohr (1784-1859) records in his diary that

> "... one rarely hears in musical circles here a serious, substantial piece of music, such as a quartet or quintet by one of our great masters ... nothing but ... *airs variés, rondos favoris, nocturnes* and similar trifles ... I ... often have the feeling of speaking to people who do not understand my language."[3]

In London this *virtuoso* violinist found that English snobbery towards musicians still persisted. In the same diary, Spohr complains bitterly about the "shabby" way in which artists were treated in London. He was particularly incensed by a visit to the Duke and Duchess of Clarence. He had known the Duchess before her marriage as a princess in Meiningen, where she had treated him with the respect and appreciation normally accorded to musicians in Germany. In England, however,

> "... [artists] were not permitted to appear among the invited company, but had to wait in a separate room until summoned to appear ..."

Spohr, following German custom, insisted on being treated as a guest, but the servants refused to serve him until told to do so by the Duke. Other performers had included

> "... the elite of the most distinguished artists and virtuosos of London ... they seemed lost upon the illustrious audience, for conversation continued without a moment's interruption ... "

The room was only quieter for an especially popular female singer. The guests were – literally – dumbstruck when Spohr took his place

"... I began to play, dispensing with the preliminary obeisance. The foregoing must have attracted the attention of the company, for there was complete silence in the room while I played. When I had finished, the Duke and Duchess applauded, the others joining in."[4]

Louis Spohr was only 14 years younger than Beethoven, but he lived a good deal longer and his career extended well into the nineteenth century. At the height of his early fame as a violinist he was regarded as second only to Paganini, but later he enjoyed another career as a composer. His music was very successful across Europe, but particularly so in England, where he became the most popular composer after Mendelssohn; the English musician Stanford (born at the end of Spohr's lifetime) used to say that in his youth many people considered Spohr a greater composer than Beethoven; and the renowned English music critic J W Davison wrote that "his influence will survive until the art is on its deathbed". He was also a renowned violin teacher (he introduced the chin-rest for the violin); and a gifted conductor (he was one of the first to use the baton for conducting); but our interest in Spohr is that his works include music for piano trio.

Spohr's five piano trios were written late in his career, after his second marriage to Marianne Pfeiffer, a *virtuoso* pianist. In his fifties Spohr re-lived some of the adulation of his earlier days by going on concert tours with Marianne, for whom he wrote a number of concert works. She brought him not only firsthand contact with the latest piano techniques, but also a reason for writing piano trios, which they performed at public concerts together with his old quartet colleague, the 'cellist Nikolaus Hasemann.

The first edition of the second Trio in F major, op.123, announces on the titlepage that it is a *Trio Concertant* – which will therefore require *virtuoso* playing from all three performers.

L Spohr: 1st movement *Allegro moderato* from Trio no 2 in F major op.123

Exposition: the movement opens with the **1st subject (1)**, divided between the piano and the strings hovering between home I and relative minor tonality:

Ex. 27.1

This is followed by a counterphrase lasting 8 bars, so that we do not hear (1) again until the violin and 'cello return to it (in parallel 6ths) at bar 13. Again the counterphrase intervenes, and the spaciousness of the movement is confirmed by a third statement over a long I pedal low in the piano. The distinctive rhythm of the first two bars then leads into the Transition, which shortly cadences on G (V of V) before rising scale figuration leads into the **2nd subject**. This theme has distinctive dotted quaver rhythms, and is first heard in the violin and 'cello in unison, low in their registers, while the piano softly drums out handfuls of notes in repeated, chromatically-rising chords.

Ex. 27.2

Again, there is a cadence on G, then the same rising scale figuration in the piano leads to another statement by the strings (soon coloured by Spohr's hallmark piano figuration: falling *appoggiatura* thirds, high in its register). This too comes back to V of V, and the piano picks up the dotted quaver rhythm. The end of the Exposition is announced as Spohr follows Mozart's example (K.548) and returns briefly to (1) – ready to return for the repeat (which is marked) or proceed on to the Development.

The **Development** is concerned entirely with the 1st subject. It begins in d minor with the 'cello plunging almost to its lowest note, well below the piano. Then all the instruments take up the dotted rhythm of the second bar. The harmonies shift until landing on the key of D in a passage of intense chromaticism, and we sense a cadence on the home V about to lead us home to F major. But our expectations are foiled by an interrupted cadence which takes us instead up a semitone to the ♭VI key of D♭; here (1) sings out softly and effectively, and then is tossed between all three instruments until Spohr lands on a chord of E major – this is held for 9 bars until suddenly he slips back into home I. (This is a highly unconventional approach – but perhaps we are to sense these 9 bars as merely a temporary interruption before the double return to home key and 1st subject.)

> **Recapitulation:** more wayward keys follow and it is not until the rising scale figuration returns to re-introduce the 2nd subject that we feel safely settled again in home tonality. The rest follows regularly, with a good deal of colourful decorative figuration in all three instruments, until the return of the 1st subject ushers in a short valedictory **Coda.**

With the benefit of hindsight, we can see both why Spohr may have been so popular in his lifetime, and also why his music has now so largely been forgotten. Of course there are good things about this movement. Spohr's music has a most appealing flow; he invents attractive themes and it is easy to follow his layout with his careful preparation for each theme. Moreover, he perfectly understands the nature and technique of each instrument. Both strings explore their wide pitch range and there are not only interesting parts for each individually, but attractive sonorities when they play together. The piano part is immensely rich and idiomatic; although it has its fair share of thematic material, at other times it fills out the texture with a constant patter of 3rd, 6th, octave or chordal doubling. Although the benign classical influence of Mozart can be felt, Spohr's style, however, lacks the hallmarks of Mozart's light contrapuntal textures and varied pace. We also miss Beethoven's sense of a dramatic narrative driving through to a final climax in the Coda, and most of all the development of thematic motifs which drive that narrative. Spohr does not develop his themes: he simply repeats them, over and over again – and after a time this becomes fatally tedious.

There were other composers as well as Spohr who wrote sonata works which built on the inherited tradition of the classical sonata form. The German Romantic opera composer Heinrich Marschner (1795-1861) wrote seven such piano trios. The established thematic framework served him and many others as a form to accommodate changing tastes and melodic fashions. These might be presented in the form of an assertive, masculine 1st subject and pretty, feminine 2nd, or as linked rhythmic/melodic motifs which added a sense of consistency to the whole. We could listen to any of these sonata form movements (and there were often two such in each trio – not only the first but the last movement as well) and feel confident that we fully understand the musical narrative, so traditionally and clearly is it presented. These composers were very competent musical craftsmen and their music was fluent and enjoyable. But it was also, almost always, *predictable* – so that it lacks the profundity and originality of Beethoven, and the melodic gifts and the element of surprise in Schubert.

So to follow the path of the gifted Austro-German mainstream dedicated to the inheritance of the traditions of Beethoven and

Schubert, we must now turn to two gifted German families, first to the Mendelssohns, and then to the Schumanns.

CHAPTER ENDNOTES

1   Schmalfeldt, *In the process of Becoming*, pp.195ff.

2   Rink, John. 'Tonal Architecture in the Early Music' in *The Cambridge Companion to Chopin*. Cambridge: Cambridge University Press, 1992, pp.78-97.

3   Spohr, Louis. *The Musical Journeys of Louis Spohr*. Modern edition transl. and ed. Henry Pleasants, Norman: University of Oklahoma Press, 1961, p.233.

4   Spohr, *ibid*, p.213.

CHAPTER 14

THE AUSTRO-GERMAN MAINSTREAM 2: FELIX MENDELSSOHN AND FANNY MENDELSSOHN-HENSEL

FELIX MENDELSSOHN (1809-1847) was born into an exceptionally cultured and cosmopolitan family. His grandfather was the Enlightenment philosopher Moses Mendelssohn (the model for Lessing's *Nathan der Weise*), his father was a successful banker and his mother had come from an equally affluent and particularly musical background. To these enviable advantages Felix himself could add a phenomenal aptitude for music; Charles Rosen describes him as

"... the greatest child prodigy the history of western music has ever known. Not even Mozart or Chopin before the age of nineteen could equal the mastery that Mendelssohn already possessed when he was only sixteen."[1]

Felix and his older sister Fanny were given piano instruction at an early age with the best teachers available. Both children also had lessons in musical theory and composition from C F Zelter, who could offer them in Berlin a peerless pedagogical link back to the music of J S Bach: his older colleague C F C Fasch had been a contemporary of C P E Bach some 60 years earlier in that same city at the court of Frederick the Great.[2] Zelter also introduced Felix to Goethe and to Hummel, both of whom were formative influences on the young composer – Goethe with his Romantic view of the dynamic importance of the arts, and Hummel as another direct link to great music of the past, this time with Mozart (he probably also gave Felix some piano lessons). A steady stream of other distinguished intellectuals and artists passed through the Mendelssohn house, in addition

204

to the musicians who came to their *Sonntagsmusik*, weekly concerts held every Sunday morning. In this way Felix was introduced to Beethoven's champion A B Marx, as well as to Hegel, whose lectures on aesthetics he later heard at the University of Berlin. Hegel's views on instrumental music must have fallen on fertile ground:

> "even in instrumental music the composer should devote equal attention to two aspects – musical structure, and the expression of an admittedly indeterminate content."

Felix had been composing music since the age of eleven. His first work was a short piano piece (no doubt proudly performed at the *Sonntagsmusik*), but it was soon followed by a stream of concertos, symphonies, sonatas, chamber and choral works. Rosen's estimate of mastery at sixteen refers to the composition of the string Octet written in October 1825. It is brilliantly scored for all eight instruments, incorporates precocious treatment of form and thematic material (it "operates like a large interconnected organic system embodying its own internal teleology and generative process"[3]) and the first appearance of Mendelssohn's famous "elfin" sound (relevant here as we shall shortly encounter this sound in a piano trio).

The general outlines of Mendelssohn's subsequent career are well-known: he wrote prolifically in almost all *genres*, both vocal and instrumental. His music was performed across Europe, often directed by the composer himself, who travelled widely and was an inspiring conductor. He is also credited with re-establishing J S Bach's choral works and generally forging a historical orientation in the concert repertoire. His music was especially popular in England, which he visited ten times, and where he became a favourite of Queen Victoria and Prince Albert. When he suffered a fatal stroke at the early age of 38 in 1847, his death was announced in *The Musical World* as the "eclipse of music" and mourned as "an international tragedy".[4]

Yet this golden reputation faded almost as quickly as it had arisen. Not long after his death – and indeed for the next hundred years or so – it became the fashion to dismiss Mendelssohn as merely a talented musician whose work was too sentimental to be taken with real seriousness.

Since 1945, however, this derogatory view has been vigorously challenged by new scholarly research. It seems that the loss of reputation had a number of contributory causes. These included the immediate and indiscriminate publication after his death of all the music which publishers could lay hands on, which included not only many works which Mendelssohn himself had already rejected for publication – he was scrupulously self-critical – but also many ephemeral pieces such as *Lieder ohne Worte* ("works whose effectiveness inhered

largely in their usefulness, and whose usefulness quickly passed"[5]).
These were probably never intended for publication and may have
distorted the record; during his lifetime Mendelssohn released "only
seventy-two numbered *opera* and an additional twenty-four minor
publications – this out of a corpus of several hundred compositions."[6]

Another contributory cause was more insidious: this was the
publication of the infamous essay *Das Judenthum in der Musik*★ only
three years after Mendelssohn's death. This was an example of the
anti-Semitism rife throughout the nineteenth century, and it may
have contributed to a misunderstanding of Mendelssohn's unique
cultural position★★ and undermined the appreciation of his music.
Returning to primary sources, modern scholars have revealed
that numerous facts and documents relating to his life have been
distorted and in some cases even fabricated. Thus since 1945 a good
deal of the accumulated lumber of ignorance and prejudice has been
cleared away, and Mendelssohn revealed again as a deeply serious
musician, a worthy contributor to the Austro-German mainstream.

Mendelssohn wrote three piano trios: the first at the age of 11
(now lost, but scored for viola instead of 'cello), and the last two not
until much later in his career – op.49 in 1839 and op.66 in 1845.
Reviewing op.49, Schumann called it

> "... the master trio of the present era, just as, in their times, were the
> B♭ and D major trios of Beethoven, and that of Schubert in E♭. It is a
> beautiful composition that years from now will delight our grandchil-
> dren and great-grandchildren"[7]

**F Mendelssohn: 1st movement *Molto allegro ed agitato*
from Piano Trio no 1 in D minor op.49**

Exposition: The home tonic key is established by the anxiously
restless **1st subject** in the 'cello – articulating at (a) the most sensitive and defining notes of d minor, *viz* the tonic, leading note and
minor third. We hear it as an initial 4-bar phrase with an answering

---

★ The author of the essay was Richard Wagner – it was first published under
a pseudonym in 1850, but reissued under Wagner's own name in 1869. The gist
of the essay was that Jews spoke German badly, and that they must therefore
be unmusical and incapable of serious musical composition. It also specifically
attacked Meyerbeer and Mendelssohn.

★★ Mendelssohn actually spent most of his life as a Christian: his father Abraham
had his children baptised as Lutherans as early as 1816, and Felix married the
daughter of a Lutheran pastor. For a thoughtful discussion of Mendelssohn's
Jewish ancestry and Lutheran conversion see Michael P Steinberg, 'Mendelssohn
and Judaism' in *The Cambridge Companion to Mendelssohn*, pp.26-41.

4 bars (although – as Schmalfeldt points out[8] – it is written out as 16 bars).

The violin responds, opening out the rising intervals as a pair of expressive 6ths, and then another distinctive phrase (a sequence of falling thirds) completes the opening material. Home tonality continues for 28 more bars – unostentatious contrapuntal scale passages passing between all three instruments – to a *ff* cadence. (1)(a) is heard again powerfully, low in piano and 'cello. Harmonies begin shifting and we recognise Classical procedures as this motif 1(a) is used as the basis of sequences which fuel a transitional passage; a beautiful 4-bar sequence of falling 7ths endorses V of V; and 17 bars later slow trills on V in each instrument usher in the **2nd subject**. This is first heard in the 'cello – a phrase of evenly-flowing crotchets which rise up the V (major) triad and then fall down to its own V.

It is taken up by all instruments in turn, finally cadencing firmly in home V. Halfway through the ensuing cadential passages Mendelssohn reverts to Mozart's practice and re-introduces (1)(a) (in V), driving to a firm cadence. There is now no giveaway double bar – so no repeat sign – but this feels like the end of a Classical Exposition, especially as the 'cello immediately embarks on the opening phrase of (1) in V.

The **Development** is skilfully managed. It begins slowly on a soft dynamic plateau, with first (1)(a) and then (2). Gradually these statements grow in intensity as the piano accompaniment accelerates into quavers, then triplet quavers, against fragments of each theme in flowing counterpoint. Finally the piano drives the chromatic motif from (1)(a) in sequences onto the home V: the strings respond with (2); a climax on home V fades over 18 bars and finally we are ready for the return of the anxious 1st subject:

The **Recapitulation** condenses the Exposition; all the original thematic material is there but with two unexpected twists: a new countersubject emerges for (1)(a), and (2) is now heard in the tonic major. By the end of the section we are back in tonic minor.

The **Coda** begins majestically with the chromatic opening motif of (1): it sounds out in three-part canon, the violin and 'cello two octaves apart against powerful chords in the piano. The strings then bring back (2) for two last *ff* statements, which metamorphose into the closing peroration, and a dramatic final statement of the first subject.

In another part of the review of this trio Schumann had more to say about Mendelssohn himself:

"He is the Mozart of the nineteenth century, the most brilliant musician, the one who most clearly sees through the contradictions of the age and for the first time reconciles them."[9]

With his customary acumen Schumann points directly to the most intriguing aspect of this movement: what Greg Vitercik has described as Mendelssohn's "reconciliation of his highly individual lyric impulse with the imperatives of sonata-form processes."[10]

Mozart is the model for this sonata form framework: where Beethoven and Schubert had ventured into new tonal areas in their sonatas, Mendelssohn remains firmly rooted in the simpler old I–V relationship. There is no double bar at the end of this Exposition, but we perfectly hear it close on that firm V cadence, just as we hear the wandering keys of the Development, and the long V preparation before all the themes come home in the Recapitulation.

Mendelssohn takes a different view of his thematic material, however. Whereas the Classical sonata, as we have seen, tended to use contrasting thematic material to underline the difference in tonal areas, and this material was subservient to the framework, Mendelssohn's themes occupy centre-stage and have become the driving force of this movement. Not long before the composition of this trio he had written to Wilhelm von Boguslawski:

"I want the [thematic] ideas to be expressed more simply and more naturally, but to be conceived in a more complex and individual fashion."[11]

Janet Schmalfeldt points out that whereas Mozartian themes are "discrete, complete and self-contained", Mendelssohn has a "capacity for obfuscating some of the formal boundaries that are so clearly

articulated in earlier classical styles."[12] We have to listen very carefully as he expands and develops motifs derived from each theme,
endlessly micro-managing the compositional process, compelling the
listener to follow his train of thought. And it is of course here that
the old pedagogue Zelter's rigorous contrapuntal training proves so
useful – counterpoint was a skill which had become a habit of mind
for Mendelssohn. As we hear those lyrically flowing lines we are
hardly aware of how cleverly the thematic ideas are being combined,
interwoven, interlocked.

Mendelssohn is in his lyrical element in the slow movement, effectively a *"Song without words"* with beautifully-balanced phrases and
a contrasting central section in the minor mode. But the following
Scherzo is perhaps his most distinctively original contribution to the
trio literature. It is written in his famous "elfin" style and there is a
great deal of technical skill beneath its quicksilver brilliance. It is not
just a simple Scherzo with a contrasting Trio: Mendelssohn shows
his easy relationship with the past by setting it in sonata form, as
follows:

**F Mendelssohn: 3rd movement Scherzo: *leggiero e vivace*
from Piano Trio no 1 in D minor op.49**

Exposition: So much of this movement is generated by the featherweight bustle of its opening notes, wittily decorating the tonic and
then the dominant triads. This is the **1st subject**, first heard in the
piano.

Ex. 28.3

It trips off through neat harmonic sequences until we hear the
harmony settling round the home V. The 2nd subject immediately
follows in the violin – skipping down from top to bottom of a scale,
only momentarily delayed by an unexpected semitone obstructing
the final note; this is rapidly circumvented and in no time the violin
is home. The bustling opening returns, briefly reinventing itself for
5 bars as a little cadence figure, and then the piano heads back into
a full statement of the 1st subject (in the home key, as though this
was going to be a repeat of the Exposition). But there are no repeat
marks and a few seconds later Mendelssohn is off in all sorts of
different tonal directions.

The extended **Development** which follows is a brilliant display of Mendelssohn's skills as a contrapuntist. All the instruments skittishly play catch with the featherweight figure, tossing it from one to another through innumerable dexterous harmonic changes and dynamic contrasts from *pianissimo* to *fortissimo*. Suddenly all goes quiet and we hear the harmonies shifting towards the home V – and shortly after the violin has us back in the Recapitulation.

Recapitulation:

The 1st subject returns, the 2nd skips down its scale as before, and then yet more intangible variants of the featherweight figure return. Finally, with gossamer lightness, and as though we had imagined it all, it fades away to nothing.

The "elfin" style first appeared in the piano figuration of some of Mendelssohn's early chamber music. It matured in the Octet, where, as Thomas Schmidt-Beste observes, "the movement appears in the autograph score without any corrections; obviously, it was written in a moment of complete inspiration."[13] Mendelssohn's sister Fanny recorded that this music was inspired by the closing lines of *Walpurgis Night's Dream* from Goethe's *Faust*:

> "Cloud and mist drift off with speed,
> Aloft 'tis brighter growing.
> Breeze in leaves and wind in reed,
> And all away is blowing."[14]

She also left an account of how Felix intended the movement to be performed:

> "The whole piece is to be played staccato and pianissimo, the tremulandos entering every now and then, the trills passing away with the quickness of lightning; everything is new and strange and at the same time most insinuating and pleasing. One feels near the world of spirits, carried away in the air, half inclined to snatch up a broomstick and follow the aerial procession. At the end the first violin takes a flight with a feather-like lightness – and all away is blowing."[15]

A year later, in 1826, Mendelssohn used the same style again to characterise Puck in his Overture to *A Midsummer Night's Dream*.

After this ethereal effervescence there follows a final Sonata Rondo movement, *Allegro assai appassionato*, in which all three instruments are given full rein for brilliant display.

Their gilt-edged cultural upbringing had given Felix and Fanny a passionate interest in all the arts, not only in music. Mendelssohn was also a gifted artist and draughtsman – his painting of Durham Cathedral, done on an early visit to England in 1830, is proof of his considerable artistic as well as musical talent. A detailed study of this picture may also enable us to draw some interesting parallels with his music.

Felix Mendelssohn, *Durham Cathedral*, 1830.
Berlin, Staatsbibliothek.

This is indisputably a romanticised representation. Mendelssohn is manipulating the scene in front of him to create his own vision of the venerable building. The stonework of the cathedral is in reality a deeper, warmer colour than this, and the trees in the foreground have surely obligingly re-arranged themselves to provide such a perfectly-shaped framework. The way in which the scene has been manipulated may tell us something about Mendelssohn's romanticising processes, particularly in his use of colour, form and detail.

To begin with colour. The subject-matter of the painting is the cathedral, so Mendelssohn depicts it in shades of pale blue-grey to give it an aura of ethereal distance. This colouring is linked not only to the sky in the background, but picked up also in the foliage of the middle-distance, and again in the stream running across the foreground. Thus Mendelssohn is using blue for both focus and integration – in much the same way as he uses theme and motif for focus and integration in sonata form.

Secondly, the use of form. The shape of the cathedral itself is in no need of manipulation, and its architectural balance and regularity are faithfully reproduced (just as Mendelssohn fulfils expectations of musical architecture with regular 8-bar themes and balanced phrases). The arching trees provide the formal setting for the building, their dark palette, not only highlighting the distant scene, but creating an arched shape through which it can be effectively viewed. The musical parallel for this is the tonal framework of the sonata movement, which creates stability for the enjoyment of each theme: the arching trees are like Transitional and Cadential passages which highlight the arrival at the next significant theme – a tonal framework for thematic display.

Lastly, Mendelssohn's use of detail. Each layer of detail is carefully arranged – distance, middle ground and foreground – to play its part in offsetting the rest. The observer's eye is caught by the detail of branches and leaves, and especially by the angular roots of the leaning tree to the left, tenaciously clinging to the rocks – a story of perilous impermanence to be compared with the permanence of the distant cathedral. The tree roots are not essential to the picture, but their irregular, gnarled shape have an unsettling beauty of their own – here is a parallel meaning for the "troubled condition" of the minor mode and the beauty of Mendelssohn's chromatic colouring.

So Felix – nurtured by his grandfather Moses's belief in "the potential of beauty to reveal the innermost nature of the human spirit", and following the German writer K P Moritz's view that "every beautiful whole from the hand of the visual artist is … in miniature a reflection of the highest form of beauty in the great wide realm of nature"[16] – perhaps romanticised the view of what he saw that day in the north of England. This was indeed in much the same way that he romanticised the sonata form framework which he inherited from Mozart – giving it a pleasing balance of different colours, thematic integration and beautiful chromatic detail, and in the process making it wholly his own.

* * * * *

Another casualty of the intervening historical record was the distortion of the close, happy and fruitful relationship between Felix and his sister Fanny Mendelssohn-Hensel (1805-1847). It was close because Fanny's aptitude for music was almost as remarkable as Felix's and it gave them a powerful bond; happy because they were also very fond of each other (as is clear from their copious early exchange of letters – in overblown language perhaps, but that was typical of the times); and fruitful because early in his career Felix relied to a considerable extent on Fanny's musical judgment and opinion of his compositions. (Marcia Citron happily dubs her his "mail-order critic".[17])

The subsequent distortion of the relationship was two-fold. Firstly, there was a suggestion that Fanny's feminine influence had been detrimental to the quality of Felix's music. A B Marx claimed that in Felix's youth, time spent in the company of Fanny and her friends resulted in ephemeral works such as the *Lieder ohne Worte* which were not the *genres* expected of a serious composer. And later the accusations flew the other way: in the twentieth century Felix was accused of disparaging Fanny's own compositions and actively discouraging her from publishing her music.

These ideas are now being rebutted. As we have seen, Mendelssohn never intended his reputation to rest on the *Lieder ohne Worte*, and it is not helpful to judge social attitudes in the early decades of the nineteenth century by the standards of modern times. We have seen that genteel women at that time simply did not perform beyond the privacy of the drawing room or salon: payment for professional performance was out of the question, and the sale of compositions for profit would not have been far behind. It would seriously have jeopardised Fanny's social standing – already at risk by virtue of her Jewish descent – to have stepped outside the conventions of her bourgeois gender role. Moreover, there is plenty of evidence to suggest that Felix encouraged Fanny in her composing. He included some of her songs in one of his own publications (readily acknowledging to Queen Victoria and Prince Albert, for instance, that they had been written by Fanny); and his supposed discouragement of publication, in a letter dated June 1837, has now been attributed to concerns for Fanny's health at the time (she had suffered a miscarriage in March of that year). Most importantly, Fanny herself does not appear to have been concerned about publication; in 1846 she wrote to a friend that "I can truthfully say that I let it [i.e. publication] happen more than made it happen".[18] (For a modern and balanced account of the relationship between Fanny and her brother Felix see Marian Wilson Kimber's chapter in the *Cambridge Companion to Mendelssohn*.)

Fanny's early musical education was identical with Felix's: they had the same tutors and she too studied theory and counterpoint with Zelter. She was an outstanding pianist – Felix regarded her as better than many of the travelling *virtuosi*. From the early 1830s most of her compositions were written for performance at the *Sonntagsmusik*, so that there are a good many *lieder* and piano pieces. Fanny also wrote a small amount of chamber music, which included one piano trio, op.11, dating from the last year of her life. She died suddenly, of a stroke, in May 1847.

Fanny Mendelssohn-Hensel: 1st movement *Allegro molto vivace* from Piano Trio in D minor op.11

Exposition: The home key of d minor is established by a turbulent accompaniment of rapid semiquavers in the piano, above which a solemn and portentous 4-note motif 1(a) opens the **1st subject** – which unfolds to pause on V after 4 bars; two falling 7th intervals in sequence complete the 8-bar theme.

Ex. 29.1

An expanded version in g minor (IV) follows, cadencing shortly back in the home key. The piano begins what now feels like an Transitional passage with a lovely 2-bar sequence ending again in falling 7ths. This moves towards the relative major key of F, passing through felicitous chromatic colouring before emerging in F major itself: we have a sense of heightened expectation that the **2nd subject** is about to begin, rewarded by a lovely *cantabile* theme 2(a) in the 'cello.

Ex. 29.2

This is repeated, and then the major mode fades away as a more restless sequel 2(b) follows in f minor, with a tailpiece of rising 7ths which again generate more satisfying sequences.

Ex. 29.3

A brief 8-bar Codetta cadences in f minor and leads (without a break) into the

Development: The turbulent semiquaver figures from the beginning of the movement return to the piano, answered softly, slowly but with increasing intensity, by the portentous 4-note motif of 1(a) in the strings. Keys range widely and the violin and 'cello engage in a fervent discourse, until all three instruments finally cadence together in f♯ minor. Again there is a sense of expectation as the motif 1(a) is heard mysteriously high in the violin: the mode slips radiantly from minor into major and the 'cello re-introduces its lovely 2nd subject 2(a). This runs its course and then the rhythm of 1(a) is heard again, insistently; the piano catches the heightened mood and answers the strings antiphonally over a powerful baseline of tramping quavers. The 4-note motif 1(a) metamorphoses into the falling 7th sequence from the Transition; it builds to an immensely powerful climax which culminates in the

Recapitulation of 1(a) back in the home tonic minor key, fully harmonised in double handfuls of 4-note chords in the piano with the turbulent semiquavers now in the strings. The thematic material follows in regular order, although with some varied instrumentation. The Transitional sequence appears again as sweetly as before, but now in d minor and in canon between the piano and the violin. The portentous 1(a) intervenes to whip up another big climax to the accompaniment of *fortissimo* rushing semiquavers; this erupts (a wonderful moment) into the blazing triumph of 2(a) (major mode) in the violin and 'cello, 2 octaves apart over sonorous *tremulandi* in the piano (a different mood from its previous appearances in the Exposition and Development). The minor mode returns with 2(b).

The final **Coda** is brief: it begins with the 4-note motif of 1(a) low in the 'cello. This mysterious and slowly unfolding passage between 'cello and piano is followed by an acceleration of the rhythm of 1(a), rising dynamically from *piano* to *forte* over 4 bars and ending robustly with turbulent semiquavers and double-stopped chords in the strings.

By any measure, this is a powerfully eloquent essay in sonata form. The listener is immediately struck by the technical brilliance of the piano part, which would have been taken by Fanny herself. But there is also abundant evidence throughout the score of Zelter's careful training in the capable counterpoint of the string parts, as well as the composer's practised understanding of the different sonorities of the two instruments.

This piano trio also makes for an interesting comparison with Felix Mendelssohn's trio in the same key. Its framework is essentially Mozartian, with conventional I and V differentiation and a structure

of expectation at key points. There is no double bar, however, and
the sectional divisions have to be heard by an attentive listener.
Fanny makes the divisions clear in a more Romantic than Classical
way, emphasising the thematic material – dramatising the introduction of the 2nd subject in the Exposition, and the anticipation of
the Recapitulation at the end of the development. She also colours
the 2nd subject themes with the 3rd harmonic shifts so beloved of
Romantic composers.

Where Felix consciously chose not to make his 1st and 2nd
subjects markedly different from each other, Fanny produces a pair
of subjects with thoroughly Romantic differentiation: the first is as
masterful and portentous as the second is lyrical and sensuous. But
Fanny also proves to be adept at deriving useful motifs for development from her thematic material: the falling 7th which she uses
to such effect seems to be derived from the second phrase of the
opening subject. She uses it especially effectively in the Transition
to the 2nd subject. It is tempting to think here that she intends a
reference to Felix's falling 7ths sequence at the same point in his
d minor trio – it is so similar in effect. Fanny furthermore seems
to have intended some significance for this 7ths sequence by using
it again at a significant point in the Development, as the tension is
building before the return to the Recapitulation she highlights it by
fusing it with 1(a) in canon; when it re-appears in the Recapitulation
she gives it academic credentials by using it again in canon. (The 7th
is an interval with as much of its own character as 3rds and 6th – it is
essentially incomplete, dissonant, restless; it longs to resolve in some
satisfactorily consonant way; Fanny clearly loves these Romantic
traits.)

The shortness of Fanny's concluding Coda is more in a Classical
than a Romantic tradition, but here paradoxically more for Romantic than Classical reasons. Fanny is clearly seeking to end her sonata
movement with a great apotheosis of its thematic material. But she
is aware that if the Recapitulation has effected all the necessary tonal
resolutions, and triumphantly repeated all the thematic material,
then there is a danger the Coda can at best only be repetitive, or at
worst over-work the material. So in this sonata she makes the Recapitulation itself the brilliant climax of the movement – by filling out
the scoring of her two favourite themes (1(a) and 2(a)) and marking
them fortissimo. After this there is little need for much more than a
figurative close, because these grander versions of the themes are all
the apotheosis that was needed.

The choice of the minor mode is of course a Romantic one,
and it follows Felix's own choice in his op.49. It also gives Fanny
the opportunity to explore the contrast between major and minor
modes, which she exploits by having two themes in her 2nd subject

group. The first, 2(a), successfully emancipates the movement from the turbulent pressure of the minor mode opening, and gives it positive momentum and lyricism; but then the second, 2(b), allows it to be overwhelmed again by the negative, troubled state of the minor mode. The listener becomes caught up in the drama of the energy driving to close in the minor mode, momentarily living the Romantic

"... sense of cosmic nostalgia, the yearning for a lost paradise, the tradition of European romanticism which believes the dream to be more potent than the reality ..."[19]

Three further movements follow. The second is in A major. Marked *Andante espressivo*, it has an attractive, carefully-crafted principal theme which hovers between A major and f♯ minor, its relative minor a 3rd below; a contrasting central section intervenes before returning to the principal theme of the first part. The third movement is short and slight; entitled *Lied*, it has no pretensions to being anything other than a songful, nineteenth-century successor to a Classical *Minuetto*. The vivacious Finale *Allegro moderato* is full of clever invention. It seems bent on closing the work in the minor mode, but near the end, after what seems like a definitive cadence in the minor mode of the home key, the principal theme returns transferred to the major mode. This sets the scene for a radiant (and wholly unexpected) return of the lovely lyrical 2nd subject theme from the first movement, and this time the major mode is triumphant to the end.

CHAPTER ENDNOTES

1   Rosen, Charles. *The Romantic Generation*. Cambridge, MA: Harvard University Press, 1995, p.569; quoted in Schmalfeldt, *op.cit*, p.159.

2   Todd, R Larry. *Mendelssohn's Musical Education*. Cambridge: Cambridge University Press, 1983, p.2.

3   Taylor, Benedict. 'Musical History and Self-Consciousness in Mendelssohn's Octet' in *19th-Century Music*, 32/2, 2008, p.136.

4   Todd, R Larry. 'Mendelssohn(-Bartholdy), Felix', *Grove Music Online*, 2001.

5   Mercer-Taylor, Peter. 'Introduction: Mendelssohn as border-dweller' in *The Cambridge Companion to Mendelssohn*, ed. P. Mercer-Taylor, Cambridge: Cambridge University Press, 2004, p.5.

6   Cooper, John Michael. 'Mendelssohn received', *ibid*, p.237

7   Plantinga, Leon. *Schumann as Critic*. New Haven, CT: Yale University Press, 1967, p.267.

8   Schmalfeldt, *op.cit*, p.164.

9   Vitercik, Greg, 'Mendelssohn as Progressive' in *The Cambridge Companion to Mendelssohn*, p.71.

10 Vitercik, *ibid*, p.72.

11 Letter to Wilhelm von Boguslawski, 19 April 1834 in *Deutsche Rundschau* 140 (1909), p.465; quoted by Schmidt-Beste, Thomas, 'Mendelssohn's Chamber Music' in *The Cambridge Companion to Mendelssohn*, p.144.

12 Schmalfeldt, *op.cit*, pp. 166 and 173; see also her chapter on Mendelssohn, pp.164-173 for detailed analysis.

13 Schmidt-Beste, in *The Cambridge Companion to Mendelssohn*, p.136.

14 Goethe, transl. George Madison Priest, New York 1941; quoted by Schmidt-Beste, *ibid*, p.136.

15 English translation from Werner, Eric, *Mendelssohn: A New Image of the Composer and his Age,* transl. Dika Newlin, London 1963, p.119; quoted Schmidt-Beste, *ibid*, p.136.

16 Bonds, *Absolute Music,* p.118.

17 Citron, Marcia. *Fanny Hensel's Letters* (1984), quoted by Marian Wilson Kimber in 'Felix and Fanny' in *The Cambridge Companion to Mendelssohn*, p.44.

18 Letter to Angelica von Woringen, from *The Letters of Fanny Hensel,* quoted by Marian Wilson Kimber, *ibid*, p.51.

19 Reed, John. *Schubert: The Final Years.* London: Faber & Faber, 1972, p.241.

CHAPTER 15

THE AUSTRO-GERMAN
MAINSTREAM 3:
ROBERT AND CLARA SCHUMANN

ROBERT SCHUMANN (1810-1856) completes a triumvirate of piano trio composers born within sixteen months of each other in the early years of the nineteenth century: Mendelssohn in 1809, Chopin in 1810, and now Schumann also in 1810.

Schumann is seen by many as a "quintessentially Romantic" composer. Two people in his early life shaped that romanticism: his father, a book dealer and author of chivalric romances, who encouraged his impressionable son to read widely and think imaginatively; and the famous pianist Moscheles, the brilliance of whose playing unforgettably inspired Schumann when he was only nine years old. At first it seemed that a literary career would emerge: he was captivated by German Romantic poets, by their reaction to Enlightenment rationalism and their cultivation of imagination and emotion, and he began to write lyrical poetry himself. The great chronicler of the sonata tradition, William Newman, says that

> "The literary interests nurtured by his father and his early environment … figured at least as much in Schumann's background and youthful aspirations as his more specifically musical interests … these literary interests matter because they contributed fundamentally to the making of one of the most discerning critics, most representative aestheticians, and most subtle symbolists, if not programmatists, of the Romantic era."[1]

Then a promising career as a virtuoso pianist opened up before Schumann and he saw the possibility of achieving a satisfying synthesis between music and literature as a composer. In 1831 he wrote 'Papillons', a sequence of pianoforte miniatures mirroring an external literary programme – the progress of a masked ball. These were ground-breaking pieces; inspired by a novel by J P F Richter and waltzes by Schubert, they were built on a classical inheritance of square-cut, 4-bar phrases, but frequently confounded listeners' expectations with their romantic whimsy and wistfulness. Denying classical expectations, they were frequently fragmentary and often – unthinkably – ended without traditional cadential closure. Schumann said they simply reflected "the half-torn pages of life".

Schumann studied the piano with Friedrich Wieck, and for some time (as Hummel had with Mozart) lived in his teacher's house in Leipzig. He cannot have been an ideal lodger. He was a wild student, living life to the full, drinking heavily (he was particularly fond of champagne) and smoking cigars; the syphilis which eventually killed him was undoubtedly also contracted during this period. It was hardly surprising, therefore, that when Schumann suddenly fell in love with Wieck's 16-year-old daughter Clara, her father violently opposed the match. It took five years of enforced separations and even a legal case before Robert and Clara were finally married in September 1840.

Schumann poured his life-experiences passionately into his music, and the anxiety and pain of those years were miraculously sublimated in composition in the final anxious months before the wedding day. Returning to the tried and tested framework of *Papillons*, he applied the same quasi-narrative device to sequences of poems from his favourite authors, which he assembled to form song-cycles. His sympathy for the poetry combined with his technical brilliance as a pianist in a perfect partnership of equals – a new synthesis between music and poetry in which he saw himself as musician become "the second poet of the poem". In eight months he wrote some 130 songs – considerably more than half his substantial total song output – in an extraordinary burst of creative activity.

The marriage turned out to be a true meeting of minds. Clara was herself one of the leading pianists of the day and their shared passion for music was a source of inspiration to them both. Robert's own hopes of a performing career having been dashed in 1832 by an injury to his right hand, Clara encouraged him to broaden his range and the Year of Song was followed by other '*genre*' years – orchestral symphonies in 1841, chamber music in 1842 and choral works in 1843. He had been used to composing at the keyboard, and although he never lost his inimitable gift for writing fresh, lyrical melodies he had to devise new methods of working on these larger canvasses: "I used to compose all of my shorter pieces in the heat of inspiration ... when I started to work out everything in my head a completely new manner of composing began to develop." Robert and Clara worked together on contrapuntal studies, taking Bach as their model: though the phraseology of poetry continued to underpin all his writing – lyrical melodies are still played out in balanced phrases – a new contrapuntal richness became added to the accompanying parts, and a concentration on motivic detail gives the onward flow of the whole an added impetus, as well as pointing towards future musical horizons.

There were always clouds on Schumann's own horizon. Throughout his life he feared an inheritance of familial mental instability, and he suffered intermittently from both physical and mental breakdowns. But from 1847 he enjoyed one last period of great productivity, which included chamber music and in turn three piano trios.

Schumann's first essay in piano trio writing had dated from his Chamber Music Year in 1842. Immediately before beginning it he had been pre-occupied with the important piano quintet Op.44, and later with its sequel, the piano quartet Op.47; in the event he did not feel that the four slight movements for piano trio written inbetween were worthy of the title of Piano Trio no.1 – they were eventually published as the *Vier Fantasiestücke* for the three instruments. The three full-scale piano trios proper were written several years later, two in 1847 and the last in 1851 – perhaps inspired by Clara, whose own very effective trio in g minor (see pp.227ff.) had appeared in 1846. The second piano trio in F major took its place alongside the piano quintet and quartet as one of Schumann's most appealing works. He had had to resign himself to working in the "higher form" of the classical sonata. In his earlier, unruly days he had resented its prescriptive formulae, but later he recognised it as a "noble musical form" and wrote that "There is no worthier form by which [younger artists] might introduce and ingratiate themselves [better] in the eyes of the finer critics."[2]

R Schumann: 1st movement *Sehr lebhaft* from Trio no 2 in F major op.80

Exposition: The brisk 1st subject is enlivened by the movement's 6/8, triplet quaver time signature – the opening motif 1(a) features displaced accents and a distinctive tonal ambivalence.

Ex. 30.1

Another statement in g minor leads back to a firm tonic cadence, and then we sense a transitional passage getting under way: a new triplet quaver figure tossed between strings and piano moves towards the V of V (encouraged by 1(a) heard again in the violin). After 3 bars of static anticipation on the V note alone, 2(a) – a soft chordal motif – is heard in the piano,

Ex. 30.2

followed shortly after by 2(b) – a phrase of triplet quavers picking out two sequences of melodic falling 3rds – also in the piano.

Ex. 30.3

The Cadence passage soon follows, again featuring 1(a). After a firm cadence in V, 4 bars of anticipatory V harmony (lifted from the Transition to the 2nd subject) lead into the

Development as the accompaniment to a beautifully mellow new theme (x) in the violin – a line of meditative dotted crotchets falling from the 5th to the tonic, incorporating chromatic decoration and a lovely falling 6th interval.

Ex. 30.4

This theme and its relatively static harmonic accompaniment dominate for some time, until interrupted by the return of the brisk rhythm of 1(a), which prompts a renewal of harmonic energy. 2(b) returns as the basis of some of the finest contrapuntal writing in the sonata we have met since Mozart; 1(a) also joins the texture, and after some time we sense the tonality moving towards V of V. Suddenly the dynamic level drops to *piano*, and the mellow theme (x) is heard again in the violin – delaying the return to the Recapitulation for some time as this theme is subjected to more fine contrapuntal treatment.

The **Recapitulation** finally begins, but not until a false 4-bar reprise (with minor mode overtones) has further delayed it. After this, 1(b), 2(a) and 2(b) return regularly, in the same order as before and now safely back in the home tonic key.

A **Coda** is preceded by the same anticipatory bars as before, introducing firstly the closing phrase of the mellow theme (x), then some intervening passagework before the opening phrase; this returns over a reassuring home V pedal and gradually accelerates into an energetic close.

This is a compact and lively movement. It neatly follows the Classical sonata framework, but fills it out with individual touches such as the new theme introduced in the Development. Although the tonal plateaux of tonic and dominant are essentially traditional, all the thematic material is constantly decorated with highly chromatic colour; Schumann's overall effect is therefore much more Romantic than Classical, a typical example of

"... the richly expressive harmonic and gestural vocabulary of Romantic music [which] tends to undercut the significance of the large-scale tonal processes that animate the sonata forms of the Classical era."[3]

Similarly, the whimsical rhythms and displaced accents of the Exposition and Recapitulation disguise a ground plan of relatively regular phrasing.

We noted that Robert and Clara enjoyed working together, studying the works of J S Bach and writing exercises in counterpoint. Once again we see the fruits of such study in the elegant contrapuntal passages of this sonata movement.

Schumann also manages the overall trajectory of the sonata narrative in this trio with a satisfying but unusual solution. The concise treatment of thematic material in his Exposition – with its fast harmonic rate and rich chromatic colour – is in marked contrast with the mood of the Development. Here the pace slows for the introduction of the new theme, but when Schumann then re-introduces the thematic material of the Exposition, extracting motifs and so skilfully interweaving them in the long passages of contrapuntal development, he is using the earlier material in a quite different way. Thus when he returns to the Recapitulation he can pick up the pace again and give us a faithful reproduction of the Exposition. When he comes to the Coda, therefore, he does not need to refer again to his 1st and 2nd subjects – he has already said all that he needs about them; instead he completes the narrative of this sonata movement by returning to the lovely Development theme. As a writer Schumann had enjoyed writing anonymously under two pseudonyms, representing the two facets of his own personality: a *'Florestan'* facet which was outgoing, active and passionate, and an *'Eusebius'* tendency towards more peaceful and introspective contemplation. It is tempting to see him giving Florestan the principal material of the movement, but allowing Eusebius to sing in the Development – and even to have the last word in the Coda.

The slow movement, *Mit innigem Ausdruck*, has some of the most ravishingly beautiful moments in the piano trio repertoire. Close your eyes as you listen to its opening bars and hear what this magician can do with a simple falling scale: Schumann begins his descent, not from the tonic note, but from the third, and when he closes an octave below, his final interval is the sensitive semitone between 4th and 3rd; three times our anticipation of the familiar sequence of intervals is tantalisingly delayed by momentary hiatuses created by the accompanying harmony.

R Schumann: 2nd movement *Mit innigem Ausdruck* from Piano Trio no 2 in F major op.80

This beautiful opening, infinitely slowly, gives out the principal theme (**A**), stated four times by the violin.

Ex. 30.5

It reappears roughly half-way through the movement (in the dominant key) and then again (back in the tonic) near the end. The three appearances are punctuated by a subsidiary theme (**B**), consisting of broken chords in the violin accompanied by simple chords in the piano. Thus the overall plan is:

A(I) – B – A(V) – B – A

This is a simple rondo pattern, easily recognised, set in a classical tonal arch-shape, and delivered in satisfying symmetry.

There is a good deal of hidden subtlety in this music. Just before the violin begins its first note of A, we hear a chromatically-rising figure low in the 'cello, immediately answered by the piano. The dotted rhythm of this figure establishes a gentle momentum beneath the slowly-falling scale (and note too how perfectly the *rising* figure balances the *fall* of the scale). This figure will reappear as the

introduction to each theme in turn – we hear it next as the preamble
to a rising scale which leads to the first statement of B. Beneath this
apparent artlessness lies a movement immensely complex both in
form and texture: for a very significant proportion of it the 'cello and
piano are answering each other in strict canon. It is music of great
richness and intensity. (For a more detailed description, see Smallman, *op.cit*, p.113.)

Schumann exercises commendable restraint by interspersing his
beautiful theme A with the statement of B. We could never have too
much of the falling scale and the chromatic harmony which colours
it so beautifully, but by limiting its reappearances he preserves its
freshness for us. This would not always be the case, as contemporary composers responded to popular demand for the gratification of
endlessly-repeated melodies.

Beethoven's sonata layout is used, so that the song-like slow movement is followed by a dance-like scherzo. But Schumann does not
call it a scherzo, and indeed this contemplative movement is far
removed from Beethoven's scherzi, and further still from those of his
own contemporary Mendelssohn – although its canonic writing may
have been inspired by Schubert's Trio in E♭ D 929. This time the
canon is not just accompaniment, it is the composite delivery of the
theme of the first section. After a contrasting central section – the
remnant of the old dance Trio – the opening canons return.

Florestan returns in the fourth and final movement, *Nicht zu
rasch*, another essay in ebullient sonata style. Critics like to complain
that Schumann overscores in his outer movements, unnecessarily
doubling the piano part with the strings in order to give the texture
extra weight. But the contrapuntal banter between the instruments is
beautifully handled, and they all dance through the movement with
great energy and verve.

★   ★   ★   ★   ★

Another remarkable woman who like Fanny Mendelssohn faced
difficult problems while maintaining a lifetime devoted to music was
Robert's wife Clara (née Wieck) (1819-1896). But the difficulties
faced by Clara were of a quite different order from those of Fanny.
She was the child of a professional musician and was positively
encouraged by her father, Friedrich Wieck, not to allow her sex to
prevent her from making a career in music (it was fortunate that she
had considerable musical talent, since he "had resolved even before
her birth to develop the child into a musician of consummate artist-
ry"[4]).

Clara was born in Leipzig and began piano lessons with her
father at the age of five; four years later she gave her first public

performance as the soloist in a piano concerto by Mozart. At the age of twelve she was taken on her first concert tour, and by 1835 had established a reputation as a brilliant executant with a stellar list of musical admirers, including Goethe, Mendelssohn, Chopin, Schumann, Paganini and Liszt. She was widely admired not only for her technical mastery, but also because of the sensitivity of her performances: "Her playing was always characterised by poetic spirit, depth of feeling, a singing tone and strict adherence to the composer's indications."[5] As well as continuing her piano studies, Clara also had instruction in singing, violin and instrumentation, and her father sent her for lessons in counterpoint with Christian Weinlig, the Cantor of the Thomaskirche (J S Bach's old post).

Clara's problems were indeed different from Fanny's. Although she was encouraged to perform and to compose, she had to endure not only the malignant rancour of her father's opposition to her marriage with Schumann, but also the tragedy of Robert's mental breakdown, his early death in 1856, and the further loss during her own lifetime of five of her eight children.

However, in 1837 that was all in the future. This was not only the year when Robert proposed to her, but also when Mendelssohn and his new wife Cécile came to live in Leipzig. He was not only a close personal friend to both Robert and Clara, but he also immeasurably deepened Clara's professional musical experience. In 1835 he had invited her to take part in a performance of J S Bach's Concerto in d minor for three pianos and orchestra; from the winter season of 1837/38 onwards he introduced his "historical concerts" of works from the Baroque to the early nineteenth century; he regularly conducted works by Mozart, Beethoven and Schubert – and directed the first performances of works by Robert. Clara appeared as a soloist in *Gewandhaus* concerts with Mendelssohn on no fewer than twenty-one occasions, and when the Leipzig Conservatory opened with his support in 1843 he encouraged both Robert and Clara to join the teaching staff. First-hand encounters with such a broad repertoire, together with the contrapuntal studies which she and Robert enjoyed so much together, become evident in the quality of the compositions she produced after their marriage, notably in the piano trio in g minor, op.17 of 1846 (her only essay in this *genre*).

Clara Schumann: 1st movement *Allegro moderato* from Piano Trio in G minor op.17

Exposition: The movement opens with a song-like **1st subject** in the violin, with a rising opening motif (a) which features the yearning semitone between 5th and minor 6th. This turns out to be the beginning of an 8-bar theme, pausing on V after 4 bars, then followed by 4 more bars which also end on V – so as to lead smoothly back into a second statement in the piano.

Ex. 31.1

Violin

This is an open-ended song, never finally cadencing in I. The home tonality of g minor is clearly felt, however, and is shortly reinforced by a rhythmically well-defined chordal progression which establishes the home key beyond doubt.

An attractive transitional passage moves towards B♭ (the relative major): after 4 bars standing on V the **2nd subject** is heard in the piano – a contrasting chordal theme, hesitating momentarily as it trips down a succession of 3 off-beats before picking itself up in a closing phrase of pianistic repeated chords.

Ex. 31.2

Piano

A Cadential passage of falling semitones ends in a double bar – and the instruction to repeat the Exposition.

The **Development:** is mainly concerned with a motif derived from the opening figure 1(a) heard forcefully, first in the 'cello, then in the violin, and ranging widely over colourful chromatic harmony in the piano. A softer passage follows, in which the strings continue a gentle contrapuntal exchange of motifs from the 1st subject. A moment of beautiful lyricism in the violin is interrupted by another forceful statement of the motif from 1(a) in octaves low in the piano; the 'cello holds a long V pedal (below the piano) as figuration above flows smoothly into the

Recapitulation. This follows regularly, turning to tonic major for the 2nd subject but returning to the minor mode for a final Coda.

Coda: the first phrase of 1(a) is heard, then the strings in a fine exchange of accelerating motifs bring the movement to a *bravura* close.

Clara's sources are clear: this is the model of Mozart's sonata form which she has learnt from Felix Mendelssohn and Robert. The Classical framework is followed even down to the inclusion of a double bar at the end of the Exposition, furthermore with an instruction to repeat. The choice of the minor mode may be Romantic, but the execution shows Classical restraint – even in the Development, where single-minded concentration on the yearning semitone motif of 1(a) is counterbalanced by its treatment in beautiful antiphonal counterpoint. The quality of Clara's training and musicianship shines throughout this movement. Her thematic invention is not strikingly original, but she works her material beautifully and the directional flow of her harmony is impeccable: listen to her bass lines and you will always know where she is going. (This is the clue to identifying the Transition's progress to 2nd subject in the Exposition: the bass tells you not to be fooled by that nice new tune in the piano into thinking you have already arrived at a 2nd subject.)

Smallman is particularly admiring of the scoring:

"What it lacks in originality it amply offsets by the excellence of its technical command, and in particular the high skill with which it is scored. It would not have been surprising if Clara, as a distinguished concert pianist, had been tempted to overload the piano's role at the expense of the strings; but in fact she shows admirable judgement, achieving a fine balance of interest in the ensemble with little or no trace of superfluous doublings."[6]

This is a full-scale sonata work, with three more movements to follow. The second movement is a mild-mannered Scherzo in B♭ major, headed *Tempo di Menuetto* and sporting three little "Scotch snaps" in its opening bars. We have not heard this favourite device of the *galant* sonata for many years. Clara contrasts it with a Trio in E♭ with more displaced accents. The third movement is an *Andante* in G major. The opening melody holds out the promise of developing favourably into beautiful lyricism, but somehow never manages to become quite as beautiful as we hope – perhaps because the harmonisation is (unusually for Clara) rather unexciting. There is a contrasting central section in e minor, the relative minor, with pungent dotted rhythms. With the last movement Clara again nails her academic colours to the mast: this is a full-blown sonata movement in g minor. It has two good themes, the first perhaps aiming to follow the same outline trajectory as the principal theme from the *Andante*, although much more chromatically decorative and rhythmically lively. The two themes are combined in exhilarating counterpoint in the Development – the motif derived from the chromatic

1st subject in particular might have been lifted straight out of a Bach fugue.

Newman says that Clara was a pioneer of the solo piano recital in the 1830s, along with Liszt and Moscheles.[7] She broke new ground also by including solo sonatas, especially sonatas by Beethoven and by Robert Schumann. Her commitment to the serious, intellectual sonata idea is evident in her piano trio. It is quite beautifully scored, full of lovely counterpoint and expertly controlled throughout. Smallman calls it a "substantial" work; it is only its lack of truly sparkling invention, making it more pleasing than exciting, that holds it back from being at the same time a "great" work.

CHAPTER ENDNOTES

1   Newman, William S. *The Sonata Since Beethoven.* 3rd ed, New York: Norton & Co, 1983, pp.258-9.

2   Schumann, Robert. *Gesammelte Schriften über Musik und Musiker,* 5th ed. Leipzig: Briefkopf & Härtel, 1914, vol.I, p.394, vol.II, p.319; quoted in Newman, *ibid,* pp. 41, 38.

3   Vitercik, *op. cit,* pp.71-72.

4   Susskind, Pamela. 'Schumann [née Wieck], Clara' in *The New Grove Dictionary of Music & Musicians,* vol.16, 1980.

5   Susskind, *ibid,* p.828.

6   Smallman, *op. cit,* p.114.

7   Newman, *The Sonata after Beethoven,* p.52.

CHAPTER 16

THE WAR OF THE ROMANTICS: ABSOLUTISTS VERSUS PROGRESSIVES

OUR LAST DIRECT encounter with musical aesthetics was in Hoffmann's review of Beethoven's 5th symphony (see p.155). We saw instrumental music chiming with Idealist philosophy and elevated to an unprecedented status above all the other arts – seen as the only one able to lift the listener beyond the limitations of language and rational knowledge into another sphere of experience. Music's very inarticulacy – not being able to express meaning through words – had suddenly become its greatest asset.

By the middle of the nineteenth century this idea was well established, fulfilling the German writer Wackenroder's prophetic statement:

> "… between the individual, mathematical and tonal relationships and the individual fibres of the human heart an inexplicable sympathy has revealed itself, through which the musical art has become a comprehensive and flexible mechanism for the portrayal of human emotions."[1]

The idea that instrumental music could express feelings and emotions was a potent one, and it took hold of Romantic musical culture after 1830. It was inevitable that sonata form, based on principles of rhetoric and essentially dedicated to an intellectual appreciation of tonal form and theme, should be challenged in this climate. With writers like Grillparzer claiming that "Where words no longer suffice, tones speak",[2] and audiences clamouring for Romantic emotional fulfilment, it was not surprising that many composers began to question the suitability of the sonata as music for such entertainment.

The principal composers driving change were Berlioz, Wagner and Liszt – who were all born between 1803 and 1813, within the same ten years as Mendelssohn, Chopin and Schumann. Although none of these three innovators wrote piano trios, their alternative solutions to musical composition affected the subsequent course of all instrumental music, chamber music as well as orchestral, and therefore we must briefly touch on their experiments as background to the piano trio *genre* in the second half of the nineteenth century.

Hector Berlioz (1803-1869) had in fact been inspired by the symphonies of Beethoven, and also by writers such as Shakespeare, Goethe, Walter Scott and Byron. In his *Symphonie Fantastique: Episode de la vie d'un artiste* of 1830, he combined the symphony/sonata idea of a recurrent theme with the Romantic notion of assigning an extra-musical meaning to that theme – thus a musical *idée fixe* represents the artist's (i.e. his own) infatuation with a Shakespearean actress. (Leaving nothing to chance interpretation, he wrote a pamphlet, no less, with a detailed description of the "programme" for distribution to audiences.) Richard Wagner (1813-1883) extended this idea of explanatory themes considerably further in his operas. A number of *Leitmotive* represent characters, objects or ideas important to the plot, and become the structural foundation of a vast, continuous texture of vocal lines and orchestral instrumental parts.

It was actually Wagner who first coined the phrase "absolute music" to describe music for instruments alone, as opposed to instrumental music with voices. But Wagner used the phrase pejoratively, and in a negative sense, saying that:

"pure instrumental music ... has been "released" or "absolved" [*abgelöst*] from its original motivation in dance ... and thereafter has "no foundation or reason for existence."[3]

The title of "Absolutists" stuck to the traditionalist composers thereafter.

Franz Liszt was also dedicated to the idea of allowing an extra-musical source of inspiration, often taken from poetry, or a painting, to inspire a musical work. He took one or two such ideas and then developed them to provide the contrasting moods which the symphony had presented in separate movements – a technique which he called "thematic transformation". Liszt was a pianist with a phenomenal performing technique which enabled him to invent and play music which could range from pyrotechnics of extraordinary volume and power (and ferocious difficulty) to expressive melodies of the most disarming simplicity. He did not write a piano trio, but his colossal technique had far-reaching influence not only on the literature for solo piano, but also on all chamber music incorporating a

keyboard instrument. Despite his colourful life and notorious theatricality, Liszt was in fact a deeply serious musician. He did write
one notable essay in the sonata idea in his Piano Sonata in b minor
(1853). On first hearing it sounds like one continuous piece, almost
half an hour in length, containing a number of contrasting sections:
these are actually the accepted *fast-slow-fast-finale* sequence of movements, running without a pause. But the whole piece is itself in an
extended sonata form, its contrasting sections simultaneously the
familiar **Exposition** (1st fast movement) – **Development** (2nd slow
movement) – (link) – **Recapitulation** (finale) of the sonata structure. Demonstrating Liszt's technique of thematic metamorphosis,
it is a brilliant *re-invention* of the sonata principles, tailored to suit
the comprehension of a different kind of audience. It will be over 60
years before we find composers of piano trios thinking "out of the
box" in this way.[4]

Like Berlioz, Liszt also frequently drew on literature as a source
of inspiration for musical ideas. A contemporary painting of 1840
shows him at the piano improvising on a literary theme to a room
full of distinguished *literati* and musicians.

Josef Danhauser, *Franz Liszt, am Flügel phantasierend*, 1840.
Berlin, Alte Nationalgalerie

Standing in the background (before a portrait of Byron) are Paganini
and Rossini, and leaning against a leather armchair to the left, Victor
Hugo. In front of Hugo, George Sand (seated in the armchair and

dressed as a man) points purposefully – and with soulful engagement – to a line in an open book held by Alexandre Dumas, *père*,
seated alongside: this must be the literary prompt for the music.
The painting was executed by Josef Danhauser (1805-1845) and
entitled *Franz Liszt, am Flügel phantasierend* ("Franz Liszt fantasis-
ing at the piano"). (The company is completed by Liszt's mistress,
the Comtesse Marie d'Agoult, appropriately seated at his feet.)
Liszt gazes directly at the face of an outsize bust of Beethoven on
the piano, as though proving that he has the master's approval of
his music. It is a disappointment to discover that this was an imagi-
nary gathering, and that the painting was actually commissioned by
the piano-manufacturer Conrad Graf as an advertisement for the
superior quality of his pianos! However, it neatly illustrates Liszt's
lifelong interest in linking music with literature, as well as reminding
us how the sonata was challenged by the easy-listening attraction of
programme music in the second half of the nineteenth century.

Two musical camps now faced each other over an increasingly acri-
monious divide: one the Absolutists, represented by Mendelssohn,
Schumann and Brahms, who continued to champion the tradition of
sonata form which they had inherited from the Viennese classicists,
and the other the new Progressives, Berlioz, Liszt and Wagner. From
the Progressive camp the composer Peter Cornelius described their
relative positions in 1854 as follows:

"The first [camp] considers music a fantastical play of tones
according to the rules of euphony and aesthetic laws derived from
the specifically musical works of Haydn, Mozart, and Beethoven
… such as unity in variety, clarity and proportion of form and
means, etc. According to this party, music achieves its effect
through itself, without the medium of accessory ideas; it elevates
the soul out of the narrowness of life to ideal heights, rinsing away
through its waves of tone, as it were, all the rot and triflings of
life … [The second camp] is no longer content to arouse vague
feelings in the layperson … It desires instead to take as its material
the rich treasures of myth, of the Bible, of history, drawing on the
inexhaustible source of one's own heart, the inner circumstances
of its love, its passions, its struggles with the world … It seeks to
renounce the freedom of absolute music and its associated servitude to conventional forms in order to win a freedom of form by
giving itself over to a specific poetic object."[5]

As we shall shortly see, such frontal attacks did not go unanswered.
But before we turn to the evidence for the defence of sonata form,
we should consider what harmful effects the popularising style of
some of the Progressives had on the quality of musical composition.

There was nothing inherently wrong with adding a descriptive title to a piece, so that it might prompt interesting expectations and interpretations in an audience: both Mendelssohn and Schumann were happy to do so, but they actually wrote the music first and added the titles afterwards. A work had to stand on its own as a piece of good music before they would attach any external description to it.

As an example of the type of association between words and music which had a harmful effect on later musical style, we should turn to Liszt's set of three piano pieces entitled *Liebesträume*, after poems by Uhland and Freiligrath. The third of these, in A♭, is perhaps one of the best-known of such pieces in the nineteenth-century piano repertoire. It is actually derived from Liszt's own setting of Freiligrath's poem as a song for soprano with piano accompaniment, the sentimental words of which he copied onto the piano score:

> O lieb, so lang du lieben kannst!
> O lieb, so lang du lieben magst!
> Die Stunde kommt, die Stunde kommt,
> Wo du an Graben stehst und klagst!
>
> *(O love, so long as you can!*
> *O love, so long as you may!*
> *The hour comes, the hour comes*
> *When you will stand by graves and weep!)*

The relationship between the song and this piano transcription brings us close to the heart of nineteenth-century popular musical culture. Commentators are fond of saying that the 4-bar phrase had a "stranglehold" on instrumental music from the 1820s, and will quote a piece such as this in evidence. But we have seen that metrical regularity had been a fundamental component of Western music since time immemorial – from Christian hymns to dance songs – and had also been an important part of the symmetry and balance of the sonata literature from John Bach onwards. Widespread enjoyment of the "quadratic syntax" of metrical regularity is reflected also in the fact that more metric poetry was read in Europe – between 1800 and 1820, and especially by women – than at any other time before or since.

It was not its 4-bar phraseology, but the superficial sentimentality of pieces of this *Liebestraum* type – so immediately effective, so easy to understand with a minimum of effort and concentration – which presented a threat to the intellectual sonata idea. Here we are in an altogether more illusory world, satirically sketched in a passage from Gustave Flaubert's novel *Madame Bovary: Provincial Lives* of 1857 (which many contemporary women reputedly thought so true to life that they claimed the heroine of the novel had been based on themselves). Flaubert mocks the romantic fantasies of susceptible females:

> "In the music lesson, in the ballads that she sang, there were nothing but little angels with golden wings, madonnas, lagoons, gondoliers, placid creations that allowed her a glimpse, for all the banality of the words and the clumsiness of the music, a glimpse of the seductive phantasmagoria of sentimental realities."[6]

We saw the dilemma for composers holding up the momentum of a sonata movement with a self-contained "tune" in the 1st movement of Schubert's E♭ trio (see p.177). How much more delicious for the salon audience to be given just the jam from the middle of the sandwich, without having to munch through all that serious sonata bread as well. Who would eat the rest when they could have neat jam? Who would sit through a sonata movement lasting 10 to 15 minutes when they could hear the whole of Liszt's *Liebestraum* in only 4½?

In time, the effect of pieces such as this was to trivialise the language of Beethoven and Schubert. The notes of the major and minor scales, those tones and semitones with their sensitive inter-relationships – "notes in love with each other" – became milked for sentimental effect. In the same way, subtle chromatic harmonies were travestied: the harmonic progression in the opening of this song, which is then repeated so often, this is the same heart-stopping progression which we heard beautifully and sparingly used by Mozart and Schubert. In the hands of a composer such as Liszt this is still well done, and the *Liebestraum* deserves its long-standing popularity, but it is easy to see how second-rate composers might turn such beauty into cliché. It was small wonder that in the context of expanding audiences everywhere, some looked for easy alternatives to sonata listening; such *salon* tastes were symptomatic of the widening rift between the "serious" mainstream sonata and other more romanticised forms of instrumental music.

The extra-musical inspiration of Berlioz, Wagner and Liszt was not going to go away. By the middle of the century, a new generation of young musicians had formed a Progressive group calling itself the New German School, and they threw themselves into compositions linking music with literature and the other arts – so-called "programme" music. In March 1860 an editorial in the *Neue Zeitschrift für Musik* claimed that "all serious musicians" of the day were part of the School.

This did not go unchallenged. The other camp put up a good fight in defence of the classical sonata idea; loyalty to sonata form was still strong amongst the Austro-German mainstream, and the very

idea that programme music might constitute the serious music of
the future was anathema to them. The young Johannes Brahms was
so incensed that he immediately circulated a "Manifesto" of protest
amongst other German musicians, seeking signatories willing to
join him in condemnation of Liszt and his hybrid concoctions as
"contrary to the innermost spirit of music, strongly to be deplored
and condemned". Most unfortunately, the text was leaked to a
prominent Berlin newspaper and it was published prematurely with
only four signatories.

Brahms was mortified, but he had an influential champion in the
person of the music critic Eduard Hanslick (1825-1904), who also
thought that Berlioz, Wagner and Liszt had "forced music beyond
its proper boundaries". Hanslick's treatise *The Beautiful in Music* of
1854 was one of the seminal books about music of the nineteenth
century. Vigorously refuting the twin notions that "the aim and
object" of music was to excite the emotions and that the emotions
were said to be "the subject matter" which "musical works are
intended to illustrate", he roundly declared: "Both propositions are
alike in this, that one is as false as the other."

Hanslick was particularly scornful of the listening habits of the
Progressives' audiences:

> "Instead of closely following the course of the music, these enthu-
> siasts, reclining in their seats and only half-awake, suffer them-
> selves to be rocked and lulled by the mere flow of sound. The
> sound, now waxing and now diminishing in strength, now rising
> up in jubilant strains and now softly dying away, produces in them
> a series of vague sensations which they in their simplicity fancy to
> be the result of intellectual action. They are the most easily satis-
> fied part of the audience, and it is also they who tend to lower the
> dignity of music.
>
> For their ear the aesthetic criterion of intelligent gratification is
> wanting, and a good cigar, some exquisite dainty, or a warm bath
> yields them the same enjoyment as a symphony, though they may
> not be aware of the fact."[7]

There will be more to say about Hanslick when we come to listen
to Brahms's own music. But this mid-century "war" between the
protagonists of programme music and the Absolutists is relevant
to the piano trio in the middle of the nineteenth century: it is the
background to be borne in mind when considering the piano trios in
the second half of the century. Composers who wanted to continue
writing sonata works were in competition with a formidable populist movement, whether they chose to continue in the old Classical
format, or in some way modify or develop it. There would be nothing

wrong with modification or development in principle – Beethoven and Schubert had indeed introduced both – but maintaining quality would be of paramount concern if the prestige of the sonata was to be maintained. After all, the sonata was still "the proof of greatness".

From this point onwards, there was no further formal modification of Sonata Form as defined by Marx and Czerny (see pp.188-89): the theorists' definitions held good for the rest of the century. We have become very familiar with the principle of the first movement and its presentation of thematic material in an inherently dramatic tonal context – from now onwards we shall be looking only for individual interpretations of the form. But before we move on, it may be helpful to summarise the *status quo* in sonata content around the middle of the nineteenth century.

1) *Thematic material:*
Melodic invention was at a premium because of the demand for originality in the sonata. Melodies might be "the smooth, songful, contemplative sort, couched in complete, well-defined phrases ... an out-and-out tune" or " ... more varied, supple, and, often, subtle in their rhythmic and pitch organisation."[8]

2) *Harmony:*
Tovey described melody as the "surface" of harmony. We have seen in all the piano trios of the nineteenth century how much the character of a tune owes to the colour of its underlying chromatic harmony – the two are often virtually inseparable. The increase in chromaticism and in dissonance is also pronounced. Newman singles out the diminished 7th chord as having "had a special significance for the early-Romantics and their successors, whether as a color harmony, a terrifying climax, a convenient modulatory agent ..., a mainstay in passage-work, a basic chord in side-slipping chromatic progressions, or a means of achieving the intentionally ambiguous and noncommittal, hence the mystical."[9] There is also a noticeable tendency to move from the minor mode of a home tonic to its own major mode, rather than moving to its relative major; this has become something of a Romantic gesture (unkindly disparaged by Wagner when used at the end of a movement as "endless victory festivals of major-mode jubilation after having endured minor-mode tribulations"[10]).

3) *Tonality:*
Modulations and keys used are often more wide-ranging than in the Classical sonata, particularly in the 2nd subject of the Exposition, and in the Development. There is also more interest amongst composers in connecting keys a 3rd apart, not only in Schubert's

favourite falling 3rd modulation, but in sequences of upward-moving 3rds.

4) *Textures:*
In the piano trio the influence of *virtuoso* pianist-composers is felt in a richer variety of figuration, not only in accompaniment figures which leave far behind the Classical period's *Alberti* bass, but in the piano parts generally (see especially the trios by Chopin, Spohr and Fanny Mendelssohn-Hensel). A similar expansion is seen in the string parts, which explore the extremes of the instrumental range more widely, and also exploit the emotional tension of melody given out at high pitch ranges. (This is as true of the violin as it is of the newly-emancipated 'cello in its tenor range.)

5) *The Coda:*
There was an increasing tendency in nineteenth-century works for composers to put the climax of a piece near the end of it: not only had Beethoven done this, but it followed the example of the dénouement of the novel, as well as the narrative trajectory of symphonic poems. This presented a difficulty in sonata form where traditionally the climax had come with the beginning of the Recapitulation, only two-thirds of the way through the movement. Thus the new Coda had to be carefully handled so that it did not upset the equilibrium of the existing three sections. Moreover, it was not clear what material it should contain. Should it simply add a *bravura* ending with impressive passage-work, or, more meaningfully, a final powerful comment on the thematic content of the movement? Solutions to the Coda problem will frequently be drivers of deviation from the traditional processes of sonata form.

Merely listing and describing these characteristics of the piano trios we have heard since the turn of the century recalls the wealth of fine composition we have found in these works, and puts into perspective the sour invective of some of the Progressives' spokesmen. A W Ambros, for instance, in 1855 wrote witheringly of the Absolutists:

> "Among creative musicians, one faction (by far the smaller) has retreated into older perspectives and forms, where it cultivates its modest plot of land according to the principles of the so-called 'classical' era. It would be presumptuous to disturb this idyllic happiness; but it is equally clear that everything such well-intentioned persons can tell us has already been said better by others before them."[11]

Happily we know that the Absolutists were far from being a spent force, and there were still many more masterworks in the piano trio *genre* still to be written.

★ ★ ★ ★ ★

It would be misleading to give the impression that from now on the Austro-German repertoire had a dwindling number of admirers. Far from it. Not all *salon* audiences had superficial tastes, and all over Europe the burgeoning middle classes were breeding a new consumer with a keen appetite for self-improvement through education. Their hunger was being fed by another new breed: the music critics. And now, again, London was developing another respectable musical culture. Some of the new English middle classes were less interested in the Italian operas or the *virtuoso* pianists favoured at the *soirées* of the old aristocracy, and more in establishing a reputation for themselves as serious connoisseurs interested in the classical repertoire of Haydn, Mozart and Beethoven. The peak of such connoisseurship was the appreciation of chamber music.

From 1835 an English violinist called Joseph Dando (1806-1894) organised the first public chamber music concerts in London. He sat his patrons "in the round" to concentrate on masterworks (albeit still mixed in with songs and lighter items). Also, in 1845 the English critic John Ella (1802-1888), who had studied in Paris with the pioneering musicologist Fétis, founded an exclusive music society known as the Musical Union, which met regularly to hear programmes consisting of just three classical chamber works. His subscribers were given analytical notes which included musical examples, and were also encouraged to follow the music in miniature scores; perhaps most significantly of all – they had to listen *in silence*. These were not isolated examples. From 1858 the managers of St James's Hall in Piccadilly ran cheaper (less socially exclusive) chamber music sessions at the Monday Popular Concerts, for which another critic J W Davison (1813-1885) also wrote analytical programme notes – which this wider audience could purchase for the price of sixpence.

It is also worth noting that Berlioz had been prompted to visit England in 1847 because he had heard that "... apparently there has been a real revolution in the musical consciousness of the nation in the last 10 years".[12]

A singular innovation, however, came from an unexpected quarter. Out of the blue, an educational establishment at the heart of the English public school system – that system dedicated to the perpetuation of the *status quo*, inculcating classical civilisation and team spirit in the sons of gentlemen, and not known for over-indulgence in any sentimental nonsense such as music or the arts – one such school made a significant appointment. In 1864, Edward Thring, the visionary headmaster of Uppingham School, appointed "a Music- and Choir-master" to teach his boys. It was the first appointment of its kind at any school in England and it established an important precedent – which other schools were quick to follow. Thring had good contacts and had chosen well – his new Choirmaster had impeccable musical credentials: he was Paul David, a godson of Mendelssohn and son of Ferdinand David (a pupil of Spohr, who had given the first performance of Mendelssohn's violin concerto). At long last, music became a respectable and socially-acceptable occupation for English gentlemen and a serious component of the educational curriculum.

CHAPTER ENDNOTES

1   Wackenroder, Wilhelm Heinrich. *Phantasien über die Kunst, für Freunde und Kunst*, 1799.

2   Grillparzer, Franz; quoted in Bonds, *Absolute Music*, p.113

3   Wagner, Richard in 'The Artwork of the Future' (Leipzig, 1849) in *Gesammelte Schriften;* quoted by Dahlaus, Carl *Between Romanticism and Modernism*, 1974; English edition transl. by Mary Whittall, Berkeley and Los Angeles: University of California Press, 1980, p.32.

4   See Chapter 9, Cobbett sonatas, pp.293-295.

5   Cornelius, Peter. Review of Richard Würst, *Preis-Sinfonie* in *NZfM* 41, Dec.1854. pp.258-59; quoted by Bonds, *Absolute Music*, p.215.

6   Flaubert, Gustave. *Madame Bovary. Mœurs de province* (1856). Modern edition transl. Geoffrey Wall, London: Penguin Books, 2009, p.35.

7   Hanslick, *op.cit*, pp.90-1.

8   Newman, *Sonata Since Beethoven*, pp.114-5.

9   Newman, *ibid*, pp.117-120.

10   Quoted in Bonds, *Absolute Music*, p.137.

11   Ambros, August Wilhelm. *Die Grenzen der Musik und Poesie*. Leipzig: H.Mathes, 1855; quoted in Bonds, *Absolute Music*, p.220.

12   Macdonald, Hugh. 'Berlioz, (Louis-)Hector', *Grove Music Online*, 2001.

CHAPTER 17

THE NATIONALISTS:
FRANCE, BOHEMIA, RUSSIA

IN ADDITION TO the challenge posed to Absolutist sonatas by the blandishments of the Progressives' easier-listening programme music, another powerful stimulus for new musical ideas arose around the middle of the nineteenth century. This was a growing sense of national identity, which had political rather than artistic origins. 1848 turned out to be a particularly unhappy year for a number of European monarchs. A contemporary Punch cartoon by Richard Doyle depicts several of them adrift in a choppy sea and crowded into a fragile boat named *L'ancien régime*, while a vast sea serpent wearing a French Revolutionary cap labelled *Liberty* bears down on them with a basilisk-stare.

THE GREAT SEA SERPENT OF 1848.

Richard Doyle, *The Great Sea Serpent*
Punch 15, 1848, pp.195-196.

In this year a series of political and social uprisings swept across Europe and parts of Latin America, but although over 50 countries were affected, almost all the revolutions were so ill co-ordinated that they collapsed, and within a year reactionary forces were back in control. Their significance for us lies not so much in the hardship and repression against which the uprisings were directed, as the cultural changes which subsequently flowed from them. The failed revolutions awoke feelings of both national and individual identity: in the great multi-national conglomeration of the Habsburg Austrian Empire, for instance, peoples such as the Hungarians, the Poles and the Czechs cherished their national identity and longed to assert their independence. In France, republican ideals re-surfaced; King Louis-Philippe was over-thrown and the Second Republic established universal male suffrage.

1. FRANCE – Franck, Saint-Saëns, Lalo, Chausson

Even before 1848, there had been stirrings of a new individuality in French music. In 1839, the same year that Mendelssohn was writing his d minor trio op.49, a serious young concert pianist in Paris was also at work on a piano trio. He was developing an idea he had heard briefly in works by Beethoven, Schubert and Mendelssohn which in the course of time would become an innovative extension of the sonata idea: this was to link the movements of a work with the same musical quotations. He had no intention of overthrowing or supplanting sonata form – on the contrary, its tonal patterns and formal framework were fundamental to him – but he had innovative ideas of his own about the sonata's presentation and development of themes. He saw thematic development as a means of linking the separate movements of the sonata to form a larger, cohesive whole. The young pianist's name was César Franck (1822-1890) and at the time he wrote his piano trio in f# minor op.1 no 1 (which introduced the principle of "cyclic" unity) he was only 17 years old.

Franck's trio has three, not four, movements. He omits the traditional opening movement in sonata form – perhaps to focus attention on the thematic material of the slow movement which opens the work, without the distractions of the expected "events" inherent in the sonata idea. Unusually, he barely departs from the home tonic key in this movement, although there is variety in the alternation between major and minor modes and in the themes presented.

C Franck: 1st movement *Andante con moto* from Piano Trio in F# minor op.1 no 1

Franck's themes unfold slowly, mysteriously, and somewhat portentously. Three strands emerge:

1) 8 bars of *pianissimo* staccato octaves low in the piano, fingering the notes of the tonic triad (A)

Ex. 32.1

2) a bald sequence of long notes in the 'cello (B), first heard against a repeat of (A)

Ex. 32.2

3) after a long (and gradually more melodic) unfolding, a third theme: a rising and falling scale sentence in the major mode (C)

Ex. 32.3

The formal outline of this movement is so simple, and these themes are repeated so often, that by the end of the movement they are thoroughly familiar: Franck now proceeds to develop them as "motto" themes by re-introducing them into the other movements.

The following Scherzo, with its two Trios, is riddled with reminders of the mottoes, particularly the scale figure (C). At the final return of the scherzo theme, in a brilliant technical twist, Franck writes motto (A) again low in the piano, cleverly incorporating it into the fast tempo of this movement by sounding it only on the first beat of each bar (but in the faster tempo this roughly equates to its original speed). In due course the Scherzo is abandoned as (A) and (B) dominate the climactic close which leads straight into the Finale.

C Franck: 3rd movement Finale *Allegro maestoso* **from Piano Trio in F# minor op.1 no 1**

The Finale is set out in orthodox Sonata Form:

Exposition: After 8 dramatic introductory bars (featuring crashing chords, double octaves in the piano and two general pauses) a proud new theme is introduced as the **1st subject:**

The **2nd Subject** is more romantically lyrical, although we can now hear motto (A) tramping through the piano accompaniment:

Later there is another new figure with a dotted rhythm pressing impulsively forward.

The **Development** section is very long – 200 bars (as compared with 164 in the Exposition, 137 in the Recapitulation and 84 in the Coda). It begins with an ostentatious return of the mottoes (A) and (B) with thunderous accompanying chords in the piano. The 1st subject intervenes, but is twice displaced. At length the more lyrical 2nd subject reappears expressively in the violin. We hear the 'cello mysteriously plucking the entire motto (A) again as a preliminary to the Recapitulation.

The **Recapitulation** is reasonably regular, but the concluding Coda is also dominated by earlier material: the scale figure of motto (C) (as it had been heard in the Scherzo), accompanied by a powerful "ostinato" figure low in the pianist's left hand (also derived from the Scherzo) – which finally provides a grandiose close to the work.

Franck's trio is bombastic, pretentious, but undoubtedly brilliant. It is an intellectual exercise but at times also intensely expressive, and his motto themes, though on first hearing perhaps unpromising, grow into a powerful presence in all three movements. In spite of ourselves, we become involved with them, and each reappearance is heavy with meaning. The emphasis on the first movement in the old sonata has shifted – the Finale is the climax of this work: a logical evolution from Beethoven's shift of emphasis from Recapitulation to Coda, and also a parallel for the climax in other nineteenth-century musical works – and of course in the novel.

The Trio's qualities were recognised by the famous musicians who subscribed to its first edition – including Meyerbeer, Liszt, Donizetti, Halévy, Chopin, Thomas and Auber. After his early career as a pianist, Franck became a distinguished organist and later a professor at the Paris Conservatoire. He was a leading figure in French musical life, with considerable influence in the second half of the nineteenth century. The principle of cyclic form would be significantly developed over the following years, not only by Franck, but also by Liszt, in whose hands it became a significant challenge to the old sonata idea. But at the time of writing this trio in 1839 it was too early for Franck to have been under Liszt's influence, and it is a remarkable work for a 17 year-old.

We should also note the title of this work – *Trio Concertans*. The uninhibited brilliance of Franck's keyboard writing required professional competence and confirms the move of many new works for piano trio out of the domestic *salon* and into the concert hall.

★   ★   ★   ★   ★

As the century progressed, a growing sense of national identity became evident amongst French composers. This was consolidated at the end of the Franco-Prussian War in 1871 by the establishment of the *Société Nationale de Musique*. Taking as its motto "Ars Gallica", it was founded with the specific intention of promoting French music. At the same time, chamber music became more widely appreciated in France. Two of the *Société*'s most active supporters were Camille Saint-Saëns (1835-1921) and Édouard Lalo (1823-1892), who both contributed piano trios to the *genre*.

Saint-Saëns wrote his first trio in 1863. He was a passionate chamber music enthusiast and had been brought up on the Austro-German repertoire. His devotion to Classical models was absolute: he did not adopt cyclic techniques nor indulge in fulsome rhetoric or chromaticism, preferring instead to write with the clarity and orderliness of the Classical style. Sonata Form was second nature to him, and it is easy to follow its framework in the elegant style of the first movement of this piano trio in F major op.18. His singular gift for musical mimicry – as well as the introduction of some indigenous French music – is also evident in the slow movement, where he parodies the sound of a hurdy-gurdy and drone accompanying a Pyreneen folk melody; he ingeniously captures the sound of the rosined wheel being turned at the end of each phrase.

Lalo was also a string player, a member of the professional Armingaud String Quartet, and did much to popularise chamber music in France. The Quartet specialised in the music of Mendelssohn and Schumann, and the romantic fluency of Lalo's last piano trio, in a minor op.26, written in 1880, clearly reflects this influence. Hugh Macdonald writes that he "has strong melodic and rhythmic elements, but" – unlike these models – "virtually no counterpoint".[1] However, his musical ideas are more striking and original than Saint-Saëns, and this is evident in the Scherzo of this trio. Its scintillating impetuosity and the effective contrast of the trio section owe nothing even to Mendelssohn, being entirely products of Lalo's own musical imagination.

It seems from these trios by Saint-Saëns and Lalo that, however intrigued French composers might be by the notion of cultivating a national idiom, the clarity and rationale of the sonata idea was fundamentally congenial to the Gallic mind. Writing with refinement and elegant lyricism, they were able to make a distinctive nineteenth-century contribution to the trio literature.

Although he produced no more piano trios, Franck continued to develop his cyclic technique. It was also adopted by a number of other French composers, such as Chausson, Roussel, Lekeu, Magnard, Ropartz and Migot. A few of these handled the quotations successfully, although others less so. With none of the imagination with which Franck had introduced and then transformed his mottoes, they simply "cut and pasted" phrases from the first movement into later stages of a work, expecting repeated but virtually unaltered statements, played ever more loudly, to have the same effect. This sort of theatricality can be heard in Ernest Chausson's (1855-1899) piano trio in g minor op.3, written in 1881.

This trio is also a good example of how a certain romantic style could become stale with over-use. Smallman describes it as "written in the somewhat over-ripe romantic style of the period ... over-reliant on second-hand rhetoric and a near-exhausted vein of melodic and harmonic expression."[2] Perhaps it finally reflects the degenerative long-term effect on musical style of the sensibility we first encountered in the eighteenth century, the insidious influence of salon culture, and a century's reading of sentimental novels from *Pamela* to *Madame Bovary* in 1857 – those novels memorably described by Flaubert as

"about love, lovers, loving, martyred maidens swooning in secluded lodges, postilions slain every other mile, horses ridden to death on every page, dark forests, aching hearts, promising, sobbing, kisses and tears, little boats by moonlight, nightingales in the grove, *gentlemen* brave as lions, tender as lambs, virtuous as a dream, always well dressed, and weeping pints."[3]

One other French piano trio might be mentioned here. It was written in 1880, the same year as Lalo's trio op.26, by an 18-year-old student from the Paris Conservatoire. He was engaged to teach her children over the summer months by Madame von Meck – better known to posterity as the generous patron of Tchaikovsky. The student was Claude Debussy (1862-1918) and he produced his only piano trio for performance one summer evening. Not surprisingly, it reflects the circumstances for which it was written, and since it bears little resemblance to Debussy's subsequent musical development, Smallman thinks "it is probably best left in decent obscurity".[4] Judged as a light *salon* sonata, and not by Debussy's own standards, it is nevertheless a prettily-melodic and rather attractive work.

This was by no means the end of the line for French chamber music, however. Two of the finest piano trios in the repertoire were composed by Frenchmen born in the nineteenth century, but they were yet to be written. Both Ravel's and Fauré's trios appeared after 1900 and will therefore be considered in another chapter.

2. BOHEMIA – Smetana, Dvořák

We go now to another nation directly involved in political upheaval in 1848. Bedřich Smetana (1824-1884) was a young man of 24 at the time of the Prague Revolution. His patriotic feelings were fervently aroused and he volunteered to man the barricades as well as to write some revolutionary marches. He remained deeply patriotic through-out his life, in due course becoming the first nationalist composer of his country, and writing characteristically Czech music in operas such as *The Bartered Bride*.

We should not be surprised therefore to find that his only piano trio, written in 1855, has a distinctly Czech flavour: both the second and third of its three movements are based on Slavonic dance rhythms. Nationalism plays only a peripheral role in this work, however. More importantly – and at the time of its composition more unusually – it is a sonata work in Liszt's "programmatic" style. Smetana was later to write a number of works inspired by an extra-musical idea, such as the symphonic poem *Má Vlast* ("My Fatherland") and the autobiographical string quartet *Z mého Zivota* ("From My Life"), but his trio is one of the earliest of such works. It was prompted by a personal tragedy: the death of his much-loved eldest daughter Bedřiška from scarlet fever when only four and a half years old. With masterly imagination, Smetana devises an affecting motto theme and with cyclic repeats of it creates a unified and profoundly moving memorial work to his child.

The "motto" is heard in the violin in the opening bars of the first movement: it is an angular figure, with strong accents stumbling down a descending melodic line. It is not inappropriate to assume that this motto represents the parents' grief – a falling melodic line in the minor mode always tends to melancholy, and especially so when it descends chromatically, in semitone steps, as it does here. (We are reminded of the chromatically-descending "ground" (bass line) used by Purcell below the grief-laden melodic line of Dido's famous lament: falling semitones have a time-honoured history of expressing desolation.)

This motto motif turns out to be the 1st subject of the opening sonata form movement. It dominates the long and dramatic Development section and also the Coda – where in the closing bars it is transformed into a descending chromatic scale, falling powerfully down a full octave. As the movement ends, we are very familiar with this motto, and we are in no doubt of its significance.

There is nothing depressing, however, about the succeeding *Polka*. It wittily transforms the motto into the duple metre of the dance, and although it is not actually the principal *polka* theme of the movement (which follows immediately afterwards), it reappears again twice. Near the close there is another chromatic scale, falling down from the home V to the tonic.

As with Franck's trio, it is the final movement which brings the emotional climax to this work. The motto does not play a large role here, partly because much of the movement's material was taken from an earlier (but unfinished) piano sonata, and partly because it is Smetana's plan to finish in an uplifting, not a morbid, mood. However, the descending chromaticism can clearly be heard at the opening, and recurs later at significant points.

B Smetana: 3rd movement *Presto* from Piano Trio in G minor op.15

Two emphatic bars introduce the falling chromatic motto at high speed: this is a Rondo movement whose principal subject (**R**) is a Czech *skočná*, a fast dance in duple meter (although we hear it against the triplet quavers of the 6/8 time signature).

Ex. 33.1

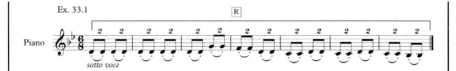

It whirls on until finally coming to rest on a low E♭ note in the piano, shortly explained as the dominant of A♭ (some distance from the home tonic). The 'cello launches into a beautiful **2nd theme**:

Ex. 33.2

It is then taken up by the violin, and a little later both strings pour their hearts out in a passage of imitative counterpoint based on the leaping intervals of this lovely melody.

The *skočná* Rondo theme returns.

It is followed again by the 2nd subject and then the imitative counterpoint. We hear hints of motto chromaticism in the flowing piano accompaniment. The pace slows, and suddenly we realise that the piano has slipped back into the minor mode, and a slower rhythm, low in the left hand, is sounding out the doleful accompaniment to a funeral march: the intervals of the beautiful theme have become a lament for the child. Chromatic semitones abound, and then – as suddenly as it had descended – the gloom is dispelled by a radiant return to the major mode of the home key. The chromatic descent of the motto can be heard, but now the lyrical melody has returned in all its beauty and will not be drowned out.

Finally the *skočná* tries to make a comeback – but its minor mode is out of place and it is rapidly drummed away by three closing bars in the major mode.

R	–	2	–	**R**	–	2	– [R replaced –	Coda
skočná				*skočná*			by 2 as a funeral march]	
i min		A♭		i min		E♭	i min	I maj

The tone of the motto theme and the inclusion of the funeral march are clearly programmatic. There will be more to say about the conflict between this view of music and the opposite view, that music is "absolute", capable of "expressing" nothing but itself, in the next chapter. But for the moment we can see that Smetana is poised between the two. He exploits his audience's familiarity with the sonata framework to present extra-musical ideas within it: it is sonata form which establishes his motto and the elegiac mood of the work, even if by the end he has altered the traditional balance between the movements by placing the emotional climax in the last movement. As well as being so touching, this piano trio by Smetana is one of the most successful trios outside the Austro-German mainstream tradition in the second half of the nineteenth century.

Arguably the finest of all nineteenth-century piano trios to emerge outside Germany, however, was not Smetana's, but one written by another Czech composer, Antonín Dvořák (1841-1904). Over the course of his lifetime, this remarkable musician progressed from simple peasant beginnings to international fame. During that time he came under a number of different influences: by the time he wrote his third piano trio in 1883 he had come through both a strict Classicist style (modelled on Beethoven and Schubert, also Mendelssohn and Schumann) and a freer, more markedly nationalistic one (drawing on Liszt and his own Slavonic heritage). In 1877 Dvořák's music was noticed by Brahms, who became his friend as well as a significant musical influence. By then his technique had developed to match his distinctive musical inventiveness, but due to contemporary political tensions between Bohemia and Germany in the 1870s his music was dismissed by his German contemporaries: he was urged by his friends to further his career by moving to Vienna, but remained loyally in Prague. However, his international reputation became cemented by his popularity in London, Russia and the USA, and by the time of his death he was fêted throughout Europe.

Dvořák's third piano trio in f minor op.65 begins with a movement in sonata form:

A Dvořák: 1st movement *Allegro ma non troppo* from Piano Trio no 3 in F minor op.65

Exposition:

We sense immediately that we are in the world of Schubert's E♭ trio: the opening **1st subject** flows easily from one bar to the next, but this is not an ingratiating 4 + 4 bar tune, but a succession of "energy-laden" motifs. The first four notes, *pp* in the strings, define the home tonic triad 1(a) then lend their rhythmic momentum to a series of copycat shapes 1(b). Next come three stamping tutti chords 1(c), with a wriggling quaver tailpiece 1(d). We do not yet realise it, but the 10 opening bars have given us much of the thematic substance of the entire movement.

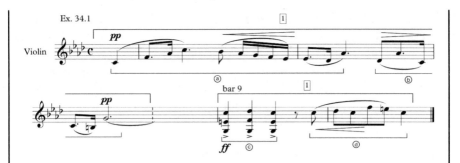

Ex. 34.1

We hear it all again, each motif spinning new development, then begin to sense keys drifting away from the home tonic in preparation for the 2nd subject.

The piano settles on the chord of the relative major of the home key – A♭ – not in its own right, however, but as the V of the distant key of D♭ (the ♭VI of the home tonic). The 'cello claims our attention and pours out a gloriously lyrical **2nd subject** over the next 10 bars.

Ex. 34.2

As it ends the piano interjects with an impatient upwardly-thrusting figure, which the violin takes up, tames and carries into its own seraphic statement of the theme, high in its register. Again the thrusting figure interrupts, and this time takes the movement into brisk cadencing figures which close the Exposition.

Development:

Faithful to classical models, this begins with the 1st subject: the strings take up all four motifs in turn, first (a) and (b), and then (c) and (d) – beginning gently, but generating increasing energy as they develop and alter the character of the originals, tossing them freely from one to the other. Finally this all subsides and three low, slow semitones in the 'cello suggest that perhaps the 2nd subject will follow. But Dvořák eschews such sentimentality (this is a classical dramatic development section) and these semitones turn out to be an ingenious transformation of (b), (c) and (d), augmented to note values of twice their original length and now the basis of a new lyrical duet between the two strings. A grand climax leads back to the

> **Recapitulation:**
>
> The 1st subject returns in its original version and with considerable grandeur. The Recapitulation proceeds, broadly following the Exposition, and certainly including the lyrical 2nd subject (now in the home tonic *major* mode).
>
> **Coda:**
>
> In a final concentrated display of energy and ingenuity all four motifs of the 1st subject play their part in driving the movement to a brilliant close.

So much of this movement is built on classical models – its rhetorical development of motifs, the dramatic energy of the Development, the triumphant return of the Recapitulation. Yet the 2nd subject poses the central dilemma of combining classical and romantic styles: as we luxuriate in this glorious oasis of lyricism it is *holding up the action* in a very unclassical way. Dvořák clearly recognises the problem and uses his melody very sparingly: it only appears twice, and not at all in the Development nor in the Coda. At each appearance we are hustled on by the thrusting figure, whose sole purpose seems to be to restore onward momentum. It is all very skilfully handled, and we may think it has enabled us to enjoy the best of both worlds.

> **A Dvořák: 2nd movement *Allegretto grazioso* from Piano Trio no 3 in F minor op.65**
>
> Dvořák replaces the classical minuet and trio with a Slavonic dance (A) and Trio. This is a typical Czech dance, in duple metre:
>
> Ex. 34.3
>
>
>
> The gently flowing quavers of the Trio could hardly offer a better contrast.

This is an admirable example of the lively cross-accented rhythms with which Slavonic dance music now enlivened the sonata literature. Its unusual accents are such that it is not easy to hear (**A**) as the simple 8-bar tune which it actually is. But if you begin counting as the piano enters (on the first beat of the bar – this is not an upbeat, although it may sound like one) 1 – 2 – 3 – 4, then you will find that (a) is indeed a simple 4 + 4 bar dance.

The slow movement is in a ternary A – B – A form, after the principle of the old Da Capo aria, but by no means so slavishly repetitive. This trio was written shortly after the death of Dvořák's mother, and the elegiac tone of this movement may, consciously or unconsciously, be a reflection of his feelings at this time.

A Dvořák: 3rd movement: *Poco Adagio* from Piano Trio no 3 in F minor op.65

A: opens with the 'cello in broken phrases, like a faltering voice trying to articulate a profound emotion. A second musical idea is more secure and the two are gently interwoven to the end of the section.

B: a brisk figure on the violin is imitated by the 'cello and surges through both strings in a series of thrilling harmonic sequences. These finally come to rest on the home V, whereupon Dvořák gives us another exquisitely romantic melody high in the violin's register (probably derived from earlier motifs – but this is hardly relevant). Its closing phrases merge into the return of section A.

A: presents its two musical ideas again, but this time in reverse order.

Coda: Dvořák bids goodbye to the movement with brief references to both the romantic melody of B and the second idea from A.

The Finale returns to Slavonic dance idioms with a sonata Rondo ingeniously based on the traditional contrasting characteristics of the Czech *furiant*. These contrasts were described by a contemporary in 1859. In the first part of the dance

"... The [male] dancer imitates a proud puffed-up farmer: his arms akimbo, he stamps with his feet, pulls his skirt outwards ..."[5]

His partner has to wait until the second part, then they dance together more slowly and to a different rhythm. Dvořák's Rondo theme depicts the puffed-up farmer's solo, and the 2nd subject the couple dance. His *furiant* also parodies the dance's traditionally complicated syncopations.

A Dvořák: 4th movement Finale: *Allegro con brio* **from Piano Trio no 3 in F minor op.65**

The opening bars present the *furiant* Rondo (**R**). Although it is written out as 6 bars in triple metre, we actually hear it as:

2 bars of 3 beats – then 3 bars of 2 beats – then back to 2 bars of 3 beats.

This captures the characteristic alternating metre of the dance. Moreover Dvořák's elastic theme is comprised of four rhythmic nuggets which fuel the ongoing vitality of the movement.

Ex. 34.4

The wife's **2nd subject** lilts like a gentle waltz, providing a delightful contrast to the farmer's robust opening.

Ex. 34.5

The two themes alternate in a classical sonata rondo format as follows:

R   –   2nd subj   –   R   –   2   –   R   –   Coda

I   ♭VI   I   I   I   I

There is a surprise return of the contours of the 1st subject from the first movement just before the final Coda – not with great significance but as an epigrammatic close to the work as a whole.

Incorporating these dance rhythms brings a pulsing life to the sonata idea, and is entirely appropriate: as we have seen, the sonata *derived* from the dance. Beethoven's scherzo had already replaced the staid minuet with idiosyncratic rhythms, and Slavonic rhythms seem an equally natural fit. Furthermore the energy of the *furiant* is well suited to the long tradition of ending suites or sonatas in a rejoicing mood with a *gigue* or rondo.

Dvořák's trio is an admirable contribution to the literature of the *genre*. The first movement is surprisingly faithful to sonata form

– although above the framework there is little division into the old tonal boxes, and the texture is more continuous. The 1st subject is not a clearly-defined theme, but a texture of constantly-developing motifs generating momentum and perpetual dynamic change. The 2nd subject is another matter: it is on a plateau of its own, stylistically quite different from the rest of the movement. It takes us back to the heart of the problem posed by Beethoven's *Archduke* and Schubert's B♭ trios: can classical rhetoric and romantic sentiment be combined in a single movement? There is no correct answer to this: it must surely be a matter of personal taste. But even for those who think "no", Dvořák's sensitive handling of the problem in this trio may be about as satisfactory a solution as possible.

With its outstanding musical inventiveness, masterly handling of Slavonic rhythms and soaring melodies, Dvořák's third piano trio is a distinguished variation on the Austro-German mainstream tradition.

3. RUSSIA – Tchaikovsky, Taneyev, Arensky, Rachmaninoff

Before returning to Brahms, there is one more distinctive strain of musical nationalism to be considered – in Russia. After Chopin's *krakowiak* and the Bohemian *skočná* and *furiant* we might expect to find here chamber music with an invigorating injection of Cossack or Caucasian dance rhythms. However, we will not find any piano trios written by the group of self-declared nationalists who established themselves in St Petersburg in the 1860s. The "Mighty Five" – Balakirev, Cui, Borodin, Mussorgsky and Rimsky-Korsakov – were self-trained musical amateurs, and deeply suspicious of the German symphony and sonata tradition, because for them it represented a much-reviled influence on what they thought of as the "true" Russian culture of the peasantry.

Russia had been introduced to western culture by Peter the Great. When he became Tsar near the end of the seventeenth century he despised what he saw as "its archaic culture and parochialism, its superstitions, fear and resentment of the West".[6] Determined that Russia should be a part of Enlightenment Europe, he had built St Petersburg as a new capital city on the edge of the Baltic Sea so that it should be "a window on to Europe" (to quote Pushkin). It became not merely a window, but an open doorway through which Europe and its culture for the next two centuries poured in to dominate the beautiful new city and the life of its gilded court and aristocracy.

The St Petersburg Conservatory was founded in 1862 by the great Russian pianist Anton Rubinstein. He had studied in Berlin and

Vienna and insisted that the basis of the new academy's curriculum should be the music of J S Bach and Haydn, Mozart and Beethoven: he dismissed Russian music as "only of ethnographical interest". Thus a thoroughly western training was given to one of the Conservatory's earliest pupils, Pyotr Ill'yich Tchaikovsky (1840-93). While Tchaikovsky was still a student, another Conservatory was established in Moscow by Anton's younger brother, Nicolay, and Tchaikovsky transferred there to teach harmony. The extrovert Nicolay became one of the young man's most devoted supporters, and his early death in 1881 was a severe blow. It prompted the composition of Tchaikovsky's only piano trio, written as a tribute "To the Memory of a Great Artist". We shall find it very different in style from the French and Czech trios we have just heard.

It will also be the longest. Beethoven's *Archduke* takes roughly 38 minutes in performance, Schubert's E♭ about 46 minutes, and Dvořák's op.65 about 40. All these trios have four movements, whereas although Tchaikovsky's has only three, even if performed with sanctioned cuts it takes some 50 minutes. It was completed in considerable haste for a first performance on the anniversary of Nicolay's death a year later, which perhaps accounts for its unedited length. The three movements are thematically linked, however, and to appreciate the work it is necessary to hear their cumulative effect, so in spite of its length we shall consider it as a whole.

P Tchaikovsky: 1st movement *Pezzo elegiaco – moderato assai* from Piano Trio in A minor op.50

Exposition: This "*Pezzo elegiaco*" ("elegiac composition") is both a recognisable sonata structure and an unconventional manipulation of the form – we shall find that it has no fewer than five distinct themes. The brooding **1st subject** unfolds powerfully in the 'cello: the opening bar decorates the dominant note with the expressive ♭6th of the minor mode (a), then falls down stepwise to the tonic. The tone of this "fatalistic" falling scale will be the inspiration for much which follows.

Ex. 35.1

After several repeats motif (a) leads a transition to the **2nd subject**, conventionally in the home V of E; this is in two parts, the first with robust chords, 2(a),

Ex. 35.2

Piano

the second a gracious lilting melody, 2(b) (both demonstrating the different, *brighter* sound of the *major* 6th).

Ex. 35.3

Violin

The concluding 4-note *motif* 2(c) is repeated at length before finally closing on the home V (classical ending for an Exposition).

The **Development** begins with another new theme (x) (related however to the falling scale *motif*), which is repeated at length over wide-ranging harmonies,

Ex. 35.4

Violin

until yet another new theme (y), *dolce espressivo* ("sweetly expressive") is introduced by the violin.

Ex. 35.5

Violin

Again this is developed repetitively, finally arriving on an expectant home V note in a brief violin cadenza.

The **Recapitulation** follows regularly with 1st and both parts of the 2nd subjects, all in tonic minor or major.

The **Coda** returns to the two new themes from the Development, but in a final postscript the piano reverts to the motto theme of the 1st subject, augmenting the notes to twice their original length as the strings close the movement with the melancholy falling scale.

This is not a movement written in the classical sonata form style of any of the great masters: the plethora of themes are extensively *repeated*, not truly developed, and the Development section does not discuss the material of the Exposition, but rather introduces more new material. The style is luxuriantly Romantic rather than Classically pithy, prolix rather than aphoristic.

The opening statement of the 1st subject also gives us a good example (for those who may be interested) of the way in which nineteenth-century composers decorated their melodies with chromatic harmony. The chart below analyses Tchaikovsky's colourful shifting harmony (although, as always, identifying the chord progressions is less important than *hearing* their colourful effect). Note also the falling sequences of 3rds from bar 10:

5 bars	–	4 bars	–	2 bars	–	2 bars	–	2 bars	–	2 bars	–	1 bar	–	2 bars
home I		IV		home V/I		III		I		♭VI		♭II		I
(a min)		(d min)		(E – a min)		(C maj)		(a min)		(F maj)		(B♭)		(a min)
		(flat side of key)				(rel major)				(interrupted cadence)		(surprise)		(home)

Fig. 10 Pyotr Tchaikovsky: 1st movement Piano Trio in A minor op.50

The second movement is exceptionally long: it is a Theme with 12 Variations, leading without a break into the last movement – in a dramatic twist, the last Variation becomes the 1st subject of the finale. It is also the emotional heart of the work, since it represents Tchaikovsky's personal links with Nicolay Rubinstein. We know that the Theme was inspired by memories of a spring day in 1873 which they spent together in countryside near Moscow, enjoying the singing and dancing of local peasants. Tchaikovsky intended the Variations to reflect this and other shared events in Rubinstein's life; he wrote to his brother Modest that they "… are only memories. One is a memory of a trip to an Amusement Park out of town, and another of a ball we both attended, and so on."

P Tchaikovsky: 2nd movement *Tema con variazioni – Andante con moto* from Piano Trio in A minor op.50

The scale of the vast movement is indicated immediately: the theme and its first two Variations are given to each instrument in turn:

Tema: *Andante con moto.* The innocuous theme (**Tema**) is presented, simply harmonised in the piano.

Piano

p cantabile

Var.I: The melody of the theme in the violin, with a running semi-quaver accompaniment in the piano.

Var.II: *Più mosso.* The 'cello takes up the theme.

Var.III: *Allegro moderato.* Picking up speed, the piano condenses the characteristic opening bars of the theme into *scherzoso* semi-quavers, punctuated by a *pizzicato* accompaniment in the strings.

Var.IV: *(minor key)* With growing pretentiousness, the strings and piano bandy fragments of the theme amongst themselves, accompanied by steadily trudging chords.

Var.V: The violin and 'cello sound a rustic drone to a new version of the theme *martellato*, high in the piano register. (This movement surely refers to that day in the country.)

Var.VI: *Tempo di Valse.* At the end of Var.V, the 'cello continues to hold its final note, then carries it on into Var.VI with a magical Schubertian key change (down a major 3rd) to A major, where it embarks on a gracefully balletic waltz. All the instruments join in turn, the piano plunging exuberantly into the distant key of C major. We begin to think this is all very delightful, but wonder what it has to do with the original theme, when suddenly we hear the *Tema* again in the strings, swaying gently on the first beat of each bar – it has been transformed as a countersubject to the waltz.

Var.VII: *Allegro moderato.* Punctuated by the strings, the piano gives us another bombastic version of the theme in chunky chords.

Var.VIII: *Fuga – Allegro moderato.* Tchaikovsky nails his European credentials to the mast with a full-scale academic Fugue. All the technical devices of this venerable form are here (formal subject and answer, episodes, canon, stretto, augmentation and so on ...): it is unexpected but exhilarating, obviously intended as a tribute to Nicolay's academic contribution to Russian culture.

Var.IX: *Andante flebile ma non tanto.* The minor mode returns as the outlines of the theme in the strings is heard through a veil of flying demi-semiquavers in the piano.

Var.X: *Tempo di Mazurka*. The piano dances through another ingenious transformation of the theme into a *mazurka*; after a mini-cadenza the strings join in too.

Var.XI: *Moderato*. With another falling third key change we are safely back in the home key, and for the first time, as the tune is sung high by the violin, we realise it is capable of lyrical generosity. The slow movement thus ends with something nearer to the original version of the theme.

3rd movement: *Variazione Finale e Coda – Allegro risoluto e con fuoco*

[Var.XII:] The Finale follows immediately, inexorably anchored to the final variation of the theme, *risoluto e con fuoco* – which indeed it is. This "resolute and fiery" version turns out to be the **1st subject** of a very long but quite straightforward sonata form movement,

Ex. 35.7

the **2nd subject** being also related to the second part of the theme:

Ex. 35. 8

The **Development** section is based on the 2nd subject. In performance, because this movement is so repetitive, a large part of both Exposition and Development are often omitted – which regrettably distorts Tchaikovsky's original formal balance. The **Recapitulation** finally builds to a momentous climax, culminating in the return of the first movement minor mode motto theme.

An immense **Coda** follows, with the strings declaiming the motto theme (1st subject) from the first movement *fortissimo*, two octaves apart, while the piano thunders out "a tumultuous accompaniment of chords and flashing arpeggios, providing the *ne plus ultra* of heavyweight scoring for trio".[7] The strings confirm the sombre significance of the fatalistic falling minor scale, and the motto is finally borne away by the solemn tramp of a funeral march receding into the distance.

This is an extraordinary work. At times, it seems to try and pour the passionate intensity of orchestral sound into the slender trio framework. Indeed, Tchaikovsky himself realised this, saying in a letter to Mme von Meck that "I may have arranged music of a symphonic character as a trio, instead of writing directly for my instruments."[8] It may not have the spindly elegance of the Classical western sonata style, but the swashbuckling nature of this elegy seems not inappropriate for the extrovert Nicolay, who died in a Paris hotel after eating a dozen oysters on his deathbed. (In defence of the molluscs – and also of the hotel – it should be pointed out that oysters were not the cause of Rubinstein's death: he was already suffering from advanced pulmonary tuberculosis.)

We sense also that this is truly *nationalist* music – that there is something very Russian about the intensity of the musical expression which Tchaikovsky brings to the western tradition. Some 60 years later, Stravinsky wrote:

"The music of Tchaikovsky, which does not seem obviously Russian to everyone, is often more profoundly Russian than that which long ago received the superficial label of Muscovite picturesqueness. This music is every bit as Russian as Pushkin's verse or Glinka's songs. Without specifically cultivating 'the Russian peasant soul' in his art, Tchaikovsky imbibed unconsciously the true national sources of our race."[9]

When we considered Haydn's musical style, we compared the architectural design of Eszterháza with the classical framework of his sonata form. It is tempting to make a similar comparison for Tchaikovsky. The historian Orlando Figes says that Tchaikovsky was "the last of the great European court composers (he lived in the last of the great European eighteenth-century states)"[10] and he was numbered amongst the intimates of the Tsar Alexander III; the Russia he knew was the westernised court of St Petersburg, the Moscow of the Conservatory and the theatres, the various country estates of his friends and relatives. He was familiar with the great palaces of the Tsars, on a much grander scale even than Eszterháza; they were too vast to be comprehended as an architectural ensemble, and could only be experienced piecemeal, one glittering room at a time. Tchaikovsky's habit of thinking in sections suggests a similarly compartmentalised approach to the sonata idea. He saw it as a secure architectural framework which he filled, not with a continuous narrative development of a few energy-laden motifs, but with a series of beautiful, self-contained musical ideas; not to be understood like the unified architectural ensemble of Eszterháza, but experienced as though moving in a steady progress from one to another of the extraordinary staterooms of the Winter Palace.

Tchaikovsky's essentially lyrical style and repetitive development technique, however, are not really suited to the conventional sonata idea: this trio gives us a sequence of sectional rhapsodies, not the narrative thrust of a sonata argument. We have seen that some composers have difficulty containing romantic melody within the sonata, but Tchaikovsky has no such difficulty because he does not even attempt to stem the flow of his musical thought, but continues piling tunes generously into the established tonal framework. (The notion of using Variations for the slow movement was a particularly good one – they introduced appropriate extra-musical associations without need for musical development.) But whatever its failings as a sonata work, this trio for Rubinstein shows us a composer with a wonderfully fertile musical imagination in the great nineteenth-century Romantic tradition, full of melodic charm and inventiveness and capable of tapping into every human emotion from high spirits to the depths of desolation.

★   ★   ★   ★   ★

Although the "Mighty Five" nationalists declined to write sonata compositions, other Russian composers were more sympathetic to classical western tradition. These included some who wrote chamber music, such as Tchaikovsky's pupil Sergey Ivanovich Taneyev (1856-1915), who wrote a single piano trio, and Rimsky-Korsakov's pupil Anton Arensky (1861-1906), who wrote two. All these are competent sonata works: Taneyev's piano trio in D major op.22 is filled with distinctive although not melodically-memorable themes, and Arensky's first piano trio in d minor op.32 is notable for its fresh inventiveness and the ingenuity of its scoring.

When Tchaikovsky died in 1893, another young Russian composer, Serge Rachmaninoff (1873-1943), immediately set himself to write a "Trio élégiaque" in his memory. Also trained at the Conservatories in St Petersburg and Moscow, Rachmaninoff's trio op.9 is broadly similar to Tchaikovsky's: its first movement is in sonata form (even more sectionalised, with an abundance of melodic ideas pouring out one after another), a set of variations (ingeniously alternating close copies of the theme with freer variations – almost in the manner of a returning scherzo with alternating trios), and a final movement dominated by the piano, culminating with a funereal motto – in that mood of profound gloom which Russian composers seemed to have made their own.

Rachmaninoff was one of the last of the great nineteenth-century concert pianists, and, to a greater extent even than Tchaikovsky's, his trio struggles with the effort of containing quasi-orchestral scoring within the confines of three single instruments. It is also diffuse and repetitive, although its stream of impassioned melody and lush harmony has a certain intoxicating effect on the listener. The old formal frameworks are as necessary as ever, since they prescribe the gratification of returning themes in tonally secure settings. But the art of listening to this music has become different, less intense, more passive. Blume describes it well:

"When most composers are not strongly purposeful about form, then form itself seems but an external housing for regions of expression and planes of colour, and … [composers] cast an additional veil over the movement and lull the listener in the magic of their sensually harmonious sound, so that he is not provoked to any co-operative interest in the music – indeed, is not even permitted to share in it. A pleasurable intoxication takes the place of Goethe's 'thinking enjoyment'. Herein perhaps lies one of the deepest contrasts between Classicism and Romanticism, since in the former the music itself demands energetic personal co-operation from the listener, whereas in the latter he is actually compelled to give himself over to a sweet passivity."[11]

The music of Tchaikovsky and Rachmaninoff represents the most extreme transformation of the sonata idea we have yet heard. So this is an appropriate moment to return to Vienna and listen to a piano trio – written within a year of Tchaikovsky's – by the last great composer in the nineteenth-century Austro-German mainstream tradition: Johannes Brahms.

CHAPTER ENDNOTES

1   Macdonald, Hugh. Article on Lalo, Édouard in *New Grove Dictionary of Music and Musicians,* 1980, vol.10.

2   Smallman, *op.cit.*, p.145.

3   Flaubert, *Madame Bovary*, p.34.

4   Smallman, *op.cit*, p.162.

5   Waldau, A in *Böhmische Nationaltänze: eine Culturstudie*, Prague, 1859, i, pp.31-2.

6   Figes, Orlando. *Natasha's Dance: A Cultural History of Russia.* London: Allen Lane, Penguin Press, 2002, p.12.

7   Smallwood, *op.cit.* p.167.

8   Letter to Mme von Meck, January 1882.

9   Cited in Taruskin, R, *Stravinsky and the Russian Traditions*, vol.2, pp.1529,1532; quoted by Orlando Figes, *op.cit*, p.558.

10 Figes, *op.cit*, p.274.

11 Blume, *op.cit*, p.155.

CHAPTER 18

THE AUSTRO-GERMAN
MAINSTREAM 4: BRAHMS

THE DETAILS OF Johannes Brahms's early life are not dissimilar from Beethoven's. Both came of somewhat undistinguished provincial musical families; because of a background in music, both were sent to study with the best teachers available; although neither enjoyed Mendelssohn's access to the teaching of first-rank musicians, both were recognised as exceptionally musically gifted, and were introduced at an early age to the music of Bach and the Viennese Classicists; and both began their musical careers as concert pianists.

Brahms's father was nothing if not a versatile musician: Johann Jakob played the flute, horn, violin and double bass. He probably himself gave the young Johannes (1833-1897) his first music lessons on the piano, 'cello and horn, but sent him at the age of seven to others for more serious piano lessons. The pianist and composer Eduard Marxsen introduced the young boy to the music of Bach and the Viennese masters, and Johannes gave his first known public performance at the age of ten in a concert of chamber music. His first solo piano recital included, in addition to the usual *bravura* pieces, works by Bach and Beethoven.

At the age of seventeen Johannes was much impressed by a concert given in his native Hamburg by a young Hungarian violinist only five years older than himself. Ede Reményi was one of a number of political refugees fleeing Hungary after the suppression of the revolution of 1848, and passing through Hamburg on their way to the USA. Johannes was impressed not only by Reményi's technical mastery of his instrument, and the quality of his playing (which was as soulful as it was spirited), but also by his repertoire of music in the *style hongrois*. This may not have been pure Hungarian folk music – it probably had a generous overlay of gypsy tradition – but its irregular rhythms, triplet figures and expressive use of *tempo rubato* were to become distinctive features of Brahms's own musical style.

Three years later, Reményi persuaded Brahms to accompany him on a concert tour of northern Germany. During the course of three months Johannes met a number of distinguished musicians who would have a profound effect on the rest of his life, both professionally as well as personally. The first meeting was in Göttingen with the brilliant violinist Joseph Joachim (1831-1907), which marked the beginning of a lifetime of collaborative friendship. The second was in Weimar with Liszt, and this was Brahms's first direct encounter with the camp of the New German School. Liszt was in the process of composing symphonic poems, and Brahms found himself profoundly out of sympathy with the aims and aspirations of the Progressives: it proved an informative and timely visit.

It was Joachim who encouraged Brahms also to visit the Schumanns. Later in 1853 the twenty-year old Johannes duly arrived in Düsseldorf clutching a sheaf of piano pieces, songs and chamber music. Robert and Clara were both deeply impressed by the young musician, and even more significant lifetime friendships were established. The following month, in another of his flashes of insight, Robert wrote in the *Neue Zeitschrift für Musik*:

"I felt certain that ... an individual would suddenly appear, fated to give expression to the times in the highest and most ideal manner, who would achieve mastery, not step by step, but all at once, springing like Minerva fully armed from the head of Jove. And now here he is, a young man at whose cradle graces and heroes stood watch."[1]

It was a two-edged accolade. It helped to establish Brahms's international reputation at a very early stage in his career, but such effusive praise from so distinguished a musician was daunting and Brahms was ever after conscious of the need to live up to such expectations. Because of Schumann, too, Brahms had to bear the burden of being widely regarded as the late nineteenth-century successor to Beethoven.

Hanslick's support for Brahms[2] in the War of the Romantics was therefore timely. The ground-breaking treatise on *The Beautiful in Music* served two important purposes: firstly, to refute the excessive emphasis on feelings and emotion in contemporary music – which was the inevitable outcome of the expectations foisted on instrumental music from the beginning of the nineteenth century (now most obviously manifest in the symphonic poems and music dramas of Liszt and Wagner); and secondly, to encourage audiences to return to understanding the *purely musical* content of music (which had after all underpinned the classical sonata idea from its inception).

Hanslick's writing will illuminate our listening to Brahms's music and we should look in some detail at what he had to say.

The opening sentence lays down the gauntlet:

"The course hitherto pursued in musical aesthetics has nearly always been hampered by the false assumption that the object was not so much to inquire into what is beautiful in music as *to describe the feelings which music awakens*."[3] [My italics.]

The essence of music, declares Hanslick, is "sound and motion", and it has "both meaning and logical sequence", but it is in "a language we speak and understand, but which we are unable to translate". This language is made up of "specifically musical" components:

"Melody, unexhausted, nay, inexhaustible, is pre-eminently the source of musical beauty. Harmony, with its countless modes of transforming, inverting, and intensifying, offers the material for constantly new developments; while rhythm, the main artery of the musical organism, is the regulator of both ..."[4]

He explains how these components are assembled:

"In all compositions the independent, aesthetically undecomposable subject of a musical conception is the theme ... the musical microcosm ... What we call the 'form' of a symphony, an overture, a sonata, an aria, a chorus, etc., is the architectonic combination of the units and groups of units of which a composition is made up; or, more definitely speaking, the symmetry of their successions, their contrasts, repetitions, and general working out."[5]

And concludes that

"The most important factor in the mental process which accompanies the act of listening to music, and which converts it into a source of pleasure, is frequently overlooked. We here refer to the intellectual satisfaction which the listener derives from continually following and anticipating the composer's intentions – now to see his expectations fulfilled, and now to find himself agreeably mistaken ... without mental activity no aesthetic enjoyment is possible. But the kind of mental activity alluded to is quite peculiar to music, because its products, instead of being fixed and presented to the mind at once in their completeness, develop gradually and thus do not permit the listener to linger at any point or to interrupt his train of thought. It demands, in fact, the keenest

watching and the most untiring attention ... truly aesthetic listening is an art in itself."[6]

This is a notable passage, giving the listener an acute perception
of music unfolding in the medium of time, and of the concentration
required fully to appreciate it. It anticipates modern thinking about
the mental processing of western music to a remarkable degree. But
we may now feel that the boundaries between music and emotion
are not so sharply divided as Hanslick thought. The line between
"the beautiful object and the perceiving subject" has been redrawn
by modern neuroscientific research, which has given us information
about the working of the human brain undreamed of in 1854. (We
shall come to this later: see pp.340-41.) We may also question the
implacable opposition to Wagner which overshadowed Hanslick's
subsequent reputation (although Wagner had his revenge in *Die
Meistersinger*, caricaturing Hanslick as the pedant Beckmesser).
Hanslick's significance for us is not in the controversies which he
aroused, but in the impact of *The Beautiful in Music* on musical
aesthetics, both at the time of its writing and since. His account of
the attention expected of a listener is timely. He has brought us back
to the habits of mind of the Austro-German mainstream composers,
with their understanding of music as *a design in time*. As we turn
to the music of Brahms we must gear ourselves to try the "mental
activity" needed for "truly aesthetic listening".

Chamber music, with its clear textures and opportunities for intricate interchange, provides an excellent medium for concentrated
listening. Brahms found it especially congenial; not surprisingly,
of his twenty-six listed chamber works, eighteen included his own
instrument, the piano. His earliest published chamber work was a
piano trio, written shortly after the momentous meeting with Robert
and Clara Schumann.

Already determined to continue in the sonata tradition, Brahms
achieves an admirable fusion of Classical principles with Romantic
style in the piano trio no 1 in B major op.8 of 1854. This is immediately obvious from the four opening bars. We have seen all sonata
composers since the eighteenth century building up 8-bar subjects
by accumulating motifs – devising motifs, repeating them, balancing
them with further repeated motifs. Here Brahms appears to begin
in the same vein, repeating the rhythm of the first two bars over and
again in a regular $(2 + 2) + (2 + 2) = 8$ bar phraseology. But there
is little Classical delicacy and decorum about the glorious melody
which unfolds in these and the next 36 bars (it tears at our heart-
strings in only the second bar, *delaying* the anticipated semitone lift
between the 3rd and 4th by overshooting onto the dominant, then
falling back on the next beat to fulfil our expectations – and then

repeating this pattern at different pitches in the following sequences).
Yet, as Walter Frisch points out, "behind its ravishing and apparently
seamless veil of tunefulness, the main theme proves to be constructed
… from continuous recycling of very concise thematic material".[7]

If we look closely at the opening bars of the 1st subject, within the
framework of repeating rhythmic patterns there are also repetitions
of melodic pattern at work:

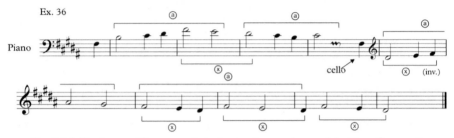

Ex. 36 J. Brahms: *Allegro con brio* from piano trio no 1 in B major op.8

Motif 1(a) is presented in the first two bars, then inverted (played
upside down) in bars 3 – 4, then repeated at a higher pitch, and so
on. Moreover, as Frisch points out, the motif (x) from bar 2 is high-
lighted in bar 9 by shifting its metrical position, "not only to create
cadential momentum but also to reveal a new aspect of the theme,
which has been hidden by the square 2 + 2 structure of earlier
phrases – this is the descending three-note figure, F♯ - E – D♯."[8]

This brief description of only the first few bars gives an indication
of the concentrated nature of Brahms's compositional process. The
three-note motif (x) continues to evolve, not only throughout the 44
bars of the 1st subject, but as a consistent feature of much of the rest
of the movement. It is an early example of what Arnold Schoenberg
subsequently called "developing variation" technique. He identified
it as a significant structural process in Western music from 1750, but
especially in the music of Brahms:

> "Variation of the features of a basic unit produces all the thematic
> formulations which provide for fluency, contrasts, variety, logic
> and unity, on the one hand, and character, mood, expression, and
> every needed differentiation, on the other hand – thus elaborating
> the *idea* of the piece."[9]

When Brahms first composed this trio he followed the long
opening theme with a 2nd subject and further textures of propor-
tionate length; many years later he decided that such length had been
youthful folly and in 1889 he undertook a substantial revision of the
work. The opening theme of the first movement happily survived
intact, but much of the rest, and the subsequent movements, were

altered. (Some of Brahms's friends seem to have approved; some preferred the original version.) The trio is generally now performed in the later version, which is described below – but listeners should be aware that the rest of this movement incorporates a number of late Brahmsian stylistic elements.

J. Brahms: 1st movement *Allegro con brio* from Piano Trio no 1 in B major op.8

Exposition: The **1st subject** unfolds beautifully, firmly establishing the home tonic key of B major.

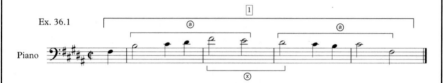

Ex. 36.1

Piano

A Transitional passage follows, based on 3-note derivatives of (x) in different rhythmic guises (ranging from three minims, a dotted crotchet version, and quavers); we also hear (1) itself; and then the harmonies shift towards D♯ as V of g♯ minor (the submediant VI of the home key). Here the 2nd subject shortly follows; it has two components: 2(a), a melodic descending 3rds phrase,

Ex. 36.2

Piano

mp

and 2(b), with off-beat versions of (x).★ After a brief Codetta featuring a new triplet quaver figure (swivelling round a succession of semitones), the Exposition closes, still in g♯ minor, with a double bar and marked repeat. (Brahms is acknowledging that all this will require careful listening to be fully understood.)

Development: The Codetta's chromatic triplet quaver is carried over the double bar and continues to be heard in both background and foreground – almost until the end of the movement. Thematically we hear the 1st subject (frequently, but especially beautifully

---

★ Brahms's love of rhythmic complexity is evident here, as described by Frisch: "Initially the listener has no doubt that all phrases and subphrases begin on the fourth beat of the bar; but … the syncopations across the barline begin to take on the character of downbeats, and the metrical grid seems to shift, now aligning with the fourth and second beats." Frisch, *ibid*, p.61.

high in the violin), and further extensions of the dotted crotchet
derivative of (x). After wide-ranging harmonies we sense a firm
cadential close in g♯ minor, where a glowing version of (1) is heard
in the violin and 'cello in unison, low in the violin's pitch range –
after 5 bars of this we realise that we have picked up on bar 21 of
the Exposition: Brahms sidles back into his home key and begins
the

Recapitulation: After its use in the Development, the 1st subject
is reduced (but now accompanied by the triplet quavers); the
Transitional passage is also shortened, and in due course the 2nd
subject material is heard in the tonic *minor*.

Coda: Returns to I in major mode. There are final tranquil references to the 1st subject (including an ethereal statement in the
violin) until the falling thirds of 2(a) gather momentum and race to
a triumphant close.

The simplicity of the 1st subject in this B major trio enables us to
hear and understand how Brahms builds up short motifs into themes,
then themes into larger paragraphs in a concentrated process which
is both logical and cohesive. "Developing variation" became a mainstay of his composing technique in the works which followed in the
next three decades of his career.

Brahms's international reputation was well established by the
time he was in his forties in the 1870s. Settled in Vienna, he held
few official posts, but lived comfortably off the proceeds of performances and publishing royalties, and established a congenial annual
routine of concerts in the winter and composing at some peaceful
resort in the summer. By the time he came to write his second piano
trio in 1882 he had completed about two-thirds of his total output,
which included not only chamber music and works for solo piano,
but also orchestral works, songs and choral pieces. These generic
titles conceal a number of sets of variations – such as the orchestral *St Anthony* variations op.56a, at least five sets of variations for
solo piano, the slow movements of two piano sonatas and two string
sextets, and the finale of a string quartet (there were five more sets
yet to be written). This was a *genre* which Brahms made very much
his own: as Beethoven had done before him, he used variation sets
to hone the skills which he employed so effectively in sonata works.

Brahms's next piano trio, no 2 in C major op.87, was written in
Bad Ischl in the summer of 1882:

J. Brahms: 1st movement *Allegro* from Piano Trio no 2 in C major op.87

Exposition: The **1st subject** in the opening 8 bars secretes four musical ideas which Brahms will open out to drive this movement. They are:

(a) the first four notes: this is far from Mozart and Schubert's tonic triad openings. (We wonder: what key are we in?)

(b) that last note is joined to the notes of the home fifth triad to make a dominant seventh arpeggio (which we might also recognise as a falling sequence of melodic 3rds).

(c) rising /falling octaves: the dominant seventh sequence ends on a rising octave, which the piano immediately picks up – rising in the left hand, falling in the right hand.

(d) semitones: the strings reply with a sequence of purely decorative chromatic semitones.

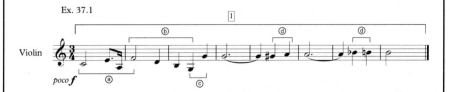

Ex. 37.1

Octaves and semitones drive forward and soon we feel comfortably established in the home key of C major. Another noteworthy phrase **(x)** in bar 21, winding upwards,

Ex. 37.2

leads back to a more ingratiating repeat of the 1st subject. A mere nine bars of Transition lead into the **2nd subject** group. This has three distinct parts, all different comments on the *semitones* proposed by 1(d) in bar 5. The first, 2(a), in the traditional V of G major with suave phrasing but intricate cross-rhythms:

Ex. 37.3

the second, 2(b), (more ambivalent about its key) with coquettish *staccato* phrases:

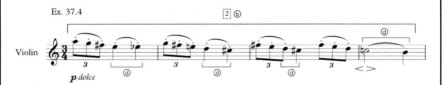

Ex. 37.4

the third, 2(c), more urgent and dramatic with a dotted quaver/two demi-semiquaver rhythm:

Ex. 37.5

The dominant 7th figure from 1(b) pulls us back to the "proper" key of the home dominant, where (over a long pedal on G – which now lasts to the end of the Exposition) an ingratiating new dotted quaver figure begins the Cadential group, and is then followed by a variant of 2(a).

The **Development** begins insouciantly with the 1st subject in the home key (as though this was a repeat of the Exposition!). But then modulations follow thick and fast as the strings press forward with the intense semitones of 2(c); a climax is reached with the violin and 'cello hammering out this dotted rhythm several octaves apart, then calling our attention with (x) to a fine tune from 1(a) and (b) (in a stroke of genius, Brahms notates them at twice their original duration, in slow tempo) in the 'cello, shortly after joined by the violin in a radiant duet. Now (x) – which has taken it upon itself to notify us of impending changes – urges the company on to a climax, culminating in a loud dominant seventh arpeggio (which is, of course, 1(b) …).

Recapitulation: The strings sing out the opening bars of the 1st subject, although the piano does not arrive in the home key until the 5th bar. Because the 1st subject has featured so prominently in the Development, no more is heard of it now. Instead – introduced by the melodic version of the dominant seventh 1(b) – a regular repeat of all three parts of the 2nd subject follow (chromatic decoration apart, all in the home I key).

Coda: Instead of remaining comfortably in the home key, the harmonies begin to drift far away in a wide-ranging piano part. The radiant string duet returns: a final apotheosis of the 1st subject

after the model of Beethoven and Schubert. Every motif 1(a), (b),
(c) and (d) plays a part, and the movement closes with a triumphant but pithy statement of (a) and (b) – the thematic nuggets
which have prompted so much of the movement.

This superb movement is surely one of those which Rosen had in
mind when he referred to "Brahms's magnificent success with sonata
form".[10] The ingenuity with which Brahms applies his developing
variation technique is extraordinary, all the more when we consider
that he builds almost the entire movement from the sparse material
of the opening bars. The 1st subject is like the secretive walnut, its
convoluted kernel so deeply embedded within its shell that the four
musical ideas concealed within it must be prised out one by one to
drive the movement. As initially heard, it is dramatic, but not immediately appealing – certainly not in the way in which the opening
of the B major trio was so appealing. Yet, by the time Brahms has
finished with it, he has turned it, as we hear it in the Development
and the Coda, into an "out-and-out tune", even casting it into regular
8-bar divisions! Furthermore, in spite of the fact that he observes all
the Classical requirements for the Recapitulation to repeat the material of the Exposition, and in between to explore that material in
the Development – with all the attendant difficulty of then handling
the Coda without its becoming an anticlimax – Brahms somehow
contrives to have the best of all worlds and enables us to enjoy the
resolution of the Recapitulation as well as the thematic apotheosis
of the final Coda. He achieves this by a masterly pacing of his material, gradually opening up the lyrical potential of his theme, yet still
holding in reserve that final outpouring for the Coda.

We saw that Dvořák – modelling his style on Brahms himself
– also generated much of his f minor piano trio's first movement
from motivic fragments, but in order to provide lyrical contrast
he invented a beautiful 2nd subject, which held up the sonata's
argument. Brahms, on the other hand, creates his lyrical contrast
by drawing it *from the same motifs*, so that his movement presents
a continuous argument. Yet it also has plenty of variety, since 1(a)
and (b) are themselves contrasted with the semitones of 1(d) and
all its interesting 2nd subject derivatives. We should not, however,
be deceived by the seemingly effortless unfolding of any of these
themes into thinking that the actual process of composition was
effortless. Brahms himself, in conversation with the music critic Max
Marshalk, declared:

"I work a long time on melodies; it is a long way from the first
inspiration to the final shaping of the melody ... A melody that

seems born of the moment is almost always the result of hard work."[11]

We can see Brahms at work on his variation techniques in the second movement of the trio, which is an Air with five Variations, in the relative minor of the home key.

J. Brahms: 2nd movement *Andante con moto* from Piano Trio no 2 in C major op.87

Theme: is first heard in the strings. It has a pervading sense of folk-like melancholy, reinforced by its accented, off-beat rhythm. It closes with a neat cadential tail-piece.

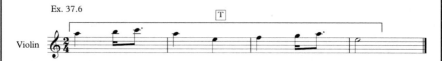

Ex. 37.6

Violin

Var.1: The piano elaborates its accompaniment in a typically Brahmsian keyboard style.

Var.2: Playing on the off-beat figures of the theme, it is skilfully split, piecemeal, amongst all three instruments, turning it into a quasi-contrapuntal texture.

Var.3: The characteristic rhythm of the theme returns in a high treble line, accompanied by triple-stopped chords on the strings, then chunky chords on the piano – a wonderfully rich sound.

Var.4: The time signature changes from 2/4 to 6/8, and the key to A major, substantially altering the character of the theme.

Var.5: The contours of the theme are heard in a mournful melody in the 'cello; followed in due course by the violin. We almost have the feeling that this is the original tune, so naturally does it flow – and that everything else we have heard has been a variation of this and not the theme we have followed from the outset.

As we expected, Brahms's genius for variation produces five highly distinctive ideas from his opening theme. Having drawn so much variety from it, he then transforms it in the final variation, so that we hear and appreciate it in a new and different way. This is the essence of his developing variation technique: we are able to *recognise* his transformations, so that they are a constant source of pleasure and admiration.

This is the moment also to draw attention to Brahms's brilliant scoring for the three instruments of the piano trio. He had played and composed for piano and 'cello all his life; his close association with Joachim as well as Reményi also gave him sensitive insights into the characteristics of the violin. His true understanding of all three instruments results in a great variety of textures and sonorities: he invents sparsely telling textures just as competently as richly romantic ones. Brahms writes superbly idiomatic and individual piano parts, but also wonderful string parts which explore the potential of both violin and 'cello with great imagination and sensitivity.

The third movement of the C major piano trio is a Scherzo and Trio which find Brahms at his most Classically correct:

J. Brahms: 3rd movement Scherzo *Presto* from Piano Trio no 2 in C major op.87

The Scherzo draws on Mendelssohn, alternating scurrying semi-quavers with chromatically-spiced dancing quavers (**S**), all in the minor mode (home tonic c minor, not relative minor).

Ex. 37.7

The Trio is in every way a contrast: it is in the major mode and rambles amiably round secure tonic and dominant triads. Later it has a second section with more chromatic colour.

After all those Bohemian dance rhythms and Russian funeral marches we return in the *Finale* to a straightforward sonata Rondo movement. Because this is Brahms speaking, however, he is not content simply to repeat Rondo and 2nd subject themes, but their rhythm and contours generate continuous movement throughout.

J. Brahms: 4th movement Finale *Allegro giocoso* from Piano Trio no 2 in C major op.87

Exposition: The third note of the opening Rondo theme (**R**) is a bit of aural fun: a jokey, chromatic F♯ which Brahms harmonises pungently but then resolves harmlessly onto the dominant note.

Equally distinctive, the **2nd subject** flows more smoothly but then drifts through several distant key changes before the end of the Exposition.

We hear both Rondo and 2nd subject in the **Development**, skilfully incorporated into a continuous texture, and then a long passage of Beethovenian dominant preparation before the Rondo theme returns, *sotto voce*, for a regular **Recapitulation**.

The **Coda** begins tranquilly, exploring a gentler side of the Rondo, but this is soon brushed out of the way in an ebullient dash for the close.

This is a fine balanced ending to follow the preceding movements: a first movement of considerable intensity, then the theme and variations, succeeded by the wicked little *scherzo* with its songful trio. Achieving a balanced finale has become harder in competition with contemporary pieces relying on dramatic props like motto themes or extra-musical associations. Working in the major mode, Brahms succeeds in combining the traditional good humour of classical Rondo finales with the chromatic harmonic colour now a commonplace in the closing decades of the nineteenth century.

Four years later, Brahms produced his final essay in piano trio writing. The first movement of his trio in c minor op.101 is immensely concentrated – it only lasts 7½ minutes – and yet it is also lyrical, prompting Joachim to exclaim "… not even you have often written anything more beautiful!"

**J. Brahms: 1st movement *Allegro energico* from Piano Trio
no 3 in C minor op.101**

Exposition: The first four bars dramatically present two ideas :

– a rising 4-note figure (x) in the pianist's *left* hand, and

– colourful chromatic harmony rising in 3rds (c minor – E♭ major
– G major).

This is the first segment of the **1st subject (1(a))**.

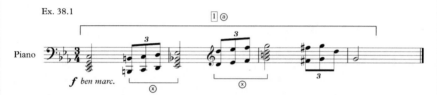

After these tonal excursions Brahms carefully establishes the home
dominant. Then the second segment of the 1st subject 1(b) follows,
exploring similarly chromatic harmony (but not identical – establishing the *principle* of chromatic colour, not the precise chords)
under a striking dotted rhythm.

The 4-note figure (x) returns, followed by a sequence of impatient
pizzicato notes in the strings, carrying us to the dominant of the
relative major key. Here the 4-note figure reappears in longer note
values, a glowing *cantando* transformation: it has become the first
four notes of an unexpectedly regular **2nd subject**, neatly packaged into a succession of 4-bar phrases in the strings, followed by
lovely falling 7ths.

Its four rising notes sound persistently through the continuation, featuring prominently over some deeply satisfying harmonic
sequences. The Exposition ends with a neat Cadential close.

The **Development** plunges back into further adaptations of the 4-note figure, first in lofty crotchets, then back into triplet quavers, and finally transformed into a new theme, quietly tripping along first in the violin and then in the piano. Then the striking dotted rhythm of 1(b) intervenes, and we hear the piano arrive on the home V note.

The return to the **Recapitulation** is tantalisingly vague. With hindsight we realise that all statements of the two 1st subject segments from the opening are omitted (because they have featured so prominently in the Development), and we have joined the Exposition at the 5th bar. We soon hear the lovely 2nd subject, now in the home tonic *major* key, sung by the violin an octave above the 'cello – both producing the beautifully rich tone colours of their lowest strings.

The **Coda** makes good the Recapitulation's omissions and returns to the 1st subject – chromatic harmony, dotted rhythms, several exalted statements of the 4-note figure – everything the listener could wish to hear again in this exultant Brahmsian apotheosis.

The most striking feature of this singular movement is the total shift it represents in the balance between tonal framework and thematic content. In both Classical and earlier Romantic sonata form works, we have heard the tonal framework as the constant factor, and composers generally accommodating their sequence of musical ideas to that given structural outline. Brahms retains the tonal framework, to be sure, but his attitude to the thematic content has developed. He has reduced the plethora of 1st and 2nd subjects, bridge passages, cadential themes, all the contents of those little tonal boxes, down to progressively fewer and fewer "energy-laden" fragments – because he can now draw all the inspiration he needs from so few ideas. Nearing the end of his composing career, this is the perfection of his developing variation technique. Frisch amplifies Schoenberg's comments on Brahms and in so doing provides us with a useful resumé of the latter's procedure in movements such as this:

"By 'developing variation,' Schoenberg means the construction of a theme (usually of eight bars) by the continuous modification of the intervallic and/or rhythmic components of an initial idea. The intervals are 'developed' by such recognized procedures as inversion and combination (e.g., two consecutive seconds make a fourth), the rhythms by such devices as augmentation and displacement. Schoenberg values developing variation as a compositional principle because it can prevent obvious, hence monotonous, repetition ... And Brahms's music stands as the most advanced manifestation of this principle in the common-practice era, for Brahms develops or varies his motives almost at once, dispensing with small-scale rhythmic or metrical symmetry and thereby creating genuine musical prose."[12]

Schoenberg enormously admired what he saw as Brahms's mastery of the technique of developing variation. Brahms's technical mastery and inventiveness, honed, like Beethoven, over the composition of many sets of variations, has enabled him in this late trio to generate an entire movement from its four opening bars, as this chart shows:

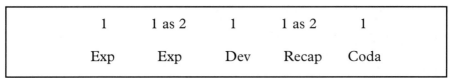

1	1 as 2	1	1 as 2	1
Exp	Exp	Dev	Recap	Coda

Fig. 11 Johannes Brahms: 1st movement Piano Trio no 3 in C minor op.101

Crucially, what we actually *hear* as we follow the developing narrative of striking thematic material transformed into the glowing *cantando* paragraph, is just that synthesis of the rational and the sensuous, of seriousness and sensibility, which we heard in Beethoven. We have seen the sonata idea teetering precariously between the two extremes of academicism and sentimentality since the middle of the nineteenth century. But as Rosen has noted, "The glory of Brahms's academicism is his almost complete transformation of his models",[13] and it is Brahms who now reclaims the sonata as a vehicle for a serious intellectual experience. The more often we listen to this music, the more we will learn to enjoy its subtlety and its variety, and the more clearly we shall recognise the perfect balance which Brahms achieves between traditional Classical rhetoric and Romantic beauty. And this is how we know that Brahms was indeed the true successor to Beethoven. Paradoxically, he answers too to the *zeitgeist* of his times as expounded by the late nineteenth-century German philosopher Nietzsche, sometime champion of Wagner, who argued that

"... the ecstatic, 'Dionysian' aspect of music was held in balance by the ordering, structuring, reflective 'Apollonian' aspect, and ... the expressive power of music, and thereby its value, emerges from the tension between these two extremes."[14]

Smallman has the last word:

"With the C major and c minor trios Brahms brought the *genre*, in its classical-romantic form, to a splendid culmination in the late nineteenth century. Many successors and imitators sought to achieve a comparable excellence in their work, but none showed the same capacity for combining profuse melodic invention with a seemingly effortless mastery of technique."[15]

Brahms is at his most profound in his chamber music. He himself took the piano part in public performances of the piano trios, and though we have no picture of him actually performing, we can perhaps get near in a turn-of-the-century painting, done by Henri Caro-Delvaille (1876-1926) in 1906, of three musicians deeply absorbed in a piano trio:

Henri Caro-Delvaille, *Trois Musiciens*, 1906.
New York, Sotheby's Picture Library (© Sotheby's / akg-images)

The three players are grouped close together on the left half of the canvas, each contributing his own intense involvement to the performance: the violinist raises his left eyebrow as musicians often do when they negotiate an especially important or expressive phrase; the 'cellist tilts his head against the scroll of his instrument, listening intently; the pianist leans towards the string players to hear and match every inflection of their playing. The viewer is drawn into the fluent arc shape of the three heads, catching their collective absorption ... This may not be a picture of Brahms himself (he had died nine years earlier), but it perfectly captures the concentration demanded of musicians engaged in realising the full subtlety of chamber music such as his late C major trio.

★   ★   ★   ★   ★

At this point we might think it would be interesting also to make contact with contemporary culture, and turn to some painting or artefact which would give us an illuminating parallel with music. But it will be difficult to find one – because in the second half of the nineteenth century, music had become *out of step with the other arts*. It may be easier for us to understand the sudden changes which overtook western music in the early years of the twentieth century if we briefly investigate this.

As the optimism of the Enlightenment and the "ennobling spirituality" of Idealism faded after the beginning of the nineteenth century, many people in Europe, including those in the prosperous middle classes, began to question some of the old certainties which had sustained their lives for so long. Fundamental and unsettling doubts were raised about capitalist society in Marx's *Communist Manifesto* (1848), and about religion in Darwin's *Origin of Species* (1859), while influential philosophers such as Schopenhauer and Nietzsche added atheism and pessimism to the mood of uncertainty. Scientific positivism and the Great Exhibition (or, to give it its full title, "The Great Exhibition of the Works of Industry of all Nations") held at the purpose-built Crystal Palace in 1851, might have extolled the progress of scientific knowledge and advances in industrial technology, but there was a growing sense that the industrial revolution had come at an enormous (and perhaps unacceptable) cost to the working classes. After the failed revolutions of 1848, also, the likelihood of much-needed social and political change still seemed a distant prospect, especially, for instance, in those nations which across the Austrian Empire still chafed under the domination of the Habsburgs.

The spirit of the times surfaced in literature: the novels of Tolstoy and Hardy and the plays and short stories of Chekhov are underpinned by tragic "characters in the grip of fate" (even Hardy's bucolic *Under the Greenwood Tree* has a destructive canker at its heart). Painters also moved from romanticism to realism, adopting a moral tone as they depicted scenes of present hardship or past times in religious and historical topics. In operas and symphonic poems, music could follow the dictates of libretto and programme and match their mood, but against such a background of realism, instrumental music might have arrived again at the same problem as in the eighteenth century: in spite of all the extravagant claims made about its ability to depict emotion, it was simply not capable of mimetic representation.

However, this, says Carl Dalhaus, was far from being a failing:

"[The romantic music] of the later part of the century was romantic in an unromantic age, dominated by positivism and realism. Music, *the* romantic art, had become "untimely" in general terms,

though by no means unimportant, on the contrary, its very disso-
ciation from the prevailing spirit of the age enabled it to fulfill a
spiritual, cultural, and ideological function of a magnitude which
can hardly be exaggerated: it stood for an alternative world ...
Thus music increased its influence because it was almost alone in
bearing the burden of providing an alternative to the realities of
the world following the Industrial Revolution."[16]

If there is a parallel to be drawn, perhaps it can be seen by
comparing music with those painters who were themselves on the
edge of realism: the Impressionists. In the second half of the nineteenth century, despite the implacable opposition of the French
Académie des Beaux-Arts to experimentation, and because of factors
such as the challenge to representative art posed by the invention of
photography, these artists became fascinated with light and determined to commit its effects to canvas. They created new visual effects
with their "broken" brush technique, introducing bright unmixed
colours, sunlight and movement into painting. We have seen a similar
fascination with chromatic harmony develop in the Romantic piano
trio literature, as composers experimented with ever more colourful
chords and more wayward excursions to foreign keys ("wandering"
tonality). Beyond the sonata literature, Liszt and Wagner pushed
tonality to its limits: the famous chord progression in Wagner's *Tristan*
has one dissonant chord resolving onto another (and how perfectly
this conveys the unsatisfied yearning of the lovers). (Debussy's music
became truly "impressionistic", but his individual style did not begin
to develop until the end of the century.)
    Pursuing the comparison, we might say that light and chromati-
cism both alleviate the discipline of form; for the painters, light illuminates and transforms the framework of representative shapes and
figures, and for the musicians, chromaticism decorates and extends
the framework of traditional tonality. But the parallel between the
two should not be pushed too far. Impressionism had clear prompts
in Paris in the 1860s, whereas chromaticism was inherent in western
tonality from the time that equal temperament tuning became established in the late seventeenth century. J S Bach had the entire spectrum of twelve-note chromaticism at his disposal – and delighted in
using it to the full.
    If we accept Dahlhaus's view, we will conclude that at the point we
have reached in the story of the piano trio, we shall not find an artistic parallel for the sonata idea. There are many works in "gloomy"
minor keys – we have heard Tchaikovsky and Rachmaninov in
moods of profound gloom – but they are still contained within the
traditional framework. We shall not find a parallel for the work of
the artist who in the 1880s began to reduce landscape painting to

a geometrically-simplified assembly of shapes: "Painters", declared Paul Cézanne (1839-1906), should "look for the cone, the sphere and the cylinder in nature." Thus began the building of the bridge leading from Impressionism to Cubism (Cézanne was "the father of us all," declared Picasso), but Brahms at this time is intent on perfecting an old tradition, not embarking on a new one. Cézanne's pioneering work to reduce painting to its fundamentals of shape and colour would be paralleled by a similar rethinking of musical fundamentals – sound in the dimension of time – but this was still some thirty years away.

CHAPTER ENDNOTES

1   Schumann, Robert. *Neue Zeitschrift für Musik*, 28 October 1853.

2   See p.238.

3   Hanslick, *op.cit*, p.7.

4   – *ibid* – p.47.

5   – *ibid* – pp.122,123.

6   – *ibid* – pp.98-99.

7   Frisch, Walter. *Brahms and the Principle of Developing Variation*. Berkeley & Los Angeles: University of California Press, 1984, p.57.

8   Frisch, *ibid*, pp.57-8.

9   Schoenberg, Arnold. *Style and Idea: Selected Writings* (1975), ed.Leonard Stein, transl. Leo Black. London: Faber and Faber, 1984, p.397.

10   Rosen, *Sonata Forms*, p.366.

11   Quoted by Trenner, Franz, *Richard Strauss. Dokumente seines Lebens und Schaffens*, Munich, 1954, pp.79-81; and quoted by Blume, *op.cit*, pp.141-2.

12   Frisch, *op.cit*, p.9.

13   Rosen, *Sonata Forms*, p.400.

14   Paddison, Max on Nietzsche's *Die Geburt der Tragödie* in 'Expression in Music, 2 After 1880', *Grove Music Online*, 2001.

15   Smallman, *op.cit*, p.128.

16   Dahlhaus, *op.cit*, pp.5, 8.

Part III

THE 20TH CENTURY

CHAPTER 19

PIANO TRIOS IN ENGLAND AND FRANCE, 1907–1923

1. ENGLAND: FRANK BRIDGE

We are used to thinking of the twentieth century as "modern", perhaps forgetting that, when it opened in 1900, over much of Europe oil lamps and candles remained the principal form of lighting and horses were still the main means of personal transport. But in the 1880's, the decade of Brahms's last two piano trios, incandescent light bulbs were nearing commercial development, and Karl Benz was patenting the first motor car. In a remarkably short space of time these inventions – along with the telephone, the radio receiver and powered flight, and advances in medicine such as X-rays and antiseptics – would transform people's daily lives. With Queen Victoria's daughters married into so many royal houses across Europe, in the opening years of the new century the prospects for comfortable and peaceful co-existence might have seemed good.

It did not, of course, turn out like that. The assassination of the Archduke Franz Ferdinand of Austria called upon existing alliances which separated the countries of Europe into two warring factions, with devastating consequences. From 1914 to 1918 the brave new technical advances were diverted to the waging of a global war in which over 15 million lives were lost. We have seen that even before the stability of life was shattered by the cataclysm of the Great War, a sense of unease had been festering in Europe for some time. In 1917 the socialist principles embodied in Marx's manifesto were adopted by the Bolsheviks in Russia, and after the War was over fundamental changes in society – and thus also the arts – were felt everywhere.

But in the first decade of the century, this was yet to come. Progressive artists might have begun to embrace a deconstruction of traditional artforms, but for ordinary people everyday life continued, and in the great capitals of Europe it seemed to do so at a feverish pace. At the turn of the century, Vienna witnessed the work of an extraordinary variety of gifted men: writers, painters and architects as well as psychologists and philosophers. Her musicians were no less gifted, and music flourished in opera house and concert hall as well as in the ballroom – where the spirit of the time was captured by the brilliance of waltzes, *galops* and polkas. The arts also flourished, and – with even more conspicuous success – in Paris, at this time widely regarded as the cultural capital of Europe.

London may have had to cede cultural leadership to Paris, but at the turn of the century Britain could lay claim to being the most powerful nation in the world, and her success and affluence were reflected in the purchasing power of the inhabitants of London and its outlying Metropolitan Boroughs. A mass public had been given access to the delights of the capital as public transport linked new housing to the City and the West End, and the new patrons were eager to spend their hard-earned cash and leisure hours enjoying themselves in the metropolis. As ever, one of the most popular forms of entertainment was the music to be heard in London's innumerable concert halls. An immense variety was available, ranging from the popular songs of the Music Halls to lofty chamber music recitals in the Queen's Hall. Many "serious" concerts were still ragbag affairs, in which distinguished singers performed *lieder* and opera extracts alongside sentimental parlour songs, but there were also a growing number of orchestral concerts conducted by a new breed of celebrity conductors. There were operas – by Léhar and Offenbach as well as Wagner, Massenet, Puccini, Debussy and Delius – and in the halls of the piano manufacturers there were virtuoso pianists who

> "performed with an extravagance of tone, interpretative flair, gesture and pecuniary expectation which was variously attributed to genius, national temperament, manipulation by grasping agents, transatlantic influence and the response of vulgar audiences."[1]

Chamber music remained the choice of the *cognoscenti*. Brahms's friend Joachim (see p.269) brought his famous string quartet to London at least once a year for eagerly-awaited concerts devoted entirely to German music from Haydn to Brahms.* On these visits he also gave lessons, and now numbered women violinists among his pupils: respectability for female violin-playing had finally been achieved by Wilma Norman-Néruda (1838-1911), later Lady Hallé, who like Clara Schumann came of a family of professional musicians. Some time later the flamboyant Guilhermina Suggia (1885-1950)

---

* Joachim also paid regular visits to Paul David and his pupils at Uppingham School – cementing both the school's reputation for music and the English link with Brahms (see p.242).

(famously painted in the flow of performance by Augustus John) achieved the same breakthrough for female 'cellists.

In 1905 the first permanent professional piano trio in Europe was established, consisting of the celebrated musicians Jacques Thibaud, violin, Pablo Casals, 'cello and Alfred Cortot, piano. These musicians already had established solo careers – they were well-matched and their trio performances became very popular. They played together for one month in every year between 1907 and 1934, building up a repertoire of some thirty trios. Their recording of Schubert's B♭ trio was one of the earliest Great Classic Recordings, made in Kingsway Hall London in 1926: it was originally issued on four 78 rpm discs and is still available as a historic recording. This is a contemporary pencil drawing of the Trio, signed by all three players and said to have been sketched from life as they performed this trio in Brussels on 3 June 1931:

Hilda Wiener, drawing of Thibaud, Casals and Cortot Piano Trio, 1931
New York, GRANGER / Alamy Stock Photo

From 1905 chamber music was given significant encouragement in England by a wealthy businessman called Walter Cobbett. He was an amateur violinist, passionate about chamber music, and eager to encourage British composers to write for chamber ensembles. He believed that chamber music "was particularly well suited to the trend of the British mind towards emotional reticence", acknowledging "the value of such a mentality in the composition of chamber music, in which the absence of exaggeration is counted a great merit." He saw a need in the concert repertoire for pieces shorter and lighter in character than the traditional four-movement sonata works, and endowed a competition for single-movement *"Phantasies"* (a whimsical revival of the title of the seventeenth-century *"fancy"* (or *fantasia*), which he understood to have been short pieces containing a number of contrasting sections).

The competitions – together with subsequent commissions – served their purpose admirably: between 1905 and 1930 some 40 new chamber pieces were written, helping to advance the careers of a number of promising young British musicians. These included Frank Bridge, John Ireland, Ralph Vaughan Williams and Herbert Howells. In 1907 prizes were offered for *Phantasies* for piano trio: first prize was won by Bridge, with Ireland and James Friskin tying in second place.

British musicians had at this time unequivocally thrown in their lot with the Austro-German tradition. Although Wagner's operas were heard in London, his dissolute lifestyle and the opulence of his music were less to the taste of the "emotionally reticent" English than the classical tradition represented by Brahms. In 1907 Frank Bridge (1879-1941) was still in his 20s. He had been a pupil of Charles Villiers Stanford (1852-1924) at the Royal College of Music. A brilliant Irishman, Stanford had been brought up on the music of J S Bach, Schumann and Brahms (whom he actually met), and had worked and travelled widely in Germany and France; he became a leading figure in a late nineteenth-century renaissance of British music. His love for Brahms's music and his rigorous teaching methods were a powerful influence on Bridge and his contemporaries, and Bridge's *Phantasie* for piano trio captures perfectly the intelligent and elegant English style which Stanford nurtured in the opening decades of the twentieth century.

Presented with a specification for a single movement containing contrasting sections, Bridge's solution was to condense the component movements of a sonata into a continuous whole – much as Liszt had done in his piano sonata of 1853. Bridge forges a connection between the sections like Liszt, by repeating the opening section at the end in the manner of a Recapitulation – thus imposing an overall sonata framework on the whole.

F Bridge: *Phantasie* Piano Trio no 1 in C minor 1907

In detail, this is heard as follows: an arresting motto theme is boldly stated, then followed by a fluent section with two separate subjects – the **1st** rich and sonorous,

the **2nd** lyrical, with wistful chromatic harmony.

With hindsight, we shall recognise this as the **Exposition**.

It is immediately followed by a **Development** section which incorporates the contrasting *tempi* and moods of a slow movement and Scherzo. The slow *Andante con molto espressivo* features another spacious theme, contrasting effectively with the crisp and sparkling Scherzo. The *Andante* theme returns briefly before:

the **Recapitulation** of the first section, so that there is a satisfying (and very classical) mirror-symmetry to the whole:

	"Exposition"	*"Development"*	*"Recapitulation"*
Theme	Motto – 1 – 2	*Andante* – Scherzo – *Andante*	Motto – 1 – 2
Key	c minor rel.maj: E♭	A major – minor – major	home c min – maj

The towering figure of Brahms the Romantic casts a benevolent shadow across this work: his idiom can be heard in its flowing melodic lines and the spacious figuration of keyboard accompaniments; in intriguing displaced accents (especially in the 2nd subject and the Scherzo) and beautiful shifts of key. Yet the *Phantasie* has a clarity – and a dissonant twang – wholly Bridge's own. He was a fine string player, with performing experience in first-rate quartets, and was also a very competent pianist. Such "inside" experience contributes to the natural fluency of the writing in this piano trio, which delighted Cobbett: he thought it was "of a remarkable beauty and brilliance" and that it stamped the young man as "one of our foremost composers for the chamber".

Bridge's *Phantasie* trio was first performed at a Musicians' Society Banquet. This might seem a curious début for a prize-winning work. It was only years later that Cobbett wryly admitted that the *Phantasies* had not turned out quite as he intended. Like Bridge, most of Stanford's eager young Brahmsian composers had seized on them as an opportunity to display their intellectual credentials by writing sonata-like movements linked together with much technical ingenuity. Cobbett, however, had had something altogether lighter in mind – suitable, in fact, for performance at banquets on festive occasions, which was how he imagined the original *"fancies"* had been performed. Instead, he wrote in 1915,

"... in these *Phantasies*, short as they are, the composers have strayed into paths which are totally unfamiliar to the average banqueting citizen; there are some of them packed pretty close with musical thought, and totally unfit for the hour of digestion."[2]

Digestible or not, the *Phantasies* were often included in chamber music concerts and became popular in their own right, so Cobbett was rewarded by their having found "an honourable place" in the chamber music repertoire. Nor should he be thought of as anything other than serious about chamber music: whatever his initial ideas for the performance of *Phantasies*, he championed the cause of good chamber music throughout his life. His encyclopaedic knowledge was incorporated into his 2-volume "Cyclopaedic Survey" of 1929, and his indefatigable support did much to encourage a fine new generation of British composers to take up composing chamber music.

2. FRANCE: RAVEL, FAURÉ

At the beginning of the sonata story we observed that three early sonata composers – Haydn, John Bach and Schobert – had been born within a few years of each other in the 1730s. Such fecund decades are a commonplace of history, but coincidence of birth dates by no means guarantees similarity of outlook, and nearly 150 years later there was far less common ground for a generation of composers born in the 1870s. If Brahms reigned supreme in London for Bridge (b.1879), Paris offered a quite different background for Ravel (b.1875).

The cultural opportunities open to Maurice Ravel (1875-1937) were as exotic as they were diverse. He had been a teenager in the French capital when *L'Exposition Universelle* was held there in 1889, and like all Parisians had been bowled over by this introduction to mystical eastern arts and musical instruments, as well as the invigorating influence of minstrel shows and ragtime from the USA. Some years later Ravel became a member of *Les Apaches* – a *fin de siècle* cultural group of painters, poets, writers and musicians who met regularly "to indulge in the usual practices of argument, tobacco, strong coffee and late nights"[3] and to exchange ideas on contemporary art and literature, as well as to listen to new music. His horizons were yet further widened by the arrival of Diaghilev's colourful *Ballets Russes* and his introduction to Stravinsky in 1909.

Yet all his life Ravel struggled to reconcile his unabashed admiration for novelty and exoticism with his innate respect for order and discipline. He began his musical training as a pianist, and from the outset was drawn to the security of writing in traditional tonal – even archaic – forms (such as his early *Menuet Antique* of 1895 and the *Pavane pour une Infante défunte*). He studied composition with Fauré at the Paris Conservatoire, and was naturally drawn to Mozart's sonata rather than Beethoven's (he declined even to play piano duets by composers with whom he was not in sympathy: "no Beethoven, Wagner or Schumann or other 'romantics'," he stipulated to a duet partner).[4] His models were Chopin and Mendelssohn and the cyclical works of his French predecessors, and in his earlier compositions he was happy to follow traditional forms – as in the overture to *Shéhérazade* (1903), which he himself described as set out in the tonal format of sonata form.

Ravel came of mixed Swiss/Basque parentage, and around the year 1911 went on holiday in his mother's Basque homeland, intending to begin work on a piece for piano and orchestra on the subject of the Basque country. It was later abandoned, but Ravel used some of the draft material in his only piano trio. The opening rhythm of the trio's first movement, with its unusual alternation of three beats with two, was described by Ravel himself as being "*de couleur basque*", and is based on a Basque dance called the *zortzico*.

M Ravel: 1st movement *Modéré* from Piano Trio 1914

The opening bars are dominated by the *zortzico* and its 5-beat rhythm. To this Ravel adds three further beats (invariably a syncopated quaver-and-crotchet figure) so that each of the four segments of his **1st theme** contain 8 quavers (3 + 2 + 3). The melodic line carrying this rhythm seems to be in the key of a minor, although it has distinctly modal flattened 7ths, and also a gently dissonant accompaniment of adjacent triads.

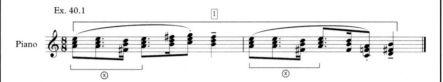

Ex. 40.1

Piano

The swaying inflections of this dance pass between all the instruments until a change of mood and a series of rushing semiquavers eventually lead to a **2nd theme** in the violin. This unfolds more slowly and lyrically and hovers between the tonic a minor and its relative major key, employing the same 3 + 2 + 3 rhythmic configuration as before.

Ex. 40.2

Violin

We are alerted to the beginning of the **Development** section by the return of the *zortzico*, mysteriously low in the piano. We must listen carefully to hear the 2nd theme, reduced to semiquavers in the piano, murmuring against the dance rhythm. The *zortzico* is taken up by both strings, and we begin to think we should expect a traditional **Recapitulation**. However, the rushing semiquavers reappear to announce the 2nd theme again in the home key (although with new harmonies). The tempo slackens as the piano re-introduces the rhythm of the *zortzico* in a low register, and the movement closes with its long-awaited return in something like its original version – finally translated into C major.

Given the date of its first performance in 1915, Ravel's contemporaries might not have been certain how to listen to this music. If they fell back on sonata form habits, they would have been reassured to hear the two distinct, returning subjects. But they would have listened in vain for a positive return to a Recapitulation, as tonal symmetry is displaced by chromatic colour and the demarcations between the sections dissolve in shifting harmonies. They would certainly not hear anything of Brahms's focus on fragmentary developing motifs. Instead, Ravel relies on repetition. This seems fitting to what is, after all, a repeating *dance*, and he scores so imaginatively for the trio medium that each repeat brings with it a new mood. In the central Development section, for instance, he passes rapidly from mystery through tender lyricism to something like menace. The wayward moods of the movement are underlined by constant changes of tempo – as though to offset the regular repetition of the dance rhythm, and prevent its repeats from becoming mechanical.

Ravel lets the form carry his content, but now it has become a nostalgic tale, an encounter between the two worlds of the dance and the sonata. Ravel resists the formal regimentation of both, drawn neither into compulsive beat nor onward narrative, but free to savour the sound of each passing moment. The movement finally ends as gently as it began.

The title of Ravel's second movement, *Pantoum*, is taken from an exotic verse-form (of Malay origin) which had been adopted earlier by several French romantic poets. The form required skilful handling: the 2nd and 4th lines of each verse must become the 1st and 3rd lines of the next; not only this, but two distinct ideas must be followed in parallel throughout the poem. For many years, nobody could understand why Ravel had adopted this title, until about sixty years later the musicologist Brian Newbould ingeniously proved[5] that Ravel had actually *followed the verse form in the music*, and moreover produced two musical ideas in parallel throughout (one a scintillating staccato opening theme, the other a yearning phrase with a triplet quaver apex, initially two octaves apart in the strings). As if all that were not enough, Ravel also reverted to sonata ideas and imposed a contrasting middle section – an *alternativo* – without a pause: thus the *alternativo* sounds through the *pantoum* verses, but in a wholly different metre. None of this artifice is evident in the music – it sounds the most natural musical outpouring in the world (although the printed score of the *alternativo* is, on paper at least, somewhat hair-raising). This is in every sense a brilliant movement, both in structural concept and in musical effect.

Ex.40 M Ravel: *Pantoum* from Piano Trio 1914

Ravel's trio was dedicated to his counterpoint teacher Gedalge, and the dedication becomes particularly appropriate in the third movement. It is built on a *passacaille* ("*passacaglia*"), or theme, followed by ten variations. This theme unfolds slowly, and takes us back to a venerable Baroque tradition – the ground bass – not variations in the mould of Beethoven and Brahms.

M Ravel: 3rd movement *Passacaille* from Piano Trio 1914

First heard low in the piano, the 8-bar *passacaille* theme (**P**) unwinds purposefully, ringing with the clarity of ancient 4th and 5th intervals.

Ex.40.4

In due course the 'cello joins in, and then the violin. Under cover of repeating rhythms the original *passacaille* is gradually transformed until by the time of the 4th variation it has taken on an invigorated new identity, rising up in the 'cello. The violin joins in and they soar together to a high climax. And then, as gradually as it had built up, the sound edifice gradually collapses: finally we are left with the piano, hollowly repeating its opening bars "as though bereft of melodic energy".[6]

This movement is another technical *tour de force*. The gradual build-up of the contrapuntal parts, their cumulatively rich sonority in the central variations, and then their eventual fading away, is handled with very considerable skill. It is also ingenious of Ravel to place the climax of the variations in the *middle* of the movement, rather than at the end – as we have seen so many sonata composers follow tradition in doing, from Haydn to Brahms. By placing it in the middle Ravel actually creates the opportunity for a beautiful mirror-image arch-shape of sound. The return to the simple *passacaille* line is perfectly handled too. But then homecomings, returning to a fundamental tonal starting-point, had been the stuff of western music for so long. A poignant sense of beginnings and endings seems to hang over the dying sounds of this beautiful movement, as though it has anticipated T. S. Eliot's lines from *East Coker V* in the *Four Quartets* (1935-42):

> "Home is where one starts from. As we grow older
> The world becomes stranger, the pattern more complicated
> Of dead and living. Not the intense moment
> Isolated, with no before and after,
> But a lifetime burning in every moment
> And not the lifetime of one man only
> But of old stones that cannot be deciphered …
> … In my end is my beginning."

The final movement of Ravel's trio was written under pressure of time. War had been declared between Germany and France on 3rd August 1914, and Ravel was determined to enlist and join the war effort. (In the event, he was turned down because, being slightly built, he was underweight; however, he did manage to become an army truck-driver.)

Smallman identifies what he sees as "a distinctive finale problem", often found in the piano trio; it is "how to achieve an effect of climax and culmination without overstepping the bounds of the chamber style". After three such immaculately suitable preceding movements, Smallman is not sure that Ravel has found the best solution in this trio: he thinks this movement is

> "… by no means a total failure; but the scale and expressive range of the preceding movements seem to demand a more expansive, perhaps more thoughtful, ending. The noisy one provided (possibly prompted by war fervour) conveys in the context an unduly conventional impression".[7]

M Ravel: 4th movement *Final – animé* from Piano Trio 1914

This movement relies rather more than the first movement on sonata form.

The **Exposition** begins promisingly, with a sort of "Chinese" lilt (brilliantly scored with featherlight touches) and wayward alternations between 5 and 7 beats in a bar.

Ex. 40.5

This opening crystallises as the **1st subject** in a discourse between the strings and eventually leads into the 2nd subject. This is perhaps where Smallman's problems begin: it seems ponderously chordal and overweight for the medium, so that the violin and 'cello can only make themselves heard with loud, high trills.

The **Development** is based on the 1st subject, so that we cannot be certain when the **Recapitulation** has begun. However, both the 1st and 2nd subjects feature in it. The movement is rounded off by a final massive and triumphant statement of the 1st subject – a "noisy" ending indeed, but perhaps understandable in the highly-charged emotional atmosphere of the time.

Listening to the four movements of this work we are bewitched by the surface attraction of the musical material: by the gently swaying rhythms of the first movement, the dazzling originality of the scoring in the second, the finely-managed ebb and flow of the third, and finally the triumphal resplendence of the *Final*. Ravel's material is so distinctive that on first hearing we may hardly be aware of the formal framework beneath. As we have seen, those frameworks are essentially traditional ones – sonata form, *passacaglia*, and the intricate *pantoum* – but Ravel's groundwork is unobtrusive, allowing us simply to luxuriate in the individual quality of his material.

Both surface material and tonal underpinning owe much to Ravel's lifelong fascination with the dance. Surface melodies in both the first and second movements are specifically enlivened by the *zortzico* and the *pantoum*: these are subtle dance rhythms which entrance the listener with their deft irregularity. But the bewitching surface is always supported by the tonal security of the dance-derived structure beneath – whose framework may now be obscured, but whose origins are frequently betrayed by long pedal notes doggedly directing the listener to secure resolutions and return.

"My objective ..." Ravel once wrote, "is technical perfection." Repeated listening to these movements will reveal hidden technical mastery at every turn. We shall find, for instance, that the opening notes of the *zortzico* – 5th–4th–5th – become a "motto" *motif* (x) for each subsequent movement: it can be heard again in the soft *staccato* opening of the *pantoum*, the first three notes of the *Passacaille*, and (on different degrees of the scale, and with pattern inverted) the 1st subject of the *Final*.

Ex. 40.6

Ex.40 M Ravel: Piano Trio 1914

As a student, Ravel was repeatedly frustrated by the hidebound attitude of his Conservatoire teachers, who insisted that technical "rules" of composition must never be broken. As harmony students know, one of the strictest of all such rules was the ban on "consecutive fifths". The opening of the first movement of Ravel's trio must have sent shivers down many a rigid Conservatoire spine: each note of the melody is harmonised by a triad, producing a whole line of consecutive fifths. These chromatically-enhanced harmonies hang decoratively below the simple melodic line – a reminder of Egon Wellesz's illuminating description of Debussy's style, which he used to say had a melody line winding like a grape vine, below which chords hung like bunches of grapes. Ravel's chords may not conform to the rulebook, but they are the source of the astringent charm of this music. They also illustrate well how Ravel succeeded in reconciling the division between his own tastes, on one hand for tradition, and on the other for exoticism and innovation; or, as Roger Nichols neatly puts it, "between knowing the rules and knowing how to break them".[8]

★ ★ ★ ★ ★

At the beginning of the Great War, Europe dominated the world stage, in finance, industry and commerce, but after 1918 nothing was ever the same again. The costs of the war were fearful, both in terms of human lives lost as well as of economies crippled; at its conclusion empires fell, the world map was redrawn and the USA emerged as a world power. In the immediate aftermath, economic hardship, disillusion and grief made grim bedfellows. The starkness of Modernism in art had been a minority taste before the War, but now its fundamental re-thinking seemed a more appropriate response to contemporary events: the *enfants terribles* had perhaps been more in tune with the times than people had realised.

It must have been hard to come to terms with such changes, especially for those who had already had a lifetime of artistic creativity behind them, but now found themselves living in another world. One such must have been Ravel's teacher, Gabriel Fauré (1845-1924) – born long before the generation of the composers of the 1870's. Mendelssohn and Schumann were still alive at the time of his birth, and Tchaikovsky and Dvořák were his close contemporaries. He had studied as an organist and choirmaster at the École Niedermeyer, and as a young man was (unconventionally) enthusiastic about the music of Liszt and Wagner; he fought a lifetime of prejudice amongst French musicians before finally being appointed as Director of the Paris Conservatoire in 1905. He lived through French nineteenth-century Romanticism, lost his contemporaries Franck (in 1890), Lalo (in 1892) and finally Saint-Saëns (in 1921), and saw a new generation (Ravel, Koechlin and Boulanger) come to take their place. He also lived through the Great War, and yet in his late seventies produced one of the finest chamber works of his life – the piano trio in d minor of 1922/3.

The piano trio is a remarkable work. In the same way that painters were paring down representational art to fundamental shapes, light and colour, Fauré too pared down his language. His texture is reduced to an absolute minimum as single lines flow to slender accompaniment figures, harmony added in light touches of colourful counterpoint. What Fauré gives us seems more vocal than instrumental: the fruits of his years at the École Niedermeyer and as an organist and choirmaster condensed into melodic lines like plainsong, with flat modal 7ths and long flowing shapes.

It is perverse, perhaps, to think of the opening movement as an instrumental sonata in a formal framework. Structurally, however, its outlines do follow what is in many ways a conventional sonata form, so here is the usual description of it:

G Fauré: 1st movement: *Allegro ma non troppo* from Piano Trio in D minor op.120

Exposition: The **1st subject** is heard first in the 'cello: it consists of a long melodious line with spacious intervals, its movement sustained by repeating rhythmic patterns.

Ex. 41.1

It is re-stated by the violin, and then with no conscious end of transition flows easily into the **2nd Subject.** This begins in the piano: it flows, too, but is made up almost entirely of adjacent notes, which give it a greater emotional intensity.

Ex. 41.2

At the end of this section the violin and 'cello in unison carry the 2nd subject to a climax on a high note C, followed by a brief sense of closure.

The **Development** follows, dealing with both themes successively and in effective combination; it builds to a dynamic climax as the **Recapitulation** returns with the 1st subject in the 'cello and piano in triumphant unison. The 2nd subject follows briefly, with wayward chromaticism. But it is the 1st subject which continues to dominate both this section and the final **Coda.**

The two movements which follow contrast well both with each other and with this opening movement. The second has a more static, songlike quality, and a particularly lovely opening theme, whereas the rondo finale combines the traditional energy of a rondo with the mischievousness of a scherzo. The rondo theme is in two parts and the rest of the movement is the story of how the two opposing ideas come together – the pent-up energy which they release is played out with great inventiveness.

Fauré's and Ravel's piano trios represent the end of the French chamber music tradition which had begun with César Franck. There is a sense of nostalgia about both works. Fauré returns to vocal, modal models, devising melodic shapes which unfold in chains of sequences and continuous, flowing lines; his textures are transparent and his writing for the piano essentially simple. Ravel, on the other hand, reverts to the dance origins of the sonata idea, distinctive rhythms enliven each movement and his textures are innovative and colourful, his writing for piano ranging magisterially from light figuration to handfuls of heroic chords. It is a measure of the adaptability of the old sonata framework that both composers continued to use it, and that the results are so different from each other. These Frenchmen use the sonata as a secure tonal framework for elegant and decorative discourse; but from this time onwards, the old framework would become a matter of idiosyncratic choice, not automatic recourse.

★   ★   ★   ★   ★

As a post-script to the early decades of the twentieth century, here is a painting of a piano trio in performance by Eugene Antoine Durenne, entitled *Sommerliche Kammermusik*. As the Great War enters its second year, it depicts a family absorbed in chamber music performance. We cannot help thinking: there is only one male figure in this room – does this family only have daughters, or are there sons too, who have gone away to the Front?

Eugene Antoine Durenne, *Sommerliche Kammermusik,* c.1915
Bremen, Kunsthalle (© akg-images)

CHAPTER ENDNOTES

1   Article on '*London Concert Life 1900-45*', *Grove Music Online*, by Cyril Ehrlich, Simon McVeigh and Michael Musgrave, 2001.

2   Cobbett, Walter. 'Obiter Dicta', *Chamber Music* 17 (1915): p.29.

3   Nichols, Roger. *Ravel*. New Haven and London, Yale University Press, 2011, p.43.

4   Nichols, *ibid*, p.43.

5   Newbould, Brian. 'Ravel's "*Pantoum*"', *Musical Times*, 116 (March 1975), pp.228-231.

6   Nichols, *op.cit*, p.175.

7   Smallman, *op.cit*, p.178.

8   Nichols, *op.cit*, p.351.

CHAPTER 20

THE GENESIS OF THE MODERN ERA: REGER, SCHOENBERG

IN CHAPTER 19 we heard notable differences between the music of Bridge and Ravel, who had nevertheless been born within four years of each other. We come now to two Austro-German composers born in the same decade, whose musical careers were pursued in yet more different directions, and with far-reaching effects – Reger and Schoenberg.

Max Reger (1873-1916) was the son of a schoolmaster and was brought up in the Bavarian town of Weiden. Sent to study with the local church organist, he received a thorough grounding in the piano music of Beethoven and Brahms, and organ works by Bach and Liszt. A seminal moment in his life occurred when he heard operas by Wagner at the Bayreuth Festival in 1888. The 15-year-old youth was overwhelmed by the chromatic musical language and extended harmony of *Die Meistersinger* and *Parsifal*, and made an immediate decision to follow a career in music. Accordingly, two years later he went to study with Hugo Riemann, the pre-eminent music scholar and theorist of the time, under whom Reger's musical education was rounded out by intense study of the music of Bach (Baroque formal types, pre-eminently fugue) and Brahms (the "sturdy oak" of the Austro-German tradition).

Reger was clever, impressionable and exceptionally hard-working. For twenty-six years until his death at the early age of 43 he performed, taught and conducted, and also composed copiously in almost all *genres* except large choral and stage works. Three distinct threads drawn from his studies run through his music: firstly, an unshakeable attachment to traditional formal structures (notably Baroque fugue, and, in his considerable output of chamber music, sonata form and variations); secondly, the technique of developing variation, which he greatly admired in the works of Brahms; and thirdly, the dense chromatic language he had encountered in the music of Wagner and Liszt.

One of his earliest works was a piano trio, in which a viola replaces the traditional 'cello. This had indicated that his development would not be on traditional lines: a contemporary commented that the variations which made up the last movement were not proper variations, because the theme could hardly be recognised. Reger saw the theme as a collection of motifs which might be disassembled to produce smaller units for immediate processing. The unwary listener was likely to lose the thread in a welter of miniature developments.

Reger's reputation as a composer grew after his appointment as teacher of theory at the *Akademie der Tonkunst* in Munich in 1904. Three years later he moved to Leipzig as *Musikdirektor* of the University, and in the same year began work on his second piano trio. Though Brahms and his technique of developing variation may have been his starting-point, by the time Reger wrote this trio for the traditional combination of violin, 'cello and piano, it no longer sounded like the music of Brahms. He had by now also been influenced by Liszt and those composers experimenting with harmonies based on clutches of superimposed minor thirds, chords of the diminished 7th, and new melodic divisions of the octave (such as the octatonic scale which alternated tones and semitones). Where Brahms used chromaticism to colour what remains fundamentally stable harmony, for Reger chromaticism – and more particularly chromatic dissonance – has become his musical vocabulary. There is still cadencing and harmonic direction in his music, but the sound-scape is a great deal less ingratiating than any we have heard up to this point.

Reger was also influenced by Wagner and the "monumental" style which, beyond the diminutive world of chamber music, was so much a feature of music in the second half of the nineteenth century, particularly in the vast orchestral canvases of Bruckner, Mahler, Busoni and Richard Strauss. The proportions of that style are evident in the first movement of this trio, which is as diffuse as Brahms's c minor trio had been condensed (it takes over twice the length of time – 15½ minutes to Brahms's 7½).

Honed by his own variation sets, Reger's application of Brahms's technique of developing variation is rigorous. It has become his compositional process, the way in which he proceeds from one bar to the next. His principal motifs are endlessly developed, and as they unfold, exhibit "a trademark of Reger's later style, namely musical prose exceeding all periodic and eight-measures bounds".[1] The sense of quadratic syntax has indeed become almost alien. This is the first movement of Reger's second trio, completed in 1908 during the last decade of his life:

M Reger: 1st movement *Allegro moderato, ma con passione* from Piano Trio no 2 in E minor op.102

Exposition: The movement opens with an enigmatic 3-note figure 1(a) in the violin and 'cello. We should hear this as two semitones decorating the keynote, E – the semitone above and the semitone below. These will be the defining intervals of this movement:

Ex. 42.1

Shortly afterwards, we hear the two semitones developed in a rising sequence, 1(b), and then as two semitones with an invigorating new rhythm, 1(c).

Ex. 42.2

These three motifs generate most of what follows and with concentrated listening can be picked out, somewhere or other, in the scoring.

Next we hear the **2nd subject** (although do not expect clear dominant preparation in this continuously-evolving texture). It comes in the unusual key of D, and is a distinctive contrast with the 1st subject motifs: it is as tonal as they are chromatic – we hear the 'cello rising expressively up a classic major triad, moving to the 6th, then falling back to the 5th before dropping again to the tonic. This is as near to two 4-bar phrases as Reger will take us.

Ex. 42.3

The chromatic fragments return and together with the opening motif end the Exposition (there is a distinct close).

The **Development** uses all the material of the Exposition including (briefly) the 2nd subject. It finally (and somewhat

inconsequentially) lands on the home tonic note (though we probably do not recognise it as such) and pauses expectantly.

The **Recapitulation** faithfully repeats most of the material of the
Exposition, tonally slanted to end in the tonic (major mode): it
begins (as the Exposition had done)) harmonising the keynote E
by turning it into the major 3rd of C major; the 2nd subject reappears briefly (first in V, then G sharp major)

The **Coda:** briefly repeats the semitone motif and its two derivatives – closing with an explicit summary of the argument of the
movement.

We need to hear this music with turn-of-the century ears, although
perhaps not those of the conservative contemporary critic Arthur
Smolian, who declared in his review of this work that it contained
"quite a lot of strange and peculiar things to hear" (although the
audience at its first performance greeted it "with lively applause").
The classical tonal pattern of sonata form is all but lost – nevertheless the work does begin and end in the "home" key of e minor, and
the Recapitulation faithfully slants the harmony of the Exposition to
end in the home tonic. In the Classical sonata, dynamic variety, the
distribution of loud or soft indications, tended to follow and endorse
the tonal framework as it presented contrasting themes or linking
passages. Here, instead, there is a febrile excitability – described by
Smolian as a "continuous shift between gloomy heroic flare-ups and
melancholy brooding" – which at first seems random but is actually
driven by the developing variation of the enigmatic opening motif. It
demands careful listening to appreciate this single-minded development, but it is just this which Reger wants the listener to hear. The
sonata form framework may still be there, and the familiar pattern
of Exposition/Development/Recapitulation may still lend its support
to the listener, but its focus has become the intense *surface interest of
thematic variation.*
   It is the loss of the tonal framework, and of the certainties and
expectations which that had generated, which mark a significant
departure from the old sonata idea in this work. To many of Reger's
contemporaries this music must have seemed distorted by ambiguous chords accompanying melodic lines, infiltrated by chromaticism
and dissonance, and lacking the traditional sense of tonal direction. Five years earlier, Reger had declared that "Any chord can be
followed by any other chord". It sounded like a declaration of war
against western tonality.

* * * * *

Reger's was not a lone voice. Only the previous year, the pianist Ferruccio Busoni had written a pamphlet raising fundamental questions about western music. Entitled *"Sketch of a New Aesthetic of Music"*, it deplored the narrowness of the western tonal vision and returned to old debates about scales and divisions of the octave:

> "We have divided the octave into twelve equidistant degrees, because we had to manage somehow, and have constructed our instruments in such a way that we can never get in above or below or between them ... Yet Nature created an *infinite gradation* ... All signs presage a revolution ... let us take thought, how music may be restored to its primitive, natural essence; let us free it from architectonic, acoustic and aesthetic dogmas ..."[2]

At the same time, increasing chromaticism had insidiously loosened the clear tonal definitions to which the nineteenth-century listener had been accustomed, so that, as the American music educator William Thomson puts it:

> " ... passages from the music of Reger, Wolf, Scriabin and the later works of Mahler only confirm the conventional wisdom: anarchic chromaticism was in the act of overturning the neat and simple controls of the major and minor scales and the modal musics of times past ..."[3]

It was at this point that another composer born in the same decade as Bridge, Ravel and Reger entered the scene. In 1908 Schoenberg became the first composer to abandon traditional western tonality, although he did not follow Busoni's proposed rejection of the twelve semitones. As it happens, although Schoenberg wrote a good deal of important chamber music, this did not include a single piano trio. But his part in leading the subsequent Modernist movement is so fundamental and far-reaching that it is necessary to understand his theories of composition in order to follow the sonata idea into the twentieth century.

Arnold Schoenberg (1874-1951) was born in Vienna in the year after Max Reger and began his musical education with violin lessons. He joined an amateur orchestra and – fortuitously – made a firm friend of its conductor, Alexander von Zemlinsky (1871-1942), another musical product of the 1870s decade. This musician had trained at the Vienna Conservatoire, and at this point in his career was much influenced by Brahms, who had been impressed by his clarinet trio. Zemlinsky proceeded to give Schoenberg his only formal training in composition, so that Schoenberg's earliest works were tonal; influenced by Brahms and Wagner, they earned the approval of Gustav Mahler and Richard Strauss. However, their tendency to chromatic dissonance did not endear them to conservative Viennese public taste.

By the first decade of the new century Schoenberg had arrived in his early 30s. Largely self-taught, he had become driven by three passionately-held views. Firstly, he had an immense distaste for much of the music being produced at the end of the nineteenth century, whose "slushy" tunes and constant repetition he regarded as decadent and inferior, and pandering to the banal taste of bourgeois audiences. "If it is art, it is not for all," he said loftily, "and if it is for all, it is not art." Secondly, he was ever conscious of the responsibility of his Austro-German inheritance. He knew and loved the music of J S Bach, Haydn, Mozart, Beethoven, Schubert, Schumann and Brahms, and he was determined to preserve the German domination of music in his own works. For him,

> "... the only logical and responsible musical developments [were] those that grow out of the tradition ... He sought, above all, to show that his music was rooted in the past, that it embodied the structural principles of the German masters, and that it was the equal of theirs in power and coherence."[4]

Thirdly, like all thoughtful intellectuals of the time, he was profoundly affected by Darwin's *Origin of Species*. The theory of natural selection had a potent message for theologians, artists and musicians as well as students of natural history: it validated the notion of constant change and simultaneously endorsed the idea of perpetual improvement. Music too was in a constant state of evolution, and it must be the composer's binding task to carry it forward to the next stage of its development.

This idea of artistic responsibility coincided with Schoenberg's encounter with the poet Stefan George (1868-1933), who inspired him with his vision of art as the highest form of human activity, the artist being the "supreme creature" of the universe. At about the same time Schoenberg met the painters Kokoschka, Gerstl and Kandinsky and himself took up painting. "This was a time," wrote Oliver Neighbour,

> "when artists and writers who were later to be called experimentalists sought to obey the promptings of the spirit ever more directly, in some sense bypassing the machinery of artistic tradition in order to reach deeper levels of experience."[5]

With hindsight we can detect such "promptings of the spirit" in Schoenberg's Second String Quartet, written between 1907 and

1908. The third and fourth movements have settings of words by George for a soprano voice; the first three movements are tonal, but the fourth movement has no structured harmony nor regulating rhythms. *"Ich löse mich in tönen, kreisend, webend ..."* ("I lose myself in sounds, circling, weaving ...") sings the soprano, as the music threads its way through dissonance and unresolved expectations, expressing the sense of the words with unbridled freedom.

Schoenberg's Quartet was heard by the artist Wassily Kandinsky (1866-1944) at a concert in 1911. Shortly afterwards he wrote to Schoenberg that

> "... what we are striving for and our whole manner of thought and feeling have so much in common ... In your works you have realised what I have so greatly longed for in music."[6]

The day after the concert, Kandinsky painted an impression of it (*Impression III (Konzert)*).

Wassily Kandinsky, *Impression III (Konzert)*, 1911
Munich, Stadtische Galerie

This painting is clearly edging towards abstraction in art: *Impression III* depicts the audience and (presumably) the large lid of a grand piano, reducing the scene to a few essential shapes, and separating the hard black lines of those shapes from the strong but simple colours of the painting. Kandinsky summed up his thought at this time in *On the Spiritual in Art*:

"That art is above nature is by no means a new discovery ... Temporal forms are ... loosened so that the objective may be more clearly expressed ... the future structure of painting lies in this direction."[7]

Comparison of this painting – in which a representational style begins to dissolve in a free association of shapes and colours – with the incipient process of tonal disintegration as Schoenberg's soprano floats unfettered by tonal chords and conventional cadences, is fascinating. "Art belongs to the unconscious! ... One must express oneself!"[8] declares Schoenberg. Music and Art are now side by side, and as painting moves away from the representational tradition, so does music loosen its ties with western tonality.

For the next decade Schoenberg was preoccupied with vocal works, but from 1920 he felt the need for a more overt connection with the process of developing variation which he admired in Brahms; indeed, he admired it so much that he took it up and adopted it for his own method of composing:

"With me, variation almost completely takes the place of repetition ... by variation I mean a way of altering something given, so as to develop further its component parts as well as the figures built from them, the outcome always being something new, with an apparently low degree of resemblance to its prototype, so that one finds difficulty in identifying the prototypes within the variation."[9]

But, as Neighbour points out,

"Where every motif is transformed before it can gather associations for the listener there can be no intensification of meaning through development; where no pattern establishes itself only extreme contrasts cheat expectation ... If Schoenberg's art of development was to develop further it needed a basis in relative stability ..."[10]

The stable basis which Schoenberg now evolved was a new technique of composition – called "serialism", it ordered all twelve notes of the chromatic scale into a non-variable sequence (also known as the "series", "row" or "set") in which each note was of equal importance. (Schoenberg was not in fact the very first composer to devise a method of composition with twelve notes – a year or so earlier another Austrian composer, Josef Hauer (1883-1959), had also done so; but Schoenberg seems to have continued to employ the technique more consistently than Hauer.) The serial technique began as the logical evolution of Brahms's developing variation and Reger's continuation of it, a line of descent acknowledged by Schoenberg himself. It began therefore with *a motif which must be varied,* involving all twelve notes in the octave; no note can be repeated until all have been heard. Furthermore the notes must be played *in the same sequence* as they are first heard, which must be maintained on every repetition. The strict rule of no note-repetition in the motif ensures that no single note is played more often than any other, so that this has the effect of dissolving tonality (as we have so often heard, it is the hierarchy of notes in the scale, constantly pulling home to tonic, which shape the sense of key in the tonal system). Furthermore, each *motif* must be continuously varied or transformed, so that the listener *cannot recognise it and begin to have expectations of it.*

> "Here is the greatest difficulty for any listener, even if he is musically educated: the way I construct my melodies, themes, and whole movements offers present-day perceptive faculty a challenge that cannot yet be met at first hearing."[11]

The word "yet" is significant. Schoenberg was by now convinced that tonality was expendable, and that over the course of time audiences would instead learn to hear and identify the tone row in its different manifestations; *the row would replace tonality as the structural basis of a piece,* heard by the listener in a succession of melodic, rhythmic, textural and timbral contrasts.

Schoenberg demonstrated his conviction in several of the serial works he wrote between 1921 and 1936 by actually setting them in old Classical forms. His third string quartet of 1927, for example, is set in the framework of sonata form. He sees the form as a three-part structure – exposition, elaboration and recapitulation – in which the "internal details may be subjected to almost any mutation without disturbing the aesthetic validity of the structure as a whole."[12] Accordingly he is content not only to abandon sonata form's tonal traditions but also to deal freely with the sequence of 1st and 2nd subjects in the Recapitulation. Not needing to resolve the dissonance between tonic and dominant keys, he can re-interpret the form by turning the Recapitulation into a mirror-image of the Exposition, reversing the order in which the 1st and 2nd subjects return so that the movement becomes an expression of his favoured "inversional balance".

As an intellectual arrangement of the thematic patterning with which we are familiar in sonata form, this is ingenious; and giving his thematic material this surface relationship with the old structure no doubt reassured Schoenberg that he was treading in the footsteps of the old masters. But twenty-five years later, Pierre Boulez was to question the association of serialism with sonata form:

> "The pre-classical and classical forms ruling most of [Schoenberg's] compositions were in no way historically connected with the twelve-tone discovery; the result is that a contradiction arises between the forms dictated by tonality and a language of which the laws of organisation are still only dimly perceived. It is not only that this language finds no sanction in the forms used by Schoenberg, but something more negative: namely, that these forms rule out every possibility of organisation implicit in the new material, the two worlds are incompatible."[13]

We shall return to the dissolution of tonality and the atonal, motivic sonata in the next chapter.

CHAPTER ENDNOTES

1   Shigihara, Susanne, writing in the accompanying booklet to the Trio Parnassus CD recording of this trio by Musikproduktion Dabringhaus and Grimm. 1998.

2   Busoni, Ferruccio. *Sketch of a New Aesthetic of Music* (1907), transl. Thedore Baker in *Three Classics in the Aesthetics of Music*, NY: Dover Publications Inc, 1962. pp.88-95; quoted in Weiss and Taruskin, *op.cit*, pp.421-423.

3   Thomson, William. *Schoenberg's Error*. Philadelphia: University of Pennsylvania Press, 1991, p.7.

4   Straus, Joseph N. *Remaking the Past – Musical Modernism and the Influence of the Tonal Tradition*. Cambridge MA, London: Harvard University Press, 1990, p.8.

5   Neighbour, O.W. 'Schönberg, Arnold', *Grove Music Online*, 2001.

6   See *Arnold Schoenberg, Wassily Kandinsky: Letters, Pictures and Documents*. Ed. Jelena Hahl-Koch, transl. John Crawford, London: Faber and Faber, 1984.

7   Kandinsky, Wassily. 'On the Spritual in Art', in *Kandinsky: Complete Writings on Art*, ed. K.C.Lindsay and P Vergo, New York, 1994, pp.208-209.

8   See *Schoenberg, Kandinsky, Letters, op.cit*, p.87.

9   Schoenberg, *op.cit*, p.102

10 Neighbour, *op.cit*.

11 Schoenberg, *op.cit*, p.102.

12 Schoenberg, Arnold. *Fundamentals of Musical Composition*. Ed. Gerald Strang, New York: St Martin's Press, 1967, p.200.

13 Boulez, Pierre. '*Schoenberg is dead*', *The Score* 6 (1952); reprinted in *Notes of an Apprenticeship*, transl. Herbert Weinstock. New York: Alfred A. Knopf, 1968, p.272.

CHAPTER 21

SHADES OF THE TONAL SONATA TRADITION IN THE MODERN ERA: SHOSTAKOVICH, MARTINŮ, DAVID MATTHEWS

ALL THE FAMILIAR habits of the western musical tradition seemed to have been comprehensively abandoned by the new "Modernist" composers who followed Schoenberg's lead. Regularity, recognition – all the old certainties of the musical language which had evolved from pulse and pitch over hundreds of years – all these were sacrificed for a new musical principle which few listeners could at first appreciate. "Consciously used, the motif should produce unity, relationship, coherence, logic, comprehensibility and fluency,"[1] said Schoenberg, but to most contemporary listeners used to western tonality, the new music was far from comprehensible. Since western ears would automatically seek out tonal melodies and listen for their return, the major and minor scales had to be scrupulously avoided; consequently all the logic of western tonal organisation went too, as consonant cadences and resolutions were replaced by unconnected dissonances. There were no more recognisable "tunes" and no more tonal boxes. Since regular rhythm was a potent factor in recognition and remembering, regular repetitive rhythms were dropped too. All sense of expectation must be dashed and ingrained listening habits thwarted.

It was some time before audiences began to adjust to the new listening required of them to appreciate this music. When Schoenberg's early atonal work *Five Pieces for Orchestra* was performed in London in 1912, the *Times* critic said it was "like a poem in Tibetan; not one single soul could possibly have understood it at first hearing". There were many in concert-going audiences who never took to it at all, so that a rift opened up between popular music and the Modernist *avant-garde*. The Modernists were accused even by moderates of snobbery and elitism: the Austro-German tradition might have reached a spectacular conclusion in the work of Schoenberg and the composers of the 2nd Viennese School, but all sense of a mainstream was now irrevocably lost.

As the twentieth century progressed, it is no longer possible to pick out a single mainstream development comparable to the old Austro-German tradition. Schoenberg had raised fundamentally important issues which no thinking musician could ignore, but reactions became irreversibly divided. In due course, Modernism splintered into a number of different schools, ranging (in roughly retreating order of rebelliousness) from Serialists, Experimentalists, Neoclassicists and Nationalists to a hard-core of Traditionalists. The introduction of Jazz from the USA and a new acquaintance with non-western musical traditions also had a considerable influence on western music, and later in the century experiments with rock music, minimalism, conceptual and electronic music added further to the bewildering variety of flourishing styles. For a time, the twelve semitones of the western division of the octave were retained, since, as Busoni had pointed out, so many instruments were tuned to it. But later, under the influence of different tonal scales from other parts of the world, new microtonal divisions of the octave became possible in electronic instruments and synthesisers, and new pitch organisations were introduced.

All these disparate groups faced the same fundamental question: could music still be tonal in the old western sense, or must it now inevitably turn to atonality? The answers ranged from that of hardcore serialists such as Schoenberg's pupil Anton Webern (1883-1945) – whose stringently atonal interpretation of serialism was adopted by the composers of the Darmstadt school (Nono, Boulez, Stockhausen and Berio) – to Schoenberg's other renowned pupil Alban Berg (1885-1935), who said that Act 2, scene 1 of his opera *Wozzeck* was in "strict" sonata form, and whose serial rows later had tonal inflections. At the other end of the spectrum was the German composer Paul Hindemith (1895-1963), who firmly believed that there was "no such thing as atonality, unless we are to apply that term to harmonic disorder"[2] and evolved his own unique tonal language using all twelve notes freely; and in England Frank Bridge's only pupil, Benjamin Britten (1913-76), who eschewed his master's later turn to atonality, becoming instead the progressive conservative father-figure of post-war British music.

Sadly for our present purposes, none of the above composers wrote music for the traditional piano trio – not even Hindemith or Britten, both of whom wrote a good deal of chamber music. (Britten did write some early pieces for piano trio in 1929, but scored them for violin and piano with viola, not 'cello.) In fact, many fewer composers were attracted to this *genre* in the twentieth century. This may in part have been because the trio's *sine qua non* – the piano itself – carried with it into the twentieth century a good deal of inherited baggage from nineteenth-century piano style. For many this was too closely associated with the immediate Romantic past from which the Modernists were so keen to escape. New ways of exploiting the performance possibilities of the piano had to be devised, avoiding the resonant chordal sounds which were too redolent of traditional harmony; the balance between the strings and piano (always problematical for trio composers) was re-thought in sparser textures devised for three equal protagonists. Few serialists wrote music for the piano trio – the British composers Alexander Goehr and Jonathan Harvey did so, but neither of their trios seem to claim a relationship with the sonata idea. Similarly there was little reference to the traditional framework in piano trios written by American composers such as Charles Ives, Walter Piston, Roy Harris and Aaron Copland, or other British composers such as Edmund Rubbra, Alan Rawsthorne, Lennox Berkeley and Kenneth Leighton.

Later in the century, minimalism offered listeners a return to tonal harmony and steady pulse, but despite the alluring soundscape of minimalist composers, their constant repetition of severely limited material and their music's lack of a goal-directed narrative had nothing to offer the dynamic sonata. Moreover, composers of a postmodernist era found many of the guiding principles of the sonata – such as adherence to formal structure and tonal unity – alien concepts in the twentieth century; they moved away to experiment instead with fragmentation and randomness, explored the use of technology, and incorporated sounds from populist and world music.

So to follow the traditional sonata idea during the twentieth century we must return to the point at which we left Schoenberg at the end of the last chapter – where his motivically-animated sonata form had aimed to succeed the old tonally-based model. The question was whether or not

"… the kind of thematic orderings Schoenberg advocated as a replacement for tonality, an organisation achieved by fastidious motivic organisation, can provide a kind of formal cohesion, a continuing sense of parts bearing kinship and of succeeding one another over a span of time."[3]

Listening to this music, did contemporary audiences have a sense of "parts bearing kinship" and "succeeding one another", and did such "thematic orderings" indeed turn out to be "a replacement for tonality"?

Enthusiasm for Schoenberg's experiments was not universal, since it became clear that the average concert-goer might not be able to identify the twelve-tone row in all its intricate variations. "Permutational arrangements are hard to learn and comprehend, when compared to arrangements based on repetition, elaboration and symmetry," says the philosopher Sir Roger Scruton, and again: "... They impose an intellectual order on sounds, but not a musical order."[4] The French psychologist Robert Frances concluded that "serial unity lies more on the conceptual than on the perceptual level ... it remains very difficult to hear",[5] and the American composer and theorist Peter Westergaard, discussing serial music by Milton Babbitt, declared that "I see no way for the ear to perceive either order or content."[6] Schoenberg's expectation that audiences would hear the tonal sets as a structural replacement for tonality was not widely fulfilled.

It turned out, as Thomson has pointed out, that there were flaws in Schoenberg's theoretical thinking about music, notably in his concept of dissonance. He was of course familiar with the physical properties of the harmonic series, but thought that the distinctions between perceived consonance and dissonance were only a matter of the immediate cultural background of the seventeenth to nineteenth centuries. Thomson suggests that Schoenberg's self-taught musical experience was narrowly limited to German music from c.1700, and that he did not know or understand the mediaeval modes, nor the ancient tonal pulls of *tenor* to *finalis* discussed in Chapter 3. He thought that modern audiences could learn to tolerate dissonance so that its perceived discordance would become "conceptually erased":

> "Dissonances are nothing else than remote consonances whose analysis gives the ear more trouble on account of their remoteness [in the harmonic series], but once analysis has made them more accessible, they will have the chance of becoming consonances just like the closer overtones."[7]

This misunderstanding meant that Schoenberg underestimated the strong tonal pull of intervals such as the octave and fifth, and the profound consonance of the major triad, which contemporary listeners would instinctively seek to extract from the set and interpret as though in a tonal context. It followed therefore that Schoenberg also underestimated the interconnected strength of the western tonal system as a means of defining form. As Thomson puts it:

"This was Schoenberg's principal error: renunciation of even the primal tonal archetypes bequeathed him by his full musical heritage, believing all the while that he was rejecting only the major-minor conventions of his immediate past. He did not understand the full ramifications of his renunciation, a denial that if followed rigorously entailed abandonment of the full range of structuring potentials of pitch ... [he assumed] that tonality was one of history's local phenomena, not one of its structural imperatives."[8]

Serial sonata forms were an interesting development of the sonata idea in the twentieth century: a highly intellectual and quite different way of presenting only the thematic, motivic events of sonata form. But to claim, as Schoenberg did, that an atonal pitch row could "replace" western tonality ignored tonality's function as the prime structural element of the tonal sonata up to that time. Furthermore, the loss of tonal direction eliminated the sense of forward narrative which had always given the sonata its dramatic momentum (the eighteenth century's association of rhetoric and sonata form was more than a matter of persuasive coincidence). This was an existential loss – the greatness of the sonata lay in its narrative of dissonance and resolution, without which it could only be a pale shadow of its former self. The music theorist Joseph N Straus's suggestion that in serial sonatas "the form emerges from new, idiomatically post-tonal musical imperatives. The form is not revived, but created anew"[9] says it all: the serial sonata had become a different animal. Sequences of surface patterns could not replace the intrinsic relationship between theme and key, and therefore the serial sonata went its own, separate way.

To follow the continuing development of the traditional tonal sonata, therefore, we now turn to three examples from composers who did – for various reasons which will become apparent – continue to write piano trios using elements of the traditional sonata idea in the twentieth century: Dmitry Shostakovich, Bohuslav Martinů and David Matthews.

1. SHOSTAKOVICH

One of the most remarkable piano trios of the twentieth century was written by the Soviet composer Dmitry Shostakovich (1906-1975). A glance at the score suggests it will be unexpectedly conventional: it is written in the key of e minor, and clearly adheres to this tonal footing. Moreover, it continues to draw on formal traditions – not only on sonata form, but also on scherzo, chaconne and rondo. It might have been expected to be sober in mood, since it is another work in the long Russian tradition of memorials to a Russian musician, but none of these facts will prepare the listener for the extraordinary power and intensity of this work. We should look behind the pages of the score to appreciate its background.

Shostakovich was born into a well-to-do family of the Russian intelligentsia in St Petersburg – one of those families which actually welcomed the revolution in 1917 because they felt that the flagrant opulence of aristocratic lifestyle did not sit at all comfortably with the harsh conditions endured by Russian peasants. Dmitry inherited his musical talent from his mother, who was an accomplished pianist, and grew up with the western repertoire of Beethoven, Schumann and Liszt as well as the music of Russian composers such as Tchaikovsky, Rimsky-Korsakov, Mussorgsky and Borodin. He was also influenced by the polymath Ivan Sollertinsky at the Conservatoire, who introduced him to the music of Mahler. Shostakovich was just beginning to make a reputation as an interesting young modernist when in 1936 his style was infamously attacked in *Pravda* as "chaos instead of music".

The article was written on the personal instructions of Stalin, the subscript being his suspicion that the dissonance of the *avant-garde* symbolised dissatisfaction. Stalin wanted the Russian people to *feel contented* under his régime; he reckoned that the consonance and lyricism of the western tradition, and the satisfying resolutions of its tonal harmony, could create an illusion of stability to cover up the political upheavals of the era. Shostakovich was privately profoundly disillusioned with the communist system, but he was presented with an unenviable decision: to escape to the west and cultural freedom (as many of his contemporary artists and musicians did), or to stay in Russia to protect his family and fulfil his belief that as a composer he had a duty to his fellow-citizens to compose. He chose the latter, and for the rest of his life fulfilled that moral obligation by becoming a voice for the suffering of the Russian people. The piano trio of 1944 shows how he was able to do this.

In 1941 German troops crossed the Soviet border and Russia was drawn into the fight against Hitler. By September, the invaders had reached Leningrad (as St Petersburg was now called), and began the notorious siege of the city. Shostakovich refused the offer of evacuation until the end of the year, when he moved to complete his 7th symphony – "a tacit memorial to the whole nation". The first performance was transmitted by radio across the country, followed soon afterwards by performances all over the Allied world as the symphony became an international symbol of resistance against Nazism. But for Shostakovich the tragedy went deeper than that. "It's not about Leningrad under siege," he said, " it's about the Leningrad that Stalin destroyed and that Hitler merely finished off."

Three years later he again put into his second piano trio thoughts far too dangerous to be articulated in words, but which music could express with greater freedom. As Figes describes it:

> "Shostakovich ... developed a sort of double-speak in his musical language, using one idiom to please his masters in the Kremlin and another to satisfy his own moral conscience as an artist and a citizen. Outwardly he spoke in a triumphant voice. Yet beneath the ritual sounds of Soviet rejoicing there was a softer, more melancholic voice – the carefully concealed voice of satire and dissent only audible to those who had felt the suffering his music expressed."[10]

The trio was dedicated to the memory of his friend Sollertinsky, who died of a heart attack in 1944. This dedication immediately "legitimised" the mood of despair which pervades the work. But it also (secretly) commemorated a Jewish pupil of Shostakovich's, who had died at the front in 1941. His death focused Shostakovich's attention on the suffering of the Jews, especially at the time of writing the trio when reports were beginning to come in of the Red Army's discovery of some of the Nazi death camps. A profound sense of unspeakable experiences permeates the opening of the first movement.

D Shostakovich: 1st movement *Andante* from Piano Trio no 2 in E minor op.67

Exposition: In a ghostly voice (produced by high harmonics and a mute), the 'cello draws the other instruments one by one into an unearthly imitative introduction. Tortured and unreal, the 'cello continues to dominate the texture with a quasi-modal, quasi-Jewish theme. Suddenly the tempo quickens, and, picking up the opening rhythm, the piano – playing with hands four octaves apart – turns it into the **1st subject**, adding two angular falling 7ths to its melodic line against an insistent repeated-note accompaniment in the strings.

Ex. 43.1   1

Piano

This rhythm continues to drive the movement forward, with the violin pushing strenuously up the degrees of a chromatic scale, until all three instruments come out into the sunshine of the **2nd**

subject in the relative major key (G): this has a falling scale introduced by an opening leap of a 9th, again incorporating the opening
rhythm.

Ex. 43.2

Development: Discussion of the 2nd subject continues into the
Development, alternating with a chromatic scale. At first the violin
part is tortuously high; later thudding off-beat chords in the piano
build to a climax.

At its peak the 1st subject duly reappears in the home key for the
return of the **Recapitulation**. The 2nd subject follows shortly. The
movement finally concludes with the artlessness of a true master:
Shostakovich reduces his material to its bare essentials – the plaintive last four notes of the falling minor scale.

We are unnerved by the ghostly sound of the 'cello in the opening
introduction – it continues to cast its macabre spell for a long time –
but once the opening rhythm has been transformed into the more
congenial 1st subject, it is easier to come to terms with what it has
to say. The regularity of the sonata form framework is offset by
moments of wilful dissonance and perverse resolutions, and in the
empty enthusiasm of the regular "subjects" and the strained height
of both string parts we sense the hidden tensions behind this unnatural semblance of normality.

The relentlessness with which a regular pulse drives the scherzo-
like second movement is all too telling: there is no getting off this
treadmill. Smallman describes its

"... air of forced jollity, its loud, emphatic themes and calculatedly
crude scoring conveying a deliberate impression of brashness and
insensitivity."[11]

It is a perfect example of Shostakovich's ability to mock and remon-
strate in music in a way which would be impossible in words.

D Shostakovich: 2nd movement *Allegro non troppo* from Piano Trio no 2 in E minor op.67

Scherzo: This bald title cannot describe the frantic gaiety of this scherzo, nor the deranged generative power with which the opening Scherzo theme (**S**) pushes the movement forward:

It constantly re-invents itself, and then returns, rondo-like, to its original version.

The Trio presents a disconcerting contrast of mood and tone. It plunges up a semitone from the Scherzo's key of F♯ major to G, where – with an imbecilic grin – it swings placidly from tonic to subdominant harmony.

The third movement takes the form of a *chaconne*, a sequence of chords with (in this case) five variations. These are in the tradition of the Baroque *chaconne* and Ravel's *Passacaille*. But it departs from Baroque practice in that its successive variations do not rely on the effect of gradually-accumulating complexity and speed.

D Shostakovich: 3rd movement *Largo* from Piano Trio no 2 in E minor op.67

A sequence of eight sombre chords is heard in the piano (**C**). Shostakovich turns this into an exercise in tonal disarray: some of its chords seem to follow each other at random, not always resolving as expected, and containing jarring discords for no apparent reason.

The violin adds a gently explorative melodic line above the chords in the 1st variation, and the 'cello its own version in the 2nd. In the 3rd variation the strings travel high in their registers, building up to a climax which then gradually fades through the 4th. In the 5th variation both 'cello and violin attempt to return to the violin melody of the 2nd variation, but neither can sustain it for more than two bars of the original before sinking down in pitch. Finally the strings drift softly up and away to dissolve into the beginning of the last movement.

The sweetness of the violin and 'cello variations at first seem to offer consolation; but at the climax they seem crushed by the impossibility of drawing the piano into consonant dialogue. The overall arch shape is not dissimilar from that of Ravel's variations, but this is a smaller, sparer arch, and finally the strings are defeated by the piano's cacophony. It is a devastating depiction of despair.

The ugliness of the chords speaks volumes: this is not how western music is meant to sound. There is a parallel here with Pablo Picasso's *Guernica*, famously painted in response to the bombing of the Spanish town of that name by German planes during the Spanish Civil War: this is not how humans nor horses are meant to *look*, either. Shostakovich gives us ravaged tonality, with jarring discords and hollow, unsatisfying resolutions (if such cadences can even be called *resolutions*); Picasso gives us ravaged norms too – figures barely recognisable as human or animal, shockingly distorted by grief and pain, the pathos of a fragile flower erupting from a dead fist still clutching a shattered sword. Shostakovich's *chaconne* has become an ugly treadmill which overwhelms the strings, preventing them from singing out in progressively more colourful variations; Picasso's painting ranges in shades of grey, each terrible figure lit by stark white light in a frame of outer blackness, devoid of all the brilliant colours of his normal palette.

Pablo Picasso, *Guernica*, 1937
Madrid, Museo Nacional Centro de Arte Reina Sofia

The philosopher-musicologist Theodor W Adorno's famous apho-
rism, *"Nach Auschwitz ein Gedicht zu schreiben ist barbarisch"* ("After
Auschwitz it is barbaric to write poetry") – even if out of context
and much derided – seems apposite here: Shostakovich and Picasso
were contemporary voices and at that moment the possibility (for
any creative artist of any nationality) of returning to joyous artistic
expression after such inhuman cruelty must have seemed remote
to both. Accordingly, each has responded with a travesty of his own
art's norms.

D Shostakovich: 4th movement *Allegretto* from Piano Trio no 2 in E minor op.67

This movement is in a modified sonata rondo form. The Rondo
theme (**R**) – with its accent on the second beat of each bar, often
referred to as being "Jewish" in character – is delivered *pizzicato* by
the strings.

Ex. 43.5

Shortly after it is followed – in a raucous reversal of roles – by the
2nd subject (2), hammered out at two octaves apart by the piano
to a boisterous accompaniment of 4-note chords on the strings
(still *pizzicato*).

Ex. 43.6

At length the strings pick up their bows again, the Rondo returns,
and then the 'cello finds its voice in the chromatically-shifting lines
of a 3rd theme.

All this is extensively developed, finally building to a terrifying and
immensely powerful climax, followed by a return of the chromatic
theme.

Suddenly there is an abrupt change of mood, and in a defining moment the piano returns to the home key, and with swirling demisemiquavers ushers in a repeat of the introduction from the first movement – shorn of its 'cello harmonics, but no less powerful.

The Rondo and 2nd subject also return, and finally the slow chords of the *chaconne* movement spread over the pitch range of all three instruments. These chords finally resolve onto the home dominant chord and lead to a peaceful close in the home tonic *major*: we have no sense that Shostakovich is placating the Kremlin in this – it is as though he cannot bear to end on a note of bleak despair, but must offer at least musical consolation to his listeners.

This is not a work one can hear too often, but neither is it easily forgotten. Its humourless themes and relentless rhythms ironically harness just those aspects of western music which in 1944 had been abandoned by *avant-garde* musicians.

★ ★ ★ ★ ★

2. MARTINŮ

As we have just seen, by remaining in Russia Shostakovich was unable to play a pioneering role amongst composers in the twentieth century. His fellow countrymen Stravinsky and Prokofiev did leave Russia, and were therefore able to develop their own style with complete freedom. But neither of them, nor any of the other leading European composers working in the second half of the century, took up the piano trio as a chamber medium – none of the Viennese serialists, not Bartók or Hindemith, not Milhaud, Poulenc or Honegger (although Bartók did write one trio, for violin, *clarinet* and piano). It is hard to know why this was so, since string quartets continued to be widely written. As we have seen, the piano trio had always been a difficult medium for composers to maintain balance between the three instruments, and perhaps the modernists found it doubly so. A certain number of piano trios were still written (notably in England, following the Cobbett compositions), but few were allied with progressive change and fewer still continued the tonal sonata tradition.

After Ravel and Fauré, the most distinctive composer to draw on tonal Classical precedents in the piano trio was perhaps the Czech Bohuslav Martinů (1890-1959). He was forced by war and political opposition to pick out a career in a number of different countries, and became typical of his displaced generation – forever far from home and yet, perversely, enriched by the breadth of his experiences as well as the character of his native music. He had been born and brought up in a Bohemian village, but his musical education began when he won a scholarship to study in Paris in 1923. Here he encountered the immensely popular new jazz and ragtime and absorbed myriad influences, ranging from the music of Stravinsky and *Les Six* to Debussy. Here too he passed through a "neoclassical" phase, studying the style of Corelli, Vivaldi and J S Bach, as well as Haydn and Beethoven. To all of this he brought his own distinctive Czech voice, with an ear for attractive melody and a lively sense of rhythm, and his music was very successful in Paris. But in 1940 he was blacklisted by the Nazis, and fled from France to spend much of the rest of his life in the USA. Martinů's third piano trio was written in New York in 1951, in the last decade of his life.

Martinů calls this work a trio "in C major". This title gives us an indication of what will follow – a work with tonal orientation and perhaps even traditional formal frameworks. We are not disappointed in any of this: the first movement is in sonata form, and the second a simple ternary form (A – B – A), and both begin and end in the same key.

However, Martinů's career in Paris had begun with a modernist style characterised by a good deal of chromaticism and dissonance, and we should not expect to find him sinking back into an anodyne musical language. Although he gives us a sense of cadence orientation, we are never sure how – or where – his chosen harmonies will carry him next. He is perhaps at his most colourful and inventive in the final movement of this trio.

B Martinů: 3rd movement *Allegro* from Piano Trio no 3 in C major H 332

For a time this exhilarating movement appears to be unwinding in a conventional sonata rondo form. A wonderful whirligig opening theme (1) opens the movement:

Ex. 44.1

This is repeated, then leads into a 2nd subject (2) which swings languidly in the strings above a continuously busy piano accompaniment.

Ex. 44.2

This all comes to an end in a sequence of syncopations, ending on a diminished 7th chord: this chord can resolve in a number of different ways, and we expect Martinů to slip skilfully from here back into the whirligig theme. However, he is having nothing to do with it. Instead, he slides into a wholly-unexpected (and quite long) free cadenza for the piano, which is then followed by a new theme, unrelated to anything we have yet heard. This proves to be a fruitful idea and Martinů develops it imaginatively for several pages. Finally it draws to a close, whereupon the whirligig opening and then its 2nd subject return – this has not been a Rondo, but a movement in ternary form. The return of the whirligig section duly closes the movement in a flourish of merry semiquavers.

There are echoes of a number of familiar conventions in this music: the motor drive of the Classical Rondo finale (and in its turn of the Baroque concerto), the time-honoured sectional contrasts of the Da Capo aria (the ternary form *par excellence*), the particularly lyrical sweetness of Czech nationalist composers, as well as an overall feeling for tonality and the framework of the sonata idea. But it also has the syncopated vigour of jazz and ragtime, and a distinctive use of dissonant notes. Sometimes the dissonance, used as it is within a fundamentally tonal framework, seems wilful and perverse: there is often a sharp edge to the piano's accompaniment figures, with dissonances thrown in for strident colour. But then this is hardly a conventional tonal movement: although the trio purports to be "in the key of C major" this *Allegro* begins in E♭ and ends in F, with little reversion to the key of C at any juncture. The framework is scarcely tonal, it is now largely thematic – and above all unpredictable. In short, Martinů now builds only on *our expectation that there will be a framework*, and that we shall follow him where he chooses to take us.

★ ★ ★ ★ ★

3. DAVID MATTHEWS

At the beginning of this chapter we referred to the bewildering variety of Modernist movements which followed Schoenberg's break with the western musical tradition. By the time the English musician David Matthews (b.1943)* was embarking on a composing career in the 1960s, the most radical forms of musical Modernism – such as the strict serialism of the Darmstadt School, aleatory (controlled by chance) and electronic music – had alienated a considerable percentage of the listening public, exposing a deeply regrettable divide between popular and serious music in western society.

Matthews has written perceptively about this:

"... for the majority of educated Westerners today, who read contemporary novels and look at contemporary art, their main experience of new music is through rock. If they are interested in classical music, it is likely to be the music of the past. Rock music, with its direct appeal to the emotions, seems to stand at the opposite extreme from contemporary classical music, which is held by most people to be 'difficult' and remote from ordinary life. But rock music, however good ... is limited in its expressive range and by its avoidance of musical complexity; it cannot plumb the depths of our experience. Classical music can do that, but contemporary classical music, it seems to most people, does not ... While the levelling-down of society in the last fifty years has tended to marginalize serious and complex music, composers themselves are partly to blame for their failure to communicate directly on an emotional level, leaving the field open for rock music to take over."[12]

Matthews is convinced that "the loss of ... accessible, singable melody in the music of Schoenberg and his successors" has been "a devastating blow to its comprehensibility".[13] He himself found the symphonies of Mahler (which were widely performed in London in the 1960s) and the music of English musicians such as Vaughan Williams, Tippett and Britten (for whom he worked as musical assistant for three years) more emotionally appealing and congenial. These composers drew him back to connect with earlier European traditions, and what he has called the "vernacular" idiom of western music "which is embedded in our consciousness" – in other words, music based on the familiar scales and cadences whose evolution

* The following discussion of David Matthews's piano trios draws on a personal interview with the composer together with information taken from his website: www.david-matthews.co.uk

we have traced throughout this book. Since familiarity facilitates the memorability and recognition which lie at the heart of the enjoyment of western music, he decided to return in his symphonies and chamber music, on his own terms, to traditional forms:

"Postmodernism ... permits a return to music of all the elements that modernism proclaimed were done with for ever. But if we are all postmodernists now, we should not be superficial in our attitude to the past, parading styles like dressing up in old clothes. Much postmodernist art ransacks the past indiscriminately, with little sense of history. A more responsible attitude is to attempt to integrate the present with the past by re-establishing a continuity with those forms from the past which contain the greatest accumulation of historical meaning. I have been much concerned ... with two of these forms, the symphony and the string quartet."[14]

To these can be added the piano trio; and Matthews has written three of them.

I have chosen to look in detail at the first, written in 1983, because it is scored with great clarity and enables the listener to follow the development of the composer's ideas, and thus understand his use of old structures, with little difficulty. We should not, however, expect a composer in the twentieth century to write in the idiom of the past. Some of Matthews' music is tonal, some is not, but his sonata movements are not always about tonality. He takes up the sonata idea where Brahms and Reger left off, and, relying on the listener's familiarity with the framework, uses it for presenting and developing thematic ideas. His harmonic context can be uncompromisingly dissonant, but his dissonance is colourful and idiomatic, often used to express tension followed by release.

D Matthews: 1st movement *Lento – Allegro moderato – Allegro con fuoco* from Piano Trio no 1 op.34

Exposition: A slow introduction focuses initial attention on the ghost of a musical idea: a descending minor triad in eerie harmonics on the violin. The tempo quickens and the strings together announce the 1st subject: a figure propelled up two octaves by an energetic rhythm, 1(a), immediately answered by a powerful falling arpeggio (based on the minor triad), 1(b).

These two ideas are tossed between all the instruments until a sudden drop to *pianissimo* announces new material – or, rather, three new ideas in quick succession: 2(a) strings playing *sul tasto* (on the fingerboard), 2(b) a romantic phrase reminiscent of Brahms and 2(c) another bold rhythmic figure tumbling down a sequence of thirds.

As though returning to repeat this concise Exposition, the 1st subject returns at its original pitch, but we are soon carried into a ruminative **Development** passage in which new triad patterns play a leading role. The strings hover expectantly on a sustained chord, after which the **Recapitulation** returns to the 1st subject (the arpeggio now falling down in the key of f# minor). This is not an exact repeat of the Exposition: it combines 1st and 2nd subjects together, and then goes on to develop the three parts of the 2nd subject. The slow tempo of the Introduction returns and finally rounds off the movement with a reverse of the opening: a sequence of *rising* minor triads, as though the initial ghostly triad, having inspired this movement, now vanishes from whence it came.

Matthews' thematic material is well defined and easily recognisable; much of it is presented by the strings in forceful opposition to the piano; but the keyboard part has its share in the continuous development, both contributing to the argument and supporting the strings, but never overpowering them.

The trio was commissioned at the suggestion of Hans Keller, the Austrian-born musician and writer. Matthews promptly dedicated the work to Keller, commenting wryly:

"Since Hans's views on the piano trio – that it is a more or less impossible medium because of the inherent imbalance between piano and strings – were well-known to me (as I'm sure he knew), there was a certain ironic humour in his suggesting the commission, so I repaid him in kind with a number of humorous (as I hope) asides in the piece ..."

(The momentary parody of Brahms we heard in the first movement was inserted to tease Keller, who disapproved of Brahms!)

"... The Scherzo second movement I intended to be a portrait of Hans, though I didn't tell him and I wonder if he guessed. It is marked 'drily humorous', it has many shifts of mood, and its main material has a deliberately Jewish character."*

D Matthews: 2nd movement Scherzo – *Allegretto* from Piano Trio no 1 op.34

This delightful movement alternates the dry humour of the sprightly but tenacious 'Jewish' theme with a quasi-'Viennese' waltz in many changing moods. It is more tonally stable than the first movement, returning often to the opening tonality of a minor. But near the close, just as we feel safely back in the home tonic, in the penultimate bar the 'cello drops slyly down to A♭ and the movement ends wickedly – and very effectively – on a *staccato* chord of *A♭ major*.

The humour of the Scherzo is followed by "a more or less literal transcription" of an earlier setting by Matthews of a visionary nature poem by Kathleen Raine, *Bright Cloud*.[15]

---

* From the composer's own programme note, reproduced in the piano score, London, Faber Music, 1984.

D Matthews: 3rd movement: *Adagio* from Piano Trio no 1 op.34

The purpose of this movement is to contrast with the tensions of the preceding movements. We have no singer nor words to follow, simply slow-moving, quiet sounds to enjoy. This is surely what Matthews intends: when composing he writes what he "likes the sound of", and we guess that we are not required to be overly analytical about structure here. We should listen (as with Schubert and Schumann) to the intricacy of the scoring: the interplay between violin, 'cello and piano, the beautiful effects in the violin's high *tessitura*, the richness of the 'cello tone, and finally the rustling arpeggios with which the strings accompany the last lingering phrase in the piano.

The *Adagio* leads without a break into the *finale*.

D Matthews: 4th movement: *Molto moderato* from Piano Trio no 1 op.34

Matthews ends his trio with a movement of classical simplicity. All tensions are dispelled by what begins as a simple diatonic melody, heard only three times as it passes in turn from violin to piano, then finally to 'cello.

Ex. 45.3

Violin

pp semplice, very pure tone

The serenity of this movement owes much to the placid opening phrase in the 'cello, which drops *dolcissimo* with a lingering trill onto a low pedal note. (Conditioned to sonata tonality, are we to hear this as a *dominant* pedal?) It lends stability to the first two statements of the lovely melody, and finally transfers to the violin; here, with the same piquant confounding of expectation as in the Scherzo (and reminiscent of Beethoven's treatment of the enigmatic C# in the *Eroica* symphony theme), it suddenly slips down a semitone to D♭. This confirms that it has indeed been a dominant pedal, for the melody is finally heard in the 'cello in the key of G♭ (enharmonically completing a tonal circle by arriving at the tonal centre of the first movement (F#)).

The character of the Finale is a striking feature of this trio. We expect another fast movement in the tradition of bouncing rondos, and the peaceful ending Matthews gives us is unusual. He describes this Finale as the last stage in a "process of gradual relaxation from the concentrated energy of the first movement". (It is no coincidence that it was conceived on the Hebridean island of Canna – Matthews inherits from Vaughan Williams the ability to be inspired by, and to capture in music, a profound sense of the peacefulness of natural landscape.)

Matthews' substitution of a slow movement as his finale is an instance of his open-minded approach to traditional archetypes:

> "The Classical symphony achieved an equilibrium between mind and body by following an initial sonata allegro, where the intellect was dominant, with a song and a dance movement; the finale was then often a movement of play: the body's energy enhanced by intellectual games."[16]

Thus we see him continuing the long tradition of the sonata idea as a synthesis of the rational and the sensuous. He still expects his listeners to devote as much intellectual effort into listening to the organic growth of his thematic material in a first movement as did Brahms; he will reward them with captivating rhythmic patterns in a dance-like movement, and with appealing, singable melody in a songful one; and if he offers peaceful catharsis instead of playful energy as a *finale*, who would deny that this might be an appropriate conclusion for listeners in the twenty-first century's frenetic times?

Two later piano trios by Matthews have become increasingly tonal in idiom. The slow movement of the second (1994), for instance, is a particularly lovely tonal elegy (poignantly *in memoriam*) and the first movement of the third (2005) ends with a strikingly effective coda in C major. All his music is written in a distinct personal style, without loss of his own integrity as a musician but nevertheless accessible to contemporary listeners.

Matthews is adamant that "Music began with song and dance, and however sophisticated it becomes, it must never lose touch with these essential human activities".[17] We have traced western music's origins from primitive pitch and pulse, through song and dance, to the cadence and pattern of the western sonata idea. There could hardly be a more appropriate comment – from a living composer of trios – to end this chapter on the piano trio in the modern era.

CHAPTER ENDNOTES

1   Schoenberg, *Fundamentals of Musical Composition*, p.8.

2   Hindemith, Paul. *The Craft of Musical Composition.* Book I, Theory. Transl. Arthur Mendel, London: Schott & Co, 1937, p.155.

3   Thomson. *op.cit,* p.176.

4   Scruton, Roger. *The Aesthetics of Music.* Oxford, Oxford University Press, 1997, pp.295, 294.

5   Frances, Robert in *Journal de Psychologie* 45 (1954), pp.78-96.

6   Westergaard, Peter. 'Some Problems Raised by the Rhythmic Procedures in Milton Babitt's Composition for Twelve Instruments', *Perspectives of New Music 4, no.1 (1965),* p.118.

7   Schoenberg, Arnold. *Theory of Harmony,* 3rd ed. 1922. Transl. Roy Carter, Berkeley, CA: University of California Press, 1978, p.66.

8   Thomson, *op.cit,* p.109.

9   Straus, *op.cit,* p.98.

10   Figes, *op.cit,* p.492.

11   Smallman, *op.cit,* p.185.

12   Matthews, David. Review: '*The Rest is Noise: Listening to the Twentieth Century* by Alex Ross', *Musical Opinion,* July –August 2009.

13   Matthews, David. 'The Rehabilitation of the Vernacular in Music' in *The Politics of Culture,* ed. Christopher Norris, London: Lawrence & Wishart, 1989, p.244.

14   Matthews, David. 'Renewing the Past, some personal thoughts' in *Reviving the Muse: Essays on Music after Modernism,* ed. Peter Davison ed, Open Library: Claridge Press, 2001. Reproduced at https://www.david-matthews.co.uk/writings/article.asp?articleid=13

15   Included in Matthews' song cycle *The Golden Kingdom.*

16   Matthews, *Renewing the Past,* see above.

17   Matthews, *ibid,* see above.

Coda: The Ulterior Effect of Past Sounds

"Unlike the architect, who has to mould the coarse and unwieldy rock, the composer reckons with the ulterior effect of past sounds"

Eduard Hanslick, *The Beautiful in Music*, 1854.

IN TRACING THE development of the sonata idea in the piano trio we have also been following the significant role played by sonata form in the historical development of western tonality. The sonata story is a thoroughgoing exploration of our music system: the notes of its scales, the dominance of home tonic sound within those scales, the comparative dissonance of a key on any other note, and the ways in which the unique phenomenon of western harmony supports these things. The physical nature of sound – or at least of our "sensory processing of sound, the harmonic series"[1] – has been a crucial ingredient of western music from the moment when primitive humans may first have heard resonating harmonics in prehistoric caves (see pp.39-40).

The conscious abandonment of western tonality at the beginning of the last century, and the subsequent failure of atonal music to appeal to the great majority of people, may have been due to the atonalists' misunderstanding of the fundamental importance of familiarity to western comprehension. If we look at the current musical scene in the western world, we will find it – broadly – represented by three distinct sectors: firstly, the followers of the "serious" *avant-garde* composers, whose music is defined by innovation and atonality; secondly, devotees of opera and the "classical" (with a small "c") concert repertoire, largely defined by their continuing enjoyment of the existing canon, with its melodiousness and tonal coherence – but who are nevertheless open to any new music with which they feel able in some way to connect; and thirdly, fans of popular music, which includes pop, rock, folk and jazz.

Numbers in the three sectors are greatly disproportionate. Admirers of the *avant-garde* are the smallest group, followed by the opera-lovers and classical concert-goers; but both are vastly out-numbered by the enthusiasts for popular music, who include the great majority of young people. The classical repertoire is largely tonal; popular music is tonal. The preferential vote for tonal music is overwhelming.

Taken at surface value, common ground between pop music and sonatas may not be immediately obvious. But if we look more closely at a typical pop or rock song, we shall find many familiar features: its melodies are tonal and underpinned by traditional western harmonies; many have at least some sturdy 4 + 4 bar phrases; all are regulated by constant beat and tempo; there is a good deal of repetition and a liberal use of sequences. The similarity between these and the European dance song is inescapable. Of course there are differences between pop songs and the use which the sonata made of the dance-song, but *au fond* the two are indebted for musical cohesion and effect to the same thing: western listeners' cultural loyalty to their tonal system.

This Coda is therefore devoted to answering two questions which now arise.

Firstly: *how* does western tonality exert its powerful effect on us as we listen to our music, and secondly: *why* should we continue to listen to a sonata repertoire which must inevitably be seen as written in an outdated idiom, since most composers no longer write tonal sonatas?

★   ★   ★   ★   ★

How does tonality exert its powerful effect on us?

Throughout the course of this book we have seen contemporary audiences exercised by the question of how they should understand instrumental music. Should it be as a carrier of intellectual meaning, or of emotional enjoyment? Or something of both? Even Hanslick recognised that music had a powerful effect on listeners which could not exclusively be attributed to intellectual enjoyment. He was perceptive enough also to realise that understanding of this problem might lie in new, scientific directions: "Psychologists and physiologists alike are fully cognisant of the truth that music acts most powerfully on the nervous system, but neither of them, unfortunately, can offer an adequate explanation," he wrote. In the state of knowledge in 1854 he can perhaps be forgiven for going on to say that: "Psychologists will never be able to throw any light on the irresistible force with which certain chords, timbres, and melodies impress the entire human organism ..."[2]

One should never say "never". Modern neuroscience and psychology are now beginning to offer explanations for the effect on the human brain of the "chords, timbres and melodies" in the western music system. When neuroscientific research first began, it was thought that music was processed by a single area of the brain. However, scientists now believe that the complex sound structures of music are decoded by "multiple successive processing stages" which are shared between the two cerebral hemispheres, and that the decoding of music "rivals the language system in breadth and complexity". In a paper of 2008, the neurologist Jason Warren wrote that music also "engenders ... powerful and neurally primitive *emotional* [my italics] responses that are fundamental to the quality of musical experience".[3] He pointed out that additionally – and significantly – parallel to the extensive cortical network for the processing of sound lies a phylogenetically much older brain circuit that mediates emotional responses. Warren says that "work in healthy subjects has demonstrated that strong emotional responses to music are associated, paradoxically, with limbic activity very similar to that elicited by basic biological drives."[4]

We should be clear what is understood in this context as an "emotional response". "Put in the simplest neuroscientific terms," says Regina Pally, "emotions organise an animal's sustained responses to rewarding and aversive stimuli ... The function of emotion is to co-ordinate the mind and body."[5] The evolutionarily ancient limbic circuitry of the brain evolved to produce responses critically related to survival – "flight or fight" reactions to predators, danger or unwelcome situations, "rest and digest" reactions to food, sex and other rewarding stimuli. It may seem something of a surprise to us to learn that music appears to trigger emotional reactions similar to such basic appetites.

A growing body of scientific evidence however is now endorsing this fact. Research in Montreal at McGill University into "musical frissons" commonly experienced by people listening to their favourite music has found that these primitive reactions – hairs rising on the back of the neck, chills down the spine – coincide at moments of peak enjoyment with the release of dopamine in the brain: dopamine is a neurotransmitter, the "feel-good" chemical released in response to rewarding human activities.[6]

Thus Hanslick's statement that "Music operates on our emotional faculty with greater intensity and rapidity than the product of any other art"[7] seems nearer the scientific truth than he could have known. However, although we may now have scientifically-supported confirmation of the outcome, can we also identify the musical prompts?

There are two theories about this. The musicologist Deryck Cooke maintained that "Melody and rhythm are primitive, elemental, natural impulses"[8] and that the intervals which underpin our western scale system are intrinsically emotional. Major or minor modes are widely acknowledged to sound "happy" or "sad", fast or slow tempi can be "lively" or "peaceful", and pulsing rhythms or soaring melodies speak directly to our emotions. The other theory is more nuanced. It suggests that the enjoyment of western music is a cultural specific, based ultimately on *familiarity*, coupled with the fact that music must operate within the dimension of time. Each individual (consciously or not) has cultural expectations when listening to music about what s/he will hear next, and *emotional reaction flows from the way in which the composer manipulates these expectations* – fulfilling them immediately, or thwarting, or delaying before finally fulfilling. The human brain has a "predilection for pleasure", and it finds it in *the flow of music through time*, which carries a sequence of tensions and releases which trigger our emotional satisfaction in western music.

The second theory is set out in a fascinating study by the cognitive musicologist David Huron entitled "*Sweet Anticipation: music and the psychology of expectation*". Much of this very detailed work is taken up by a general theory of expectation, but it is also applied to music. "The sweet anticipation of future pleasure," says Huron, "is one of the main motivators for engaging with music,"[9] and he demonstrates how pleasure is derived from a number of the features of music, ranging from tonality and cadence to metre and syncopation. Statements such as "The positive feelings evoked by the tonic pitch and by the downbeat are artefacts of accurate prediction, not objective properties of the stimuli themselves"[10] prompt us to look back in the light of this theory at some of the music we have heard during the course of this book, to understand how it makes its effect.

We have found that melody (which lends individuality to *theme*, that important ingredient of sonata form) is one of the most characteristic components of western music. "Scale degree," says Huron, "is almost certainly the most musically important mental representation of accurate prediction related to pitch for Western-enculturated listeners."[11] We found that our western major and minor modes evolved from ancient rising and falling chants, and our modern scales developed from modal melody; we understood how the characteristic relationships of goal-orientated scales set up expectations which can only be resolved by tonic tonality. Melody has "significant and intentional connection," said Schopenhauer; it is "one thought from beginning to end".[12] We have only to remember the tantalising hiatuses in the harmony with which Schumann accompanies his falling scale to realise how profoundly we are affected by "savouring" each interval, and the glow of release on arriving home each time the scale is heard (cf p.225). (We might also note here, in passing, the soothing effect of a *falling* scale, and compare the exhilarating effect of a sequence of *rising* notes, as in the theme of the variations in Beethoven's *Archduke* Trio.) Such effects are naturally also intensified on each repetition.

Repetition is another obvious trigger for anticipation. Our music is phenomenally repetitive. "We are attracted to repetition, even as adults," says the neurologist Oliver Sacks; "we want the stimulus and the reward again and again, and in music we get it."[13] Huron measured a cross-cultural sample of 50 musical works and found that "94% of all music passages longer than a few seconds in duration are repeated at some point".[14] Perhaps human pleasure in hearing tunes repeated was embedded by the endless repetition of dance music, driving step patterns round and back down the centuries. Familiarity is pleasing, and western music has used it as a happy structural framework from time immemorial – in ballads and *carole* refrains and Da Capo arias – long before sonata form took it to another level of appreciation. The sonata form idea is a sophisticated exercise in anticipated repetition, its effects dependent on the listener's *recognition of what has been heard before*.

Repetition is also highly enjoyable on a small scale: we have often come across sequences – pleasing phrases immediately repeated at another pitch – and they are one of the most emotionally satisfying of all repetition techniques. "We are pattern-seeking creatures,"[15] says Gilbert Rose, and musical sequences satisfy both our intellect and our emotions.

If repetition sets up such expectations of predictability, so too does pulse and the regulated beat of repeating rhythms. If we listen again to J S Bach's *gigue*, but then suddenly pause it in mid-flow, we may be surprised by the strength of the momentary shock felt on being unexpectedly deprived of its anticipated pulse. As we saw in Chapter 2, it was music for dance which first introduced this compulsive element into "serious" western music. It created a double expectation: firstly the stress on the first beat of each bar (defining duple or triple time to suit the particular dance), and secondly the grouping of bars into 8-beat sections (to fit the patterns of the dance). The expectations raised by the familiar patterns are not fulfilled until the final note sounds on the final beat. (This is perhaps one of the reasons why a lengthy and regular "tune" does not make a good sonata form subject: we want to hear it again, and in full, on every appearance, and we will not be satisfied with less – but inevitably this holds up the dramatic thrust of sonata narrative.)

All sonata movements are governed by regular pulse, but nowhere more than in Rondo finales. After the traditional "rejoicing" triplet rhythms inherited by Classical Rondos (as in Mozart's K.548) came the lively folk rhythms of nationalist composers (Chopin, Smetana, Dvořák). Expectations can often be thwarted by unexpected off-beat stress and syncopations. These little surprises create momentary tensions which are then released by reversion to the main beat – all the more enjoyable for having been temporarily withheld.

Although surprises are usually only temporary, they are significant creators of tension. Chromaticism is a surprise; that is the secret of its effectiveness. Mozart loved introducing splashes of chromatic semitone decoration, Haydn relished inserting unexpected chromatic chords, both momentarily diverting our attention and causing us to enjoy all the more the following *expected* consonant note or chord. After Beethoven and Schubert, chromatic harmony and the wayward inclusion of "foreign" keys add more tonal variety to the framework of the sonata idea as the nineteenth century progresses, but we become acclimatised to it; by the twentieth century we can accommodate new levels of chromatic tension and release (Ravel, Shostakovich, Martinů). Sets of variations are a succession of surprises: we can only be sure of the main theme, and after that we must rummage for the tune in the tantalising aural rubble which surrounds it; when Mozart recasts his theme in the minor mode, that is a surprise; Beethoven's, Tchaikovsky's and Brahms's variations are full of them.

Dissonance may be a less palatable surprise, but again it is often only temporary and serves to enhance the subsequent resolution. Suspended notes are especially effective carriers of temporary dissonance: a note first heard as a *consonance* over underlying harmony, becomes a *dissonance* if it continues to be held after that harmony changes, and the eventual delayed resolution is all the more rewarding for being so delayed. The most ubiquitous chord in the western repertoire is a dissonant one: the dominant 7th. Hidden in the texture, it longs for a sweet resolution onto the tonic 3rd at cadence points. In tonal sonata literature – it tends to get it. And as we heard in the Classical period, the functional harmony which defines important cadences is constantly enhanced by the preparation of chromatic Neapolitan and dissonant 6th chords (cf p.103).

Cadences bring us to tonality, the anticipated stability of which is a major source of the emotional satisfaction to be derived from listening to western music. We rely on satisfying cadences perhaps more than we realise. Virginia Woolf drew a telling analogy with music when complaining about an inconclusive story by Chekhov which left the reader "hanging in the air":

"But is it the end, we ask? We have rather the feeling that we have overrun our signals; or it is as if a tune had stopped short without the expected chords to close it ... Where the tune is familiar and the end emphatic ... we can scarcely go wrong, but where the tune is unfamiliar and the end a note of interrogation ... we need a very daring and alert sense ... to make us hear the tune, and in particular those last notes which complete the harmony."[16]

We should not be surprised. Playford's dances showed us how the "figures" of dance matched the pattern of dance songs, and how these wired tonal cadences – half-closes on the dominant, and full closes on the tonic – into the musical subconscious of western Europe (see pp.34-35). We recall again Rosen's comment that "the cadence is the basis of all western musical form", and perhaps now understand more clearly why and how cadence and tonality have defined all the music we have heard – from the neat thematic "boxes" of Classical sonata trios, and the demarcations of Exposition/Development/ Recapitulation, to the glowing melodies of Schubert, Dvořák, Tchaikovsky and Brahms. The pattern and symmetry of the sonata idea is dependent on key relationships and the final return to the "home" key; and as Virginia Woolf well understood, we rely on cadences to reinforce sonata symmetry and fulfil our expectations. Conversely, the "free" nature of the Development section and our consequent lack of clear expectations, coupled with the disappearance of the home key and rapid harmonic change, significantly raise tensions. Composers often play up to this and delay the return to the Recapitulation with long passages of anticipatory dominant preparation, so that the eventual return is a doubly welcome release.

Tonality also underpins climax, another of the composer's most effective tension-inducing techniques. A musical climax must reach a tonally-satisfying place or it will not be effective. But climaxes can also be ingeniously engineered: they can be accentuated by pulse (especially if accompanied by acceleration), *crescendi* and rising pitch. ("Like emotion," says Pally, "music is expressed in pitch, timbre and frequency."[17]) A musical climax is a sophisticated manipulation of multiple expectations. If we can bear it, we should flick the pause button just before the climax arrives – the physical shock of disappointment we experience will confirm how primitive is our emotional reaction to music.

Huron's theory of expectation has been recognised as a landmark in the cognitive science of music. He offers a plausible analysis of how western music might be processed by the limbic circuitry of the human brain to evoke the emotional effect of music which is so widely acknowledged, and gives fascinating insights into the processes of tension and release which work on us as music unfolds in time. But even Huron's comprehensive scrutiny does not give us all the answers: music still has some magical mysteries. He has not told us, for instance, why we all feel that the minor mode is *sad*. But he may have found an answer to the apparent paradox propounded by Sacks, that although Dido's lament "makes one experience pain and grief more intensely, it brings solace and consolation at the same time".[18] Here we have the notes of the minor scale and its expressive semitonal arrangement of "notes in love" finding their anticipated conclusion – showing that even the most ragged emotions can be ordered in the *emotional closure* of a cadence. And there may be a scientific explanation for the "instability" of the intervals of both the minor third and the semitone: both are so high in the harmonic series that the human ear processes them as *unstable – un*predictable, triggers for concern – in association with the tonality of the funda-mental note.

The character of the third note of the scale, whether it is major or minor, is very specific. The major 3rd is as positive a sound as the minor 3rd is dolorous, and owes its strength to its prominent position in the harmonic series. During the course of the nineteenth century, composers became taken with Schubert's falling 3rd modu-lations, which trigger another emotional reaction which may defy predictive analysis. As we have observed, this is a "pleasant" surprise, but it might be hard to define how or why we feel that chords on the "flat side" of a key, the 4th, 6th and ♭6th degrees of the scale, have a dreamier, more romantic tendency than those on the robust dominant side. But perhaps, again, this is due to our western culture, that once we have accepted an opening key as our home tonic, we only hear subsequent keys *in relation to this home*; and therefore, since the "flat" keys are built on notes/harmonics more distant from the fundamental, we sense they are "distant" and aurally process them as such.

It is over a century and a half since Hanslick identified "the irresistible force" of "certain chords, timbres and melodies", and modern research is now leading to better understanding of such matters. There will undoubtedly be further revelations to come, but neuroscience and psychology have already revealed the extent to which western listeners enjoy their music *because it is their aural cultural inheritance*. This may seem self-evident: early folk dancers would scarcely have thought of their favourite dance songs as cultural treasures – for them they were simply familiar tunes. But layers of sophistication were added to a simple dance tune as it trav-elled from the village green to the ballrooms of the gentry, and many more again as it became transformed into the instrumental sonata. After describing melody and rhythm as "primitive, elemental, natural impulses", Deryck Cooke concluded by saying: "but harmony has been a consciously-willed, complex invention of western man – there is always something intellectually calculated about it."[19] The sonata idea is perhaps the ultimate intellectual calculation of the western musical tradition.

We have seen by pursuing Huron's theory how the "natural impulse" of melody in conjunction with the "complex tradition" of harmony created a musical language governed by expectation and fulfilment. Sonata form realised the potential of that language, in all its melodic, metrical and tonal variety, so that Huron's theory seems to have identified many of the ways in which tonality exerts its powerful effect on us as listeners.

★ ★ ★ ★ ★

We come now to consider the second question posed on p.340 – *why* should we continue to listen to a sonata repertoire written in an outdated idiom no longer used by most contemporary composers?

There are many reasons why we should do so, the first two being very simple. Firstly, not to do so would be as ludicrous as throwing out all the plays, poetry and novels of western literature for the arbitrary reason that they are not written in twenty-first century vernacular, or pulling down all buildings built before (say) 1960 because they are not "modernist" in style. The tonal sonata repertoire, in all its many manifestations, is a rich and significant part of our musical heritage, capable – as Huron's theory has just demonstrated – of giving great emotional as well as intellectual enjoyment.

Furthermore, that enjoyment is second nature to us because the western musical idiom is our cultural inheritance. Familiarity is here the key. Familiarity with the western scale and its expressive potential, and familiarity (conscious or not) with the "positive feelings evoked by the tonic pitch".[20] Western tonality is a "given" to those brought up in the west; it begins to be absorbed by the unborn child *in utero*, and it is the foundation of folk dance and popular music as well as the classical repertoire. All that is needed is more focused teaching and appreciation of the structures of music for forms such as sonata form to be more widely recognised, understood and enjoyed.

In passing, we might note here the following hard-hitting comment by the brilliant but sometimes controversial musicologist Richard Taruskin, addressing a seminar in Chicago in 1989:

"In the West, a century-long tradition [in the 20th century] of reckless, socially irresponsible and self-absorbed avant-garde behaviour ... coupled with an ever-increasing passivity on the part of an audience that is deprived by its education and by the growth of the recording industry of participatory skills in music, has led to the extreme apathy that threatens the continued existence of art music in our culture."[21]

There is of course a great deal of modern music, not written by inscrutable *avant-garde* composers, which is much enjoyed by contemporary audiences. The post-tonal repertoire is immensely varied, there are now many more types of music than sonata works and they are written for a variety of instrumental ensembles other than the piano trio. We are at a disadvantage here in that this book has been limited to considering the sonata idea in the piano trio, which did not continue to flourish in the twentieth century as vigorously as other chamber music ensembles.

The question we might now ask is whether there is some sort of tonal work which might continue the sonata tradition – perhaps even in the piano trio – into the twenty-first century. "The real problem for the composer in our time," writes Scruton, "is how to respect the principles of tonal organisation without writing music that is either banal or short-winded," and he goes on to commend the work of David Matthews in this connection: "… the importance of David, for me and for many others, is that he has faced up to that problem, and set an example that can be followed."[22]

Matthews himself writes:

"… if tonality is to regain its full power, it must be used dynamically again … To write a movement in sonata form is somewhat daunting, as you are competing with – and almost inevitably failing to equal – the many supreme examples of such movements from the past. But it gives you access to a world where meaningful contradiction has been practised for two-and-a-half centuries. Although many of the devices of confounding expectation have been over-exploited and have themselves become clichés, it is not impossible to renew them by inner conviction; and there are still new games to play."[23]

We heard Matthews' own dynamic use of theme and tonality in his first piano trio: the first movement is filled with colourful themes and we are drawn to listen carefully, to satisfy our curiosity as to what will become of them. The sonata idea accustomed audiences to following the progress of its musical content in this way, for it is indeed itself – as Nicholas Cook puts it:

"… a kind of plot, functioning rather analogously to the stories on which ancient Greek plays were based – stories that the audience knew beforehand, so that what they were interested in was not *what* the play presented but *how* it was presented."[24]

Plays, novels, rhetoric – and to this list we should add sonata form – are all driven by the human instinct to follow a thread of meaning and to understand and rejoice in its conclusion. "Whatever human rationality consists in," says Mark Johnson, "it is certainly tied up with narrative structure and the quest for narrative unity."[25] And so here is another compelling reason why we should continue to listen to and enjoy a tonal sonata literature: because it has this deeply satisfying sense of a *musical narrative* pursuing its course to resolution.

The narrative experience was there from the beginning of the sonata idea. Hepokoski and Darcy put it in specifically musical terms:

> "The sense of drama within eighteenth-century sonata practice is ingrained in the genre's striving to articulate cadences in a spotlighted, quasi-theatrical, or narrative way. One way of understanding a sonata is to interpret it as a dramatized musical activity that by means of fluctuations of energy seeks to pass through an ordered set of rhetorical and tonal gateways ..."[26]

From this it is clear moreover that the sonata's narrative was intrinsically dependent on western *tonality*, the dénouement being brought about by the return of the home tonic key. "The fact that it is tonality that is the deepest current in the river of true symphony [or sonata movement], means that the flow of the whole depends on it,"[27] writes Robert Simpson. When the words of dance songs were jettisoned, instrumental music adopted tonality as its "agent of form",[28] and it is tonality – that "sensory processing of the harmonic series" – which provides the narrative thrust which carries the thematic material of the sonata to emotional satisfaction in the return of the home key. This is not just wishful thinking tempering instinct; it has been corroborated by the analytical work of the great nineteenth-century Austrian theorist, Heinrich Schenker:

> "... the basis of a Schenkerian analysis is seeing music as directed motion in time, and for Schenker this was tied up with an almost metaphysical conception of music being a temporal unfolding of the overtone [harmonic] series which exist as a simultaneity in all natural sounds. More specifically, Schenker saw music as the temporal unfolding, or *prolongation*, of the major triad 'chord of nature', as he called it, since it exists as the first five partials of the overtone series ..."[29]

The changing nature of the surface of the tonal sonata may obfuscate, but it never undermines the strength of this tonal underpinning. Where the eighteenth-century sonata introduced theme as a

means of identifying the tonal difference between tonic and dominant, and found its solution in the tonal unity of the Recapitulation,
the nineteenth-century sonata allowed the thematic surface to take
centre stage; but however much chromatic harmony or however
many obscure key areas later intervened, none could take the place
of the final tonal homecoming. For, as Straus observes, "thematic
disposition is not as profound an element of musical structure as
harmonic polarity."[30]

What we hear as a *tonal narrative*, however, has yet another, deeper
meaning, which leads us to a final cogent reason for listening to the
tonal sonata: because in both the eighteenth and the nineteenth
centuries music could offer through tonality a profoundly inspiring
metaphor for contemporary philosophical thinking.

Devised in the rational era of the Enlightenment, sonata form's
logical and symmetrically-balanced presentation of tonality answered
to the eighteenth century's demand for ordered entertainment.
Such orderliness and stability proved their worth in the emotionally
charged artistic world of the nineteenth century, for when Enlightenment optimism faded it was realised that rationalism and scientific
knowledge would not provide immediate answers to all humanity's
problems. As people searched for philosophical answers, the wordless logic of music seemed to speak eloquently to the listener "from
another and higher sphere: it is not the here and now ... that speaks
to us through music, but another world, whose order is only dimly
reflected in the empirical realm."[31] Music could not only sing of joys
and sorrows, but its tonality could *control* disorderly emotions and
bring the listener to reassuring resolutions. Brian K. Etter, professor
of Humanities,[32] describes it thus:

"The tonal order ... was able to ground objective accounts of
emotional expression, precisely because of its intrinsic order ... it
is not just that dissonance is a metaphor for pain, or minor keys
a metaphor for sorrow, but rather that these states of negative
emotion were indeed expected to *resolve* [my italics] in a piece of
music."[33]

We encountered Idealist philosophy as background to Beethoven
at the beginning of the nineteenth century. Etter describes it as
follows:

"The aesthetic of idealism was grounded in the belief that human
existence is meaningful, and that it is ordered by a larger good.
Such a good is defined by the ideal character conceived as the
nobility of heroism, sacrifice and virtue, and the ideal of happiness
conceived as tranquillity ..."[34]

We can sense here the direction in which a good many nineteenth-century novels and opera plots were headed. There will be many in the twenty-first century who will feel little connection now with Idealist philosophy, but such thinking was undoubtedly the aesthetic background to the nineteenth century and, if we will allow it to do so, can give us an illuminating insight into the significance of sonata form: and why – as Rosen has told us – it came to be "the proof of greatness".

★ ★ ★ ★ ★

We can now see that a number of significant strands came together in the sonata idea: firstly, a propulsive narrative, "… the essence of the concept of the musical work",[35] and secondly, a permeating tonality, which ordered the narrative and gave it structure; thirdly, the formal orderliness of sonata form itself, which drove towards consonance at a local level as well as final resolution in the home tonic key; and fourthly, the Idealist vision, which saw resolution and reconciliation as leading to an ideal of tranquillity in resolution.

So this was more than just a desirable outcome of musical events: *resolution* itself had deeper meaning. The individual listener could find in the resolutions and reconciliations of sonata form a metaphor for human efforts to make peace with the world, for as Etter points out, "directed order, in the Western philosophical tradition, has always been associated with the category of goodness … The historical links between philosophy and music, are crucial for understanding the normativity of the kinds of order classical music possesses."[36]

In the twentieth century musical composition was deeply affected by the pessimistic writing of Adorno, who said that "Music must give up the attempt to design itself as a picture of the good and the virtuous …".[37] One can only speculate on what direction the music of the future will take, but, as Etter says, "perhaps it is time to seek an expression of the good adequate for a new century." Western tonality is still a live and flourishing tradition and music can still "satisfy the deepest needs of the human spirit for the presentation to itself of the beauty of goodness and truth."[38]

Sonata form is one of the great archetypes of western music. Its tonal narrative carries as much intrinsic meaning as the novels and plays of the western literary canon, underpinned by the same traditions of western philosophy. For this reason it is a notable archetype also of the western artistic canon, and should be valued right up there with the sonnet and the Classical temple, the paintings of Leonardo da Vinci and the plays of Shakespeare. If only more people could be taught to know and understand it – and thus ensure that it will continue to be heard and admired and loved as it deserves. For "as long as the canon is preserved, there will be the aural evidence of the goodness of order, represented in the compelling beauty of the works composed according to the principles of tonality."[39]

* * * * *

When Hanslick writes that "the composer reckons with the ulterior effect of past sounds" he has given precise directions for listening to music, and especially to sonata music. The "past sounds" of the western music system fashioned around those ringing natural harmonics – heard, imitated and made familiar, then systematised, combined and compulsively enjoyed – these "past sounds" have a profoundly "ulterior" effect, some thousands of years in the making, on how we hear and sensorily process western music. At the same time, the shorter-term "sounds" of each individual sonata movement must be heard, identified and followed and their resolutions anticipated and savoured in order that the "past sounds" of each work can have their own full "ulterior effect" on the listener.

Thus conscious of the sonata's fundamental debt to its ancient beginnings, it seems appropriate to end as we began, with a painting of the life-affirming vitality of humans dancing in a ring, for "Society spreads its image before itself," says Scruton, "in poetry, architecture, image-making and music."[40] In this final painting, Henri Matisse vividly captures the energy of the circling dance (see opposite). But it is hardly what the painter saw as he looked out of his studio window: sky was never so blue, nor grass so green, and people did not generally dance with such naked abandon – certainly not in 1910, when this was painted. The painting is not about a conventional dance, but about an idealised vision of dancing.

This image of society belongs to music, too. It depicts the circularity which music also derives from the dance, drawing us into the experience of a shared ancestry: the lively movement of the dance expressed in the rhythmic momentum of music, the constant pattern of *8 steps to the left, then 8 returning steps to the right* defined by tonal anticipation and resolution. The circular, returning tonality of the dance is at the heart of the sonata's emotional effect.

Henri Matisse: The Dance, 1910.
The Hermitage, St Petersburg

As we read in the Introduction, Adam Smith in 1795 admired the proficiency with which instrumental music had replaced the graphic nature of words with a musical narrative of its own:

> "In the contemplation of that immense variety of agreeable and melodious sounds, arranged ... into so complete and regular a system, the mind in reality enjoys not only a very great sensual, but a very high intellectual, pleasure, not unlike that which it derives from the contemplation of a great system in any other science."[41]

Our intellectual pleasure lies in perceiving the sophisticated use and development of theme and variation, in hearing the tonal detours and return at the heart of the sonata idea. But at the same time we draw deep emotional satisfaction from expressive arrangements of the notes of the western scale, and luxuriate in the relief of home-coming generated by the closure of the final cadence. It is because it achieves this satisfying synthesis of the rational and the emotional sides of our human nature that the sonata form of the western tonal tradition, in all its manifestations from the middle of the eighteenth century onwards, continues to give us such profound pleasure in "the ulterior effect of past sounds".

CHAPTER ENDNOTES

1   Thomson, op.cit. p.177.

2   Hanslick, *op.cit*, p.79.

3   Warren, Jason. 'How does the brain process music?', *Clinical Medicine*, vol.8 no.1, February 2008, pp.32-36.

4   Warren, *ibid*, drawing on A J Blood, R J Zatorre, 'Intensely pleasurable responses to music correlate with activity in brain regions implicated in reward and emotion', *Proc.Natl.Acad.Sci*, 2001; 98:11818-23.

5   Pally, Regina. *The Mind-Brain Relationship*. London and New York: Karnac Books, 2000, p.73.

6   Salimpoor, Valorie N, Benovoy, Mitchel, Larcher, Kevin, Dagher, Alain, Zatorre, Robert J, 'Anatomically distinct dopamine release during anticipation and experience of peak emotion to music', *Nature Neuroscience*, 2011, DOI:10.1038/nn.2726.

7   Hanslick, *op.cit*, p.77.

8   Cooke, Deryck. *The Language of Music*. Oxford: Oxford University Press, 1959, p.193.

9   Huron, David. *Sweet Anticipation: Music and the Psychology of Expectation*. Cambridge, MA and London: MIT Press, 2006, p.329.

10 *ibid*, p.356.

11 *ibid*, p.129.

12 Quoted by Oliver Sacks in *Musicophilia: Tales of Music and the Brain*. London: Picador, 2007, p.211, fn.7.

13 Sacks, *ibid*, p.47.

14 Huron, *op cit*, p.229.

15 Rose, *op.cit*, p.96.

16 Woolf, Virginia. *The Common Reader*. London: Hogarth Press, 1925.

17 Pally, *op cit*, p.109.

18 Sacks, *op cit*, p.301.

19 Cooke, *op cit*, p.193.

20 Huron, *op. cit*, p.314.

21 Taruskin, Richard. Lecture: 'Et in Arcadia Ego; or I Didn't Know I Was Such a Pessimist until I Wrote This Thing', given at the Chicago *Seminars on the Future*, 13 April 1989; published in *The Danger of Music and Other Anti-Utopian Essays*, Berkeley and Los Angeles: University of California Press, 2009, p.5.

22 Scruton, Roger. 'The Emancipation of the Consonance', contribution to *David Matthews: Essays, Tributes and Criticism*, ed. Thomas Hyde, London: Plumbago Books, 2014, p.108.

23 Matthews, *Renewing the Past*, pp.9,12.

24 Cook, Nicholas. *A Guide to Musical Analysis*. Oxford: Oxford University Press, 1987, p.262.

25 Johnson, Mark. *The Body in The Mind: The Bodily Basis Of Meaning, Imagination, And Reason*. Chicago: University of Chicago Press, 1987, p.172.

26 Hepokoski and Darcy, *op. cit*, p.250.

27 Simpson, Robert. Introduction to *The Symphony: Vol. Two*, Harmondsworth: Penguin Books, 1967, p.11.

28 Scruton, Roger. *Music as an Art*, London: Bloomsbury Continuum, 2018.

29 Cook, *op. cit*, p.39.

30 Straus, *op. cit*, p.97.

31 Scruton, *Aesthetics of Music*, p.489.

32 Brian K Etter held the post of Associate Professor in Humanities in the Department of Liberal Studies, Kettering University, Michigan, USA.

33 Etter, Brian K. *From Classicism to Modernism*. Aldershot: Ashgate, 2001, p.65.

34 Etter, *ibid*, p.114.

35 Etter, *ibid*, p.114.

36 Etter, *ibid*, p.49.

37 Quoted by Etter, *ibid*, p.232.

38 Etter, *ibid*, p.233.

39   Etter, *ibid*, p.229.

40   Scruton, *Aesthetics of Music*, p.478.

41   Smith, *Essays on Philosophical Subjects, p.*235.

Appendix A:
List of Major and Minor Keys

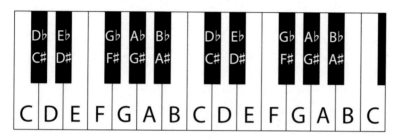

simple scale:
d minor (harmonic)

D E F G A Bb C# D

♯ KEYS					♭ KEYS			
Key	Key signature	Domi-nant	Rela-tive minor		Key	Key signature	Domi-nant	Rela-tive minor
C		G	a		C		G	a
G		D	e		F		C	d
D		A	b		Bb		F	g
A		E	f#		Eb		Bb	c
E		B	c#		Ab		Eb	f
B		F#	g#		Db		Ab	bb
F#		C#	d#		Gb		Db	eb

Appendix B:
Glossary of Musical Terms

This is a select set of terms to cover those used in this book. It includes the Italian terms widely used by composers to indicate tempo (speed), dynamics (volume of sound) and musical expression.

accidentals – symbols used for chromatic alterations to a scale or key: sharp (♯), flat (♭) and natural (♮)

adagio (*literally* 'at ease') – slow, at a comfortable pace

Alberti bass – a stereotyped accompaniment (usually broken chords) for a pianist's left hand

allargando (*literally* 'broader') – becoming gradually slower

allegro, allegretto (*literally* 'cheerful', 'merry') – quick, lively

allegro agitato – quick and agitated, excited; *allegro con brio* – quick and spirited; *allegro energico* – quick and energetic; *allegro giocoso* – quick and playful; *allegro maestoso* – quick and majestic; *allegro ma non troppo* – quick but not too quick; *allegro moderato* – moderately quick; *allegro risoluto* – quick and resolute, determined; *allegro vivace* – quick and lively, vivacious

andante – at a walking pace

animato – animated, lively

appassionato – passionately

appoggiatura (from *appoggiare*, 'to lean upon') – an ornamental note, often sounding as a dissonance with its underlying harmony, but then moving to an adjacent consonance; usually heard on a strong beat, an expressive, yearning ornament

assai (*literally* 'much', 'very') – as in *Allegro assai* – very quick

augmentation – a theme presented in *doubled* note values ('augmented', twice as long), a device often used in counterpoint; *see also* 'diminution' augmented intervals – perfect and major intervals are said to be 'augmented' when extended upwards by a semitone; *see also* 'diminished intervals'

Ausdruck (Ger) – expression (*mit innigem Ausdruck*, with real (sincere) expression, feeling)

bar (*also* 'measure') – the convenient division of music into regular metrical units, as prescribed by time signatures (eg 3/4 = 3 crotchets to each bar)

binary form – a two-part musical structure, which can be on either a large or small scale:

1) whole-movement binary forms are in two sections divided by a double bar, modulating to the dominant key at the end of the first part, and returning to the tonic at the close

2) a miniature version of the binary principle, the 8-bar period structure of dance songs and (often) sonata themes may follow a similar tonal pattern

cadence – a cadence functions in music similarly to line-endings in poetry or punctuation in speech: cadences define both temporary pauses and distinct closes, delineating short phrases as well as musical paragraphs and whole movements. Cadences are emphasised by a chord progression of (at least) two chords. There are four types: 1) 'perfect' ('authentic', 'full close'): V – I; 2) 'plagal' ('weak close'): IV – I; 3) 'imperfect' ('half-close'): I – V; 4) 'interrupted' ('deceptive'): V – VI. Cadences are important carriers of the sense of tonality – defining 'home' key as well as movement away from 'home' to another key (i.e. to an area of contrasting tonality)

canon – a technique of composition in which a musical phrase is sung or played and then strictly repeated once or more in other voices

cantabile, cantando (from *cantare*, 'to sing') – in a smooth, singing style

chaconne – see 'variations'

chord – a chord is a group of three or more notes sounding simultaneously

chromatic – the introduction of 'chromatic' (irregular) notes into a scale may be for temporary colour, or to lead into different keys; *see also* 'diatonic'. The 'chromatic scale' consists of 12 notes and moves in semitone steps up and down the 12 semitones of the octave

coda – a concluding section, typically added to the 1st movement of a sonata, especially from the beginning of the nineteenth century; a coda adds a display of brilliant technique or further exploration of thematic material

common practice period – the era of the western tonal system in music from c.1650-c.1900. Its distinctive features are: use of major and minor keys, supporting harmony and metrical regularity

con – 'with', as in con espressione, with feeling, expressively; con fuoco – with fire; con moto – with movement, keeping moving

consonance – notes played together making a pleasing, agreeable sound (eg an octave, a third), as opposed to a dissonance, which is displeasing, disagreeable (eg a second, a seventh)

contrapuntal – see 'counterpoint'

counterpoint (literally 'point against point') – a technique of composition which combines two or more melodic lines simultaneously; 'contrapuntal' writing has a long history in the western tradition, dating from mediaeval times but notably practised by Baroque masters; 'contrapuntal' exercises have long been regarded as a useful discipline for composers and music students

crescendo – gradually growing louder

diatonic – the term 'diatonic' is generally used to describe the natural notes, such as can be found in the white notes of a keyboard (see p.49): both major and minor scales are produced from this sequence of tones and semitones (note: the same scale sequences can of course begin on any other one of the keyboard's 12 notes.) Any other note introduced into these scales is described as 'chromatic'. It may be helpful to think of chromaticism in the first instance as a 'colouring-modification' of diatonicism; see pp.102-03, also 'chromatic'

diminished intervals – perfect and minor intervals are said to be 'diminished' when reduced by a semitone; diminished seventh – see p.103, footnote; p.239; see also 'augmented intervals'

diminuendo – gradually getting softer

diminution – a theme presented in halved note values ('diminished', half as long), a device often used in counterpoint; see 'augmentation'

dissonance – see 'consonance'

dolce – sweetly

enharmonic – an 'enharmonic' note is like a literary pun: its meaning depends on its context. Thus in equal temperament tuning F♯ and G♭ sound at the same pitch; although they may be approached from different key areas, either from sharp keys or flat keys, they are 'enharmonically' equivalent; see Appendix A equal temperament – equal temperament tuning deviates from the tuning of 'pure', acoustically correct intervals. The western tonal system uses the 8-note tones and semitones arrangement of the natural scale but draws them from an acoustically-compromised octave of 12 equal semitones. The compromise of equal temperament tuning results in a sequence of 12 fifths (the "circle of fifths") coinciding with a sequence of 7 octaves, and gives composers a considerable ability to move freely from one key to many others. *see* pp.48-50; *see also* Appendix A

flebile – plaintive, mournful

functional harmony – the use of chords (principally the primary triads I, IV and V) to endorse tonality in a piece of music; *see* 'cadence', *also* pp.47-48

giusto – regular, with exactitude

grazioso – gracefully, prettily

interval – the distance in pitch between two notes. Intervals may be melodic (heard successively) or harmonic (heard simultaneously)

inversion – a theme played 'upside down', so that upward-moving intervals change to move downwards, and downwards move upwards, producing a mirror-image of the original

key – the sense of 'home' tonality engendered by the 'home' tonic note/ chord, endorsed and supported by functional harmony. Any note in the chromatic 12-note scale may function as a 'keynote' or tonic

largo (*literally* 'breadth') – very slow

lebhaft (Ger) – lively, brisk

legato (*literally* 'bound together') – very smooth

leggiero – played lightly, gracefully

lento – slow

martellato – played like hammer-blows

meno – 'less', as in *meno mosso*, less quickly

mode – in both ancient Greece and the mediaeval church, 'modes' were the tonal basis of music: each mode had its own characteristic sequential pattern of tone and semitone intervals. The western major scale is derived from the Ionian mode (the ecclesiastical XI Tone), and the minor scale from the Aeolian mode (the IX Tone). The

362   PAST SOUNDS

word is still used in differentiating between the major and the minor 'mode' of a key.

modulation – the harmonic process of moving from one key (tonal centre) to another, usually by introducing notes chromatic to the original key

monothematic – using the same thematic material for both 1st and 2nd subjects in a sonata movement

mute – a small clamp temporarily fixed to the bridge of a string instrument, used by string players to reduce the intensity of the sound

Neopolitan 6th – a decorative chromatic chord; *see* pp.103, 344

note – (English usage) both the musical sound and the printed symbol for a pitch

ostinato – a distinctive melodic phrase persistently repeated; *see* 'variations'

passacaille, passacaglia – *see* 'variations'

pedal – a long sustained note in the bass line, deriving its name perhaps from the pedal board of the organ (although sustained 'pedal' points are also found in early vocal music)

phrase, period – terms used to describe sections of music: short 'motifs' or 'figures' can be combined to build 'phrases', 'periods', 'tunes', 'melodies' or 'sentences' into lengthier structures

pitch – describes the 'highness' or 'lowness' of a sound; musical instruments are tuned to a constant pitch in order to play together (standard pitch is 440 Hz for A above middle C)

pizzicato – indicates to string players that they should produce notes by plucking the strings with their fingers, not by using the bow

poco (*literally* 'a little') – *poco a poco,* little by little, gradually

presto – very fast

scales – the major and minor scales are the two scales used most commonly in the western tonal system of the common practice period. Both are made up of 8 notes (including the higher octave) and both are diatonic scales (using the tones and semitones arrangement of the natural scale); *see* 'tone, semitone', pp.43–46; *see also* 'mode' and Appendix A *scherzo (literally* 'jest', 'joke') – a light-hearted movement replacing the staid minuet as (usually) the third movement of a sonata; like the minuet, the scherzo is followed by a trio before being repeated

semitone – *see* 'tone, semitone'

semplice – simply

sequence – repetition of a phrase or motif at a different pitch

sforzando (literally 'forced') – a sudden, strong accent

sostenuto – maintaining, sustaining the tone

staccato (literally 'detached') – played as short, separated sounds

strophic – description of a song in which all verses are sung to the same music

subject – a term used in analysing a piece of music to describe a significant musical idea or theme

tema – theme

tempo rubato (literally 'robbed time') – a performance technique which relaxes the strictness of a regular beat for expressive purposes, either accelerating or slowing down the tempo

ternary form – a three-part structure, A-B-A, with the third part largely repeating the material of the first (the vocal *Da Capo* aria – repeating 'from the beginning' – is a classic example)

tessitura – the most comfortable pitch range for a singer or instrumentalist

tonality, western tonality – *see* 'common practice period'

tone, semitone (also called 'whole tone', 'half tone') – the interval building blocks of western scales, inherited by European music from the systematic division of the octave by Pythagoras in ancient Greece – his tuning system was based on the natural harmonics

triad – a vertical combination of 3 notes sounding simultaneously, called a 'triad' or 'chord'. Triads are the building blocks of western functional harmony; *see* pp.46-47

variations – a musical form based on the presentation and subsequent decorative treatment of a theme, from c.1750 usually (although not always) retaining its original melodic outline and harmonic plan. The *chaconne* and *passacaglia* were earlier Baroque variation forms based on a succession of chords or a bass line ('ground' or '*ostinato*')

Suggested Reading

The following is not intended to be a comprehensive list, but rather further reading for those who may be interested in exploring in more detail some of the topics discussed in the text.

Reference Sources

Grove Music Online: authoritative source of information on music and musicians, with new articles and article revisions added every year. Available online at *www.oxfordmusiconline.com*

Cambridge Companions to Music, informative series published by Cambridge University Press. Individual volumes on composers, instruments and musical topics. Information online from *www.cambridge.org*

The Oxford History of Western Music. A narrative history of music from the 'earliest notations' to the late 20th century, by Richard Taruskin. 5 vols, Oxford: Oxford University Press, 2005.

Music in the Western World: A History in Documents. ed. P Weiss, and R Taruskin. New York, Schirmer, 1984.

Pre-History and the Middle Ages

Apel, Willi. *Gregorian Chant.* Bloomington & Indianapolis: University Press, 1958 (Midland Book, 1990).

Devereux, Paul. *Stone Age Soundtracks: The Acoustic Archaeology of Ancient Sites.* London: Vega, 2001.

Garfinkel, Yosef. *Dancing at the Dawn of Agriculture.* Austin: University of Texas Press, 2003.

Georgiades, Thrasybulos. *Music and Language: the Rise of Western Music as Exemplified in Settings of the Mass.* Publ. in German 1974; English edition *transl.* M L Göllner. Cambridge: Cambridge University Press, 1982.

Hutton, Ronald. *The Rise and Fall of Merry England: The Ritual Year, 1400 – 1700.* Oxford: Oxford University Press, 1994.

Lewis-Williams, David. *The Mind in the Cave.* London: Thames & Hudson, 2002.

Menocal, María Rosa. *The Arabic Role in Medieval Literary History.* Philadelphia: University of Pennsylvania Press, 1987.

Mithen, Steven. *The Prehistory of the Mind: A Search for the Origins of Art, Religion and Science.* London: Thames & Hudson, 1996.

Nettl, Bruno. *The Study of Ethnomusicology: Thirty-one Issues and Concepts.* 1st edition 1983; new edition Urbana and Chicago: University of Illinois Press, 2005.

Stevens, John. *Words and Music in the Middle Ages: Song, Narrative, Dance and Drama, 1050-1350.* Cambridge: Cambridge University Press, 1986.

Wallin, N L, Merker, B, Brown, S *et al. The Origins of Music* (contributions to an international workshop held in Florence in May 1997). Cambridge MA: MIT Press, 2000.

Dance

Ehrenreich, Barbara. *Dancing in the Streets.* New York: Metropolitan Books, 2006.

Flett, J P and T M. *Traditional Dancing in Scotland.* London: Routledge and Kegan Paul, 1964.

Playford, John. *The English Dancing Master: or Plaine and easie Rules for the Dancing of Country Dances, with the Tune to each Dance [1651 – c.1728].* Modern edition: *The Complete Country Dance Tunes from Playford's Dancing Master, ed. Jeremy Barlow.* London, Faber Music, 2007.

Rust, Frances. *Dance in Society: An analysis of the relationship between social dance and society, in England, from the middle ages to the present day.* London: Routledge and Kegan Paul, 1969.

Sharp, Cecil J. *The Country Dance Book*, Parts I – VI. London: Novello, 1909-22.

Sharp, Cecil J and Oppé, A P. *The Dance: An Historical Survey of Dancing in Europe* (1924). Republished Wakefield: E P Publishing, 1972.

Instruments

Rowland, David, ed. *The Cambridge Companion to the Piano.* Cambridge: Cambridge University Press, 1998.

Kolneder, Walter. *Amadeus Book of the Violin.* Cleckheaton: Amadeus Press, 2003.

Isacoff, Stuart. *Temperament.* London: Faber and Faber, 2002.

Sonata

Caplin, William E. *Classical Form: A Theory of Formal Functions for the Instrumental Music of Haydn, Mozart and Beethoven.* New York: Oxford University Press, 1998.

Hepokoski, James and Darcy, Warren. *Elements of Sonata Theory: Norms, Types, and Deformations in the Late Eighteenth Century Sonata.* Oxford: Oxford University Press, 2006.

Mellers, Wilfrid. *The Sonata Principle* in *Man and his Music*, Part III. London: Barrie & Rockliff, 1957.

Newman, William S. *The Sonata in the Classic Era.* Chapel Hill: University of North Carolina Press, 1963.

Newman, William S. *The Sonata Since Beethoven.* 3rd edition, New York: Norton & Co, 1983.

Rosen, Charles. *Sonata Forms.* New York, London: W W Norton, 1980.

Tovey, Donald F. 'Sonata' in *Encyclopaedia Britannica,* vol.xv. Tovey's articles on music from the *Encyclopaedia Britannica* were published by Oxford University Press/Humphrey Milford in 1945.

Webster, James. *Sonata Form.* Article in *Grove Music Online.*

18th Century

Bonds, Mark Evan. *Wordless Rhetoric*. Cambridge, MA: Harvard University Press, 1991.

Burney, Charles. *A General History of Music, Parts One and Two*, 1776, 1782. Modern edition New York: Dover Publications, 1957 (republishing the modern edition prepared by Frank Mercer, 1935).

Leppert, Richard. *Music and Image*. Cambridge: Cambridge University Press, 1988.

McVeigh, Simon. *Concert Life in London from Mozart to Haydn*. Cambridge: Cambridge University Press, 1993.

Outram, Dorinda. 'The Enlightenment' in *New Approaches to European History*. Cambridge: Cambridge University Press, 1995.

Porter, Roy. *English Society in the 18th Century*. Revised edition London: Allen Lane/ Pelican, 1990.

Rosen, Charles. *The Classical Style – Haydn, Mozart, Beethoven*. Revised edition London: Faber and Faber, 1976.

Terry, Charles Sanford. *John Christian Bach*. 2nd edition (with a forward by H C Robbins Landon), London: Oxford University Press, 1967.

Till, Nicholas. *Mozart and the Enlightenment*. London: Faber & Faber, 1992.

19th Century

Blume, F. *Classic and Romantic Music: A Comprehensive Survey*. Transl. M D Herter Norton. New York and London: W.W.Norton, 1970.

Bonds, Mark Evan. *Absolute Music: The History of an Idea*. Oxford: Oxford University Press, 2014.

Bonds, Mark Evan. *Music as Thought: Listening to the Symphony in the age of Beethoven*. Princeton and Oxford: Princeton University Press, 2006.

Dahlhaus, Carl. *Between Romanticism and Modernism: Four Studies in the Music of the Later Nineteenth Century*. Transl. Mary Whittall. Berkeley and Los Angeles: University of California Press, 1974.

Figes, Orlando. *Natasha's Dance: A Cultural History of Russia*.
London: Allen Lane, the Penguin Press, 2002.

Frisch, Walter. *Brahms and the Principle of Developing Variation*.
Berkeley & Los Angeles: University of California Press, 1984.

Hanslick, Eduard. *The Beautiful in Music (1854)*. 7th edition, transl.
Gustav Cohen. New York: Liberal Arts Press, 1957.

20th Century

Etter, Brian K. *From Classicism to Modernism*. Aldershot: Ashgate,
2001.

Ross, Alec. *The Rest is Noise: Listening to the Twentieth Century*.
London: Fourth Estate, 2007.

Schoenberg, Arnold. *Style and Idea: Selected Writings* (1975). Ed.
Leonard Stein and transl. Leo Black. London: Faber & Faber, 1984.

Straus, J. *Remaking the Past: Musical Modernism and the Influence of
the Tonal Tradition*. Cambridge MA: Harvard University Press, 1990.

Thomson, William. *Schoenberg's Error*. Philadelphia: University of
Pennsylvania Press, 1991.

General

Ball, Philip. *The Music Instinct*. London: Bodley Head, 2010.

Blacking, John. *How Musical is Man?* Seattle: University of
Washington Press, 1973.

Blanning, Tim. *The Triumph of Music: Composers, Musicians and their
Audiences, 1700 to the present*. London: Allen Lane, 2008.

Cook, Nicholas. *Music: A Very Short Introduction*. Oxford: Oxford
University Press, 2000.

Cooke, Deryck. *The Language of Music*. Oxford: Oxford University
Press, 1959.

Huron, David. *Sweet Anticipation: Music and the Psychology of
Expectation*. Cambridge MA and London: MIT Press, 2006.

Láng, Paul Henry. *Music in Western Civilisation*. London: J M Dent,
1942.

McClary, Susan. *Conventional Wisdom: the Content of Musical Form.* Berkeley and Los Angeles: University of California Press, 2000.

Meyer, Leonard B. *Emotion and Meaning in Music.* Chicago: University of Chicago Press, 1956.

Patel, Aniruddh D. *Music, Language and the Brain.* Oxford: Oxford University Press, 2008.

Pendle, Karin, *Women and Music – a History.* 2nd edition, Indiana: Indiana University Press, 2001.

Reti, Rudolph. *The Thematic Process in Music.* London, Faber & Faber, 1961.

Sacks, Oliver. *Musicophilia: Tales of Music and the Brain.* London: Picador, 2007.

Scruton, Roger. *The Aesthetics of Music.* Oxford: Oxford University Press, 1997.

—— , *Music As An Art,* London : Bloomsbury Continuum, 2018.

Smallman, Basil. *The Piano Trio.* Oxford: Clarendon Press, 1990.

Storr, Anthony. *Music and the Mind.* London: Harper Collins, 1992.

Audio Clips of Music Discussed in Text

Recordings of all the piano trios discussed in this book are widely available.

Figures in Text

Illustrations

General Index